THE RELIGIOUS HISTORY
OF AMERICA
Revised Edition

THE RELIGIOUS HISTORY
OF AMERICA
Revised Edition

EDWIN S. GAUSTAD AND LEIGH E. SCHMIDT

HarperOne
An Imprint of HarperCollins*Publishers*

HarperOne

An exhaustive effort has been made to locate all rights holders and to clear reprint permissions for all illustrations. This process has been complicated, and if any required acknowledgments have been omitted, or any rights overlooked, it is unintentional. If notified the publishers will be pleased to rectify any omission in future editions.

HarperCollins books may be purchased for educational, business, or sales promotional use. For information please write: Special Markets Department, HarperCollins Publishers, 10 East 53rd Street, New York, NY 10022.

HarperCollins Web site: http://www.harpercollins.com
HarperCollins®, ■®, and HarperOne™ are trademarks of HarperCollins Publishers.

Cover: Queena Stoval, *Swing Low Sweet Chariot*, 1953, oil on canvas, 28 x 40 inches. Collection of the Maier Museum of Art, Randolph-Macon Women's College, Lynchburg, Virginia.

FIRST HARPERCOLLINS PAPERBACK EDITION PUBLISHED IN 2004
Library of Congress Cataloging-in-Publication Data is available upon request.

ISBN: 978-0-06-063056-0

12 13 14 RRD(H) 20 19 18 17 16 15 14 13 12

With great gratitude and boundless love,
we dedicate this book to our respective families.

Contents

Preface to the Revised Edition

Edwin Scott Gaustad's *A Religious History of America* first appeared in 1966, taking its place as a prime successor to the leading text of the previous generation, William Warren Sweet's *The Story of Religion in America*. Through subsequent revision and elaboration, Gaustad's history has remained a standard introduction to the field for more than a quarter of a century. With this new edition, the hope is to make that distinguished narrative available to another generation of readers.

Such accessibility required more than simply reissuing the last edition. Given the swirl of changes in American religion and culture over the last decade and more, the text obviously needed updating. To start, that entailed substantially augmenting and reworking the final section on the period from World War II to the new millennium. Also, given the rapidly shifting and expanding scholarship dedicated to making sense of American religious history, all the bibliographies required renovation. On a larger scale, the organizational design of the narrative itself warranted some restructuring. In the place of the five distinct ages—from the Age of Exploration to the Age of Limits—that patterned the story before, the current incarnation places more explicit emphasis on specific historical markers. In an era that resists the grand narrative and the panoramic vision and that embraces fragmentation and dispersion, the "Age of" this or that has a noticeably discordant ring. In keeping with recent revisionist concerns, cultural encounter and religious conflict have been accented; also, added attention has been given to religious practices, visual materials, pluralism, and spiritual seeking.

The main intent of the book as well as the bulk of the narrative remain faithful to Gaustad's original design, namely, to offer a wide-ranging sketch of the variable shapes and the diverse powers of religion throughout

American history. Though this new edition necessarily introduces some of the rougher edges of more recent scholarship about American religious life, I hope that much of the old storytelling polish of the earlier editions remain. I also trust that much of Gaustad's hopefulness about the American experiment—the working out of religious freedom, pluralistic dialogue, and national community—has survived my own editing and rewriting.

This history remains, above all, Gaustad's story, but he now has been brave enough to allow the voice of one of his own students into the text alongside his own. I have long been interested in the double-voiced talents of ventriloquists, and this new edition is perhaps worthy of such a tricky enterprise as containing two authorial voices in the body of one text. But of course the success of this exhibition is to be measured not by the harmony of those two voices but by the range of religious voices it makes audible.

Daniel Sack and James Hudnut-Beumler of the Material History of American Religion project deserve thanks for their interest in the visual dimensions of this project. The book is richer in appearance and interpretive detail because of that support. Acknowledgment and thanks are extended as well to Jennifer Wiley Legath and David Passiak for the time they spent as research assistants and sounding boards. Stephen W. Hanselman, John Loudon, Kris Ashley, and Priscilla Stuckey at Harper San Francisco improved and eased the production of this new edition in countless ways.

Leigh Eric Schmidt
Princeton, New Jersey
Summer 2001

Part 1

RELIGION IN THE COLONIAL ERA

CHAPTER 1

Beginnings

"I'm tired of all these pilgrims, these puritans, these thieves." So sings the pop artist Jewel on her compact disc *Spirit*. It is a fatigue that historians of American religion know well, finding it not just among their students but also among themselves. Long gone are the days when New England Puritanism stood as the dominant emblem of America's religious past, let alone its present. Stories of Pilgrim landings and first Thanksgivings now leave a syrupy taste, while any reexamination of witchcraft crises, religious persecutions, and Indian slaughters only replaces the yawn of those grown tired of Pilgrims and Puritans with a look of horror and disgust.

Plymouth Rock itself now seems not so much a relic of holiness—the consecrated place on which the Pilgrim forefathers landed, the great ancestral altar of liberty—as a quaint artifact, a tourist curiosity, perhaps more befitting a minivan side trip (the Plymouth Voyager) than the Mayflower Compact. Long fenced in to protect it from being chipped away by souvenir seekers, Plymouth Rock sits now as a half-hallowed shrine that bears witness to the very invention and historical malleability of these Pilgrim forefathers. Throughout the nineteenth century and into the twentieth, much of the magical power of the rock came from the desire of many Americans to identify themselves closely with these Pilgrims and Puritans, to cherish them in all their piety and courage as the forefathers of the nation. "Standing on this rock," as one lover of the Pilgrims wrote in 1832, ushers "us into the presence of our fathers." But, what happens now in the twenty-first century when so many have grown weary of Pilgrims and Puritans, when so many find Anglo-American relations with Indians to be thievish or worse, when so few in this polyglot and multiracial nation identify with them as fathers, let alone as mothers? Where should a religious history of America begin when the old New England stories of origin now seem so contrived, so narrow, so political?

1. By the early nineteenth century Plymouth Rock had become a New England shrine that marked off the Pilgrim forefathers and their landing as sacred. The enclosure was later made more monumental to augment the grandeur of the modest-sized rock. *Library of Congress*

Stories told about historical beginnings remain especially significant, and it is important to recognize at the outset that there are multiple birth narratives in American religious history, just as there are for the making of the nation as a political entity. Many of these stories, though certainly not all, will be found in these pages. Among them, for example, is the prominence of Alaska as the eighteenth-century birthplace of Russian Orthodox Christianity in America. As one twentieth-century Orthodox Christian recalled, "Alaska is for Orthodox Christians the oldest part of Orthodox America and the source of their spiritual roots in this land." Other groups tell other stories of their religious roots in America—the organization of the first Jewish synagogue in 1729 in New York City; the formation of the first independent African church in the early 1770s, a Baptist congregation in Silver Bluff, South Carolina; or the emergence of the Christian restorationist movement in 1801 out of a giant revival meeting at Cane Ridge, Kentucky, a location recurrently celebrated as "the birthplace of a faith." Then there are Roman Catholic claims about American beginnings, many of which center on St. Augustine, Florida, settled already with Spanish adventurers and Catholic missionaries in 1565. "St. Augustine was founded forty-two years before the English colony at Jamestown, Virginia, and fifty-five years before the Pilgrims landed on Plymouth Rock in Massachusetts," boasted a recent partisan, "making it the oldest permanent European settlement on the North American continent."

There is no such thing as immunity from the past, William Faulkner wrote in *Requiem for a Nun* in 1950. "There's no such thing as past either. . . . The past is never dead. It's not even past." The contentiousness and solemnity that so often surround American stories of religious beginnings show just how apt were Faulkner's observations. This religious history opens with Native American, Spanish, and French stories before turning to English colonization, but those beginnings are, in turn, nested within other beginnings that emerge all along the way. Again, these narratives range widely, whether Mormon visions of primordial origins in ancient America or African American Muslim stories of roots that go back to Africa and move through and beyond the devastation of slavery.

NATIVE AMERICAN RELIGIONS AND COLONIAL ENCOUNTER

The "New World" clearly was not new to those who had inhabited it for tens of thousands of years before any Europeans arrived. Long before pharaohs sat on ancient Egyptian thrones, long before Moses led his people out of that Egypt, and long before Homer wrote *The Iliad* or Rome rose to mighty power, inhabitants of the Americas had hunted and fished, planted and reaped, loved and given birth, danced and mourned their dead. These inhabitants had also ordered their lives in accord with socially prescribed patterns of behavior and explained their existence and their universe in accord with cosmological principles of understanding. In other words, they had developed complex systems of religious ritual and belief.

The religions of these indigenous peoples were as diverse as the places of their settlement, as varied as the tribal groups themselves. If one is inclined to think of pluralism as a phenomenon of the modern world, it is important to recognize that the American continents were never so pluralistic as in the centuries before European discovery and exploration. Pluralism was reduced, not enhanced, by the "invasion of America." No single religious institution, no single sacred book, no unified priesthood or common creed, no core group of rituals can be found in the mottled patterns of the lives of these indigenous peoples. It was only centuries into colonization that a pan-Indian or Native American identity emerged and, likewise, that intertribal religious movements (such as the Native American Church, with its peyote-based ritual observance) came into being. Even then, the new encompassing identity fostered by such pan-Indian movements was fiercely contested.

Misunderstanding between Europeans and indigenous peoples came early in the application of the name Indian, since Christopher Columbus thought he had reached the outermost islands of India. It is important to recall that the European construct of "the Indian" and the abstraction designated as "Native American religion" are both artificial labels suggesting a unity that is nowhere to be found. When we borrow such shorthands, we are really referring to the Arapaho, Blackfeet, Chumash, Delaware, Eskimo, Flathead, Ghost Dancers, Hopi, Iowa—and so on through the rest of the alphabet right to the Yuma and Zuni. Each tribe had to come to terms with its own specific environment, whether of woodlands or plains, seashores or deserts, and indeed the close bond between place and people has often been of primary religious importance in native traditions. As one contemporary Apache man says, "The land looks after us. The land keeps badness away."

Each tribe also had to discern and repeat the stories, often in song and dance, that explained to themselves who and why they were. In exploring the significance of a people's place in the world, tribal storytellers pursued many different paths, even as the underlying questions often repeated themselves: How, in the beginning, did the world come to be as it is? Where did we as a people come from? What happens after death? What things are permitted or forbidden for us to do? What separates us from, or unites us with, other peoples of other places or ancestries? What rules the sun or the seasons? What heals the ailing body or brings the blessings of fertility? What do dreams and visions signify? What will the future bring? And while such questions were (and are) widely shared—indeed, they were common across European, African, and Native American cultures—in the answers lay inevitably a rich diversity.

Cherokees of the Southeast, for example, regarded the earth as "a great island floating in a sea of water" and suspended at its four extremities "by a cord hanging down from the sky vault, which is of solid rock." Pimas in the Southwest saw the "Earth Magician" as the creative agent who shaped the world; "Round and smooth he molds it."

> Earth Magician makes the mountains
> Heed what he has to say!
> He it is that makes the mesa.
> Heed what he has to say.

Tsimshians in the Northwest explained the light of the sun with a story of the One Who Walks All Over the Sky. This divine figure wears a mask

2. At the end of the sixteenth century an early English settler, John White, portrayed the ceremonial life of the Indians he encountered. *Library of Congress*

of burning pitch that warms and illumines as he makes his way from east to west. Sparks flying out of his mouth at night account for the stars, while the moon receives its light from the face of the sleeping sun. When the sun paints his face with red ocher, that redness visible in the evening tells the people that the weather will be good the next day. And in the Northeast the Iroquois elaborated their account of Sky World, Earth, and Underworld with stories that explained not only where people came from but also where, after death, they would go.

In addition to painting cosmological pictures that helped make sense of the world, indigenous peoples also wove a rich tapestry of rituals of community, transformation, and vision. Rites of passage, such as those surrounding childbirth or death, have been especially critical to Native American religions, just as they are in Judaism or Christianity. Zunis of the Southwest, for example, present the eight-day-old infant to the sun after a ceremonial washing by the women of the father's clan. With cornmeal as a sacrificial offering, the elders dedicate the child, praying to "our sun father" that his blessing might rest upon the infant and indeed upon the whole community: "May you help us all to finish our roads." Among the Chinooks of the Northwest, concern is directed toward the pregnant woman, who is forbidden to wear certain jewelry or eat certain food or do anything that might endanger her life or the life she bears within. "She does not look at a corpse . . . [or] at anything that is dead." "She does not look at anything that is rotten." And the husband, too, is placed under careful restrictions, being also forbidden to look at a corpse, to kill animals related to the clan, or "to eat anything that has been found." Every precaution must be taken, not least precautions with the spiritual world.

Tribal communities also supervise and sanction the transition of boys and girls from their status as children to the more responsible role of adults. In the Chinook puberty ceremony for girls, several days of fasting were required, and the girl remained "hidden for five days." And for a period of one hundred days she had to wear a specified garment, refrain from picking fresh fruit, and bathe only at night. For the boys, puberty ceremonies required arduous or even painful initiations that would become the mark of manhood. Among the Delawares, the young man's first successful hunt signaled the moment when he should be ceremonially accepted into the tribe and instructed in his proper duties. A Moravian missionary to that tribe, David Zeisberger (1721–1808), reported that the felling of the first deer "proves the occasion of a great solemnity." First the deer, if a buck, is given to one of the male elders in the tribe, if a doe, to an older woman. The animal is then skinned and brought back to the village by the whole hunting party. As the group nears the village, one hears "a prolonged call, which is the old man's or old woman's prayer to the deity in behalf of the boy, that he may always be a fortunate hunter." A meal follows, in which the boy is instructed "regarding the chase and all the circumstances of his future life." Afterward, alone in the forest, the boy, on the verge of manhood, might have a spiritual vision of an "old man in a gray beard," who will assert his power over all things upon the earth and will promise the neophyte that he, too, will have much power: "No one shall do thee harm and thou needest not to fear any man."

The grim fact of death once more marshaled all the resources of the community to affirm that the unfriendly forces responsible for this individual death would not destroy the community and that hostile spirits would not trouble the family of the departed. This world and the world beyond were not separate or independent. An aged Pueblo Indian, for example, might leave this world only to return in another form, as a cloud or as a kachina doll. The death of a young person or a child, on the other hand, could be much more ominous, implying an imbalance between the forces of good and evil. Among the Kwakiutl, when a child died, the greatest concern was to see that the spirit did not return to haunt or to hurt. The purpose of the ceremony was to insulate and protect the living. By contrast, among the Hurons any infant who died was buried near the road so that the young spirit might enter the womb of some passing wife, thus to be born again.

When an Ottawa warrior was on his deathbed, the family dressed him in as fine a garment as could be procured; they then painted his face and dressed his hair "with red paint mixed with grease." The priestly leaders or medicine men gathered around him as his weapons were brought in and laid at his feet. When the moment of death seemed near, the person was helped to a sitting position so that he might look alive and thus defy death a little longer. When death finally conquered, the burial was public, the period of mourning carefully stipulated, and the feasts of reaffirmation and remembrance held. The ceremonies of death were not private but part of the collective life of the community.

Before Europeans learned much about the inhabitants of the New World, they often romanticized and idealized them as symbols of innocence, as the true inheritors of the Garden of Eden before the Fall. Even in the eighteenth century the aboriginal Indian maiden was a preferred artistic symbol of America: richly blessed by nature, unsullied by civilization. This idealization did not fare well in toe-to-toe combat, in hostilities provoked by relentless European advancement, in misunderstandings on both sides of a cultural chasm. The tendency of Europeans to sentimentalize the earliest Americans was always matched by a tendency to brutalize and exploit them, and that predilection only increased as time went on. In the nineteenth century, the period of most rapid European sweep across the North American continent, racial stereotypes of white man versus red man intensified as the Indian was thought of chiefly in terms of a problem requiring a solution. To many, the solution was assimilation through education and Christianization; to others, the solution was removal to a reservation; to still others, the only enduring solution was warfare and extermination. To the last group, the only good Indian was a dead Indian.

In early America indigenous peoples were dealt with largely in terms of their potential for trade, for labor or land, for military attack or alliance, and for conversion. These were the chief points of contact between the old inhabitants and the new arrivals. Trade was often the least disruptive form of contact, for its success generally depended upon leaving Indian cultures and religions intact. This was true all through the eastern half of North America: from the French along the St. Lawrence River to the

Dutch along the Hudson River, from the English in the Carolinas to the Spanish in Florida and along the Gulf Coast. But as European settlement swelled, successful trading alliances gave way to wider contests over the possession of land and the demarcation of private property.

The English, gradually developing a system of black slavery in Virginia, experimented, without success, with making the Indians into slaves. Unlike blacks, who had been completely uprooted from Africa, Indians still had cohesive cultural support, still had a nearby refuge to which they could flee. But land, more than labor, became the sticking point in relationships between Europeans, who wanted to settle and possess the land, and Indians, who found the notion of private property alien. The two sides usually talked past each other, since traditional patterns of behavior were so different and basic assumptions so far apart. The English even ran into trouble explaining to themselves why they had a perfect right to take over whatever Indian land they happened to occupy. Did they have a title from King James or King Charles? And if so, who had given the Indians' land to those English sovereigns? Did the Indians forfeit their land by being "uncivilized" or by merely passing over it rather than surveying, marking, fencing, and "improving" it?

John Winthrop (1588–1649), founder of the Massachusetts Bay Colony, argued that land "which is common to all is proper to none. This savage people ruleth over many lands without title or property; for they enclose no ground, neither have they cattle to maintain it, but remove their dwellings as they have occasion." In other words, since Massachusetts woodlands did not look like English villages, all that territory was available for the taking. Besides, Abraham was called forth by God to leave his own homeland to "go and take possession" of the land of others. So may English Puritans, with similar justification, possess this land to which they had been called. "Why may not Christians," Winthrop asked, "have liberty to go and dwell amongst [the Indians] in their wastelands and woods?" It was a question whose affirmative answer led to repeated conflict and warfare between migrating Europeans and previously settled Native Americans.

Wars in Virginia, in New England, in Canada, and elsewhere set the tone of Indian-white relationships through most of the colonial period of American history and well beyond. Adversaries in war rarely try to understand the opposition but instead only misrepresent and caricature each other. One Anglo-American advocate in the 1780s argued that Indian land claims were meaningless and absurd: "I would think the man a fool and unjust," Hugh Henry Brackenridge (1748–1816) wrote, "who would exclude me from drinking the waters of the Mississippi River because he had first seen it. He would be equally so who would exclude me from settling in the country west of the Ohio, because in chasing a buffalo he had been first over it." In fact, Brackenridge added, the Indian and the buffalo have about the same claim to all this vast continent. "To see how far the folly of some would go, I had once thought of supplicating some of the great elks or buffaloes that run through the woods, to make me a grant of a hundred thousand acres of land and prove he had brushed the weeds with his tail, and run fifty miles." Indian as noble savage had become Indian as enemy and foolish exponent of outrageous claims. Such Indians, if they could not be silenced or moved or assimilated, had to be slain.

Christianity, the prevailing religion of the traders and settlers, sometimes moderated and sometimes only intensified European severity and hostility toward the Indians. Christianity could be used, for example, to label Indians as idolaters and hence worthy of slaughter, as was the case in the Puritan war with the Pequots already in 1636–1637. Questioned by some back in England as well as by the Pequots about the brutality of killing women and children, Captain John Underhill simply replied, "We had sufficient light from the word of God for our proceedings." One minister, after the Puritan victory, gave thanks, announcing that God himself had "subdued" the Pequots.

From top to bottom, the encounter between Europeans and Indians was fraught with struggle, and this was especially the case in the relationship between Christian missions and indigenous religions. The missionary is now regularly dismissed as one who showed no sensitivity to tribal tradition, who regularly violated tribal integrity, and who could barely discern a distinction between Christianity as a religion and Western civilization. Often, indeed, the missionary imperative meant not only new practices of prayer or scripture reading, but also new modes of agriculture and dress. Conversion meant, especially for English missionaries, a wholesale cultural transformation. Yet missionaries also served often as cultural buffers, moderating the effects of the many detrimental agents in these colonial zones of contact. Some offered sharp critiques, for example, of the greed and immorality of traders who dealt in whiskey and guns. Quaker John Woolman (1720–1772), roaming across New Jersey and Pennsylvania, worried that English settlers and hunters were depleting the "wild beasts" upon which the Delaware Indians depended for subsistence and that traders were inducing them "to waste their skins and furs in purchasing a liquor which tends to the ruin of them and their families." For Woolman love was "the first motion" that compelled him to spend "some

3. The Sun Dance, a leading religious rite of regeneration among a number of tribal groups across the Great Plains, tested the bravery and perseverance of those who bound their own flesh to the pole at the center of the dance. *Library of Congress*

time with the Indians, that I might feel and understand their life and the spirit they live in." He came, he wrote in his *Journal* in 1763, "to receive some instruction from them"; the gospel light to which Woolman testified was inseparable from such love and empathy.

Missionaries were also brokers of tribal traditions to wider European audiences, sending back descriptive reports, however unsympathetic, on indigenous religions. Much of our modern knowledge of native traditions comes from sifting through these sources, both Catholic and Protestant. Often vast in scale and gritty in detail, such missionary reports include, for example, seventy-three published volumes of Jesuit accounts of their travels and labors in New France from 1610 to 1791. Other missionary-oriented groups, such as the Moravians, were similarly zealous observers, reporters, and record keepers. Missionaries, to be sure, generally regarded the Indians as "heathen" and therefore fit subjects for conversion, but this represented a clear advance over the harsh alternative of regarding the Indians as subhuman and therefore fit subjects for extermination or enslavement. As an early clergyman declared, "The Israelites had a commandment from God to dwell in Canaan; we have leave to dwell in Virginia. They were commanded to kill the heathen, we are forbidden to kill them, but are commanded to convert them." In understanding motivations, it is also important to recognize that missionaries, in transmitting Christianity to the "heathen," believed that they were bestowing a great gift: a blessing, not a curse, a sacramental community in this life and an eternal communion of saints in the life beyond. Modern scales of value may well put more emphasis on cultural integrity than on eternal felicity, but the superimposing of these priorities upon an earlier time distorts history more than illumines it.

It does little good to replace the vicious stereotype of cowboys and Indians as seen in the old Hollywood movies with a missionaries and Indians stereotype that makes arrogant villains of the former and hapless victims of the latter. The fateful clash between Europeans and Native Americans was ultimately far more complicated than any simple morality tale will allow. Above all, Native American cultures and religions proved far more resilient and enduring than most missionaries ever imagined. Again and again Indians resisted Christianity outright: would-be missionaries were scoffed at for telling their stories about Satan or the resurrection of Jesus, and indigenous conjurers often emerged victorious as healers and visionaries over this alien religious power. At other times Indians creatively absorbed the missionary religion into native traditions, making room for new indigenous forms of Christianity. The Trinity of the Father, Son, and Holy Ghost became the Fire, Earth, and Water; or the Holy Spirit became an eagle with good eyes. Jesus, a Narragansett man told an eighteenth-century Congregationalist minister, was a "handsome Man," who had as companions in heaven many spirits "Resembling Butterflies of Many Colours." The Narragansett man knew this, much to the minister's dismay, because of his own visionary travels across the threshold into the spirit world.

What is finally most notable is the mixing of religions and cultures that took place through colonial contact. The religion of the invaders became the occasion for layering old with new, for preserving native religious practices in hybridized Christian forms. The ceremonial use of gourd rattles among the Winnebagos in Nebraska was preserved, for example, even as the gourds were inscribed with images of Jesus and the cross. This mingling was evident as well in the account of one Winnebago man from 1893 who, caught up in the new peyote religion, consumed eight peyote buttons one evening and "saw God." Then, sitting quietly, he offered up this prayer: "Have mercy upon me. Give me knowledge that I may not

4. Chanting and fasting remain important parts of the visionary rituals of many Native American religions, just as they were for this Sioux practitioner in the early twentieth century. *Library of Congress*

say or do evil things. To you, O God, I am trying to pray. Do thou, O Son of God, help me, too. This [peyote] religion, let me know. Help me, O medicine grandfather, help me." The result of such cultural tenacity and inventiveness has been that Native American traditions and religions live on across North America despite the long history of war, disease, forced removal, reservation, poverty, boarding school education, and Christian "civilizing."

SPANISH COLONIAL VENTURES AND MISSIONS

Christopher Columbus (1451–1506), native of Genoa, wanted to go east by sailing west. He wished to find a new route to India, one that did not follow the medieval pattern of hugging a coastline, never allowing land to drop from sight until one's proximate goal was reached. His vision was to strike out daringly across an uncharted ocean, a sea of unknown breadth, until at last India came into view. Portugal having declined to sponsor him (the Portuguese seamen much preferring to hug the African coastline until they came to its end), Columbus left Lisbon in 1485 for the port of Palos in the southwestern corner of Spain. By May of the following year he was granted an audience with Queen Isabella. He made his plea, and Isabella made her move: she chose to refer the whole complex matter to a committee.

The committee to which Columbus's proposal was sent consisted of Catholic churchmen, for in the fifteenth century most educated men—whether doctors or lawyers or astronomers or cartographers—also held ecclesiastical titles. And churchmen for centuries had carried on endless debate about other lands beyond the "known world"—known to Europeans, that is. Did lands exist on the other side of the earth? And if so, were such lands inhabited? And if inhabited, did Christ appear to them sometime after he had appeared to people on "this side," to people who dwelled in the middle of the earth, that is, the Mediterranean world? But if Christ had not appeared to such people, were they then without hope of salvation until somehow European Christians could carry the gospel to them? Or perhaps God in his wisdom had so ordered the world that lands on the other side of the earth (if such really existed) would not be populated until the means for reaching those lands, called the Antipodes, had been developed or revealed. For a thousand years or more the discussion, entirely theoretical, raged back and forth until that day when it would no longer be a proposition for debate but a matter of sustained exploration and encounter.

To succeed, what mariners like Columbus needed most was the financial backing that would enable them to outfit a fleet of ships, complete with crew and ample provisions. Columbus, therefore, waited anxiously for the committee to issue its report. The wait was long, and the results were bad. After a leisurely four of five years in studying the problem, the committee concluded that the proposal to reach the East by sailing west was vain, impossible, and deserving of rejection. The reasons for so negative a reaction were these: (1) such a voyage would take at least three years; (2) the western ocean might be without limit; (3) even if Columbus were lucky enough to reach the Antipodes, he could never get back; (4) it was quite possible that there was no land to be found anyway on the other side of the earth; and (5) because such presumed islands had not been known before, it is most unlikely, this long after Creation, that they could be discovered now.

Deeply discouraged, Columbus waited another half-year to see if the queen would summon him into her presence. No summons came. Shaking the Spanish dust from his boots, Columbus determined to set out for France in order to give King Charles VIII the opportunity to support what Queen Isabella had turned down. At this juncture, two people intervened on Columbus's behalf. The first, Franciscan friar Juan Pérez, persuaded Isabella to meet with Columbus one more time and appoint one more committee. Although this committee also reported negatively, it concluded that such a voyage might indeed be possible were not the cost too high. At that point General Treasurer Sanchez entered the debate on the side of Columbus. True, one took risks in backing such a novel venture, yet, Sanchez argued, the potential rewards were great. This daring expedition, Sanchez told the queen, "could prove of so great service to God and the exaltation of his Church" that to decline the option would be "a grave reproach" to that divine order.

If such a voyage were truly possible and if the risks were truly acceptable, then nothing remained but for Queen Isabella to give reality to Columbus's ambition. On April 30, 1492, she commissioned her "Admiral of the Ocean Sea": "Whereas you, Christóbal Colón, are setting forth by our command . . . to discover and acquire certain islands and mainlands in the ocean sea . . . it is our will and pleasure that you" shall discover and acquire the same for the glory of God and the wealth of God's great nation, Spain. After three more months of careful preparation, Columbus, with ninety men aboard the *Niña, Pinta,* and *Santa Maria,* turned from the known waters of Palos to the unknown waters of the Atlantic Ocean. Seventy days later Columbus and his men knelt on an island of the Bahamas. To that island they gave the name San Salvador, Holy Savior, thus making the religious renaming of the New World's landscape one of the voyage's first objects.

This expedition was an affair of state but clearly also of church. The most loyal Roman Catholic nation in Europe at this time, Spain took seriously its responsibility to the pope and to maintaining the purity of its faith. For eight hundred years Catholics in Spain had warred against Muslims, finally driving them back across the Strait of Gibraltar to Africa. For centuries Spain had sought to convert or isolate the Jews; now, in the very year that Columbus sailed for parts unknown, more than 100,000 Jews were exiled from their homeland in a new diaspora. The Spanish Inquisition, known for its rigor in seeking out all heretics, had performed its task with cruel efficiency, purifying the national faith by fire. Spain's colonial endeavors in the New World were but an extension of the Crusades, which had taken place for centuries in the medieval world: claiming land and riches in the name of God and of his Church.

Columbus shared the religious vision of Catholic mission even as he shared the conviction that God ruled human history. A regular communicant, given to daily prayer as well as to the study of religious writings, the mariner interpreted his expedition in scriptural terms. "God made me," Columbus reported, "the messenger of the new heaven and the new earth of which he spoke in the Apocalypse of St. John, after having spoken of it through the mouth of Isaiah; and he showed me the spot where to find it." To the general treasurer who had rendered such timely help, Columbus wrote in 1493 that his success was due not to his own merit "but to the holy Christian faith, and to the piety and religion of our Sovereigns." The faithful response to such great discoveries should not be prideful boasting but humble thanksgiving, Columbus insisted. Let us all "give thanks to our Lord and Savior Jesus Christ, who has granted us so great a victory and such prosperity. Let processions be made and sacred feasts be held, and the temples be adorned with festive boughs." Then, striking a note that was to be heard again and again as European nations justified their occupation of already-occupied lands, Columbus added, "Let Christ rejoice on earth, as he rejoices in heaven in the prospect of the salvation of the souls of so many nations hitherto lost." The discovery of America was the climax of a great pilgrimage, the end of a noble spiritual quest as well as the opening of new millennial epoch in salvation history.

Spain moved quickly to secure its position, discovering more islands that turned out not to be islands at all but peninsulas of enormous land masses of a size almost beyond comprehension. Spain discovered so much so fast that its neighbor, Portugal, felt that it was being bypassed in this greatest of all land rushes and crusades. After all, Portugal was a Roman Catholic country, too, and a faithful one as well; Portugal had already explored a good portion of that ocean sea, having appropriated the Azores, the Canaries, and the Cape Verde islands. Should Spain now take the lead from their own explorers? Portugal appealed to the Holy See, the papacy in Rome, to settle the competitive tension between the two Catholic nations so busy in exploring and claiming new lands. Pope

Alexander VI responded by drawing a north-south line west of which all lands "discovered or to be discovered" would belong to Spain, east of which all such lands would belong to Portugal. This "papal line of demarcation," first drawn in 1493, was moved, by the terms of the Treaty of Tordesillas in 1494, farther to the west, thus favoring Portugal. The new line also intersected the "hump" of Brazil, giving Portugal an important foothold in South America.

The Spanish, who benefited most from this papal division of the spoils, proceeded rapidly with their exploration, planting on each new bit of soil both flag and cross. By 1511 a twenty-six-year-old Hernando Cortés (1485–1547) was in Cuba, making preparations for his conquests of Mexico and Peru. In 1513 Ponce de León (1527–1591), sailing out of Puerto Rico through the Bahamas, made his way to a peninsula to the north and west. Making landfall on Easter Sunday (in Spanish, *Pasqua Florida*, Easter of the flowers), he gave the name Florida to what he believed at the time was another large island perhaps about the size of Cuba. The following year Spain's King Ferdinand appointed de León governor of the "island," urging him to lead the native population "by all the means you may be able to devise ... into the knowledge of Our Catholic Faith." Another Spanish explorer, Vásquez de Ayllón (1475?–1526), in 1521 ventured into northern Florida (naming the St. Johns River) and far beyond to the Chesapeake Bay. He, too, received imperial encouragement to bring the Indians "to understand the truths of our holy Catholic faith, that they may come to a knowledge thereof and become Christians and be saved."

Once Mexico City, formerly the capital of the Aztec civilization, was transformed into the major center of Spanish power and population, land expeditions from that point northward penetrated the vast continent into what would become much later the states of Texas, New Mexico, Arizona, and California. In 1539 Brother Marcos of Nice (d. 1558), a Franciscan friar, walked over three thousand miles on such a journey, erecting a small cross near the Zuni pueblo at Cibola and claiming all in the name of Spain. To the Indians that he met he promised humane treatment, not enslavement, not slaughter. Such a promise represented a commitment on the part of some churchmen to support barbaric treatment no longer.

In 1516 a Dominican missionary, Bartholomew Las Casas (1474–1566), received the title of "Defender of the Indians" for venting his fury against his countrymen because of their cruel treatment of the native peoples. "In God's name," he cried, we must consider whether our tortures and murders of Indians "do not surpass every imaginable cruelty and injustice!" He asked "whether it could be worse to give the Indians into the charge of the devils of hell than to the Christians of the Indies." Keeping up a steady campaign for recognition of the common humanity binding European and Indian, Las Casas finally found his position validated in a papal bull, *Sublimis Deus* ("The Sublime God"), issued in 1537. There Pope Paul III declared that the Indians were, in fact, human beings, not subhuman beasts. Indians were not to be deprived of their liberty or their property and should not "in any way be enslaved" whether they chose to become Christians or not. While even this minimal ideal often failed to be put into practice, it could not be violated with utter impunity by those who saw themselves, in some way or another, as emissaries of the Catholic faith.

Missionary and native tensions were keen in New Spain as elsewhere. In 1597 Indians on St. Catherine's Island, off the coast of Georgia, justified their rebellion against Spanish overlords by explaining that their whole culture was being condemned and subverted. The friars "obstruct our dances, banquets, feasts, celebrations, fires, and wars, so that by failing to use them we lose the ancient valor and dexterity inherited from our ancestors." The missionaries also "persecute our old people, calling them witches," and they "always reprimand us, injure us, oppress us, preach to us, call us bad Christians, and deprive us of all happiness." As was so often the case under colonial contact, Christianity represented a repudiation of all ancestral ways. Such a radical abandonment pushed these and many other Indians into postures of rebellion and resistance as they tried to hold off the Spanish campaign to extirpate native religious traditions and supplant them with the cross.

The southeastern corner of the North American continent proved generally inhospitable to both Spanish missions and Spanish settlements. Louis Cancer (1500–1549), a Dominican preacher who came fresh from missionary work in Central America, was determined to win equal victories in Florida. Sailing into Tampa Bay in 1549, he and several companions debarked, only to be slain the moment they reached shore. In 1565 Pedro Menéndez de Avilés (1519–1574) managed to retake north Florida settlements from exiled French Protestants (Huguenots), who were ruthlessly slain in the New World as heretics and enemies of the true Christian faith just as they had been in the Old World. But, in his efforts to conquer territory to the north, the Carolinas and Virginia, Menéndez met with great resistance from the Indians and was also defeated. Accompanying him were members of the Society of Jesus, the Jesuits, who shared in the defeat and discouragement. By 1571 the general of the Jesuit order, Francis Borgia (1510–1572), decided that the cost was too high and the number of lives lost too great to justify continuing efforts even in Florida, much less to the

5. Colonial Spanish missions dotted the Southwest as well as Florida and made for an enduring Catholic presence in those regions, as was evident in this late-nineteenth-century feast
day at the San Estevan del Rey Mission in New Mexico. *Library of Congress*

north. We can count on the fingers of one hand, said Borgia, the number
of our converts, and even some of them have relapsed into their former
ways. Since the Jesuits had too much to do elsewhere and too few missionaries for the task, "not only is it not fitting to keep the Society in that
land, but it must not be done."

Spain's ecclesiastical forces left a much more enduring imprint on the
American Southwest. Franciscans (the Order of Friars Minor), building

upon the earlier travels of Brother Marcos and others, entered New Mexico as well as Texas and Arizona quite early. The royal city of Santa Fe (Holy Faith), established in 1610 (three years after Jamestown, Virginia), developed into the political and religious capital for the surrounding region. Such development, however, came at high cost. The initial governor, Don Juan de Oñate (1549?–1624?), leading his first expedition in 1595, visited great cruelty upon the New Mexico pueblo dwellers. A Franciscan friar in 1601 wrote to the Spanish viceroy to protest Oñate's totally unjustified behavior as he robbed and plundered, burned villages, and killed men, women, and children. What Oñate has managed to do, the friar reported, is alienate an entire population, when it would have been possible for a more intelligent and compassionate commander to control this whole territory with fifty men, if only the conquest had been effected "in a Christian manner without outraging and killing these poor Indians, who think that we are all evil and [that] the king who sent us out here is ineffective and a tyrant."

Such undeserved treatment also played havoc with the missionaries' reason for being in the New World. Because of Oñate and his like, the Franciscan acknowledged, "We cannot preach the gospel now, for it is despised by these people on account of the great offences and the harm we have done them." That was the short-term effect of the brutality. The long-term effect was an Indian revolt in 1680 led by the Indian shaman Popé. Santa Fe was virtually destroyed, with over four hundred lives lost, many of those Franciscan. Spain prevailed, however, with Diego José de Vargas leading a powerful military force into the region a dozen years later. The capital city was rebuilt, even as missions arose once more on the desert landscape. Here as elsewhere, however, the cost of early European cruelties was high, coloring all future contacts among conquerors, missionaries, and Indians.

New Mexico, though a conspicuous center of Spanish missionary activity in North America, did not stand alone. On both sides of that territory, Franciscans and others labored long and hard. In Texas mission efforts began along the Neches River, with the creation of the San Francisco de los Texas mission in 1690. Father Damien Massanet reported that in the eastern woods of Texas he found "a delightful spot close to the brook," and within three days enough ground had been cleared and enough of a "roomy dwelling" had been built to permit Mass to be said "with all propriety." Massanet, like other missionaries, was quick to make the terrain itself Catholic: "I called this place San Antonio de Padua, because it was his [saint's] day. In the language of the Indians it is called Yanaguana."

One of these Texas missions, San Antonio de Valero, founded in 1744, achieved special fame a century later as the Alamo where Texans died in their struggle against Mexico for independence. In Arizona it was the Jesuit Eusebio Kino (1645–1711) who above all others left a palpable Spanish mark upon that land. Almost as much geographer as preacher, Kino traveled through northern Mexico (Sonora) as well as southern Arizona, mapping as he went, learning Indian languages, baptizing, and building chapels. In 1697 he founded his largest and best-known mission, San Xavier del Bac. When Kino died in 1711, much of the Christianizing effort in Arizona slowly withered away. A half century later, however, Spanish Catholicism made a powerful resurgence in California.

Under the direction of Franciscan Junípero Serra (1713–1784), a long chain of missions stretched from San Diego (1769) in the south to San Francisco (1776) in the north. Serra's last mission was founded at Ventura in 1782, two years before his death. Serra and his companions, walking from Lower or Baja California into what is now U.S. territory, spent many days crossing plains and gullies to get to that port of which they had heard. On the first of July in 1769, he recorded in his diary as follows: "We started early in the morning on our last day's journey. Already the beginnings of the port we were seeking are partly visible. . . . We therefore continued on and finally arrived at said camp . . . a little before noon. . . . Thus was our arrival, with all in good health, happy and content, thanks be to God, at the famous and wished for Port of San Diego." Here, as elsewhere, native peoples struggled through the incursion of the missionaries, both resisting and appropriating the Catholic faith. All of this cultural contact and ecclesiastical activity on the Pacific Coast in the 1770s and beyond took place without reference to the tumult on the Atlantic Coast, as thirteen British colonies entered the struggle for their own independence from England.

Spain's presence in North America never equaled that so firmly fixed in Central and South America, but the Hispanic presence north of the Rio Grande was strong and enduring. The Catholic missions of the sixteenth through eighteenth centuries laid the foundation for a vigorous Hispanic Catholic culture in the United States in the twentieth and twenty-first centuries. It also remapped the landscape on Catholic terms, with the names of saints marking settlements from St. Augustine, Florida, to San Francisco, California. As Anglo-American and Protestant cultures moved west and south, they, too, would feel deeply the presence of these Catholic beginnings, at once reviving the Spanish colonial past for their own romantic purposes and reviling Hispanic Catholic culture as in desperate need of Protestant civilization. Whether in California, Florida, New Mexico, or Texas, Anglo-American Protestants, Hispanic Catholics, and indigenous peoples long found that there was no immunity from this colonial past. More recently, even Hindu immigrants in Norwalk, California, have found there is no immunity now either; a local planning commission instructed them to build their new temple in a manner more befitting the Spanish style of neighborhood architecture.

FRENCH TRADE AND CATHOLIC FAITH

Newfoundland's fishing banks first drew France's attention to the New World. Breton fisherman crossed the northern Atlantic to net as great a catch as their tiny vessels could safely carry back. Then in 1534 Jacques Cartier (1491–1557) sailed from St. Malo with sixty men and two small ships past those fishing banks into the strait located between Newfoundland and Labrador. He explored inlets and small bays, made contact with natives of the Algonquian linguistic family, and took two Indians back home with him to learn French. The next year Cartier returned with three ships, over one hundred men, and his two "interpreters" to carry on even more serious exploration.

Like other Europeans, the French were charmed by the idea of a Northwest Passage, a waterway shortcut from Europe to Asia. Every bay or gulf or broad river raised hopes that it would prove to be this much-sought-after passage. On his 1535 voyage Cartier can be forgiven for believing that he had in fact found it. What he did find was the Gulf of St. Lawrence and then the St. Lawrence River, which led in a southwesterly direction into the interior of a vast continent. Discovery of the St. Lawrence River, while it did not lead to Asia, did lead to exciting possibilities of a profitable fur trade and of significant French settlement far within North America. Other French explorers would learn later that this major river would bring them within easy reach of the Great Lakes and even the headwaters of the Mississippi River. With access to waterways such as these, France could draw a cordon around the entire eastern half of the continent. Catholic France to the north and Catholic Spain to the south could divide the New World between them.

The promise far outran the reality. A settlement effort in the early 1540s proved disastrous as relations with the Iroquois turned sour, as supplies ran short, and as the cost of this entire venture proved exorbitant. All the money was flowing out, and none was flowing back in. France, moreover, found itself seriously distracted at home, as the Reformation, which had divided Germany between Protestant and Catholic segments, threatened to do the same in France. Ultimately, France was not so fragmented, but for most of the second half of the sixteenth century that nation teetered on the edge of a full-scale religious war. The Edict of Nantes, issued in 1598, brought a measure of peace to that troubled land, even as it enabled France once more to turn its attention to that great contest among the European nations for colonial control of the New World.

The seventeenth century opened with commercial and colonizing ventures directed by Samuel de Champlain (1567?–1635). While the earliest efforts at settlement here turned out as unhappily as those some sixty years earlier, a fort built at the first narrowing of the St. Lawrence River evolved into the town of Quebec, and soon a bit farther up the river the village of Montreal had its beginnings. Political control was unsure, however, and population growth was insignificant in the first half of the seventeenth century. By the 1660s only about 3,000 French colonists dwelled in Canada, this at a time when about 40,000 English colonists inhabited New England alone. French affairs in the New World ended up being directed much more by the Society of Jesus than by the government itself.

The Jesuits, since their founding in 1540 by Ignatius Loyola (1491–1556), had become one of the most rigorous missionary instruments of the Catholic Counter Reformation, and they proved as bold as ever as they moved out from their North American base at Quebec. Exploring, mapping, translating, and reporting on Algonquian and Iroquois tribal life at great length, the Jesuit missionaries sought, with death-defying sacrifice, to win converts from among the Indians to their own Christian faith. That hope often ended in frustration and spirited resistance, just as it had for their Spanish counterparts laboring among the Seminoles in Florida. Jean de Brébeuf (1593–1649), arriving in 1625, lived and worked with the Hurons (in the general neighborhood of the lake, which bears their name) for two years without winning a single convert. Brébeuf had few illusions about the difficulty of the task before him, and he did not wish other missionaries to arrive unaware of the enormous challenge that confronted them.

After having worked with the Hurons for more than a decade, Father Brébeuf in 1636 advised potential missionaries to dispense with all illusions about the beauties and bounties of a wilderness life among the Indians. You will have, he wrote, no bed but the earth, no roof but the stars, and for dinner "a little corn crushed between two stones and cooked in fine clear water." By day the sun burns you, he warned, and by night the mosquitoes torment you. If you fall sick, expect no earthly help, for from what source could it be obtained? And if your illness is such as to make it impossible for you to keep up with the Indians in their journeys, "I would not like to guarantee that they would not abandon you." Then you confront the horrendous task of learning a totally distinct language in this wilderness. "The Huron language will be your Saint Thomas and your Aristotle," and despite the fact that you are likely a most clever person, you will do well to remain silent for weeks if not months. "You will have accomplished much if, at the end of a considerable time, you begin to stammer a little." In short, Brébeuf concluded, do not come to New France unless your soul burns with such a sacrificial fire to imitate Christ's sufferings that no other vocation will satisfy you.

If all these hardships were not enough, still greater suffering lay ahead. In 1649 war broke out between the Hurons and the Iroquois, with the latter victorious. Hundreds of Hurons were slain, and Brébeuf himself was captured. The Iroquois grievances against the Jesuit were several: he was an intruder, a Frenchman; he was an enemy to the Iroquois god, Areskoui; and he was a friend to the Iroquois enemy, the Hurons. On him, therefore, their full fury fell. He suffered slow and agonizing torture, which after some four hours brought a death that could only have been merciful. Father Brébeuf, who had counseled his fellow Jesuits to have "sincere affection for the Savages," had surely demonstrated the sincerity of his own.

One of those fellow Jesuits, Isaac Jogues (1607–1646), had arrived in Quebec in the 1630s determined to assist in that missionary venture among the Hurons. No sooner had his work begun, however, than an epidemic broke out, striking Indian and French alike. For weeks Jogues himself hovered between life and death. The Hurons reasoned that since the plague arrived soon after the priests did, the latter were responsible for this most unwelcome disease. As Huron chiefs deliberated the proper time and the proper means for putting the missionaries to death, the Jesuits (fully aware of these discussions) continued their ministry to the sick and dying. The threat of reprisal passed, the fevers subsided, and Jogues himself eventually recovered.

In 1641 the Chippewas invited Jogues to establish a mission in their midst. In the peninsula between Lake Michigan and Lake Superior, the Jesuit father established Sault Sainte Marie, which ultimately became a major settlement. Though eager to press westward where no European had yet been, to preach to the Illinois, the Sioux, and other western tribes, Jogues remained near Georgian Bay and the mission at Sault Sainte Marie. Here for a time his work progressed without serious incident and with modest success. But the next year, in 1642, Jogues accompanied some Indians back to Quebec for supplies. The journey, after portage, up the St. Lawrence was hazardous enough with rapids, waterfalls, hunger, and exhaustion. To these normal hazards, however, was added the menace of Iroquois warring parties along the banks of the river. Jogues and his party managed to make it to Quebec safely, but on their return he and several others fell into Iroquois hands. As prisoners of war, they received much abuse and repeated threat of execution. "Amid these dread and alarms," Jogues later wrote, he died many a death or ended up living "a life harder to bear than death." During his several months of captivity, "I made no effort to study the Iroquois tongue, for why should I learn it, since I believed I was about to die at any moment?"

A year later, Iroquois guards brought Jogues to the Dutch trading post at the juncture of the Mohawk River with the Hudson, the site of present-day Albany, New York. There fellow Europeans tried to secure his release but without alienating those Indians upon whom the Dutch depended for their fur trade. The Dutch Reformed pastor, Johannes Megapolensis (1603–1670), granted Jogues a rare moment of joy by returning to him his lost service book (or breviary), which the Dutch rescued from a Mohawk trying to use it in barter. Father Jogues, however, was obliged to return with his captors to their village, though the Dutch continued to explore the possibility of arranging for his release or escape. Months later, the Dutch assisted him in getting aboard a ship bound for Europe, and Jogues set sail down the Hudson for Manhattan (being the first Catholic priest to visit that Dutch settlement) and then home.

But his story does not end there. Back in France, Jogues made plans to return once more to the mission field where he had labored for nearly a decade. By June of 1644 he was back in Quebec, ready to do whatever needed to be done. What was needed most at that time was a way to encourage the Indian groups to make peace with one another. The Iroquois, especially the Mohawks, carried on almost ceaseless war against the Hurons. At the request of the latter, the Jesuit agreed to be an emissary for peace to the Mohawks. Unfortunately, the diplomacy went awry as a band of young Mohawks, ever ready to blame the French for their troubles, captured Jogues and a companion. This time, in October of 1646, the torture and abuse did result in death, a martyrdom that eventually led to Jogues's canonization, along with Brébeuf's, in 1930.

Probably in the very village where Jogues met his death, the daughter of an Iroquois chief and an Algonquian Christian mother converted to Christianity in 1676 when she was twenty years old after receiving guidance from Jesuit missionaries as well as native converts. So strong was her discipline of chastity, so thoroughgoing her mortification of her own flesh, and so active her life of prayer that Kateri Tekakwitha (1656–1680) soon impressed both native Christians and French missionaries. Though she died before she was twenty-five, her grave site became an object of pilgrimage and veneration, a Catholic shrine on North American soil. Many stories of miraculous cures came into circulation and have long continued to multiply. In 1980 Pope John Paul II beatified Tekakwitha, the "Lily of the Mohawks," the first Native American so honored, and she continues to serve as a focus of reverence and devotion: "Kateri, lily of purity, pray for us." Through Tekakwitha, the legacy of the French missionary encounters live on in contemporary Catholic devotionalism.

French labors in the Mississippi Valley also left a significant imprint on the interior of the North American continent. In 1669 a Jesuit named Jacques Marquette (1637-1675) arrived as a missionary in Wisconsin; from that base he assisted in exploring the upper Mississippi River. His 1673 journey with Louis Jolliet gave Marquette such fame as an explorer that his long missionary labors among several Indian tribes in Wisconsin and Illinois were virtually obscured. Speaking at least six Indian languages and eager to reach new tribes to the south, Marquette proved the ideal traveling companion for Jolliet. The two men together hoped to find that ever-elusive route to the great western sea and thence to Asia. What they found instead was a silt-laden, widening river that flowed not to the Pacific but to the Gulf of Mexico. France now laid claim to the very heartland of

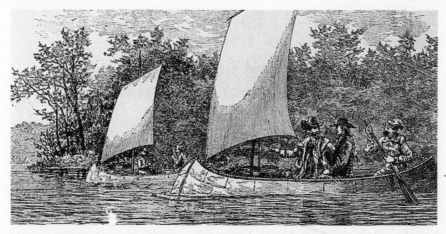

6. The early French expeditions into North America left a lasting imprint up and down the Mississippi River; here Father Jacques Marquette and explorer Louis Jolliet sail down that river in 1673. *Library of Congress*

America, from the mouth of the St. Lawrence River in the north to the mouth of the Mississippi in the south. And France's church now had before it a mission field of staggering dimension.

In 1682 Sieur de La Salle (1643–1687) completed the exploration of the Mississippi River south to the broad delta, proving its navigability all the way from the Illinois River to the Gulf of Mexico. For two decades, however, no French settled along the lower Mississippi. One reason for the delay was somewhat embarrassing: the French had trouble finding the river when coming by way of the gulf. La Salle tried in 1684 but ended up in Matagorda Bay off the coast of Texas. In another attempt three years later, La Salle was murdered by his own mutinous men. By 1700, however, Jesuits arrived in what is now Biloxi, Mississippi. Father Paul Du Ru (1666–1741) saw before him a missionary challenge that daunted even the most self-sacrificing. Confronted by the vast diversity in languages and the difficulties of learning even one, Du Ru exclaimed, "If one would want to ask God for a miracle in their favor, it would be the gift of tongues."

In 1702 Mobile, Alabama, was founded, this becoming the oldest French town on the Gulf Coast—since Biloxi was only a fort. And in 1718 the settlement called New Orleans came into being, this destined to become the major center for French missionary activity and the political capital for all the Louisiana Territory. Like the Spanish, the French quarreled among themselves over economic and religious priorities, these disputes frustrating the mission effort. The superior of the Jesuit mission, Father de Beaubois, in 1726 concluded an agreement with the responsible French company, making possible a more extensive missionary enterprise. Jesuits were joined by other Catholic clergy—Capuchins, Carmelites, Récollets—as well as an order of nuns, the Ursulines, in their labors in and beyond New Orleans. For nearly a half century, however, Jesuits took the lead, reaching out to the Yazoos by 1726 and to the Arkansas, the Choctaws, and the Alibamons in successive years.

Yet two major events, unrelated except in time, brought an end to the extensive Jesuit effort and to much French dominance of interior America. The first event of 1763 was the French suppression of the Society of Jesus. The order had become so powerful and wealthy as to arouse jealousies and fears within both the wider Catholic Church and the royal family. With a shattering suddenness Jesuit property was sold, seized, or transferred to the Capuchins. Jesuits themselves sought the first available passage back to France, there to be reassigned or pensioned off. Whatever the justifications for this French action (a decade later the pope abolished the

Society of Jesus everywhere, though restoration came in 1814), the effects on New France were devastating and never really overcome, especially in the Mississippi Valley. The Jesuits had been the leading religious organization in New France, and without them much of the Catholic enterprise dwindled.

The same ship that arrived in New Orleans to bring news of the Jesuit suppression brought word of the end of the Seven Years' War between England and France. By the terms of the Peace of Paris in 1763, France ceded to England all territory east of the Mississippi River (except New Orleans) and to Spain all territory west of that great river. After 1763 the French religious presence in the entire interior valley could only be described as ghostly, a presence that lingered on largely in place-names and missionary memoirs. Nonetheless, even in the late twentieth century the largely Protestant southeastern United States contained within it a powerful Roman Catholic presence in Biloxi, Mobile, and southern Louisiana, these strongholds still offering testimony to those French beginnings hundreds of years earlier.

CHAPTER 2

English Exploration and Anglican Establishment

For England, as in continental Europe, the Protestant Reformation was steeped in both politics and blood. Papal authority, monastic lands, vernacular Bibles, and fine theological distinctions over the sacraments, among other doctrinal points, soon became a matter of life—and of death—for the ordinary villager, the humble family, and the local parish. In England King Henry VIII took the first political steps in the 1530s, with Parliament at his bidding passing a series of measures that accomplished the separation of the Church in England from the pope in Rome. Henceforth Henry would be the earthly head of England's national church: that much was clear. Far less clear was how Protestant or how Catholic that English church should be. For the next century and more England would seethe with divergent answers to that question.

The blood of religious division was shed only in small amounts during Henry's reign (1509–1547), and the nation as a whole escaped widespread persecution and recrimination. During the brief reign of the "Boy King," Edward VI (1547–1553), England shifted sharply in the direction of Protestantism, then in the equally brief reign of Mary I (1553–1558) turned sharply back toward Roman Catholicism. That reversal made the more convinced Protestants reel; it sent many of them into exile, some going to Geneva where they were schooled further in the rigors of Protestant reform and discipline, and it sent others to their death. These turbulent, unsteadying, and often brutal years made the nation yearn for religious peace and settlement, if such could be found in the sixteenth century. A new and youthful queen, Elizabeth I, came to the throne in 1558; for the hope of bringing steadiness to this religious tumult, her years of rule were fortunately long (1558–1603). Her policies, though

30

bound to disappoint both Catholics and the more ardent Protestants, were carefully calculated to seek a middle way in religious matters.

Elizabeth did not rule long enough, though, to see English colonies successfully launched in the New World. That outcome would await her successor, the first of the Stuart line of monarchs, James I, who reigned from 1603 to 1625 and who chartered the companies that launched both Plymouth and Jamestown. These enduring ventures were built on decades of preparation, exploration, and boosterism, which Elizabeth had encouraged. Virginia especially, named for Elizabeth as the Virgin Queen, would be the initial flowering of the English colonial endeavor, the first and ultimately most successful establishment of the Church of England in North America. The power of the Church of England, while severely challenged by the growing number of religious dissenters in the 1740s and 1750s, would be supreme in Virginia right up to the Revolution.

FOR "THE GLORY OF GOD AND THE GOOD OF MY COUNTRY": THE PROMOTION OF ENGLISH COLONIZATION

In the late sixteenth century it appeared that the colonial bravado and early adventuring of other European nations were eclipsing England's sun. From the perspective of devout English Protestants, that eclipse would have darkening religious effects, for it would mean that England's gospel in all its Protestant glory would fall far behind the missionary advances being made by Portugal, Spain, and France—Catholic nations all. Would England ever join the colonial chase with sufficient fervor to forestall these Catholic giants?

To be sure, England had not been sound asleep. John Cabot (1450–1498), for example, had sailed for King Henry VII at the close of the fifteenth century. Cabot, together with his son Sebastian (1476?–1557), moved in for a closer look at Newfoundland and the Atlantic coastline. Like other explorers, they hoped that this closer look would reveal an opening to the Orient and all its riches. The voyages of the Cabots did give England something of a claim to North American lands, but they did not result in any steady development of colonies or forts, missions or trade.

The notorious Francis Drake (1540?–1596), knighted by Queen Elizabeth in 1581, also indulged in some exploration of the continent, just so long as "scientific observing" did not interfere with the more profitable enterprise of piracy. As English and Spanish hostility increased in the 1580s, Drake became a major maritime nuisance to the ships from the

Spanish Main. He wrecked many a Spaniard's fortune, lined many an Englishman's pocket, and took the view—with utter seriousness—that all his efforts constituted a kind of Protestant crusade. Like Columbus before him, Drake enforced regular religious services aboard his ships, and his boats carried Bibles, prayer books, and that most Protestant of all English books, John Foxe's *Book of Martyrs*, which offered blood-chilling accounts of the Protestant sufferings under the Catholic Queen Mary I. Drake believed that any blow against Spain was a blow on behalf of England and of England's own Protestant church. In 1588 came the most disastrous blow of all as the English (with God's help, they believed) defeated the Spanish Armada, thereby destroying Spanish naval supremacy and hampering Spain's largely unchallenged ventures into the New World.

A little more than a decade before that defeat, Sir Humphrey Gilbert (1539?–1583) had argued for even more of the Drake type of activity. Gilbert contended, in effect, that heaven helps only those who help themselves and that England should seize every opportunity to get ahead of its enemies or, as he put it, to "annoy the King of Spain." "The safety of States, Monarchies, and Commonwealths," Gilbert stated, "rests chiefly in making their enemies weak and poor, and themselves strong and rich." He added that God had placed opportunities for strength and wealth in Elizabeth's hands "if your highness shall not overpass good opportunities for the same." Put not your trust in foreign treaties, Gilbert advised, but only in God. And Christian princes can never be justified in making league "with such as are at open and professed war with God himself," that is, Catholic Spain itself. What Gilbert chiefly proposed was an attack upon Spanish shipping anywhere and everywhere and by every means legal or otherwise. It is a wise, lawful, and Christian policy, he concluded, to prevent mischief ahead of time rather than avenge it too late.

Even more important than stopping Spanish trade and plundering its gold, other Englishmen argued, was planting an English foothold firmly in the New World. All that territory does not by some natural right belong to Spain or France: England had its explorers, too! To establish colonies in North America would advance the national interest just as surely as it would advance the Protestant cause. And two Protestant clergymen, Richard Hakluyt the Younger (1552?–1616) and Samuel Purchas (1577–1626), made that argument with particular force and effect.

A graduate of Christ Church, Oxford, Hakluyt maintained a dual loyalty to religion and geography. This was not an unreasonable combination when accurate cartography and improved navigation were so necessary to the spread of the gospel. And if it were to be the right gospel, "true and sincere religion" in Hakluyt's words, then it must be Protestant England and not Catholic Spain that should bear the Christian message to North America. Working closely with Walter Raleigh in 1584, Hakluyt presented to Queen Elizabeth *A Discourse on Western Planting*. Here he pleaded for what was to become England's distinctive approach to the New World: settlements and towns rather than trading posts and forts. If the nation's energies were devoted to genuine colonization, he argued, then conversion of the Indian would go forward more surely than had been the case with both Spain and France. Missionaries would have the opportunity first to learn the language and the customs of the natives, then they could proceed diplomatically to "distill into their purged minds the lively liquor of the gospel." Otherwise, the Oxford graduate noted, "for preachers to come unto them rashly without some such preparation for their safety, it were nothing else but to run to their apparent and certain destruction."

England was called by God to this task, Hakluyt assured Elizabeth, just as surely as "the blessed Apostle Paul" had been called to be an apostle to the Gentiles. In his letter to the Christians in Rome, Paul asked, "How shall they believe in Him of whom they have not heard? And how shall they hear without a preacher? And how shall they preach except they be sent?" The parallel, in Hakluyt's mind, was exact. The Indians would remain heathen as long as they did not hear the (true) gospel; they could not hear unless missionaries came to them; and missionaries could not reach them unless the larger community sent them. Kings and queens of England had been called "Defenders of the Faith," Hakluyt noted, and by this "title I think they are not only charged to maintain and patronize the faith of Christ, but also to enlarge and advance the same." The time for such enlargement, he insisted, was now. Spain and France were already well ahead of England, and England could not delay any longer.

To the argument that the pope, by his line of demarcation, had already divided the New World between Catholic nations, Hakluyt responded with scorn and utter indignation. The pope had no "lawful authority to give any such dominion at all." To establish this point, the Protestant preacher appealed to the Bible, to history, to the voyages of the Cabots, and to common sense. Besides which, in that century as in later centuries, possession made all the difference. Let's not waste time arguing about who has a right to what, he said; let us go out, lay claim to the land, and take it as our own. "This enterprise may stay the Spanish King from flowing over all the face of that vast [land] of America, if we seat and plant there in time, in time I say."

To overcome any inertia and timidity, Hakluyt mounted a promotion campaign rarely matched in Western history. He goaded his people by reminding them of the great daring exhibited by the English in the past, of heroic adventures at home and abroad, of long-forgotten feats of courage and lionhearted conquest. Hakluyt searched, probed, and pushed in order to gather all such records that "lay so dispersed, scattered, and hidden in several hucksters hands that I now wonder at myself to see how I was able to endure the delays, curiosity, and backwardness of many from whom I was to receive my originals." But he did not stop until he had enough to fill one volume, then three, with wondrous stories of *The Princi-pall Navigations, Voyages, Traffics, and Discoveries of the English Nation, Made by Sea or Over Land.*

First published in 1589, this widely read, greatly cherished book became England's epic for an age of exploration, discovery, and coloniza-tion. It inspired the country, stirring the imagination and emboldening adventurers. Consider, Hakluyt argued, if so much had been so grandly done by so few in the centuries past, how could contemporary English-men and -women continue to rest in "sluggish security"? In his dedica-tory letter preceding the work, Hakluyt confessed to his sorrow and shame that he heard other nations "miraculously extolled for their discov-eries and noble enterprises," while England was at the same time either "ignominiously reported or exceedingly condemned." Many of his read-ers agreed: sluggish security was unbecoming to so proud a nation with so rich a past. Those who did not read could simply watch the indefatiga-ble Richard Hakluyt as he celebrated the entry of Protestants into Florida, as he encouraged the voyages of Martin Pring to New England, as he urged the formation of the Virginia Company of London, and as he enlisted as a charter member of the Northwest Passage Company. Author, editor, booster, geographer, and preacher, Hakluyt gave his whole being to that "most godly and Christian work" of imprinting the Protestant gospel of England upon America.

When he died in 1616 his successor was already hard at work. Fellow clergyman Samuel Purchas published the first edition of *Purchas his Pil-grimage* in 1613, a large four-part volume that roamed the globe to demon-strate the universality of religion and the indisputable necessity of clerical hierarchy and order of the English variety. In his often-reprinted work, Purchas mixed geography and theology, anthropology and economics, piety and politics. The conglomeration was characteristic of the age, since all these forces were mingled in the minds and motives of those who pro-moted and those who planted and those who preached. As Walter Raleigh

(1552?–1618) so aptly put it, "Men have traveled, as they have lived, for religion, for wealth, for knowledge, for pleasure, for power and the over-throw of rivals." Purchas intended his book to be a history of the known and the about-to-be-known world, with good chronology and accurate geography but with full recognition that the soul of that world was reli-gion. Thus he would study "heathen" lands but with the comforting hope that their "worn-out rites or present irreligious religions" would all be washed in "the purer stream of sacred baptism."

From the vantage point of universal history, Purchas noted that so little of the world was Christian. Moreover, even that small part that was Chris-tian was divided into "sects and superstitions," the Reformation being only a century old when he composed his opus. Even when Purchas looked at Protestant England itself, he found much to discourage him. Mostly what he saw was ingratitude and sedition, "the beastly sin of drunkenness, that biting sin of usury, that devilish sin of swaggering. . . . These are payments we return unto the Lord, instead of prayers for and loyalty to his majesty; peaceableness and charity to each other; modesty and sobriety in ourselves." His book of universal history contained these sermonic sentiments because the fate of the world depended upon such truths being heard and heeded. In his note to the reader, Purchas dedi-cated his book "to the glory of God and the good of my country." In order for that glory to be reached and that good attained, Purchas said, England now must exchange lethargy for liturgy. She must rise up and become a colonial and missionary power.

The promotional efforts of Hakluyt and Purchas did pay off, though the early English attempts at colonization gave little encouragement to either investor or preacher. Hakluyt's contemporaries, the half-brothers Gilbert and Raleigh, not only joined him in the promotion but also took steps toward execution. After many delays, Gilbert set sail for Newfoundland in 1583, boldly claiming all that he saw on behalf of England. His venture, unfortunately, displayed more vision than careful preparation; only one of the five ships completed the voyage as planned, and Gilbert was not among those who returned. His expiring patent or governmental grant was transferred to Raleigh, who immediately backed an expedition to the North Carolina and Virginia coasts. Raleigh's two ships returned late in 1584 to report that they had seen a land full of deer, rabbits, and fowl; waters alive with fish; soil "the most plentiful, sweet, fruitful and whole-some of the whole world"; and Indians who were "a kind and loving peo-ple." This extravagant report, written by Arthur Barlowe, a captain under Raleigh's direction, was only the first of a series of inflated advertisements of the delights of America, reports that regularly and sometimes tragically misled prospective settlers. Some who came to the New World expected not to work but only to reap the natural bounty all around them.

Actual settlement efforts got under way in 1585. Seven ships, commanded by Sir Richard Grenville and Sir Ralph Lane, left 108 settlers on Roanoke Island (off the North Carolina coast) in August of that year. But when Francis Drake (now Sir Francis) drifted by the following June, he found the weary colonists ready to accept passage home. Among other difficulties, the relationships with the Indians had deteriorated rapidly, with little love and kindness evident on either side. Two of the settlers, Thomas Hariot and John White, carried back detailed reports, Hariot in prose and White in drawings. These men believed that even though their first effort had collapsed, a more carefully planned, a better supplied, and a more advantageously situated colony could actually succeed.

Thus encouraged, Raleigh sent three small ships from Plymouth, England, for the North Carolina coast once more, the party setting sail on May 8, 1587. The settlers, numbering 150 and this time including women and children, made landfall in early August, with the first recorded Protestant service being held on Roanoke Island that month. August saw another first, as John White's daughter Elenor, wife of Ananias Dare, gave birth to the first English baby born in North America: Virginia Dare. Shortly after this domestic event, John White (1540?–1593), who had been named governor of the colony, found it necessary to return to England to ensure that urgently needed supplies reached the struggling settlers. Incredibly, it took him four years to get back, the chief cause of delay being the outbreak of war between Spain and England. When at last White did secure passage back to the Carolina coast, he searched and searched but found no trace of family or friends. Some four centuries later, the "lost colony of Roanoke" has still not yielded up all its secrets. Despite the disappearance of the Roanoke group and the failure of early colonizing efforts, promoters like Hakluyt and Purchas only redoubled their zeal and held to their grand vision of English exploration and expansion.

"ALMIGHTY GOD HATH OPENED THE GATE": THE ANGLICAN ESTABLISHMENT IN VIRGINIA

In 1606 King James I chartered two companies to support settlements in North America. One, the London Company, was granted exclusive right to settle in (and, everyone hoped, make a profit from) land between the thirty-fourth and forty-first degrees of latitude, with the company's authority extending westward over land one hundred miles and eastward over the ocean for the same distance. The other company, named Plymouth, received a similar grant farther to the north. In January 1607, the London Company sent forth its first expedition, the group of three small ships sighting the Virginia coast near the end of April. The first permanent settlement, Jamestown, bore the name of England's monarch, and, with an appropriate sense of history as well as gratitude, the title of honorary rector of the first parish formed at Jamestown was given to Richard Hakluyt.

As one would expect in a visibly religious age, with the Reformation itself not yet a century old, religious motivations received explicit acknowledgment in the Royal Charter of Virginia. So daring an adventure was to be carried on only "by the providence of God," and the propagation of the Christian religion to those who "as yet live in darkness and miserable ignorance of the true knowledge and worship of God" remained a prime motivation. Also as John Rolfe observed on behalf of the settlers, the group saw itself as "a peculiar people, marked and chosen by the finger of God, to possess [the land], for undoubtedly He is with us."

For many years, however, these colonists no doubt wondered in Job-like questioning whether God indeed was with them. Jamestown came perilously close to meeting a fate similar to that of Sir Walter Raleigh's group. The total number of settlers, a little more than a hundred in May of 1607, had been reduced by half by the following September. Indians attacked even before the first fort could be finished. And when it was completed, fire broke out, destroying that fort along with several houses, the church, and Chaplain Robert Hunt's (c. 1568–1608) entire library. Food rotted, rats invaded, supplies disappeared, and mutiny threatened. Sickness, always on the heels of famine, spread in the "malarial swamp" where the settlers lived. More settlers arrived along with more supplies, but these augmentations were themselves to be followed by more tribulations. An especially severe "starving time" in the winter of 1609 to 1610 so decimated the young colony that it seemed doomed to failure. But, asserted the explorer, governor, and historian, Captain John Smith (c. 1579–1631), God "would not that it should be unplanted."

Whatever the motivations of the Englishmen who came to Virginia, the expectations were out of all proportion to the reality. The Spanish had found gold and silver in their colonies; these first Virginians found none. Neither did they find other natural resources to exploit or profitable crops to raise for export. The Indians, not surprisingly, refused to become a docile labor force, and English gentlemen were disinclined to assume the necessary and obvious burdens of subsistence farming. The population of the struggling colony had reached about two thousand in 1622 when an Indian counteroffensive resulted in the deaths of about one-fifth of the settlement. Profits were nonexistent, and the potential even for survival was not promising. In 1624 the king took over control of the colony to improve its direction and to prevent its demise. Virginia was saved, however, not so much by its new status as a royal colony as by its cultivation of a crop that promised to make the economy work at last: tobacco. Although James I vehemently condemned the vile weed and its corrupting effect in English society, Virginians found in exporting it the nearest equivalent to the gold of Spanish conquest.

Religious progress was no speedier than economic improvement. After Jamestown, a second parish was organized in 1611 in Henrico, where the rector, Alexander Whitaker (1587–1617), proved himself an able propagandist in the tradition of Hakluyt and Purchas. His sermon, "Good News from Virginia," found an eager audience in England, especially among the parish poor who were ready to believe that some better lot could be theirs in a new and promising land. Whitaker also won a place in Virginia's early history by performing the celebrated marriage in 1614 between John Rolfe (1585–1622) and Pocahontas (1595?–1617). Rolfe took pains to emphasize that his courtship came not from "carnal affection" but from his concern "for the good of this plantation, for the honor of our country, for the glory of God, for my own salvation, and for converting to the true knowledge of God and Jesus Christ an unbelieving creature: namely Pocahontas." Rolfe did confess, however, that he found his thoughts and emotions tangled up, caught "in so intricate a labyrinth that I was even awearied to unwind myself thereout." Rolfe nonetheless declared, in words that many of his fellow colonists would also affirm, that "Almighty God . . . hath opened the gate and led me by the hand that I might plainly see and discern the safe paths wherein to tread." While the marriage did promise for a time to improve relations between the English and the Indians, Pocahontas died in 1617, still in her early twenties, while Rolfe was killed five years later in the Indian resistance.

Before Rolfe's death, the Virginia legislature took its first steps in 1619 toward making the Church of England the officially established and solely supported church in Virginia. Parishes were laid out, glebe lands (acreage that could be used to raise crops for the support of the church) were set aside, and support for the clergy was promised. Again in 1642 and 1662, in language ever more explicit and prescriptive, the legislature provided for a re-creation in Virginia of the familiar national church at home. Only one doctrinal standard would be tolerated, namely, the Thirty-Nine Arti-

7. The Church of England was built upon a carefully structured liturgical life, embodied in the Book of Common Prayer with its set readings, prayers, and calendar. Elegant communion ware and careful catechesis were also fixtures of the established Anglican order in the seventeenth and eighteenth centuries. *Library of Congress*

cles of the Church of England; only one ministry would be accepted, namely, that sent out by bishops back in England. Any clergyman arriving in Virginia was obliged to present his credentials to the royal governor sitting in Jamestown. The governor would then induct the properly ordained and properly commissioned minister into his parish, "and if any other person pretending himself a minister shall, contrary to this Act, presume to teach or preach publicly or privately, the Governor & Council are hereby desired and impowered to suspend & silence the person so offending." The state, however inchoate, would protect and defend the church, however tentative its own development.

In addition to laying out the geographical boundaries of the parishes, assuring the purity of doctrine, and guaranteeing a ministerial monopoly in Virginia, the legislature in 1662 provided for the governance of each local parish through the creation of a vestry of twelve "of the most able men of each parish." This board would be responsible not only for the ecclesiastical affairs as such, but also for wider concerns in the community. It would oversee administration of charity in the area, and the leading men who sat on it would be directed to conduct the "orderly managing of all parochial affairs." Such men were required, of course, to pledge their loyalty not only to the king of England but to the king's church as well, swearing their conformity "to the Doctrine & Discipline of the Church of England."

A half century after the Jamestown settlement, the legal structure for a truly official church had been set into place. One might expect to see in the Virginia of the 1660s, therefore, the typical English church presiding over the typical English village in such serenity as to convince the English emigrant that he or she had never left home. That, however, is not the way it worked out. No typical English towns arose along the banks of Virginia's broad and navigable rivers. Parishes were measured not in yards but in miles as they stretched in narrow bands along the James or the York or the Rappahannock Rivers. Potential congregations were so widely scattered as to make the gathering of a significant number difficult and, in bad weather, impossible. Covering even a single parish of such imposing breadth proved a formidable task, but because of scant population, a harried minister might find himself assigned to two or more of these sprawling and expansive parishes. A minister could hardly offer regular services in each parish or be on hand for all the christenings, weddings, and funerals where his presence was expected. In the absence of the minister and sometimes in the absence of a church building, the plantation home and the plantation cemetery could become more the center of sacred life, as they already were in secular life.

The parish church, therefore, was often both literally and figuratively at the edge rather than at the center of community life in the seventeenth-century Virginia. The church's marginality was aggravated by a shortage of clergy, especially of well-qualified and well-motivated ones. The colony in its early years offered little to potential ministers but personal hardship and a meager livelihood. Aware of this problem, the legislature tried from time to time to strengthen the position of the clergy and to assure their income, but salaries paid in tobacco and corn could never be stable since the market price of these products fluctuated so widely. Some parishes failed to provide even a modest dwelling for their ministers so that Governor William Berkeley (1605–1677) found it necessary at midcentury to instruct each congregation that had installed a minister to "build for him a convenient Parsonage House." The glebe lands were to be cultivated for the benefit of the clergyman and his family as well as for the support and upkeep of the parish. But a dozen years later an English observer in Virginia reported that the ministers there were condemned to "see their families disordered, their children untaught, the public worship and service of the great God they own neglected."

For their part, the parishes could complain that some of the clergy received better support than they deserved. Ministerial quality throughout the seventeenth century proved a problem virtually beyond solution. For a time it seemed that only those clergy left England who wished to escape bad debts, unhappy marriages, or unsavory reputations. In 1632 the Virginia House of Burgesses felt obliged to decree as follows: "Ministers shall not give themselves to excess in drinking, or riot, spending their time idly by day or night playing at dice, cards, or an other unlawful game; but they shall ... occupy themselves with some honest study or exercise, always doing the things which shall appertain to honesty, and endeavor to profit the Church of God." Furthermore, they should keep in mind their solemn obligation to be a model, "to excel all others in purity of life and ... be an example to the people to live well and Christianly." A visitor two decades later concluded that the legislation had not had much effect: Virginia's reputation was so bad in England, John Hammond wrote in 1656, that the young colony managed to get only those clerics who, by turns, "babble in a pulpit" and "roar in a tavern."

This dreary picture, overdrawn even for its own time, gradually improved over the second half of the seventeenth century and sharply improved in the eighteenth. Yet it could not be denied that the Church of England in early Virginia did not enjoy anything like the good health that its legislative favor would seem to ensure. An anonymous pamphlet appearing in 1662, carrying the title *Virginia's Cure*, pointed the sickly patient toward a path of renewed health. If Virginia had no towns, if her population was widely scattered and without education, if her clergy were few in number and deficient in quality, obviously some heroic measures

8. When the capital of Virginia moved from Jamestown to Williamsburg at the end of the seventeenth century, the Bruton Parish Church took on greater importance; this building reached its present form with the addition of the tower in 1769. *Library of Congress*

must be taken. Towns must be created, artificially if necessary, where the women and children at least may live while the plantation master and his laborers work the land. (The latter can come into town on weekends.) With such towns, schools can be supported and attended; parish churches can be, as they must, the true center of religious life. With respect to the clergy, "Virginia Fellowships" must be offered in England that will pay for the education of worthy young men who, in exchange for their education of seven years, will agree to spend a minimum of seven years in Virginia, elevating the morals of the people and giving real substance to the Anglican church in that wilderness. The advice, while it had much merit, was not followed until some forty years later when Thomas Bray (1656–1730) marshaled the forces of private philanthropy in England to create societies that would send both literature (Society for Promoting Christian Knowledge, 1699) and clergy (Society for the Propagation of the Gospel, 1701) to all the English colonies in North America.

By mid–seventeenth century about thirty Anglican parishes had been created in Virginia, that number doubling by the end of the century, with the greatest number created in the period from 1640 to 1660. Parishes in the most settled portions of the Tidewater region ranged from twenty to forty miles long and five to ten miles in width. Though this was enough of a challenge to a single clergyman, parishes farther to the west or south of the James River might be a hundred miles or more in length. Just as the territory varied widely from parish to parish, so did the population and the ability, therefore, of any given parish to employ a minister, build a church, maintain a regular schedule of services, and care for the widows, the orphans, and the poor. Despite the considerable difficulties that Anglicanism faced in Virginia, the church steadily improved its position. By the middle of the eighteenth century parishes numbered more than one hundred, and Anglicanism was stronger in Virginia than anywhere else in North America.

Alone among the southern colonies, Virginia even had its own college, founded in the final decade of the seventeenth century. Under the prompting and coaxing of Anglican cleric James Blair (1656–1743), the audacious idea for a college became a positive movement. Blair petitioned the Virginia legislature for approval of the idea, raised money in support of the notion, and sailed to England to win royal sanction and an official charter. In 1693 the College of William and Mary received its charter so that Virginia youth might "be piously educated in good letters and manners"; so that the Church in Virginia might be provided "with a seminary of ministers of the gospel"; and so that "the Christian religion may be propagated amongst the Western Indians, to the glory of Almighty God." The college never managed to attract the Indians, and neither did it prove an effective training ground for clergy since all young men still had to journey to England for ordination. But particularly in the eighteenth century, the school did educate many who would play significant roles in the formative years of the new nation.

Just as Anglicanism in Virginia grew steadier, stronger, and more confident, new challenges confronted this legally sanctioned, state-protected church. A direct religious challenge came in the form of dissenting (that is, non-Anglican) churches, which, despite the legal prohibitions, began to infiltrate the colony of Virginia. Early penetrations in the seventeenth century by Puritans and Quakers met with such stern resistance and open hostility that these challengers did not grow to any strength. In the eighteenth century, however, first Presbyterians, then Baptists, and finally Methodists battered against the wall of the Anglican establishment. In general these dissenters settled not in the eastern Tidewater where Anglicanism dominated but in the foothills and the backcountry of more western, more mountainous Virginia. These dissenters also shared a fondness for evangelical religion, for religion more intense, kinetic, and personal than that often found in the formal liturgy and printed prayers of Anglicanism. That revival-charged movement, which took off in New England and the Middle Colonies in the 1730s and 1740s, rode into the hinterlands of Virginia with mounting force in the 1750s and 1760s. The Anglican establishment would never be quite the same after the evangelicals arrived.

The Presbyterian preacher Samuel Davies (1723–1761) heralded this upsurge when he came into the colony from Pennsylvania in 1747. Finding himself outside the law, unable to perform marriages, unauthorized to travel from community to community, and unwelcome in the eyes of all authorities, civil and ecclesiastical, Davies protested again and again that Virginia was exceeding the prohibitions even of England. More than a half century before when the cosovereigns, William and Mary, came to England's throne in 1689, they had issued a Declaration of Religious Toleration that granted some measure of recognition to Protestant dissenters. Now Virginia, even though it boasted a college that bore these monarchs' names, resisted the implementation of their liberality. As Davies evangelized widely, among both blacks and whites, political authorities grew fearful, resentful, and finally determined to stamp out dissent on their home turf. Back in England, however, the authorities were not nearly so alarmed by this influx of dissent. Concerned about the economic growth of the colony, the London-based Board of Trade advised that "a toleration and free exercise of religion is so valuable a branch of true liberty and so essential to the improving and enriching [of] a trading nation, it should ever be held sacred to His Majesty's Colonies." The board advised Virginia, therefore, to do nothing that would "in the least affect that great point."

Such a forceful policy declaration did not immediately wipe away all impediments of law and custom, but it did make the colonial authorities somewhat more circumspect in their harassment and persecution. Many more years would pass, however, before "free exercise" would become a meaningful and effective phrase throughout Virginia. Meanwhile, Davies continued to preach, continued to push, continued to win converts to evangelical religion in general and to Presbyterianism in particular. Davies also took seriously, more so than most Anglicans, the obligation to see that the gospel reached Virginia's blacks, who in 1750 numbered over 100,000. In that year Davies reported that he had personally baptized "about forty of them in a year and a half, seven or eight of whom are admitted into full communion and partake of the Lord's Supper."

Africans had been brought to Virginia as early as 1619, and once they proved to be an effective labor force, blacks were shipped in ever-increasing numbers to Virginia's shores. Soon *blackness* and *slavery* became interchangeable terms, even though a few free blacks managed to maintain their own farms on Virginia's eastern shore. Anglican catechizing and religious instruction among this large proportion of the population (about 40 percent by 1750) was impeded by several factors: resistance of the plantation owners to giving their workers sufficient time off for religious education; fear that a Christian baptism might change their civil status from that of slave to a free person; widespread illiteracy among the slaves with few opportunities for any education open to them; and even, at the lowest level of rationalization, the baleful argument that blacks had no souls. With some rare exceptions, Anglicans did not make significant progress in converting the slave population to Christianity. A 1730 report from London deplored the lack of progress, even on the part of missionaries dispatched for that very purpose.

Evangelical religion, on the other hand, made the gospel appear more accessible, more liberating, more emotionally satisfying. It was a version of Christianity that could be sung, shouted, and even danced. It offered an effective contact point, far more so than Anglican forms of catechizing, between Anglo-American religious beliefs and indigenous African traditions. Early in the movement, evangelicalism rarely put on the airs of hierarchy and refinement, offering a spiritual egalitarianism that soon opened up paths to black leadership, preaching, and organizing. Two black preachers, one named Gowan Pamphlet and the other simply known as Moses, had even organized their own independent African Baptist Church in Williamsburg by the 1780s.

It was Baptists like Pamphlet and Moses who, following in Presbyterianism's wake, created the second and most powerful wave of evangelicalism in Virginia. From New England, Shubal Stearns (1706–1771) arrived in 1754 to spread the notion of a free church without a confining or authoritarian hierarchy, of a ministry that depended upon no credential or ceremony other than the call of God, of a baptism by immersion not of infants but of adult believers who heard a gospel that they were ready to accept and profess. Though Stearns himself soon left for North Carolina, he left behind many to continue the evangelical outreach. So many continued in such force that one Anglican leader in Lunenburg County warned in 1759: this "shocking Delusion . . . threatens the entire subversion of *true Religion* in these parts, unless the principal persons concerned in that delusion are apprehended or otherwise restrained." Some forty to fifty Baptist preachers were jailed or "otherwise restrained" over the next fifteen years or so, usually under the charge of disturbing the peace. Many more were mocked, spat upon, assaulted, and otherwise abused. The arrest in 1774 of a half-dozen "well-meaning men" near the home of James Madison (1751–1836) in Orange County set the future president on a career dedicated to religious liberty. At the age of only twenty-two, Madison wrote to condemn that "diabolical, hell-conceived principle of persecution." No Baptist himself, Madison was ready to make common cause with them and other dissenters who found themselves arrested and jailed for no reason other than the assertion of their religious opinions.

John Leland (1754–1841), another New England Baptist who came south, was for his part ready to join Madison in the pursuit of religious liberty. Arriving in Virginia in 1776, Leland quickly identified himself with the cause of evangelical religion and religious liberty. Baptists joined with Presbyterians in petitioning the Virginia legislature for relief from oppressive laws that favored Anglicanism and discouraged all dissent. Baptists joined with Jeffersonians in urging government to do the best thing it can for religion: simply leave it alone. As Leland observed, state establishment of religion has done more harm to the cause of Christ "than all the persecutions ever did." Official government support of religion, like a bear, "hugs the saints but corrupts Christianity," while persecution, like a lion, "tears the saints to death, but leaves Christianity pure." In his travels all across Virginia, Leland created many new churches and led in the rapid development of the Baptist denomination.

Women as well as men assumed prominent roles in Baptist worship, and this also alienated and horrified the Anglican establishment. Denunciations were thundered against a sect so disorderly that it allowed women to pray in public, permitted "every ignorant man to preach who chose," and encouraged "noise and confusion in their meetings." Shubal Stearns's sister, Martha Marshall, even took to the pulpit and on "countless occasions melted a whole concourse into tears, by prayers and exhortations." The improvisational quality of evangelical worship, the accent placed on testimony and exhortation, opened up spaces for women to talk publicly about their religious experiences and to enjoin similar holiness upon others. Though the openings for such speech slowly narrowed and were often closed down, early Baptists remained an unpredictable group, a nursery for ragged prophets and independent visionaries, acting as a wedge to undermine the predictable social hierarchies of Anglicanism.

Methodists achieved independent denominational status in America only after the nation itself had won its independence from England. Well before American Methodism's "Declaration of Independence" from the Church of England in 1784, it made itself felt in Virginia. Launched by the brothers John (1703–1791) and Charles (1707–1788) Wesley, Methodism in England began as an effort to recall the Church of England from its formalism, to strengthen personal piety, and to reach the common laborers who seemed to be abandoning the national church in ever-larger numbers. Methodism was, in other words, initially a little church within a larger church, a holy club within, not apart from, the Church of England. In Virginia Methodism used some of the Anglican churches as a natural base of operations, and at least one Anglican clergyman, Deveraux Jarrett (1733–1801) of New Kent County, found himself caught up in the fervor of this evangelical force.

Most Anglicans found Methodism even more disturbing than the other dissenting forces, since these Wesleyans were boring away at the establishment from within. They threatened, or at least many Anglicans believed, to turn the whole Church of England upside down, to alter its liturgy through open-air revivals and itinerant evangelism, and to transform its mode of Christian living through a rigorous devotional diet of small class meetings and near constant prayer. Despite harsh condemnations and even passionate pleas from the bishop of London to stop this virulent plague from spreading, Methodism continued to make inroads in Virginia—and elsewhere. And, after its formal break with the Church of England in the 1780s, the Methodist denomination grew even more swiftly.

So Presbyterians, Baptists, and Methodists all beat against that stout civil wall that surrounded and protected the Anglican church. It is doubtful, however, if that wall would have fallen if major political factors had not come into play. First among these was, of course, the American Revolution itself. In fighting a war against England, most Americans were disinclined to seek or preserve any special favor for the Church of England. The Revolution threw Anglicanism on the defensive, but not so much because Anglicans opposed the Revolution, though outside of Virginia large numbers did oppose it. Most Virginia churchgoers supported the Revolution, yet had to acknowledge that the very nature and government of their church was intimately joined with England: England's civil and sacred authority were interwoven; the Church of England's liturgy and even its calendar offered blessings upon the monarchy. In 1776 when so much was happening in America on the political front, many Virginians began to take steps to sever those bonds that had identified the colony all too closely with its "Mother Church."

Thomas Jefferson (1743–1826), though nominally an Anglican himself, led in the battle for a full and free exercise of religion in Virginia. Proposing a "Bill for Establishing Religious Freedom" as early as 1779, Jefferson had to wait for many forces to coalesce before some seven years later his bill finally became law. One hundred and fifty years or more of an establishment tradition were not readily overturned. Virginia's legislature tended to be dominated still by the Tidewater region where Anglicanism was so strong and a pattern of church-state connection so fixed. Indeed, that long-standing pattern led some patriots to argue that if the Church of England were no longer officially supported, then at the very least Christianity must be declared the state religion. Patrick Henry (1736–1799) took the lead in trying to get such a bill passed in the 1780s, a bill that would affirm that "the Christian Religion shall in all times coming be deemed and held to be the established Religion of this Commonwealth." James Madison took the lead on the other side in seeing that such a bill never became law. In 1785 he presented his famed Memorial and Remonstrance against the Henry proposal, arguing (like Baptist John Leland) that the government establishment of religion, since the days of Constantine, had always been bad for religion. Such special favor created "pride and indolence in the Clergy; ignorance and servility in the laity; in both, superstition, bigotry, and persecution."

It might seem now with more than two centuries of hindsight that James Madison's victory over Patrick Henry in this contest was assured and that the Anglican walls in Virginia were fated to come tumbling down under the force of a democratic Revolution. The Church of England, to be sure, was knocked off its lofty perch, becoming only one more denomination (the Protestant Episcopal Church) among many denominations, and initially not a particularly robust one as it had to face up to the ruins of war. Just as notable, though, is how powerful and privileged a role the Church of England had come to play in colonial Virginia for over a century. From out of the frailest of settlements had emerged a viable and long-lasting Anglican establishment. That was the good news for the Church of England; the bad news was that the Anglican successes in Virginia, however subject to challenge and attenuation, were harder to come by elsewhere in the colonies.

CHAPTER 3

Puritan New England

While some English citizens labored to transplant the established Church of England to Virginia, the Puritans labored to transform the English church into a more thoroughly Protestant institution, an institution closer to the one John Calvin (1509–1564) had brought into being in sixteenth-century Geneva. At the same time, still stricter Protestants, despairing of any genuine reformation of the state church, resolved to separate themselves completely from it in order to create a true and pure Christian church according to their understanding of what the New Testament required. Whereas the Puritans hoped to bring a dramatic redemption to the liturgy, theology, piety, and governance of the Church of England, the more avowed Separatists (initially embodied in the Pilgrims) envisioned a radically new church model of independence from the state, a complete reformation without tarrying for any. The latter wanted to start all over again with a gathered body of believers who were free from state power and royal control, who made the church a small and protected garden separate from the entangling weeds of lordly magistrates and bishops.

From the nagging presence of Baptists to the even more disturbing presence of Quakers, the strength of this sectarian religious bent proved considerable in New England. It forced the Puritans repeatedly to confront the divisive and heterodox dimensions of their own movement, their own separatist leanings. For all the vigor and power of New England's Puritan order, such impulses toward a "free church" ultimately proved uncontainable. They reached quintessential expression within the bounds of New England itself in Roger Williams's Rhode Island, which became both receptacle and refuge for independent-minded dissenters from the more establishment-minded Puritans in Massachusetts and Connecticut.

THE ARRIVAL OF PILGRIMS AND PURITANS

Those who in American history have been dubbed Pilgrims and who are forever associated with the crossing of the *Mayflower* determined, while still in England, to go their own ecclesiastical way. In the early seventeenth century this was both illegal and dangerous. To be identified as a nonconformist, that is, one who did not conform to the national church and its Book of Common Prayer, was to fall not only into social disgrace but also into the hands of the nearest sheriff. A small congregation of Separatists in Nottingham, north of London, met secretly in the early years of the seventeenth century, trying to hide from the eyes of the law, trying to decide what was right in the eyes of God. If they stayed in England, they would have to either compromise their consciences or lose their estates and possibly their lives. If they left England, where could they go?

Holland presented the likeliest option, being only a few miles distant across the English Channel. Also Holland provided a greater measure of religious toleration in the early 1600s than did any other European country. So around 1607 this congregation, which had been meeting weekly in the home of William Brewster (c. 1566–1644) always with a lookout posted to warn of the sheriff's approach, determined to migrate, as a church, to a land "they knew not but by hearsay, where they must learn a new language, and get their livings they knew not how." But for greater freedom of worship they would pay the price, take the risk, and leave their farms and homes.

Amsterdam, a major commercial port, was their first new residence. The city, however, proved too full of temptations and seductions for this ascetic band, so the group, under the leadership of John Robinson, removed to the smaller town of Leyden, "a fair and beautiful city, and of a sweet situation, but made more famous by the university with which it is adorned." This voluntary exile was assumed to be a temporary one. The Separatists thought they would remain in Holland only until England came to its senses, until demands for religious conformity would become less stringent, until England, like Holland, would grant some measure of toleration to the religious dissenter. The Pilgrims waited, then waited some more.

The hoped-for changes did not come. Meanwhile, all was not going well for this congregation in Holland. Making a decent livelihood was not easy. Parents watched their children grow up not in familiar English ways, but with Dutch habits and customs. Some of their children, they feared, were even "drawn away by evil examples into extravagant and dangerous courses." The Sabbath was not honored on the continent any better than it was being honored in England under James I. The more they were immersed in such a strong and thriving foreign culture—one of cosmopolitan sophistication and commercial vibrancy—the more the unity and purity of their own fellowship seemed threatened. For the sake of their original religious principles, it seemed time to move on.

But where could they go? Not home, since, as Separatists, they would be fined or whipped or jailed or forced to conform. As Englishmen and Englishwomen, however, what other choice did they have? To stay in Holland would mean slowly losing their religious and cultural identity; to return to England would be to face all the old persecutions again. Neither alternative held any appeal, and yet the hard dilemma offered no other way out. But what if they could return to English soil without returning to England itself where sheriffs were so near and bishops so powerful? Could they cross a furious ocean and remove themselves from the immediate force of intolerable laws yet not remove themselves from England's flag, language, or culture? Was immigration to America possible? How great would be the cost? What chance of royal permission did they, nonconformists still, possibly have?

Answering those tough questions took many years. Complex negotiations were required to gain the approval of the Virginia Company and of the king. The latter proved more difficult than the former, since James I found the notion of religious liberty no more acceptable thousands of miles away than close to home. These Separatists had to prove that they were loyal God-fearing subjects, not radicals, not hostile to the nation's interests, not likely to subvert the whole colonial enterprise. The Pilgrims came as close as they could to asserting their orthodoxy and loyalty; the king came as close as he could to recognizing their liberty; the Virginia Company came as close as it could to underwriting the costs of the voyage. Thus in July of 1620, not the whole Leyden church but a portion of it left Holland for England, where two ships were readied for the Atlantic crossing. The two ships left Southampton in August, but one proved unseaworthy; the remaining ship, the *Mayflower*, put in at Plymouth to try again, now with more supplies and more passengers. On September 6 the single ship set out for "northern Virginia" with 102 passengers aboard. Sixty-six days and four deaths later, the crew sighted land off Cape Cod, far north of where they had planned to land. But weary Pilgrims had no intention of sailing any more: if this was where God wanted them to be, here they would settle, here they would farm, here they would worship, here they would establish another Plymouth in the New World.

William Bradford (1590–1657), governor of this small colony for thirty years, recorded the bleakness of that November arrival. We had, he wrote, "no friends to welcome [us], no inns to entertain or refresh [our] weather-beaten bodies." No houses awaited them, and the wilderness that did await them seemed filled only with "wild beasts and wild men." What could sustain us in this winter season, Bradford asked, "but the Spirit of God and His grace?" He dared to hope that future generations would be willing to say, "Our fathers were Englishmen which came over this great ocean, and were ready to perish in this wilderness, but they cried unto the Lord, and He heard their voice and looked on their adversity."

The Plymouth Colony began to plant, to fish, to hunt, to cut and saw. Like colonists in Jamestown, those in Plymouth found that first year almost too much to bear. Of the twenty-six men with families, only twelve survived into the spring. Of eighteen married women, only three lived through the winter. It was a small and terribly depleted group that survived to give thanks for the first harvest in the fall of 1621.

The Plymouth colony never grew by great leaps. In 1630 the population was only a few hundred and a decade later barely 1,000. In 1660 only 2,000 inhabited the colony that, a generation later, was absorbed into the much larger Massachusetts Bay Colony, located a few miles farther north. This latter settlement, which began in the 1630s with massive migration from England to the bay around Boston, reached a population of 20,000 by 1660 and nearly three times that number by the end of the seventeenth century.

These Puritans at Massachusetts Bay who came in such strength regarded themselves as still very much part of the Church of England, the vastly purer part that in a *new* England would be able to demonstrate what a truly revitalized Church of England ought to be. They had hoped, while still in England, to move the entire state establishment in a more Calvinist, less Catholic, direction. But like the Pilgrims, they found the bishops too strong, the inertia too great, and the penalties of law too heavy. Unlike the Pilgrims, however, they did not take the outright step of schism from the established church; rather, they took the bold step of emigration, carrying with them their own charter for the Massachusetts Bay Company. On this aspect of church polity, if on few other matters, the Puritans remained akin to Anglicans in maintaining the value and necessity of an established church.

John Winthrop (1588–1649), many times governor of the Bay Colony (as Bradford was of Plymouth), outlined the motives and the vision of these Puritans as in 1630 they sailed into what would become "their" bay. We come as a dedicated community, Winthrop declared, as a true and pure church, as members of a covenant one with another and with God. "We must love one another with a pure heart fervently; we must bear one another's burdens"; and above all we must keep faith with our God, for "we are a Company professing ourselves fellow members of Christ." We have made a contract, pledged ourselves to an agreement; "we have taken out a Commission." And we must not fail. God has promised to do certain things for us; in turn, we have promised to do certain things for him. "Now if the Lord shall please to hear us, and brings us in peace to the place we desire, then hath he ratified this Covenant and sealed our Commission." Our duty is set before us, Winthrop noted, and if we neglect it, "the Lord will surely break out in wrath against us [and] be avenged of such a perjured people and make us know the price of the breach of such a Covenant." "We must consider," Winthrop continued, "that we shall be as a city upon a hill. The eyes of all people are upon us."

That stern warning would be repeated over and over during the course of the next several generations, as these Puritans built their city upon a hill, conducted their errand into the wilderness, sought "a due form of Government both civil and ecclesiastical," and labored to "work out our Salvation under the power and purity of his holy Ordinances." And though the Puritans initially thought of themselves as still part of the Church of England, that part gradually became so distinctive that it ultimately acquired an independent life and a new name: Congregationalism. An early and prominent Boston clergyman, John Cotton (1584–1652), set down what he regarded as the major Puritan complaints against the national church, and in these complaints one can see the beginnings of the Congregational or the New England Way.

In the national church, Cotton noted, the rule exercised by the bishops and the rigid conformity demanded by the law had become burdens too onerous to bear. The use of the Book of Common Prayer, moreover, violated the Second Commandment, which forbade men to bow down before the work of their own hands. Further, Cotton declared that the authority of the church should be congregational, not episcopal; the highest human authority is neither king nor archbishop but the local minister and congregants themselves. If that gave great power to the members, they for their part must prove themselves worthy of such power by giving evidence in their lives of their genuine conversion, of their having been chosen by God for eternal felicity with him. Finally, the church (said Cotton) is created not by legislative action from above but by contractual agreement from below. Church members must covenant together to create a fellowship of the redeemed. The church is not a consecrated building but a gathering of the faithful who, in the words of the Salem group, "covenant with the Lord and with another; and do bind ourselves in the presence of God to walk together in all his ways, according as he is pleased to reveal himself unto us in his blessed word of truth."

In the colony of Massachusetts, then of Connecticut, and later of New Hampshire, the New England Way took shape, molding itself with such firmness and care that it stamped upon that region a way of thinking and living that would endure far beyond the colonial period. The immigrants themselves built Congregationalism or Puritanism into the fabric of their lives. London did not direct the enterprise, approve the clergy, or enforce the doctrine. While the Virginia Company hoped for profits in Plymouth and the Massachusetts Bay Company shared similar dreams for Boston, the saints who made up a new Bible commonwealth came to the colonies out of reasons of faith, not to serve the commercial or mercantile interests above all else. They came for the due observance of the Sabbath and the sacraments, for the proper organization of the local church, for the enforcement of moral discipline, for the full explication of Calvinist doctrines, and for the instilling of the proper habits of piety.

The Puritans came as well for the freedom to practice their religion. It is important to understand that they never intended to launch a colony that would be open to all people of all religious persuasions—or of none. The Puritans came to create a pure church and to conduct a holy experiment free of opposition, distraction, and error. They were not hypocrites who demanded freedom of religion then denied that same freedom to others. Freedom of religion across the board was never the plan, never the commission or errand. They came to prove that one could form a society so faithful, a church so cleansed, that even old England itself would be transformed by witnessing what determined believers had managed to achieve many thousands of miles away. That was the vision to be steadily pursued, without weakening or wavering, without transgressing or backsliding, without ever forgetting the awesome obligations of a covenant with God.

PURITAN THEOLOGY, WORSHIP, AND EDUCATION

Within the context of the Protestant Reformation, Puritanism identified with that broad tradition known as Calvinism. John Calvin and those who followed after him emphasized above all else the absolute sovereignty of God. God, not humanity, was in charge of the universe, and from that fundamental proposition all other theology must flow. As the Puritan poet Edward Taylor (1645?–1729) inquired:

9. John Bunyan's *Pilgrim's Progress* (1678) was the archetypal Puritan narrative of the Christian's hard-fought spiritual journey toward the heavenly city. *Library of Congress*

Lord, Can a Crumb of Dust the Earth outweigh
Outmatch all mountains, nay the Chrystall Sky?

Humankind is that dust, more the folly than the glory of the universe, and the Lord of all the heavens above or below exercises a dominion, a power, that pathetic worms cannot contend against. God rules, and people obey or, more often, given their fallen condition, disobey that divine sovereign.

In the all-important matter of salvation, therefore, one would expect the Puritan to hold that this is an affair wholly within the power and purview of God. And so it is. Men and women do not choose God, but, acting with divine grace, God chooses them. That otherwise inscrutable process of election is ordered in accord with the terms of a covenant agreed to by both parties. Samuel Willard (1640–1707), Harvard class of 1659 and Massachusetts clergyman, wrote glowingly of the covenant of grace and its inestimable benefit. God and humanity "strike hands in an everlasting covenant" by the terms of which "God bindeth himself in a promise that eternity, which should have been spent in executing his wrath upon them, shall be employed with the entertainment of them with the highest expressions of an infinite love." Once one enters into this saving covenant with God, "nothing shall ever make a separation between them." Since salvation is given by God, not earned by women or men, it is safe, secured, assured forever. Come what may, those among God's chosen will persevere; once within the covenant, once among the "elect," there is no falling away. "God hath cast all their sins behind his back, blotted them out as a cloud." Thus is the divine side of the agreement fulfilled. On the human side, all the redeemed find "their hearts are engaged to him, devoted to his praise, and so fixed in their love to him, that all waters of affliction cannot extinguish it."

If salvation of the elect was set and certain, Puritan society itself was not therefore similarly set and stable. Both political and religious leaders of the second and third generations grew anxious about the declining faith, the cooling zeal. Would the children and grandchildren of the original settlers prove worthy of their noble inheritance? Or would they fall into a kind of indifference, taking for granted that for which parents and grandparents had been prepared to die? Churches began to relax their requirements for membership, no longer insisting that all newcomers tell the whole congregation of their own personal, intense experience of conversion. Some ministers, partly out of a desperate desire to increase participation in communion, began to divorce the privilege of the sacrament of

10. Puritans were sparing in their use of iconography, but seventeenth- and eighteenth-century gravestones in Congregational New England often included decorative work such as representations like this one of an angel. *Library of Congress*

the Lord's Supper from the requirement of a conversion narrative. Perhaps, they reasoned, the power of the sacrament itself would spark the much-desired conversions.

Amid these fears of religious decline and socioeconomic change, Puritans often resorted to a more insidious side of their theology, namely, confronting the dangers of Satan and his minions. Witchcraft, demonic possession, curses, and necromancy were theological no less than biblical realities, and they were regularly inserted into one social conflict after another, sometimes with terrifying results. This became especially evident in the notorious witchcraft episode at Salem, Massachusetts, in the 1690s. There the evidence for witchcraft, even if taking spectral form, seemed all too abundant in the testimony of the afflicted, and the biblical commandment remained all too clear: thou shalt not suffer a witch to live. In Salem in 1692 twenty people, so accused and then judicially found guilty, met their deaths, most by hanging, none by fire. As the frenzy of accusations subsided, the long process of self-recrimination began. One of the judges,

Samuel Sewall, stood before his church in 1697, acknowledging his blame and shame and asking the pardon of both his fellows and his God that this sin "and all his other sins" would be forgiven.

The story of the decline of piety followed by reformation and renewal was one that Puritans regularly told themselves. In the first half of the eighteenth century that familiar Puritan story line received its arch embodiment in the form of religious revivals and awakenings. Once again, out of the supposed pit of pious decline, New England was recalled in the 1740s by a wave of religious excitement and revivalism, a movement that eventually came to be known as the Great Awakening. Among the many significant consequences of this revival was its bringing to the fore New England's most brilliant theologian: Jonathan Edwards. Born in Connecticut in 1703, Edwards entered Yale College at a very young age, concluding his work there in 1720. After a brief pastoral charge in New York City, Edwards returned to Yale as a tutor and then assumed the leadership of the Congregational church in Northampton, Massachusetts. While there he not only took an active role in the revivals but also reflected deeply on their meaning in such influential works as *A Faithful Narrative of the Surprising Work of God* (1737) and *The Life of David Brainerd* (1749). After a painful dismissal from his Northampton charge, Edwards and his large family moved to Stockbridge, about forty miles west of Northampton, to minister to the Indians and others in the area. In Stockbridge he wrote the major philosophical and theological treatises that won for him so wide a reputation. In 1757 he was invited to become president of the College of New Jersey (later Princeton) and took over the duties of his office early the next year. Unhappily, he died soon thereafter as a result of complications from the still-new technique of smallpox inoculation.

The passions aroused in the course of the Great Awakening—and passions were aroused both for and against the revival—stimulated Edwards to reflect on the essential character of religion itself. "There is no question whatsoever that is of greater importance to mankind," Edwards wrote, "than this: What is the nature of true religion?" In a *Treatise Concerning Religious Affections,* published in 1746, Edwards offered his answer to that question in what emerged as the most subtle and sophisticated defense of the Awakening and the role of emotion in the religious life. Deep emotion not only was legitimate in religion, he argued, it was essential to genuine religion. For without the emotions or "affections," one is not moved, one's life is not altered. Religion was not a matter of intellectual apprehension alone, Edwards declared, not a matter of doctrinal knowledge alone, not a matter of mere propositions. Faith rested upon knowledge but moved beyond the faculty of understanding to the faculty of the will or what we often speak of as the heart. Edwards explained that to have a change of mind was not the same thing as to have a change of heart. The latter involved deep feeling, new direction, transformed life. There was a great difference, he said, between being told that honey is sweet and having the experience of tasting honey. The latter knowledge is direct, intuitive, certain, and rests upon experience that can be neither doubted nor denied. This knowledge comes to us by what may be called a "sense of the heart." "Spiritual wisdom and grace is the highest and most excellent gift that ever God bestows on any creature," Edwards declared. Furthermore, "it is not a thing that belongs to reason ... it is not a speculative thing, but depends on the sense of the heart." Edwards joined Puritan theology to evangelical piety and practice, and that made for a forceful blend that long shaped the religious and intellectual life of New England.

Puritanism was not only a theological movement but also a liturgical one, deeply concerned with reshaping the ceremonial life of the Church of England. What went on in the national church seemed to the Puritan far too Catholic, too "papist." Worshipers should not kneel when receiving the sacrament of the Lord's Supper, for that suggested a kind of idolatry, an acceptance of the Catholic idea that the wine and the bread were in fact transformed into the very body and blood of Jesus Christ. Instead, communicants should sit together as a community at a great feast. Vestments should not be worn, for they implied a spiritual distance between clergy and laity—as if those persons belonged to separate castes. Academic gowns might be worn, for that indicated a special training or preparation but not a higher spiritual order. If one reads the New Testament carefully, the Puritans argued, one finds no ground for the high office of bishop with such special prerogatives as the rites of confirmation and ordination. Indeed, in the Puritan view, one could find no justification for a whole host of Catholic and Anglican ceremonies, including even the exchange of wedding rings and the celebration of Christmas.

For Puritans, as for most Protestants, the list of Catholic sacraments narrowed from seven to only two: baptism and communion. Baptism represented an initiation into the Christian community; it could be bestowed appropriately upon infants, properly sponsored by their natural parents (church members, of course). Infant baptism was a pledge for the future by all who witnessed it: to support and sustain this child, nurturing his or her faith and bringing that youth into a full and faithful participation in mature Christian life. The Lord's Supper sustained the Christian community, as ordinary food sustained the common life. Bread was the most basic food, the "staff of life"; similarly, the bread served in the Lord's Supper was basic to one's spiritual life. Wine, said Samuel Willard, symbolized the work of Christ: "Wine is a cordial, it comforts the heart, recruits the fainting spirits, and greatly refresheth them that drink it." These sacraments were observed because Christ commanded that they be; they served as key community moments, dense with meaning and no small danger. Those who communed unworthily, Puritan ministers and catechisms warned, ate and drank their own damnation. It was no wonder that some Puritans, anxious about their worthiness and readiness, fearfully avoided the sacrament of the Lord's Supper.

The minister was no intermediary standing between the worshipers and their God, and the Catholic saints and the Virgin Mary had no special intercessory role to play. Sunday was a holy day, to be strictly observed. It was not a time for frivolity or sports or unnecessary travel and labor, and God was known to strike down the Sabbath breaker with ferocious judgments. At the same time feast days, saint days, and the whole church year from Advent through Easter to Pentecost had no special sanctity and called for no special observance: that would be popish, that would be worship uncleansed of the remaining taints of Catholicism. No priest or bishop should "intermeddle" in the personal piety of the Christian; no altar should suggest that the sacrifice of Christ must be repeated over and over; no statues or pictures or stained glass windows should tempt the faithful to honor anything other than God. Worship should be filled with supplications from the heart, not fixed in accord with the Book of Common Prayer or with any other book except the Bible. One came to church to praise God with psalm singing and to hear the scriptures expounded and interpreted, not ritually intoned or read without comment (the latter was called "dumb reading").

All of this took place in the meetinghouse, which was the center not only of ecclesiastical life but also of social and political life in the seventeenth-century New England town. It was the place of "meeting," whether the purpose was a call to worship or a call to the militia. On Mondays citizens met to decide what roads or fences needed to be repaired, what bridges must be built, whose pigs required better control, and what new land should be surveyed. The meetinghouse belonged to the town, for the whole population of the town (whether church member or not) contributed to its support and paid for its repair. Congregationalism was the official religion of New England, not just one denomination among many; the alliance between the civil and ecclesiastical authorities was both intimate and strong. Ministers did not rule the colonies of Massachusetts and

Connecticut; there was no theocracy. But clergy and magistrate, governor and people, worked in mutual understanding of common obligations all carried out under the watchful eye of God.

The settlement patterns of New England, differing markedly from the "scattered plantings" of Virginia, centered on the creation of towns, just as those towns centered on the meetinghouse. Ironically, New England did better at re-creating the parish life of old England than did Virginia, which had set such a re-creation as its goal. And New England ended up as the most thoroughly "churched" region of colonial North America. By 1740 Congregationalists had well over 400 churches, concentrated largely in Massachusetts, Connecticut, and southeastern New Hampshire. Anglicanism at that same time had little more than half that number, spread all throughout the South as well as widely scattered in colonies north of the Chesapeake. No other denomination began to approach these two in number of churches, and no group, not even Anglicanism, rivaled Congregationalism in its ecclesial saturation, authority, and power.

The revivalism of the 1740s may have "awakened" many New Englanders to a more earnest and committed spiritual life, but it also divided their churches into two "armies" (as Jonathan Edwards said), the New Lights, who favored the revivals, and the Old Lights, who opposed them. Revivalists and itinerant ministers, foremost among them Britain's George Whitefield, alarmed and alienated many. Whitefield challenged the standing order and questioned the conversionist zeal of its clergy. The neat and orderly pattern of one church in one town with one minister solemnly appointed thereto was threatened by noisy and critical itinerants who preached where they had not been invited, who left in their wake angry ministers and divided towns. One itinerant from New Jersey, who toured New England on Whitefield's tails, wrote of "The Danger of an Unconverted Ministry," an inflammatory and disturbing tract that suggested that regularly ordained pastors might not even be Christians! A New England minister responded with "The Danger of an Unqualified Ministry," suggesting that many of the itinerants were obnoxious and mindless troublemakers who simply did not know what they were talking about.

Such fiery tracts hardly settled matters, but they did point to the sharp divisions that ultimately spelled doom for the Congregational monopoly in New England. Many of the New Light churches, separating from the town's control, argued that only a zealous ministry and a regenerate membership faithfully reproduced the pure Christian church of New Testament days. A large number of these Separate New Light churches turned to the Baptist denomination, making that non-Congregationalist group suddenly a powerful force in New England and well beyond. Even before the Awakening, other unwelcome religious forces, such as Anglicanism and Quakerism, had invaded the Congregationalist domain. Quakers initially received the harshest treatment, and four of them had been hanged in Boston Common in the second half of the seventeenth century. Since Anglicans had the force of all England behind them, they could not be hanged, but they could be resisted. One Boston pastor, Jonathan Mayhew (1720–1766), ridiculed the absurd practice of having Anglican missionaries sent to New England. The very thought was appalling. Why, Mayhew exploded, missionaries have been sent into those very towns "where the public worship was regularly upheld, and his word and sacraments duly administered." Anglicans, as much as Baptists, seemed hell-bent on subverting the orderly and established New England Way.

By the end of the colonial period Congregational worship still dominated New England and still infused the culture of the region, but it no longer exercised anything close to a monopoly. The revival movement especially disrupted Congregational consensus about pure worship and regularly split up village churches over these matters. Many now thought that itinerant evangelists, new hymns, lay exhorters, extemporaneous sermons, outdoor revivals, and instantaneous conversions were the height of godly worship. Many others found such innovations to be the epitome of fanaticism and disorder. By the mid–eighteenth century, Catholic and Anglican liturgies could still stoke the older Puritan polemic, but most on-the-ground battles were fought now over evangelical styles of worship.

In New England, where no bishops ruled but Bibles did, education always had a high priority. The first ministers in the great migration of the 1630s were themselves university-educated men, chiefly from Cambridge University in England. So far as meager resources would allow, the Puritans resolved that education in New England would not be inferior to that available in Old England. In Massachusetts, each town of fifty households or more would maintain its own teacher of reading and writing; each town of a hundred or more families would be required by law to build and support its own grammar school. Connecticut soon followed suit with similar demands so that by 1671 all Puritan New England—alone among the American colonies—had its own public system of compulsory education. As one proponent exclaimed, "Lord, for schools everywhere among us! That our schools may flourish!"

Grammar schools constituted a good and necessary beginning, but grammar schools were not enough, certainly not for a colony that dreaded

11. The commitment of New England Puritans to education was epitomized in the founding of Harvard (1636) and Yale (1701), a commitment that was renewed with the chartering of Dartmouth College (1769). Carved out of the forests of New Hampshire, the fledgling college served in part as a missionary venture to the Indians. *Billy Graham Center Museum*

"to leave an illiterate ministry to the churches, when our present ministers shall lie in the dust." Very soon after the Puritans' arrival, therefore, leaders began to plan for some higher form of education. As Thomas Shepard (1605?–1649), pastor in a new community on the Charles River, reported, "The Lord was pleased to direct the hearts of the magistrates . . . to think of erecting a School or College, and that speedily to be a nursery of knowledge in these deserts." The Puritans' "nursery of knowledge" was placed in Shepard's town, promptly renamed Cambridge in honor of the English alma mater so many of the immigrant ministers called their own. The college itself took the name of Harvard when a young citizen died, unexpectedly leaving a legacy of nearly £800 and an entire library. Founded in 1636, a mere half-dozen years after the beginnings of Massachusetts Bay, Harvard testified to the keen commitment that the Puritans made to education.

No mere Bible school or parochial seminary, Harvard from the beginning was dedicated to the "advancement of all good literature, arts and sciences." Students were obliged to know Latin and Greek, not in order to graduate, but in order to be admitted. Of course, the school was permeated with the religious commitment that characterized the colony as a whole. A 1646 rule stipulated that every student "shall consider the main end of his life and studies to know God and Jesus Christ which is eternal life." Students had to read their Bibles twice every day, studying the scriptures carefully and being prepared "to give an account of their proficiency therein, both in theoretical observation of language and logic, and in practical and spiritual truths."

Two generations later, in 1701, Connecticut followed with Yale College. Longing for "a nearer and less expensive seat of learning" than that at Harvard, Congregationalists in the "land of steady habits" launched their school first at Saybrook, then in 1716 moved the infant institution to New Haven. In 1718 the "Collegiate School" took the name of Yale after a wealthy trader, Elihu Yale (1649–1721), who, responding to a plea from Cotton Mather (1663–1728) and others, made a significant contribution to the institution that then agreed to bear his name. Mather's argument was that bestowing his name upon the school would prove, years hence, to be a better monument than even an Egyptian pyramid. The argument of the colony's colonial agent in London (where Elihu Yale then lived) was that even if the school were not Anglican, as its benefactor was, what better way to convince young men of the truth of the Anglican cause than to make them "sensible of it by giving them good learning." Yale, like Harvard, dedicated itself from the beginning to "the liberal and religious education of suitable youth ... under the blessing of God." The founding trustees declared in 1701 that for too long they had neglected their "grand errand" to "propagate in this wilderness the blessed reformed Protestant religion in the purity of its order and worship." Yale, like Harvard, would be a vital instrument directed toward the achievement of that end.

New England Congregationalists, by means of these and other educational efforts, gave a distinctive coloration to their own culture and made a lasting imprint upon the later nation. Given the educational programs at Harvard and Yale and given the systematic qualities of Reformed theology, the intellectual legacy of colonial New England was far clearer and more defined than the legacy of any other region. The New England theology, even if internally conflicted and externally buffeted, exercised a lasting influence on American culture, evident, for example, in its extensive impact on nineteenth-century literature (including on such luminaries as Nathaniel Hawthorne, Harriet Beecher Stowe, and Herman Melville). It was evident, too, in how deeply the new nation internalized notions of chosenness and covenant. Right through to Ronald Reagan and beyond, the United States would be imagined as John Winthrop's beacon of light unto the world, the city on the hill. As President Lyndon B. Johnson remarked in 1965, our forebears "made a covenant with this land. . . If we keep its terms, we shall flourish."

"A FULL LIBERTY IN RELIGIOUS CONCERNMENTS": RHODE ISLAND

The phrase "Puritan New England" deliberately excluded Rhode Island, and all Puritans would have preferred it that way. The tiny colony of Rhode Island, founded in 1636, never became part of the New England Way and never pursued a religious conformity or uniformity. Nonetheless, this much-despised colony managed also to leave its imprint upon a later nation, that mark relating to a new and daring liberty in religion.

The efforts of the Massachusetts Bay Colony to maintain strict religious conformity exacted a high price: intolerance, persecution, and exile. One of those whom Massachusetts sought first to silence, then found necessary to expel, was Roger Williams (1603?–1682). Coming to Boston in 1631 as a Puritan minister, Williams soon found his views diverging from those of the other Puritans. In the first place, he did not believe that one could claim, in good conscience, to be still part of the Church of England while pursuing distinctly different paths of worship and thought. You cannot have your cake and eat it, too; or in Williams's words, you cannot build a square house on top of a ship's keel. And if you were so foolish as to try, the result would never be "a soul-saving true ark or church of Christ Jesus."

Massachusetts Puritans were trying to walk some invisible narrow line, trying to find some imaginary middle path wherein they could walk not totally inside the Church of England but at the same time not totally outside it either. No such path exists, Williams asserted. "This middle walking" was really nothing more than a dangerous if not fatal compromise: one must make a clean break, separating the "holy from the unholy, penitent from impenitent, godly from ungodly." To do anything less was to betray the primitive purity of the gospel.

In the second place, Williams was disturbed to discover that the first immigrants from England had simply taken over and occupied the land without any reference to or acknowledgment of the Indians. No one paid for the land or bartered for it. No one asked permission of the Indians to occupy it on terms that might be mutually agreeable. Puritans in general thought this notion utter nonsense: the Indians neither farmed nor fenced most of the land. They roamed here and there, hunted and fished; now and then they planted some corn. One could hardly believe that they actually held title to specific parcels of land, as Englishmen did. Besides, the land had been assigned to them quite legally: King Charles I, by terms of their charter, had given them the land on which they had built. Agreed, said Williams, but pray tell, who had given the land to King Charles?

Williams saw a third and even more unsettling difficulty regarding the New England Way. Puritans had fled England to escape the cruel penalties of law and the religious persecutions resulting from it. Yet in Massachusetts they forged the same kind of fatal alliance between the civil and the ecclesiastical authorities. "It has been England's sinful shame," Williams wrote, "to fashion and change [its] garments and [its] religions with wondrous ease, as a higher power or a stronger sword has prevailed." Would Massachusetts repeat that folly? Nothing is more absurd, Roger Williams contended, than "the setting up of civil power and officers to judge the conviction of men's souls." If history teaches us any lessons at all, it teaches us that force applied to religion creates not a purity of faith but a river of blood.

The Massachusetts authorities listened, at first with patience, then with incredulity, and finally with horror. Here was a man gone mad, a zealot who heeded neither the voice of reason nor the voice of God. Williams had gone so far as to declare that their churches were impure, their title to the land unclear, their enforcement of true religion both cruel and absurd.

As Cotton Mather later wrote, he was reminded of the story of a Dutch town where a violent wind caused the windmill to whirl around so fast that it overheated the millstone, setting first the mill and then the entire town on fire. "But I can tell my readers," Mather noted, that "there was a whole country in America like to be set on fire by the rapid motion of a windmill in the head of one particular man." That man, Roger Williams, must not be allowed to burn all of Massachusetts.

The colony's General Court therefore ruled in 1635: "Whereas Mr. Roger Williams . . . hath broached and divulged diverse new opinions against the authority of the magistrates and churches here, . . . it is therefore ordered that the said Mr. Williams shall depart out of this jurisdiction." This opinion was rendered as the harsh winter season approached, so the court agreed to allow Williams to stay until spring if and only if he would keep silent with respect to these "diverse new opinions." But as the sun cannot stop shining or the ocean cease its roaring, so Williams could not stop speaking to those who visited him in his home. In January the authorities made plans to arrest him and set him aboard a vessel bound for England. When Williams heard of these plans he left home "in the bitter winter season," making his way on foot out of the bay colony's jurisdiction to the headwaters of the Narragansett Bay. There he established a settlement that he called Providence "in a sense of God's merciful providence unto me in my distress." And so another colony was born, a colony whose official name remains Rhode Island and Providence Plantations.

Williams's complaints against Massachusetts were much on his mind as he founded his new colony. He therefore (1) bought the land from the Indians; (2) helped to organize a separated church; and (3) determined that the civil government would have nothing to do with religion except to maintain a peaceable social order. He and others spent many years seeking guarantees for the colony's territorial borders and assurances that their "livelie experiment" in religious liberty could be pursued. Finally in 1663, a generation after its founding, Rhode Island received from King Charles II a charter that declared without equivocation that the experiment could indeed continue. "No person within the said colony," the royal charter affirmed, "shall be any wise molested, punished, disquieted, or call[ed] in question for any differences of opinion in matters of religion." On the contrary, the colony would be founded on the premise—no, on the conviction—"that a most flourishing civil state may stand and best be maintained . . . with a full liberty in religious concernments." No other colony, state, or nation had yet dared to make a claim of such frightening extravagance.

Williams, concerned about his own religious liberty, was equally dedicated to the religious liberty of all others. His colony would be a haven for
all dissenters, for people of all shades of religious opinion or of no religious opinion at all. Whoever wished might come. And come they did, in
considerable number and variety.

One year after the colony's founding, Anne Hutchinson (1591–1643)
fell afoul of those same authorities that had banned Roger Williams. Like
Williams, Hutchinson saw herself as a very good Puritan, perhaps a
somewhat better or more insightful Puritan than many of those around
her. More purely theological than ecclesiastical in her concerns, Anne
Hutchinson wished to magnify the role of God's grace, to clarify the distinction between religion and morals. Unlike Roger Williams, Anne
Hutchinson thought she was only explicating the theology of her pastor,
John Cotton, only drawing out implications already present in Puritan
thought. But in drawing out those implications, she went further than the
fathers were willing to go, and certainly further than those fathers were
willing for a woman to go. Hutchinson talked too much, knew too much,
and presumed too much; she did things not "fitting for your sex."

So she, too, was brought to trial before Boston's General Court, and
she, too, found it necessary to flee to Rhode Island. Her enemies, employing loaded scare words of the seventeenth century, brought two charges
against her: she was both an antinomian and an enthusiast. Because she
regarded "good works" as unrelated to the evidence of salvation, she
undermined the social order of New England and destroyed all basis for
moral law. In this sense she was "against the law," which is what the word
antinomian literally means. To be an *enthusiast* in that early day meant
much more than being excited or zealous: it meant that one presumed—
the grossest presumption of all—to be inspired directly by God. Anne
Hutchinson, during the course of her trial, confessed that some of what
she knew and taught came to her by "immediate revelation." That seemed
to bypass the Bible, the clergy, and the Church, thereby once again threatening the entire social fabric of New England. As the court deliberated,
with the outcome never really in doubt, the defendant declared, "You
have power over my body, but the Lord Jesus hath power over my body
and my soul." Exercising what power it had, the court found her guilty
and exiled her from the commonwealth, while her church cast her from its
fellowship. Removing to Rhode Island in 1638, Anne Hutchinson and her
family remained in the colony until 1642; then she departed for Long
Island, where the following year she and some of her children were slain
by Indians.

During those same years Baptists took advantage of Rhode Island's liberty and settled there in significant numbers, this a full century before Baptists reached Virginia. The Baptists, emerging as another radical Separatist branch of English Puritanism early in the seventeenth century, settled in Providence in 1638 and in Newport shortly thereafter in 1639. Roger Williams participated in the founding of America's earliest Baptist church in Providence, though he remained within the denomination only a short time. He left the Baptists not for any other church, but on the conviction that a truly pure church must await the return of Christ and the initiation of a new apostolic age. In Newport the physician and clergyman John Clarke (1609–1676) gave steady and significant leadership to the infant denomination throughout the colony and beyond. When in 1651 Clarke and two companions journeyed to Massachusetts to help advance the Baptist cause, Bay Colony authorities quickly arrested all three. Four years earlier Massachusetts had passed a law against Baptists as having historically been "the incendiaries of commonwealths and the infectors of persons in main matters of religion." Such people would be banished from the colony, or if they did not live in the colony, some other form of punishment would be inflicted.

One of Clarke's companions, Obadiah Holmes (1607?–1682), learned just what that clause meant. Publicly whipped with thirty lashes in Boston's Market Street, Holmes responded by declaring that he was pleased to share in the kind of suffering that Jesus knew "so I may have further fellowship with my Lord. [I] am not ashamed of His sufferings, for by His stripes am I healed." Roger Williams was enraged at such treatment, specifically objecting to the handling of Clarke's case. Protesting to Massachusetts Governor John Endicott, Williams again made the point that the civil magistrate has no business meddling "in matters of conscience and religion." Further, if you persecute everyone who disagrees with you on any point, sooner or later, Williams wrote, you will end up persecuting Christ himself. Ask yourself this question, John Endicott: "I have fought against several sorts of consciences; is it beyond all possibility and hazard that I have not fought against God?" Not until 1682 did Boston concede the right of Baptists to hold their own services of worship there.

Long before then, Baptists had established themselves firmly in Rhode Island, but not so firmly that they enjoyed a religious monopoly. Roger Williams's colony was open to all others as well. The Society of Friends, or Quakers, shortly after their founding by George Fox in England in 1651, moved in large numbers to Rhode Island, settling especially near Newport.

Soon they were strong enough to dominate the colonial government and to become, in the words of an Anglican missionary in 1676, "the Grandees of the place." Authorities of Puritan New England, horrified that a sanctuary for Quakers existed so close to their own borders, urged authorities in Rhode Island to shut their doors against them. But that colony's General Assembly serenely declined, asserting that "freedom of conscience we still prize as the greatest happiness that man can possess in this world."

Cotton Mather was not amused. Rhode Island had become a sink, a cesspool, a latrine into which all the refuse of the world could be dumped. Never in history had there been "such a variety of religions together on so small a spot of ground," wrote Mather. One could find there anything that fancy might conjure up: "Antinomians, Anabaptists, Antisabbatarians, Arminians, Socinians, Quakers, Ranters—everything in the world but Roman Catholics and real Christians." What for Mather was a shattering indictment was for Williams and others a cherished freedom: "a full liberty in religious concernments."

Rhode Island never matched its neighbors in either population or wealth. In 1700, when Massachusetts was over 50,000 strong and Connecticut over 25,000, Rhode Island had fewer than 6,000 inhabitants. Seventy years later, it had only one-fourth the population of Massachusetts and about one-third that of Connecticut. By then Rhode Island Baptists and Quakers had been joined by Anglicans, Congregationalists, and Jews, among others. Under the auspices of the Society for the Propagation of the Gospel, Anglicanism established its first outpost in Newport in 1704. By 1726 Anglicans there had sufficient strength to erect a magnificent wooden church near the water's edge, and one year later the missionary in Newport joined with other nearby Anglican clergy to write London that England's national church did much to produce "a great reformation in life & manners, & vice and immorality." But Rhode Island, they admitted, was quite a challenge. "That fertile soil of heresy & schism" somehow found new strength to resist the Anglicans, and this sad fact was due in no small part to having Baptists and Quakers in the highest civil offices of the colony. But if London could only send them a bishop, they wrote, all would be well.

London did not send them a bishop in 1727 or at any later date. From Ireland, however, came an ecclesiastical dignitary who gave them some hope and encouragement. George Berkeley (1685–1753), who as a younger man had written philosophical works of lasting brilliance, determined to build in the New World a college that would be a fountain of learning and religion for all the colonies. From 1730 to 1732, while waiting for Parlia-

12. Rhode Island throbbed with religious dissent and diversity in the heart of Congregational New England, and that openness found one expression in the Touro Synagogue in Newport, which was built in 1763 and is the oldest synagogue building in North America. *Library of Congress*

ment to fulfill its pledge of a major grant, Berkeley lived near Newport. As an Anglo-Irish clergyman and dean of Londonderry, Berkeley often preached in that handsome wooden church, Trinity, and offered comfort to the Anglican clergy seeking a friendly following in a hostile land. Berkeley's sojourn in America gave special encouragement to a philosophical soul mate in Connecticut, Samuel Johnson (1696–1772), who later became the first president of King's College (forerunner of Columbia) in New York City. Berkeley's own college, however, was never built, as Parliament reneged on the grant and Berkeley returned in disappointment to his native Ireland.

Congregationalists, while disdainful of Rhode Island's wild and willful varieties of religion, by the 1720s felt some obligation to see that "real Christians" be introduced there, too. From Boston's Old South Church, Josiah Cotton (1703–1780) came as a "missionary" to Providence, where he organized a church in 1728. In Newport, Ezra Stiles (later president of Yale) exercised an effective ministry from 1755 to 1776. A man of broad sympathies and even broader intellectual capacities, Stiles (1727–1795) helped move Congregationalism out of its theological shell toward a more vigorous participation in cosmopolitan forms of Enlightenment rationalism and critical inquiry.

Jews also took advantage of the colony's offer of religious freedom. Arriving in the seventeenth century, Sephardic Jews, that is, Jews whose liturgical practices stemmed from Portugal and Spain, had to wait many decades before their numbers and resources permitted the building of a synagogue. They finally broke ground in 1759, completing in 1763 the finest of colonial synagogues and one that is still in use. Home of the Congregation of Jeshuat Israel, Touro Synagogue, named after its rabbi at the time of construction, had its plans drawn by Peter Harrison (1716–1775), distinguished master builder and designer who also gave to Newport other notable buildings. A tiny fraction of America's colonial population, Jews also opened synagogues in New York City, Philadelphia, Richmond, and Charleston. The first federal census of 1790 showed just how modest Jewish population was prior to the major immigrations of the nineteenth century: only 1,200 could be tabulated in the expanse from Maine to Georgia.

In 1764 the colony of Rhode Island acquired a college that ultimately came to reside in Providence under the name of Brown University. With the support of Baptists from Pennsylvania and New England, Brown took as its mission to educate young men "for discharging the offices of life with usefulness and reputation." Furthermore, the original charter, in an effort to remain true to the spirit of Roger Williams, stated, "Into this liberal and catholic institution shall never be admitted any religious tests; but on the contrary, all the members hereof shall forever enjoy full, free, absolute and uninterrupted liberty of conscience." Williams would have been pleased. Over a century earlier he had written, "Having bought truth dear, we must not sell it cheap—not the least grain of it for the whole world."

CHAPTER 4

Middle-Colony Diversity

Pluralism is not a product of the last half century alone. New York and New Jersey in the seventeenth century displayed a remarkable variety in religion without anyone having really planned it that way and without laws that officially recognized the bubbling diversity. Freedom in religion there, never complete, arrived in spite of efforts to prevent it and in spite of theories that condemned it. As in so much of American history, diversity itself set the agenda. In the earlier periods of that history, the presence of many religious options, a novelty for most seventeenth-century Europeans, demanded notice. It astounded, it amused, it offended; chiefly, however, it prevailed. And in the grand Quaker endeavor in Pennsylvania, it more than prevailed. There, from the colony's founding, the principled pursuit of the liberty of conscience yielded a lush religious variety. Across the Middle Colonies an eventful experiment with religious pluralism took place that was at once deliberate, fortuitous, and turbulent. That very diversity, if largely Protestant in its contours, is a reminder that Protestantism itself was far from homogenous. It functioned instead in early America as a religious prism through which ethnic difference, sectarian multiplicity, theological controversy, and iconoclastic fragmentation found expression.

"RELIGIONS OF ALL SORTS": NEW YORK, NEW JERSEY, AND DELAWARE

Under the auspices of their West India Company, the Dutch in 1626 sailed into the mouth of the Hudson River then later up the river to establish trading posts that would bring to Holland some share of New World riches. A major seafaring power at this time, Holland ignored the overlapping English claims of the Virginia and Plymouth Companies to purchase Manhattan Island from the Indians and moved upriver, far north of Man-

13. This Dutch Reformed Church was erected in 1715 in Albany, New York, an early center of Dutch presence in North America. *Library of Congress*

hattan, to establish Fort Orange near the present-day site of Albany. Here furs could be received from Indians to the west, in or near the Mohawk River valley, and from here oceangoing vessels could sail down the Hudson to that larger port called New Amsterdam. Trade with Europe and throughout the Caribbean would make Holland a major player, along with France, Spain, and England, in the markets of the world and in the search for that elusive shortcut to India.

While the company's interest was clearly commercial, merchant promoters urged that ministers be sent to instruct both the few settlers and the many Indians "in religion and learning." Those ministers would naturally represent the Dutch Reformed Church, Holland's legal religious institution. Amsterdam's company would direct the economic life, while Amsterdam's church (more specifically its synod or classis) would direct the spiritual life. The first ordained clergyman, Jonas Michaelius (1603–1670), arrived in April of 1628 to find "a rather rough and unrestrained people" and Indians whom he characterized as "entirely savage and wild" as well as "proficient in all wickedness and godlessness." If these comments suggest that Michaelius was not wholly charmed by the delights of New Amsterdam, the hints are correct. Neither was the West India Company wholly charmed with him. In four years he sailed for home, with little regret expressed on either side.

In 1629 the Dutch Reformed Church received official recognition as the established church of New Netherland, an establishment technically excluding the presence of other religions. Just as in Holland, however, the company preferred to follow a relaxed policy that would not make religion an issue of such difficulty or magnitude as to interfere with commerce and economic growth. Peter Stuyvesant (1592–1672), who in 1647 took over as the director-general of the colony, had trouble understanding or applying that liberal company policy. In his view, the populace of New Amsterdam was in 1647 an undisciplined mess. The town had too many nationalities, too many languages, too many religions, and not nearly enough strict Dutch obedience. Stuyvesant would clean it all up, making New Amsterdam look like the neat Dutch village it ought to be.

Already dismayed by the presence of Lutherans, Quakers, Presbyterians, and Catholics, Stuyvesant was in no mood to put up with a couple dozen impoverished Jews who arrived in his city in 1654. Thinking only of the good of "this weak and newly developing place and the land in general," Stuyvesant reported to the company, he "deemed it useful to require [the Jews] in a friendly way to depart." Accustomed to a broader tolerance in old Amsterdam than they found in New Amsterdam, the Jews protested to the West India Company. From these merchants, they received the assurance that they could "travel and trade to and in New Netherland and live and remain there, provided that the poor among them shall not become a burden to the company or to the community." Jews did live and remain there, first holding religious services in their homes, then purchasing land for a cemetery, and finally (in 1729) organizing America's first synagogue, the Congregation Shearith Israel, in what by that time had become New York City.

Stuyvesant had even greater difficulty with the Quakers. For years he tried to stamp out this "abominable heresy," though the more he stamped the more the young sect grew. Outside the law, as the Pilgrims had been in England, Quakers also met in private homes and kept their newfound faith alive and flourishing. In Jamaica on Long Island, Stuyvesant was informed in 1662, a majority of the citizens gathered on Sundays in secret Quaker meetings. An outraged director-general arrested the man in whose home such meetings had been held, hauled him to New Amsterdam for trial, and quickly found him guilty of harboring and encouraging a religion that "vilifies the magistrates and preachers of God's Holy Word, that endeavors to undermine both the State and Religion," and that seduces "others from the right path with the dangerous consequences of heresy and schism." The Quaker, John Bowne (1628–1695), was fined, a penalty he refused to pay; he quickly found himself, therefore, thrown in prison. But Bowne, like the Jews, argued his case (in person) before the West India Company, which, once more, took Stuyvesant to task. Old Amsterdam, the company noted, "has always practiced [a] policy of moderation and consequently has often had a considerable influx of people." New Amsterdam should do no less.

Stuyvesant fought against not only his own company but also the temper of his own people. In 1657 the inhabitants of Flushing protested his edict that any ship daring to bring a Quaker into his colony would be confiscated and anyone allowing a Quaker to spend the night in his home would be fined fifty Flemish pounds, with half of that amount going to the informer. The residents of Flushing, deciding they had had enough, issued a Remonstrance, which took a different stance: it advocated that "love, peace, and libertie" be extended "to all in Christ Jesus." Whether we talk of Quakers or Baptists, Independents or Presbyterians, "we cannot in conscience lay violent hands upon them." Any and all shall have the right of free entrance into our towns and our homes "as God shall persuade our Consciences."

Meanwhile, Swedish Lutherans had settled along the Delaware River near the modern city of Wilmington. Like the Dutch, the Swedes saw the New World as a potential source of wealth and trade, but again like the Dutch, the national church would go wherever merchants and governors went. The governor who arrived in the small colony in 1643, John Printz (1592–1663), was instructed to "exert himself to obtain a good breed of cattle," to obtain all kinds of sheep, to plant grapes and make wine, to search for metals and minerals, and to consider "what kind of advantages may be expected from oak-trees and walnut-trees." But in the midst of all this economic preoccupation, the governor should "above all things . . . consider and see to it that a true and due worship, becoming honor, laud, and praise be paid to the Most High God in all things." Worship would be conducted according to the "unaltered Augsburg Confession" and the "ceremonies of the Swedish Church."

While the colony of New Sweden represents the first formal introduction of Lutheranism to North America, the real strength of that European denomination had to await the arrival of much larger numbers from Germany in the eighteenth century and from Scandinavia in the nineteenth century. The few hundred Swedes who lived at Fort Christina (named in

14. The Swedish colonial venture up the Delaware River in 1638 has a continuing witness in this "Old Swede's Church" located in Wilmington, Delaware. *Keystone-Mast Collection, University of California, Riverside*

honor of their nation's seventeen-year-old queen) could not greatly advance the Lutheran cause, though one minister, John Campanius (1601–1683), tried to gather in the Delaware Indians by learning their language and by translating the catechism of Martin Luther into the "American-Virginian" tongue. When in 1654 a few hundred more Swedes arrived in such strength as to enable the colony to take over a nearby small Dutch fort, Stuyvesant to the north reacted with predictable outrage. He led seven armed vessels from New Amsterdam down to the mouth of the Delaware, then up the Delaware, where he forced the surrender of Fort Christina.

While the Swedish flag came down, the Swedish mission itself remained until the American Revolution. In New York Peter Stuyvesant's effort to guarantee a Dutch Reformed monopoly soon became academic, as the Dutch outposts fell to the English in 1664. In September of that year, England landed its soldiers at Gravesend "and marched them over Long Island to the Ferry" opposite Manhattan. British ships "came up under full sail . . . with guns trained to one side." "They had orders," reported the Dutch Reformed Minister Samuel Drisius (1600–1673), "if any resistance was shown to them, to give a full broadside on this open place, then take it by assault, and make it a scene of pillage and bloodshed." Wisely, the Dutch surrendered, and New Netherland became New York. Drisius gratefully reported, however, that the Articles of Surrender provided "that our religious services and doctrines, together with the preachers, shall remain and continue unchanged."

English authorities were prepared to acknowledge another national church, that of Holland, as being more or less on a par with their own Church of England. They were not prepared, any more than Stuyvesant had been, to look with favor on the religious hodgepodge all around them. Governor Edmund Andros (1637–1714) in 1678 painted the shocking picture: we have here, he wrote, "religions of all sorts, one Church of England, several Presbyterians and Independents [Congregationalists], Quakers and Anabaptists of several sects, some Jews." Eight years later, nothing had improved, according to Governor Thomas Dongan (1634–1715), who found also Catholics, preachers male and female, lots of Quakers (both "singing Quakers" and "ranting Quakers") and much besides: "In short, of all sorts of opinion there are some, and the most of none at all." To Dongan, it was the worst of both worlds: wild religious variety coupled with widespread religious indifference.

Early in the eighteenth century an arrogant governor, Lord Cornbury (1661–1723), resolved to harass or persecute, penalize or imprison in order to make the establishment of Anglicanism more the true reality and not simply the theoretical ideal. He turned against even the Dutch Reformed, who up to this time had been left rather alone (as indeed the Articles of Surrender required). When Dutch churches lost their ministers, Cornbury arbitrarily appointed Anglican ones in their places. When Dutch ministers arrived directly from Holland, Cornbury refused to grant them licenses to preach or to recognize a congregation's right to install them. The Dutch naturally protested that Cornbury had changed the rules that had been in

15. Colonial New York bustled not only with religions of all sorts, but also with those unin-terested in the churches. Effective Christianization was thin, especially outside New England, and one colony after another was a fertile field for Christian anxiety about wantonness and unbelief. *Library of Congress*

effect since 1664, but the governor replied that what had been done before was by mere courtesy, not by right. He, on the other hand, had the right and would exercise it to the hilt to establish the Church of England fully and firmly.

If Lord Cornbury treated the Dutch Reformed Church with contempt, one can readily imagine the scorn that fell upon other dissenters. In 1707 he took on the Presbyterians, arresting Francis Makemie (1658–1708) and John Hampton for preaching without a license. When these traveling preachers claimed the protection of England's 1689 Declaration of Religious Toleration, Cornbury calmly replied that the benefits of this act did not extend to New York. Makemie held out for a trial by jury, where he argued that he was "morally persuaded there is no limitation or restriction [of] the Law to England." English law, he added, had been extended to Barbados, to Virginia and Maryland; why not to New York? Unimpressed by precedent, Cornbury did admit that in general English law took effect in the colony of New York, "but the Act of Toleration does not extend to the Plantations by its own intrinsic virtue . . . but only by Her Majesty's Royal Instructions signified unto me."

Cornbury, who felt no obligation even to read the act, declared that it had been passed precisely to prevent "strolling Preachers" such as Makemie. The latter, who had read the law, observed that it contained "not one word against traveling or strolling Preachers." At Cornbury's request, the judge directed the jury to render a verdict of guilty. With minds of their own, the twelve jurors found Makemie innocent. Cornbury was soon recalled to England, having done the cause of Anglicanism more harm that good.

Anglicanism in New York prospered more in spite of Cornbury than because of him. The city's first Anglican church, Trinity, was chartered in 1697; a mere half century later, New York had twenty such churches with an additional eighteen in New Jersey and fourteen in Delaware. By mid-century New York Anglicans felt strong enough to consider the possibility of a college that would represent their cause in the North as the College of William and Mary did in the South. New York's General Assembly in 1746 authorized a public lottery "for the advancement of learning and toward the founding of a college," while the city's Trinity Church donated farmland for this purpose. In 1754 King George II granted a charter to "the College of the Province of New-York in the City of New-York in America." Calling their school King's College, Anglicans launched an institution that would in 1784 take the name of Columbia.

Presbyterians and others protested that New York's one college was too distinctly Anglican in liturgy and in rule. Since the colony was mixed religiously, so should the rules and regulations of the college reflect that heterogeneity. William Livingston (1723–1790), Yale graduate and Presbyterian lawyer, led the forces opposed to a strictly Anglican school. He pointed out that Congregationalists, Presbyterians, and Dutch Reformed were all more numerous than Anglicans in the 1750s; moreover, in New York also were "Anabaptists, Lutherans, Quakers, and a growing Church of Moravians, all equally zealous for their discriminating tenets." To give any one group exclusive control of King's College, Livingston argued, would "kindle the jealousy of the rest, not only against the persuasion so preferred, but the College itself." Livingston lost the battle but won the war. While the school's trustees, the majority of whom were Anglican, specified that morning and evening services would be conducted every day according to the liturgy of the Church of England and that the college president would be an Anglican "forever hereafter," diversity would not be denied. All academically qualified New Yorkers were eligible to attend, and by the time of the Revolution the very idea of an Anglican school lost any chance of continued public support. "Columbia" was clearly a more patriotic name than "King's," as the Church of England suffered from its intimate identification with the authorities against whom Americans went to war.

Far more than in Virginia or the South generally, Anglicans in New York and New Jersey opposed the Revolution and clung to England's side. The clergy, almost all missionaries sent out by the Society for Propagation of the Gospel, put down only the shallowest of roots in America, seeing England as their home and their "exile" in America as merely temporary. As they regarded it, their main mission was not to identify with American interests or condemn the Stamp Act or argue for a larger degree of local liberty. Rather, their task was to advance the cause of Anglicanism everywhere; that meant loyalty to the king no less than to his church. It also meant, from their point of view, that sending a bishop to America had the highest urgency. A New Jersey Anglican, Thomas Bradbury Chandler (1726–1790), wrote in 1767 *An Appeal to the Public* in which he declared that "arguments for sending Bishops of the Church of England to America" were so strong, so rational, so readily apparent that none could resist. Bishops were necessary for Anglicanism to conduct its affairs, including such basic rites as the ordination of new clerics, and to deny this church its bishops was to deny its religious freedom. Bishops would neither persecute other religious groups in America, Chandler promised, as they might have done in England, nor necessarily require support by taxes and other public monies. And then in an argument that could hardly have appealed to a large segment of the American public in the late 1760s, Chandler gave his case away by asserting, "Episcopacy and Monarchy are, in their Frame and Constitution, best suited to each other. Episcopacy can never thrive in a Republican Government."

Thomas Bradbury Chandler was right. As republicanism spread throughout the colonies, the Church of England did not thrive, and it would not thrive until it reconstituted itself with American-elected bishops, who had no more taste for monarchy than did their fellow citizens. Bradbury found it expedient to return to England in 1775, while his fellow clergyman in New York City, Charles Inglis (1734–1816), hung on to continue, even in 1776, the plea for a bishop and to condemn the American Revolution in no uncertain terms as "one of the most causeless, unprovoked, and unnatural" rebellions "that ever disgraced any Country." Inglis proudly reported to London that the clergy of his colony as well as those in New England and New Jersey retained their loyalty to the king; in the South, he conceded, it was another story, but "I never expected much Good of those Clergy."

While Anglicanism suffered, other denominations took up any slack that appeared: Baptists, Methodists, Quakers, Lutherans, and especially the Scots-Irish Presbyterians and the long-suffering Dutch Reformed. Colleges founded in New Jersey reflected the prestige and strength of the two latter groups. Following in the wake of the revivals of the 1730s and early 1740s, Presbyterian forces sympathetic to this "great and general awakening" established in 1746 the College of New Jersey, which later took the name Princeton. Aided by the support of Presbyterians in all the colonies as well as of many in the British Isles, Princeton suffered no reversal during the Revolution. On the contrary, it identified itself wholly with the patriotic cause, and its clergyman president, John Witherspoon (1723–1794), was the only minister to sign the Declaration of Independence. And Scots and Scots-Irish Presbyterians, who took much of their identity from the long history of Scotland's conflict with Anglicanism and English power, made the revolutionary cause their own, so much so that an English statesman was provoked to call the Revolution "a Presbyterian rebellion." The Synod of New York and Philadelphia, organized in 1758, directed the growth of Presbyterianism in all the Middle Colonies, a large proportion of that growth resulting directly from the hundreds of thousands of Scottish immigrants from both Scotland proper and the Ulster Province of Northern Ireland.

The Dutch Reformed, like the Presbyterians, participated in the larger revival movement and benefited from it. Under the leadership of

Theodore Frelinghuysen (1723–1760?), churches found new strength and membership during the course of the Dutch version of evangelical or pietist revival. A later Frelinghuysen in 1755 directed the plan for a Dutch Reformed college, the church's synod affirming their resolve "to strive with all our energy, and in the fear of God, to plant a university or seminary for young men." Like the Puritans who founded Harvard, the Dutch desired to raise up and educate their own young men so that they might "enter upon the sacred ministerial office in the church of God." Queen's College, subsequently Rutgers University, resulted a decade later from this resolve, training ministers but also offering a broad education to all its students. While the Dutch Reformed Church never swept across the country in the manner of the Presbyterians or Methodists, it continued to be a major cultural force in New York and New Jersey, where a century and a half earlier Dutch adventurers so tentatively had explored the reaches of the Hudson River.

Quakers also survived and prospered in New York and New Jersey, despite the determined efforts of both Stuyvesant and Cornbury. But Quakers flourished most dramatically in a colony of their own, founded across the Delaware River from New Jersey. And when it came to encouraging "religions of all sorts," Pennsylvania far outdistanced what even New York and New Jersey had managed to do.

"IN NO WAYS MOLESTED OR PREJUDICED": PENNSYLVANIA

Pennsylvania came into existence not in the early decades of the seventeenth century but many decades later. This timing deserves emphasis, for much more than simple chronology is involved. Penn's colony, founded in 1682, had the advantage of learning from all the others: learning above all else what mistakes to avoid in bringing a new colony into being. Thus the Quaker colony avoided the "starving time" of Jamestown and the similar struggle for survival in Plymouth. It avoided encouraging any and all to emigrate to the New World, expecting bounty without labor, harvest without planting. As Penn wrote in 1681, he would have all prospective settlers to understand "that they must look for a winter before a summer comes; and they must be willing to be two or three years without some of the conveniences they enjoy at home." Penn encouraged none to venture across the ocean with a "fickle" mind or without due reflection but to consider carefully "the providence of God in the disposal of themselves." But for those willing and ready to work, a rich land promised rich reward.

William Penn (1644–1718), born in London and a student at Oxford in the early 1660s, turned in 1667 to the Society of Friends (the Quakers). Entering an active ministry on their behalf in England and elsewhere, Penn first tried to reform his own nation and its church then, like the Pilgrims, tried to save the small sect itself from harsh persecution and possible extermination. In 1670 Penn wrote a lengthy treatise, *The Great Case of Liberty of Conscience,* in which he argued against the senseless intrusion of civil power into the tender area of religious conscience. A great and good God has given us reason, understanding, and judgment to use in matters religious, he wrote. These instruments, not sheriffs or armies, courts or jails, properly decide ultimate matters of the soul.

So Penn argued vigorously but largely in vain for a far more liberal policy of toleration in England, making his argument long before England took such a step in 1689. Before that date Penn found in the New World an even happier solution. King Charles II owed a large debt to Penn's father, who had served him in a military capacity. Charles discharged that debt by giving to the son a vast tract of land on the west side of the Delaware River. Pennsylvania (or "Penn's woods") would offer English and Irish Quakers a refuge from persecution and a path to prosperity. These things it would offer not only to them, however, but also, in the words of the 1682 Frame of Government, to "all persons living in this province who confess and acknowledge the one almighty and eternal God to be the creator." All such citizens, agreeing "to live peaceably and justly in civil society," would "in no ways be" molested or prejudiced for their religious persuasion or practice in matters of faith and worship, nor shall they be compelled at any time to frequent or maintain any religious worship, place, or ministry whatever." Thus the Holy Experiment was set upon a path that would avoid another earlier and common mistake: religious harassment and persecution. Penn's colony would grant not merely "moderation" in the Dutch manner or "toleration" in the English fashion, but a much bolder invitation to freedom in religion. And to the amazement of all, the colony did not suffer thereby; on the contrary, it quickly prospered.

Another mistake that William Penn wished to avoid pertained to the Indians. Both Virginia and Massachusetts had offended and alienated different tribal groups; both had suffered from costly Indian wars. Even before coming to America, Penn sent agents ahead to let the Delaware Indians know of his intention to occupy the land only "with your love and consent." I am well aware, Penn added, "of the unkindness and injustice" that Indians have suffered from previous English settlers and traders. "But I am not such a man, as is well known in my own country." Penn sent presents as well as promises that when he himself arrived he would seek a fair treaty and "a firm league of peace." And in laying out the city of Philadelphia ("brotherly love"), Penn charged his commissioners to "be tender of offending the Indians . . . but soften them to me and the people; let them know that you are come to sit down lovingly among them." The treaty itself, finally concluded in 1701, set Pennsylvania on a course of better relations between Indian and English than any other colony had known. Not all problems were solved or all tragedies avoided, but Penn at least had made a far better start.

Quakers settled in large numbers in Philadelphia, William Penn's carefully laid out "green country town," and in nearby lands along the river. German emigrants soon added to the ethnic and religious mixture, founding Germantown (a section of some six thousand acres) in 1683. Later, Mennonites and Amish, Anabaptist groups who had suffered terrible persecutions across post-Reformation Europe, moved into Lancaster County, west of the early Quaker settlements. Still later, in the 1730s and beyond, many German Lutherans and German Reformed (Calvinist) developed farms and churches in the region, planting further seeds for an enduring German American folk culture. Near Lancaster, in Ephrata, a German communitarian group of Seventh-day Baptists took root in 1732. Founded by pietistic visionary Conrad Beissel (1690–1768), the sect practiced celibacy, wore simple and uniform clothing, and became a major publisher of German religious works in the colonies. That enterprise at Ephrata was matched by the activities of another German-speaking pietist group, the Moravians, who set up their own closely governed community at Bethlehem. To the mottled quilt of German groups were added Scots-Irish Presbyterians, Welsh Baptists, free African Methodists, Irish Catholics, and missionary Anglicans. It was a staggering, if still predominantly Protestant, diversity.

Earliest settlers and administrators soon learned that the "blessings of liberty" also seemed to carry a few curses. For Penn himself, disappointment followed disappointment. Quakers even quarreled among themselves, while trusted deputies mismanaged their funds and abused their positions. Many mistook liberty for license and freedom for the equivalent of moral anarchy. In a sobered mood Penn later noted, "Liberty without obedience is confusion, and obedience without liberty is slavery." While he continued to work earnestly for "a blessed government and a virtuous, ingenious, and industrious society," Penn felt the reins of his Holy Experiment slipping from his grasp. Even his own family embarrassed him, and at last disease disabled him; in 1718 Penn died a dispirited and saddened man.

16. Quakers were renowned both for the place of silent meditation in their worship and for their acceptance of women preaching and testifying. Here a woman rises up in a meeting to relate an opening of light from God. *Library of Congress*

Nonetheless, the colony flourished economically and proved by 1750 to be the major center for Lutheranism, German Reformed, and Presbyterianism. Lutheranism, largely German at this time, found strong leadership in Henry Mühlenberg (1711–1787), who arrived in Philadelphia in 1742. An accomplished linguist, Mühlenberg could preach in English and Dutch as well as German, doing so far beyond the confines of Pennsylvania. He journeyed to New York, New Jersey, Delaware, Maryland, the Carolinas, and Georgia. Everywhere he went, he not only preached in whatever language seemed most appropriate, but he also conducted catechism classes, settled congregational disputes, introduced some measure of Lutheran liturgy and discipline, and carried on an extensive correspondence with those whom he could not reach in person.

As Mühlenberg noted in his valuable and voluminous journal, his willingness to minister to any and all he encountered left some people unsure whether he was even a Lutheran. The German Reformed thought he was one of them, he observed in his journal, because "I had not reviled and run down" all other denominations "but simply preached the order of salvation." An Anglican clergyman came to him, convinced that some sort of coalition could be worked out between them. The Anglican minister "expressed the opinion," Mühlenberg recorded, "that this was just the most suitable period in which to establish a bishop in America. And if this were to come to pass, native German sons of good intelligence and piety could be educated in the English academies, ordained, and usefully employed for the best welfare of the Church of Christ in both the German and the English languages." Mühlenberg listened to what must have been a surprising proposal, commenting only that one "could travel from one pole to the other in a few minutes on a map, but in practice things went much more slowly and laboriously." Such a diplomatic reply revealed Mühlenberg to be a pastor of a broad and practical spirit.

One aspect of Quakerism, however, got under his skin, as it did that of many other Pennsylvanians; namely, pacifism. Quakers believed that the command of Christ to "love your enemies and bless them that persecute you" meant at the very least that followers of Christ could not in good conscience take up arms for the purpose of killing those enemies and persecutors. In addition to the Quakers, Pennsylvania was filled with other pacifists whose roots went back to the radical Reformation of sixteenth-century Germany, Switzerland, and Holland: Mennonites, Amish, Schwenkfelders, Dunkers, and more. This disproportionate number of people unwilling to bear arms threw the burden of defense upon those who were left, a burden sometimes resented and protested. When during the course of the French and Indian War (1756–1763), some frontiersmen murdered twenty Conestoga Indians, then marched defiantly upon pacifist Philadelphia, the Quakers—according to Mühlenberg—at last were willing to bear arms, not against the French or the Indians, but against their fellow colonists! It was amazing, Mühlenberg stated, to see these "pious sheep" who had sat out the long war comfortably and who "would rather have died than lift a hand for defense" now arm themselves to "shoot and smite ... suffering fellow inhabitants and citizens from the frontier." A great many of those frontier fighters were Scots-Irish Presbyterians who fully shared Mühlenberg's impatience and would have welcomed his biting sarcasm if they had known of it.

Pacifism proved even more difficult, of course, during the equally long American Revolution, which lasted from 1776 to 1783. Benjamin Franklin (1706–1790) in that troubled period advised all pacifists to render some kind of service on behalf of the united colonies: to help care for the wounded, to provide food, or to form emergency fire brigades. If they only sat on their hands like "pious sheep," their neighbors would understandably feel great hostility against them and perhaps even give vent to it. In a petition to the Pennsylvania Assembly in 1775, Mennonites indicated that they were quite ready to accept such advice "with Cheerfulness towards all Men of what Station they may be—it being our principle to feed the Hungry and give the Thirsty Drink." A few Quakers overcame their scruples long enough to enlist in the Revolutionary Army, but most did not, holding themselves aloof not only because of pacifism but because of doubts about the colonial cause. Earlier English kings had befriended the Quakers and made Penn's colony possible; now they would stand by the present king. The Philadelphia Yearly Meeting in 1774 reminded its members that they were indebted to King George III "and his royal ancestors for the continued favour of enjoying our religious liberties."

German Reformed immigrants, like the Lutherans with whom they shared an ethnic bond, displayed no fondness for pacifism. Moving first into the upper Hudson River valley in 1708, German Calvinists made Pennsylvania the place of their largest settlement. By mid–eighteenth century, over sixty German Reformed churches had been planted in Pennsylvania, far more than in all other colonies combined. And like others who arrived a half century or more after the colony had been founded, these Germans settled farther to the west, in such counties as Montgomery, Lehigh, Northampton, Berks, and York. In their earliest years, feeling especially estranged in a land of many religions and tongues, these Calvinists often joined with Lutherans, who spoke a common tongue and shared a common national heritage. In the 1730s, for example, Lutheran and Reformed together rented "an old and dilapidated butcher's house," sharing the space and sometimes even the minister until each group gathered sufficient strength to establish its own church and hire its own clergy.

Presbyterians moved in force toward the colony's western frontier, many of them migrating from that point down the valleys into the backcountry of Virginia and the Carolinas. Enjoying unencumbered religious freedom in Pennsylvania, they continued to press beyond the Susquehanna River into the Cumberland Valley and along the banks of the Juniata River. England at the conclusion of the French and Indian War tried to halt all overland migration across the Allegheny Mountains, but Presbyterians would not be halted. In 1773 Presbyterian minister David McClure (1748–1820) made his way into the "western country," observing that the many families he overtook displayed "a patience and perseverance in poverty and fatigue" that he could only admire. They looked forward, he said, to abundant land, full freedom, and "happy days." Already twenty

SCHUYLKILL

17. Baptists distinguished themselves especially by the rite of adult baptism by full immersion, which was often made a matter of public spectacle in rivers and streams. *Billy Graham Center Museum*

years earlier, at midcentury, Presbyterians counted over 200 churches throughout America, the largest number being in Pennsylvania and New Jersey.

The earliest Baptists in Pennsylvania came from Wales, settling in or near Philadelphia before the end of the seventeenth century. In 1707 Baptist churches banded together to form the Philadelphia Association, the first such interchurch fellowship among Baptists in America, and one of enduring strength both before and after the Revolution. By 1750 Pennsylvania was second only to Rhode Island in its number of Baptist churches, and by the time of the Revolution Pennsylvania (along with much of the South) had moved well ahead of Rhode Island. Baptists, who spoke much of liberty, found the rhetoric of resistance to all tyranny, civil or ecclesiastical, congenial to their interests and readily adaptable to their theology.

Spilling over from nearby Maryland, as well as disembarking directly at Philadelphia, Roman Catholics also freely conducted their services of worship in Penn's colony. Much of colonial America continued throughout the eighteenth century to keep doors against Catholics tightly shut, but not Pennsylvania. In 1750 Catholics counted thirty churches in the colonies, all but four of these in Maryland and Pennsylvania. Even these colonies, however, could not escape rumors of "popish plots" and "Jesuit intrigues." In 1757, during the early years of the French and Indian War, many feared that Catholics would make common cause with France against the interests of England and its colonies. Prompted by this concern, British authorities ordered that a census of Pennsylvania Catholics be taken, which showed a grand total of only about 1,400 in the entire colony, the majority being German. In the Revolution, France's status shifted from enemy to ally, thereby helping to soften the near-automatic suspicion of all things Catholic.

Philadelphia also became a major center for Jews in America. Though synagogue services did not begin until the middle of the eighteenth century, the Philadelphia Jewish community grew by the end of the colonial period to be the largest in the new nation. The social and economic status of this community enabled it to erect the Cherry Street Synagogue in 1782 and to remodel that structure early in the nineteenth century in the Egyptian revival style, giving Philadelphia its first example of this architectural mode. Much later in the nineteenth century, Rabbi Isaac Leeser (1806–1868) would make Philadelphia an important center for Jewish educational and theological life in America.

After the Revolution Methodism made its presence felt in Pennsylvania as it did everywhere else. But Philadelphia was uniquely important in the organization of and ministry to black Methodists. In 1787 Richard Allen (1760–1831), along with other African Americans, led an exodus from the white-controlled St. George's Methodist Episcopal Church in Philadelphia, where blacks had been confined to the gallery and suffered from various indignities of white hubris. A few years later Allen, who was born into slavery and who eventually rose to the office of bishop, founded Bethel Church as a fellowship for others of his own race, this "mother church" of African Methodism being dedicated in 1794. Here the seeds were planted for what was to become the first independent black denomination in America: the African Methodist Episcopal Church. For a time Allen had hesitated between remaining with the Methodists or turning to the Episcopalians but opted for the former, explaining, "I was indebted to the Methodists, under God, for what little religion I had" and was "convinced that they were the people of God." A companion of Allen's, Absalom Jones (1747–1818), did accept ordination in the Episcopal Church, taking over in 1796 the ministerial duties of the African Episcopal Church of St. Thomas in Philadelphia.

The Anglicans had built only a single church in Pennsylvania prior to 1700, but after Thomas Bray created his Society for the Propagation of the Gospel, prospects sharply improved. By 1750 nineteen Anglican churches had been erected in the colony, concentrated in its southeastern corner.

18. Late-eighteenth-century Philadelphia became a center for the development of independent black churches, especially the African Methodism of Richard Allen. *National Portrait
Gallery, Smithsonian Institution/Art Resource, NY*

Anglicanism seemed headed for even larger successes in the prosperous
colony when it foundered on the hard rock of anti-English sentiment in
general, antibishop sentiment in particular. Like Anglicans elsewhere in
the Middle Colonies and New England, Pennsylvania's clergy felt unable
to cope with all the religious diversity and indifference unless strengthened and supported by a resident bishop. And when revolutionary passions rose, these clergy who had taken oaths of loyalty to the king found
themselves placed upon a cruel rack. On the one hand, they could not in

good conscience omit offering the prescribed prayers for the king and the royal family; on the other hand, if they did offer such prayers they placed themselves and their churches in danger from angry mobs. What to do? Most solved their dilemma by simply closing their churches, continuing to minister in a private fashion as best they could.

Even that strategy failed to save them from all public outrage. As Thomas Barton (1730?–1780), society missionary in Lancaster, reported to London in 1776, "I have been obliged to shut my Churches to avoid the fury of the populace." By the end of 1776 when Barton's letter was written, passions ran high. Even though he had acted with all prudence and tact, Barton noted, "yet my life and property have been threatened upon mere *suspicion* of being unfriendly to what is called the American cause." And with respect to his fellow clergy, what indignities had been heaped upon them! "Some of them have been dragged from their horses, assaulted with stones & dirt, ducked in water; obliged to flee for their lives, driven from their habitations & families, laid under arrests & imprisoned!" Certainly, the year 1776 was no time to indicate any hesitation with respect to "the American cause" or to reveal any sympathy with either England's Parliament or king. Neither was it a time, in the words of Philadelphia's Thomas Paine (1737–1809), to put up with the summer soldier or sunshine patriot who, when the going got rough, would surrender his rifle and shed his patriotism.

Anglicanism suffered not only from its identification with England but also from its strong distaste for the wide diversity in religion so flagrantly manifest in Pennsylvania. Anglicanism adjusted far more readily to those situations in which it alone bore the title of Church, while all other groups, if present at all, were identified as dissenters or nonconformists or worse. Thomas Barton, in his capacity as missionary to all of Lancaster County, could find no more than 500 Anglicans there. The rest, he glumly reported, "are German Lutherans, Calvinists, Mennonites, New Born, Dunkers, Presbyterians, Seceders, New Lights, Covenanters, Mountain Men, Brownists, Independents, Papists, Quakers, Jews." Then, obviously out of breath as well as patience, Barton added a final "et cetera." Clearly, the Church of England had little chance to make its way "amidst such a swarm of sectaries." Barton would hang on, he would pray, and he would try to hope, but the society's headquarters back in London simply had to understand that Pennsylvania posed a challenge unlike anything his church had ever been called upon to face.

For the direction that America would later take, Pennsylvania made two critical contributions. First, it offered religious liberty on a wider scale than had been available anywhere before, that offer being accepted by a greater number than had been the case elsewhere. Second and probably even more important, Pennsylvania demonstrated that religious liberty and economic progress could go hand in hand—a conjunction that caught the eye of even so august a theorist as Adam Smith in his *Wealth of Nations* (1776). Despite all that diversity, Pennsylvania prospered in a most remarkable fashion. Though it began a half century after Massachusetts and even longer than that after Virginia, Penn's colony by the time of the Revolution had caught up with both. And Philadelphia by then had become the cultural capital of America, a center of light and learning as well as of prosperity. All this success came despite a rampant religious variety. Or could it just possibly be, as Adam Smith surmised, that such success was a result of the disestablishment of religion and the pursuit of an open religious marketplace?

CHAPTER 5

From Maryland Catholics to Georgia Evangelicals

Alone among the British colonies in North America, Maryland came into existence under Roman Catholic auspices and served as a haven for English Catholics. Just as relations between Catholics and Protestants were stormy in England, so that turbulence characterized most of Maryland's colonial years. As Maryland shifted toward Anglican establishment, this Catholic "haven" hardly remained secure. Likewise, the Carolinas and Georgia presented other locations for the exercise of Anglican power. Sometimes that power proved significant, as it was in South Carolina, but equally often it proved frail and tenuous. This was especially evident in Georgia, a belated effort of British imperial design to thwart the ambitions of Spain along the border with Florida. By the time of the American Revolution, more notable than Anglican structures were evangelical inroads from the Methodist advance along the Delmarva peninsula to the incursion of George Whitefield into Georgia.

MARYLAND

In 1632 King Charles I granted a charter to Cecil Calvert (1605–1675) for lands on both sides of the Chesapeake Bay. Calvert, who inherited from his father the title of Lord Baltimore, thus became the founder of the first proprietary colony in America, a colony in which all the land legally belonged to Calvert himself. As landlord in a quite literal sense, Calvert hoped his colony would attract many settlers and quickly become an economic success. To that end he encouraged both Protestants and Catholics to emigrate, even on the first ships, the *Ark* and the *Dove*, which set sail for the Chesapeake in 1634. He instructed his fellow Catholics aboard those ships to "preserve unity and peace among all the passengers," giving neither scandal nor offense to any of the Protestants. All occasions of Roman Catholic worship aboard ship were to be conducted as privately as possible, with all Catholics instructed "to be silent upon all occasions of discourse concerning matters of religion." If diplomacy and tact were the keys to religious harmony, Maryland's future seemed assured.

Jealousy, suspicion, and political cabal, however, prevented serenity both in Maryland and back home. In England many protested the very notion of giving land to a Catholic family, such a grant inevitably offering encouragement to a religion against which the kingdom had set its face. In 1633 the proprietor and his friends tried to soften the protests by explaining that sending Catholics off to Maryland was not necessarily doing them any great favor. "Banishment from a pleasant, plentiful, and one's own native country into a wilderness among savages and wild beasts" perhaps was not such a fair exchange. True, Catholics were persecuted in England, but an exile in colonial backwaters possibly meant departing "from one persecution to a worse. For diverse malefactors in this Kingdom have chosen rather to be hanged than to go to Virginia." Besides, some political service could be rendered to England since English subjects, even if Catholic, rather than foreigners would possess the land. No one should worry about some sort of Catholic coup in British territory, Lord Baltimore pointed out, for already three times more Protestants lived in Virginia and New England than did Roman Catholics in England. In that respect, Calvert spoke more truly than he knew: Protestant coups, not Catholic ones, would threaten his royal grant.

In March of 1634 the two ships with their nonquarreling passengers arrived at the mouth of the Potomac River then made their way northward up the Chesapeake Bay to St. Clement's Island. One member of the group, Jesuit Father Andrew White (1579–1656), offered the first Mass on the twenty-fifth of that month, then he and his fellows, bearing "a huge cross, moved in procession to a spot selected" where "we recited with deep emotion the Litany of the Holy Cross." Soon after this solemn event, the Jesuits directed the building of the first Catholic chapel in St. Mary's City, the original capital of Maryland.

Father White attempted missionary work among the Indians, but their unyielding resistance made his recall to St. Mary's mandatory. Still, Jesuit missions among the Indians remained a major objective in and around the settled areas. "It is more prudence and charity," White related, "to civilize and make them Christians than to kill, rob, and hunt them from place to place, as you would do a wolf." Again, the alternative to Christianization was extermination, not cultural and religious integrity. Like other priests and ministers, White saw the colonial venture as a hallowed opportunity to expand the cause of Christ among both Europeans and Indians. "The English nation," he stated, "never undertook anything more noble or glorious than this. Behold, the lands are white for the harvest, prepared for receiving the seed of the Gospel into a fruitful bosom."

That harvest fell into "enemy" hands quite soon, as Protestants in the early 1640s wrested control from Lord Baltimore and expelled the Jesuits from their own land. In 1646, when lawful authority was restored, the Jesuits returned to resume their labors. In an effort to prevent future religious conflict, the Maryland Assembly in 1649 passed a Toleration Act (well before England's Act of 1689), which guaranteed to all Christians the right of free worship and immunity from all coercion in religion. This would seem to have been enough to keep the neighbors at bay, but it was not. England's Civil War, the execution of the king, the ascendancy of Oliver Cromwell—all these events afflicted Maryland. A Protestant rebel named William Claiborne (1587?–1677?) managed to win full control of the colony by 1655, moving quickly to bar Roman Catholics from any civil office and to restrain anyone from practicing "the popish (commonly called Roman Catholic) religion."

When in 1660 the monarchy was restored to England, Calvert regained his authority and a comparative peace settled once more upon Maryland. But England was not finished with its turbulence or Maryland with its distractions. The Glorious Revolution of 1688, which brought William and Mary to the throne, brought a resurgence of anti-Catholic feeling both at home and abroad. In 1692 Maryland lost its proprietary status forever, becoming a royal colony under the control of very Protestant sovereigns and a very Protestant Parliament. Maryland's own assembly in that same year hurried to pass an act that provided "for the service of Almighty God and the establishment of the Protestant religion." For much of the seventeenth century the Calverts had tried to balance delicately the competing interests of Catholic and Protestant, of nation and church; they had tried a policy of open immigration and religious toleration. To no avail. By the final decade of that century Maryland, like its neighbors to the south, had become just another Anglican colony, with officialdom moving quickly to make England's church as strong and unchallenged as it could possibly be.

In 1696 the three Anglican clergy in Maryland wrote to the bishop of London, complaining that Anglicanism suffered from the presence not only of Roman Catholics but also of Quakers and "wandering preachers" who "deluded not only the Protestant Dissenters from our Church but many of the Churchmen [Anglicans] themselves by their extemporary prayers and preachments." Furthermore, new immigration augmented the Catholic presence, with "great numbers of Irish Papists brought continually into this province" and even, in disguise, a few Irish priests. Some Catholics were so misguided as to think that Lord Baltimore's authority would be restored, the Anglicans reported; thus they refused to be quiet and subdued. So even though the Church of England now enjoyed official status, it did not enjoy a great deal of respect. The solution? The Maryland churchmen, like those in New York and Rhode Island, wanted England to dispatch a bishop without further delay. What Maryland required above all else was "an Ecclesiastical rule here, invested with such ample power and authority . . . as may capacitate him to redress what is amiss, and to supply what is wanting in the Church." If no such rule were established, the clergy noted with mournful despair, Maryland would soon be overrun with "enthusiasm" (that is, Quakerism and its radical Protestant cousins) and with "idolatry" (that is, Roman Catholicism).

As was the case elsewhere, Maryland received no bishop. The colony did receive, however, Thomas Bray (1656–1730), who came as a commissary or bishop's representative at the very end of the seventeenth century. He was already identified in the public mind of England as a man thoughtfully concerned about ways in which to advance the Anglican cause. Anglicanism in the colonies, he argued, needed more than mere legislative fiats, which created parishes on paper but failed to give those parishes any real life or force. In 1695 Bray had set down his "Proposals for Encouraging Learning and Religion in the Foreign Plantations." These proposals pointed to the real weakness of Anglicanism throughout so much of North America: insufficient attention to any means for education and inadequate supply and inappropriate quality of clergy. A graduate of Oxford, Bray was a gifted student, pastor, and teacher who, when appointed a commissary by the bishop of London, took his responsibility with singular seriousness. It would not be enough to travel to Maryland, observe the deficiencies, deplore the weakened condition of the church, and come home to detail the same in a report that no one would ever read. Bray conceived of a corporation, perhaps two, that would be empowered to receive gifts, collect monies, dispatch goods and services: in short, he proposed creating agencies that for the first time would really take charge of a situation for which no one in England felt any keen obligation. And it was about time, Bray concluded, that someone did.

In 1699, therefore, Bray founded the Society for Promoting Christian Knowledge, which would go into the book business, not for England's sake but for the sake of its colonies, its "foreign plantations." This society would print and distribute literature, would encourage the creation of parish libraries, and would resolve to make each Anglican church a center of education and religious training. While noble in its intent, this society did not make the impact in colonial America that Bray's second agency did: the Society for the Propagation of the Gospel in Foreign Parts, founded in 1701 after his return from Maryland. This body, he announced, would attack the clerical problem and try mightily to solve it. On its own it would hire ministers, send them as missionaries where they were most needed, continue to support them financially as long as necessary, and continue to give them all the encouragement possible from home. To sell England on the idea Bray painted a picture of religion in the colonies darker than it really was but dark enough certainly with respect to the fortunes of Anglicanism. We are credibly informed, King William III declared in the charter of 1701, that many of the foreign plantations "are wholly destitute and unprovided of a maintenance for ministers and the public worship of God." Indeed, "many of our loving subjects" appear to have been abandoned "to atheism and infidelity"; to correct that deplorable circumstance, the society was therefore constituted and ordained.

In some respects Bray did not exaggerate. The effectiveness of the ministry to Indians, blacks, and backcountry settlers was virtually nil, for Anglicanism in the colonies showed a consistent weakness in reaching beyond its own social and geographic strongholds. Bray's society tried to change that, actively assisting those that "shall most hazard their persons in attempting the conversion of the Negroes or native Indians." A generation later, however, the secretary of the Society for the Propagation of the Gospel had to report most regretfully that little progress had been made. David Humphreys, writing in 1730, noted that while some converts had come into the church, "what hath been done is as nothing with regard to what a true Christian would hope to see effected." Humphreys added that slaves rarely had enough time off to receive religious instruction, Sunday being their only time to clear ground and plant crops "to subsist themselves and families." Masters, moreover, did not take seriously any obligation with respect to the conversion of their slaves. "Some have been so weak as to argue [that] the Negroes have no souls; others, that they grew worse by being taught and made Christians." Distressing reports these were, so much so that Humphreys felt obliged to add that he would not even mention them "if they were not popular arguments now," arguments that had "no foundation in reason or truth."

By 1750 Anglicanism was far ahead of all other religious groups in Maryland, but Catholicism had not been extinguished. One Catholic family in particular, the Carrolls, gave Catholicism a political and social visibility that enhanced its status, especially during the revolutionary years and beyond. Charles Carroll (1737–1832), a wealthy and eloquent spokesman for the Catholic cause, served as an adviser to the First Continental Congress and a delegate to the Second, in which capacity he became the only Catholic to sign the Declaration of Independence. Like Cecil Calvert a century and a half earlier, Charles Carroll manifested more tolerance and forbearance than he received. Attacked by fellow Marylander Daniel Dulany (1727–1797) for his Catholicism, for his presumed sympathies with the Stuart kings, for his being a threat—as Dulany saw it—to religious and civil liberty, Carroll responded that he despised "knaves and bigots" of whatever sect or denomination. And he added that Dulany "would make a most excellent inquisitor."

John Carroll (1735–1815), cousin to Charles, played an even more powerful part in rescuing Catholicism from the widespread suspicion with which it was regarded. Educated abroad, Carroll returned to his homeland in 1774, just as tension between England and its colonies reached the point of war. His sympathies residing wholly with the American cause, he joined in efforts to win France's aid and to keep Canada (which had bounced back and forth between France and England) at least neutral in the event of war. In 1784 Carroll was named vicar apostolic for the new nation, this title a prelude to his being elevated to the dignity of America's first Roman Catholic bishop. Carroll chose Baltimore as the site for his cathedral, and there Benjamin Latrobe (1764–1820) designed a classical structure in the style of the Pantheon in Rome. In 1785 Carroll reported to Rome on the state of Catholicism in America: a grand total of only about 25,000 members in the entire country, the vast majority of them in Maryland and Pennsylvania. Clergymen were few, but Carroll wisely warned that it was better to have no priests at all than "incautious and imprudent" ones, especially in a country ever ready to find fault with a religion still widely feared and distrusted. Catholicism enjoyed no great strength in the new United States when Carroll became bishop in 1789; upon his death in 1815 he left behind a far more vigorous ecclesiastical body than he had found.

Maryland, the colonial center for Catholicism, became also—more surprisingly—the colonial center for Methodism. Emerging out of the Church of England as an evangelical movement dedicated to revival, personal holiness, and all-consuming devotion, American Methodism was spread in its earliest years by the efforts of dedicated laymen and laywomen. Thus in 1766 Robert Strawbridge (d. 1781) first introduced the Methodist

19. John Carroll, the first bishop of the Roman Catholic Church in the United States, built upon the earlier labors of Father Andrew White and the large hopes of Cecil Calvert. *National Portrait Gallery, Smithsonian Institution/Art Resource, NY*

message in Maryland. The "cradle of Methodism" in America, Barrett's Chapel near Frederick, soon resulted from Strawbridge's lay preaching. A Methodist conference meeting in 1773 reported more Methodists in Maryland than in any of the other colonies, though Methodism swiftly spread south into Virginia and north into Delaware, Pennsylvania, New Jersey, and New York. In 1774, however, over half of the colonial Methodist membership still lived in Maryland.

One decade later Methodists gathered in Baltimore to declare themselves separate from the Church of England and to begin an American denomination that would reach far beyond the borders of Maryland.

Francis Asbury (1745–1816) emerged as the leading voice from that Christmas Conference in 1784 and also as the leading itinerant in advancing the Methodist gospel. Setting the example as an itinerant preacher or "circuit rider," Asbury traveled incessantly, as so many others would do after him. Methodist clergy did not settle into a single parish but moved across great expanses, visiting isolated settlements and families and pulling people into the evangelical orbit more successfully than any other movement. Methodists seemed always on the move, growing so rapidly in so many places that observers trying to keep up were flabbergasted. The Methodists, Jedidiah Morse (1761–1826) reported in 1792, number somewhere around 40,000, but then again, who knows? Every time one turns around, they seem to be in some other place where they had not been before, and every new account places them well above the numbers of only a year or two before. "It would be a matter of no small difficulty," Morse concluded, "to find out their exact amount."

While this was true up and down the Atlantic Coast, it was conspicuously true in Maryland, where Methodists soared in number, reaching both blacks and whites, using both laity and clergy, employing devout women no less than zealous men. In 1787 the General Conference exhorted its ministers to make a special effort to reach the slaves. That effort paid off as blacks, both slave and free, responded warmly to a gospel made accessible to them. Former slave Richard Allen, who was aided in winning his freedom through the preaching of the Methodist itinerant and antislavery advocate Freeborn Garrettson (1752–1827), explained: "The Methodists were the first people that brought glad tidings to the colored people. I feel thankful that ever I heard a Methodist preach." He added that African Americans were "beholden to the Methodists, under God, for the light of the Gospel we enjoy; for all other denominations preached so highflown that we were not able to comprehend their doctrines." Unmistakably, early Methodism moved in charismatic power across racial lines, across the categories of class and gender, and across age hierarchies based on youthful deference.

Maryland provided an important base of organization and initial strength for both Roman Catholics and Methodist evangelicals. That made Maryland an augur of an important part of the new nation's emerging religious demography. By the 1830s Catholics and Methodists had grown to become the two largest religious bodies in the land, and they would remain so for decades thereafter.

THE CAROLINAS

When the monarchy was restored to England in 1660 and Charles II elevated to the throne, the English moved to repudiate the religious chaos that had characterized the turbulent Cromwellian period. Stability and order, it was now widely assumed, lay in unquestioning loyalty to the king. Republican experiments and religious innovations had to be left to the past. All land was the king's, and if he so chose he could grant large portions of it to merchants and planters and loyal supporters. In 1663 Charles did bestow land between the latitudes of thirty-one and thirty-six degrees, extending from the Atlantic Ocean in the east to those mythical "South Seas" of the west. Honoring the king, that whole territory would take the name of Carolina, and if the Latin form were not enough, the major settlement and port would be called Charlestown, the only real city in the colonial South.

Settlement did not come swiftly, and by 1670 fewer than 200 people lived in the colony. By the end of the century, however, the numbers had risen to around 8,000, with half of those being black. The slave population, mostly imported from Barbados, continued to grow even more rapidly than the white, with the result that South Carolina became the only colony in which the white settlers were a minority. (In 1750 the colony numbered about 64,000, of whom nearly 40,000 were slaves.) The larger numbers of blacks, together with the whites' heavy dependence on slave labor, especially in cultivating rice, helps to account for a sharp severity in the slave code. Blacks knew both harsh treatment and cruel punishments; life expectancy in Carolina, as in the Caribbean, was low. For their part white settlers, knowing what deprivation of freedom could ultimately mean, jealously guarded their own liberties and asserted their own freedoms.

Population centered on Charlestown ("Charleston" after 1787), which served as center for the trade in furs and slaves. Immigrants from France, Germany, and Ireland as well as from the Caribbean and England poured into the town. Settlers came even from New England. And once again diversity simply defied all careful plans to reproduce an English society and a unified Anglican establishment in an American environment.

One element of that diversity resulted from a coincidence of timing. The Edict of Nantes, which had granted a measure of toleration to Protestants in France, was revoked in 1685. Finding it both prudent and necessary to flee their homeland, French Protestants, or Huguenots, sought safer shores. Carolina, at that time still in its earliest years of settlement, presented itself as one welcome possibility, with the result that about 500

Huguenots had settled there by 1700. Many of these were artisans, following trades in the New World that they had learned in the Old: blacksmiths, coopers, gunsmiths, and clock makers. And many were young and newly married, a younger population being more willing to undertake the long and dangerous ocean voyage. These French-speaking settlers quickly moved into the political life of the young colony and also quickly organized their own church in Charleston.

Both political and religious instability kept the French community disquieted and unsure of the best path to follow. Some Huguenot ministers thought it best to develop close relationships with official Anglicanism, even seeking ordination in that church. Others who recognized the need for an accommodation of sorts nonetheless determined to maintain their own liturgy, their own language, and their own Calvinist theology. One clergyman, John La Pierre (d. 1755), found Anglican pressures for conformity so irksome that in 1726 he took the unusual step of complaining by letter to the bishop of London concerning his mistreatment by the leading Anglican clergymen in the colony, Commissary Alexander Garden (1685–1756). This man, La Pierre affirmed, has charged me with "open contempt and defiance of the ecclesiastical laws and constitutions" of Carolina. La Pierre's crime, if such it was, consisted of his having baptized an infant within Garden's parish and without Garden's consent. Garden reported the offense to both the governor and the bishop of London, leaving La Pierre dismayed that he was not given an opportunity "to have made him all reasonable satisfaction in a meeting of the clergy, as our former custom was." The case has significance as a symbol of the uneasy relations between the Huguenots and the Anglicans in a colony that certainly could have used some bridges of understanding between its many religious groups. Huguenots, nonetheless, maintained a visible presence in and near Charleston, as they did much farther to the north, in New Rochelle, New York.

The Church of England struggled through many political shifts, from the initial charter, which had offered a large measure of religious toleration, to a proprietary establishment of the Church of England, which made few concessions to dissenters, to a royal colony (after 1719), which again granted to non-Anglicans some latitude for their own worship and some relief from harassment. Missionaries sent out by the Society for the Propagation of the Gospel filled their reports with complaints about the difficulties of their assignments, the disinterest of English settlers, the resistance of Indians and blacks to their preaching, and the irrepressible growth of "libertines, sectaries, and enthusiasts," particularly in the Carolina backcountry. One such missionary, Gideon Johnston (d. 1716), noted in 1710 that he lived in the midst of hardship, poverty, and disease, with the prospects for the Church of England depending on empty promises of better pay, better crops, and a better life. Johnston thought little of such promises, seeing around him in Charleston mainly "the Vilest race of men upon the earth" who have "neither honour, nor honesty nor Religion enough to entitle them to any tolerable Character."

Years later Alexander Garden found the population somewhat improved but the prospects of the Anglican church still greatly dimmed by all the unchecked competition, which, like weeds, choked out its normal development. The Huguenots along with other dissenters troubled him, but when one of his very own fellow Anglicans, George Whitefield, came bounding into the colony in 1740, preaching to and even encouraging all the dissenters, Garden exploded. That explosion is made more understandable by Whitefield's explicit attack upon Garden and upon the general spiritual state of Anglicanism in Carolina. Whitefield attended one service in Garden's church then advised the people to worship instead in the dissenting meetinghouses "since the Gospel was not preached in the Church." The revivalist added that perhaps the society should send no more missionaries to the Carolinas since those that had been sent were such poor representatives. "The Established Church is in excellent order as to externals," Whitefield wrote in 1740, but its chief ministers were "bigots." Of course, they were only raging against Whitefield for his raging against them.

Commissary Garden succeeded in summoning an ecclesiastical court in Charleston and tried to suspend Whitefield from exercising the ministerial office of an Anglican minister. Garden informed the bishop of London that if it were in his power he would excommunicate Whitefield altogether, for this evangelist only weakened the church further, holding it up to ridicule, encouraging illiterate and untrained men to imitate him in a traveling ministry, and creating the illusion that salvation was "a sudden, instantaneous Work" rather than "a gradual and cooperative work of the Holy Spirit, joining in our understandings and leading us on by Reason and Persuasion." But it was not in Garden's power either to excommunicate Whitefield or to prevent his continuing ministry. He did succeed in driving Whitefield even more fully into the arms of the dissenters, and Charleston's Baptists, Presbyterians, and Congregationalists welcomed him warmly.

The Great Awakening proved therefore another trial to Carolina's Church of England, even as dissent and indifference had been trials from the beginning. Nonetheless, Anglicanism could boast of at least sixteen churches in 1750, some of them impressive structures. An Anglican observer in 1766 thought that the church was healthy enough to turn down more mission money, carrying on its work in such grand churches as St. Phillip's and St. Michael's, the former being, by one estimate, the "most elegant Religious Edifice in British America." But Anglicanism still had to endure a revolution (Charleston, like New York City, was long occupied by the British), survive disestablishment, and absorb, by 1790, a "free exercise and enjoyment of religious profession and worship."

Much later to be settled were the regions well to the north of Charleston, regions that would eventually be designated as North Carolina. To the extent that these lands were ruled at all in the seventeenth century, that rule came from Charleston. In 1711 North Carolina had its own governor and in 1729 its full status as a distinct royal colony. If South Carolina seemed inhospitable to the careful cultivation of religion and morality, North Carolina, by contrast, made its southern neighbor took like a model society. Both Virginia and South Carolina regarded the wilderness that lay between them with hostility and derision. Virginia's acerbic William Byrd (1674–1744) in the 1730s spoke of North Carolinians as not knowing Sunday from any other day. This would be a great advantage, he added, if only they were industrious. "But they keep so many Sabbaths every week that their disregard of the Seventh Day has no manner of cruelty in it, either to Servants or Cattle." Missionaries on occasion had ventured into that wild land, but, wrote Byrd, "unfortunately the Priest has been too Lewd for the people, or ... they too Lewd for the Priest." Under these circumstances, no reformation in either doctrine or morals would ever take place.

Anglicans were not reassured when in 1707 a Quaker was named deputy governor of the province. Quakers had migrated down from inhospitable Virginia, finding in this region of Carolina no government strong enough or near enough to persecute them or drive them away. By the early years of the eighteenth century they had become a significant body in North Carolina, the only southern colony in which a Quaker presence endured. John Archdale (1642?–1717), the Quaker deputy governor, tried to play down the issue of religious distinctiveness, arguing that what really mattered was whether colonists could clear and develop the land. "For cannot Dissenters kill Wolves and Bears, etc. as well as Churchmen; as also fell Trees and clear Ground for Plantations, and be as capable of defending the same generally as well as the other?" To Archdale, the answer was obvious. And the reality of the dissenters' abilities could be

20. Scots and Scots-Irish Presbyterians, who in the middle of the eighteenth century moved into the southern backcountry, used communion tokens to ensure that only the properly prepared were admitted to the Lord's Supper. *Presbyterian Historical Society, Presbyterian Church (USA), Montreat, North Carolina*

demonstrated if only the Anglicans did not try to take too seriously their legally privileged status. To those who wished to argue that North Carolina could never prosper if dissent were not checked, Archdale had a ready response: look at Pennsylvania. Surely it "can bear witness to what I write." Let the Scottish Presbyterians flourish here as they do there, he said, for these were people "generally Ingenious and Industrious ... a People generally zealous for Liberty and Property, and will by no Persuasion be attracted to any [place] where their Native Rights are invaded." Let the dissenters come, and let us all leave their religious scruples alone.

Dissenters did come to North Carolina, arriving in such force and variety as to scandalize Virginia and South Carolina even more. By 1750 Baptists had built more churches than Anglicans, and they joined with Quakers and Presbyterians, with Moravians and German Reformed, to make that colony a rich repository of religious dissent. And if Anglican observers were sometimes encouraged by the progress of the Church of England in South Carolina, their reactions to what passed for religion in the northern province were precisely the contrary. Everything about the evangelical Baptists and Presbyterians in North Carolina offended one especially acerbic Anglican cleric, Charles Woodmason (c. 1720–1776), who found himself in something of a guerrilla war with backcountry dissenters. They mocked him, stole his horse, and noisily disrupted his preaching, "halloing and whooping" outside the church doors. They tore down the handbills announcing the places and times of his worship services and sometimes even put up fake ones to misdirect the Anglican faithful. At one point some hooligans broke into one of his churches and placed a pile of "their Excrements on the Communion Table."

Aside from the outrage of such subversive actions, Woodmason thought that these evangelicals got Christianity all wrong. These "new-born" Christians placed all too much emphasis upon religious experiences. "It seems that before a Person can be dipped he must give an Account of his Secret Calls, Conviction, Conversion, &c. &c." These testimonials, in Woodmason's view, were either hilarious or blasphemous; many were "too horrid" to be repeated. He insisted that these Baptists, with their elaborate river baptisms with women in scanty white dresses, had their liturgical life all wrong as well. If outdoor baptisms and ecstatic revivals were not bad enough, young men and young women gathered in the evenings at "what they call their Love Feasts and Kiss of Charity." In Woodmason's estimation, these apostolic gestures inevitably became occasions for much more than just religious instruction. "Lasciviousness, Wantoness, Adultery"—these were more common now than they had been before these new "Holy Persons" arrived, Woodmason commented with disgust. Indeed, he concluded, religion had been "brought into Contempt," and if steps were not taken to make the Church of England stronger in North Carolina, then all would see "the End of Religion: Confusion, Anarchy, and every Evil Work."

This was a harsh judgment, indicative of the intensity of the conflict between weakly established Anglicans and upstart evangelicals across the southern colonies. But Woodmason was interested in making a larger point, namely, that without an official church the colony was doomed and much of American religion along with it. Yet, as it turned out, it was Woodmason's sense of true religious order that was doomed. Baptists, spurred by the ongoing simmering of evangelical revival and the gathering strength of revolutionary politics, raced all across North Carolina and eventually through all of the South.

In Salem, North Carolina, a close-knit communitarian body, the Moravians, made their mark as they had in Bethlehem, Pennsylvania. This pacifistic, intensely devout European group had escaped persecution for a time by taking refuge in Saxony on the large estate of a leading pietist, Count Nicholas von Zinzendorf (1700–1760). America promised to be both a larger mission field and a more lasting refuge for these settlers. The North Carolina settlement resulted from their purchase of a large tract of wilderness in the northwestern portion of the colony, a land they named Wachovia. Salem became the "capital" of Wachovia, as in 1766 the Mora-

21. The German pietist group called Moravian Brethren built an enduring community in Bethlehem, Pennsylvania, pictured above, and another strong enclave to the south in Salem, North Carolina. *Library of Congress*

vians began to build their community store and tavern, their homes and "congregation house." We "were rejoiced and strengthened," a Moravian writer reported in that year, "by the safe arrival of the first company of Brethren and Sisters coming to us direct from Europe by way of Charleston." Resources were scarce and numbers few, "but for this small beginning we thank our Heavenly Father, and He will help us further next year." The promise of better times "next year" kept many a knot of believers clinging to their small plot of ground and subsisting on their meager harvests.

As the Moravians settled more firmly in North Carolina, they became ever more intertwined, like other religious groups in the region, with the institution of slavery. They used slave labor on their farms and in their shops, and enslaved Africans became indispensable partners in the building of the Moravians' sanctified community. A number of black Moravians, still enslaved, many of them German speaking, incorporated themselves into the spiritual life of this tight fellowship of pietist conversion and holiness. Despite their acceptance of the slave economy, the Moravian Brethren also affirmed the spiritual equality and fundamental humanity of slaves, that they "were no less creatures of God and beneficiaries of the promise of eternal salvation, bought by the blood of Jesus Christ, than were the Whites." "After death," one slave, who listened attentively to Moravian preaching, said, "we will be with God, and there we will all be equal."

This African and German encounter in the Piedmont in North Carolina was a small one compared with the vast plantations, where far harsher social relations and deeper antagonisms reigned. In the Carolinas, as in Virginia, missionaries reported the reluctance of many masters to see their slaves become Christian at all, and in the Carolinas more than in Virginia, they also reported barbaric cruelties practiced upon the slaves. Francis Le Jau (1665–1717), Anglican missionary in the Goose Creek parish near Charleston, wrote early in the eighteenth century that he had great difficulty watching one of the white overseers kneel in his church in an attitude of prayer when he knew of that overseer's merciless treatment of his slaves. Some maimed or crippled, others whipped and chained, and still others placed in a coffin where they "could not stir" for several days and nights—these and other horrors Le Jau recounted. Mistreatment was so severe that it caused slaves to commit suicide when the opportunity presented itself, but, Le Jau noted, I and much of my congregation look upon those deaths as nothing less than murder.

Nonetheless, and it is an incredible *nonetheless*, many slaves, well beyond the small group of Moravians, turned to the Christian religion and its promises of a loving and just God, one who would ultimately punish iniquity and comfort the afflicted. After careful examination and instruction ("I do nothing too hastily in that respect"), Le Jau baptized some slaves and carefully supervised their behavior thereafter. He would have baptized more, he wrote the society's headquarters back in London, but for the masters who "seem very much Averse to my Design." They continue to argue that "Baptism makes the Slaves proud and undutiful," while Le Jau continued trying to "convince them of the Contrary from the Example of those I have baptized." In a plaintive tone, Le Jau urged the society to publish something "to induce the Masters to show more Charity towards their Slaves." He also tried to reach the nearby Indians with his Christian message but confessed that the Carolina practice of "fomenting of War among them for our people to get Slaves" doomed his efforts from the start. Indeed, the behavior of the English with respect to both Indian and black "afflicts and discourages me beyond Expression."

GEORGIA

Thomas Bray, whose societies made such an impact on all of North America, was even more intimately involved in the founding of Britain's last colony on American soil. Bray's idealism by itself could never have brought Georgia into being, but that idealism joined with certain social and political necessities in England could make it happen. Britain needed another military outpost against Spain, whose forces threatened to creep up from Florida all the way to the very borders of Carolina. (The imminence of this Spanish Catholic threat made Georgia an inhospitable place for Catholics, who were denied religious liberty there.) Britain also needed some place to send the "worthy poor" with whom its debtors' prisons were filled to overflowing. Bray in the 1720s received a bequest specifying that monies derived therefrom be "employed in the erecting [of] a School or Schools for the thorough instructing in the Christian Religion the young Children of Negro Slaves & such of their Parents as show themselves inclinable & desirous to be so instructed." Bray, now aged and ill, formed yet another organization, this one known as Dr. Bray's Associates, which would oversee the expenditure of this money and, as it turned out, also oversee the founding of the colony of Georgia, named after King George II, who reigned from 1727 to 1760.

Launched with great idealism, Georgia was initially under the control of trustees from 1732 to 1752. This body of men decreed that Georgia should be free of slavery, free of liquor, and profitable to England. None of these ideals endured. By the time Georgia became a royal colony in 1752, it began to resemble its neighbors farther north, with an established Anglican church, the adoption of slavery, and the usual quarrels about land, profits, and losses. Population, moreover, remained sparse, with scarcely more than 2,000 souls by then in Georgia's vast expanse, most of these huddled around Savannah.

In its brief experimental period, Georgia did prove a haven not only for the "worthy poor" but also for the persecuted from Europe. Lutherans from Salzburg, Austria, escaped their tormentors and, under the sponsorship of Bray's Society for Promoting Christian Knowledge, made their way in 1734 to the just-launched colony. These "Salzburgers" emigrated as a religious community, led by their pastor, Johann Martin Boltzius (1703–1765), who conducted services aboard ship, sustained the faltering, and led the entire group in a service of praise when land was sighted on the fifth of March after two months at sea. "The Sixty-sixth Psalm, which came next in order of our readings, brought us great pleasure because it fitted our circumstances exceedingly well. At last we read from the fifth chapter of Joshua, with the admonition that those who needed it should use the last few days at sea to open their hearts."

Though it had not been planned for Jews to be part of the early colony, they nonetheless came in 1733. James Ogelthorpe (1696–1785), resident governor, not only welcomed them but also gave them land, and soon synagogue services were heard in Savannah. Scottish Presbyterians were encouraged to settle farther to the west where they could defend against Spanish encroachment. Moravians also arrived early but were less interested in serving as part of a military defense against anybody and soon moved northward to Pennsylvania. And the poor came, lured by the promise of land abroad and driven by the harshness of life at home. In the words of an early chronicler of Georgia's first years: "No wonder then, that great numbers of poor subjects, who lay under a cloud of misfortunes, embraced the opportunity of once more tasting liberty and happiness." The account continued, speaking of others who soon arrived: "Jews, attracted by the temptation of inheritances, flocked over"; also "Germans, oppressed and dissatisfied at home, willingly joined in the adventure." And then even "gentlemen of some stock and fortune willingly expended part of the same in purchasing servants [indentured whites, not slaves], tools, commodities, and other necessaries."

With these gentlemen came, of course, the Church of England, which later found official protection in laws passed by the Georgia Assembly. This church's progress, like that of the colony as a whole, was painfully slow. Even John and Charles Wesley came to Georgia in 1736 as young and devoted Anglican missionaries, John laboring in Savannah and Charles on St. Simon's Island. Neither found much satisfaction in his labor in Georgia, and John with his devotional rigor for sacramental requirements fared especially poorly (one woman even tried to shoot him and then chased after him with a pair of scissors). The brothers soon returned to England, having done little for the Anglican cause, but their contact with the Moravians through their Georgia travels had a lasting impact, proving crucial for the devotional dimensions of the Wesleys' soon-to-emerge Methodist movement.

As the Wesleys left Georgia, itinerant evangelist George Whitefield arrived, making a much greater impact there than his predecessors and putting an evangelical stamp upon the colony. In 1740 he started an orphanage named Bethesda near Savannah, raising money (and suspicions) for that project up and down the Atlantic Coast. After his first visit to Georgia in 1738, he noted in his journal that he left it with great regret.

22. From New England to Georgia, the revivalist George Whitefield attracted enormous crowds to hear his dramatic preaching. Even in death Whitefield displayed a power to inspire people, as he was immortalized in poetry and statuary. *University of Pennsylvania*

For in his opinion, he wrote, it was "an excellent school to learn Christ in." He had particularly high hopes for Savannah, "because the longer I [was] confined there, the larger the congregations grew. And I scarce knew a night . . . when the church house has not been full." But Whitefield's evangelical hopes for Georgia rightfully stirred Anglican fears of subversion. The two leaders of Whitefield's orphanage, who actually ran this House of Mercy in the itinerant's absence, were noted for the censorious judgments they heaped upon "unconverted" Anglican priests. Not surprisingly, Anglican critics saw Whitefield's operation in Georgia as "a Nest for the Enemies of the Church."

While Georgia may have been "an excellent school to learn Christ in," the learning came much too slowly for most. The solitary Anglican clergyman in Augusta complained in 1768 of "a famine, not a famine of bread, nor a thirst for water, but of hearing the word of the Lord." Savannah offered no more promise, for the colonists there "seem in general to have but very little more knowledge of a Savior than the aboriginal natives." At midcentury Georgia harbored only a scattering of churches and by the time of the Revolution a population of fewer than 50,000. The youngest of the colonies was in 1776 still too young to have its religious patterns fixed. After the Revolution, the learning came more quickly, especially as taught by Baptists and Methodists, black and white, who delivered on Whitefield's evangelical optimism for Georgia.

Suggested Reading for Part 1: Religion in the Colonial Era

Almost all of the topics covered in this book have their own historians, often in abundance, who have produced the kind of scholarship upon which general narratives like this one depend. Each of the sections on suggested reading contains a solid sampling of that scholarship, which can lead the reader quickly into wider circles of inquiry. General bibliographic resources, such as encyclopedias on American religion, are noted at the end of the book.

For leading works that highlight the complexity of historical memory and commemoration, see John D. Seelye, *Memory's Nation: The Place of Plymouth Rock* (Chapel Hill, 1998); John R. Gillis, ed., *Commemorations: The Politics of National Identity* (Princeton, 1994); David Glassberg, *American Historical Pageantry: The Uses of Tradition in the Early Twentieth Century* (Chapel Hill, 1990); and Matthew Dennis, *Red, White, and Blue Letter Days: Identity, History, and the American Calendar* (Ithaca, 2002).

On the clash of cultures and religions in the age of colonization, see, for example, James Axtell, *The Invasion Within: The Contest of Cultures in Colonial North America* (New York, 1985); Peter C. Mancall and James H. Merrell, eds., *American Encounters: Natives and Newcomers from European Contact to Indian Removal, 1500–1850* (New York, 2000); Karen Ordahl Kupperman, *Indians and English: Facing Off in Early America* (Ithaca, 2000); John Demos, *The Unredeemed Captive: A Family Story from Early America* (New York, 1994); John Thornton, *Africa and Africans in the Making of the Atlantic World, 1400–1680* (Cambridge, MA, 1992); Ramón A. Gutiérrez, *When Jesus Came, the Corn Mothers Went Away: Marriage, Sexuality, and Power in New Mexico, 1500–1846* (Stanford, 1991); and William B. Taylor, *Magistrates of the Sacred: Priests and Parishioners in Eighteenth-Century Mexico* (Stanford, 1996).

On the history of the religious life of Native Americans more generally, one would do well to consult Joel W. Martin, *The Land Looks After Us: A History of Native American Religion* (New York, 2001). On the capacity for creative mixings of native and Christian traditions, an excellent case in point is Michael D. McNally's *Ojibwe Singers: Hymns, Grief, and a Native Culture in Motion* (New York, 2000). The work of the missionaries, from earliest contact to the twentieth century, is explicated in Henry W. Bowden, *American Indians and Christian Missions* (Chicago, 1981). The Roman Catholic missions in New Spain and New France are well surveyed in John Tracy Ellis, *Catholics in Colonial America* (Baltimore, 1963).

Important overarching works on religion in the British colonies include Patricia U. Bonomi, *Under the Cope of Heaven: Religion, Society, and Politics in Colonial America* (New York, 1986), and Jon Butler, *Awash in a Sea of Faith: Christianizing the American People* (Cambridge, MA, 1990). Both have much to say on many of the topics that follow below. They are good places to begin.

Louis B. Wright gave full attention to England's religious motivations in his *Religion and Empire: The Alliance between Piety and Commerce in English Expansion, 1558–1625* (Chapel Hill, 1943). England's earliest attempts at colonization receive detailed treatment in David Beers Quinn, *Set Fair for Roanoke: Voyages and Colonies, 1584–1606* (Chapel Hill, 1985). On Anglicanism in the colonies, see the survey of John F. Woolverton, *Colonial Anglicanism in North America* (Detroit, 1984). The power and the travails of the Anglican establishment, along with the evangelical insurgency, are examined in Rhys Isaac's masterful book, *The Transformation of Virginia, 1740–1790* (Chapel Hill, 1982). An architectural historian, Dell Upton, has given life to the bricks and mortar of colonial Anglican churches in *Holy Things and Profane: Anglican Parish Churches in Colonial Virginia* (New York, 1986). For especially lively observations on the Church of England and its competitors in the 1760s, see Richard J. Hooker, ed., *The Carolina Backcountry on the Eve of the Revolution: The Journal and Other Writings of Charles Woodmason* (Chapel Hill, 1953).

The literature on New England's early religious history is especially vast; a few of the authoritative guides to it are the following: Charles L. Cohen, *God's Caress: The Psychology of Puritan Religious Experience* (New York, 1986); E. Brooks Holifield, *The Covenant Sealed: The Development of Puritan Sacramental Theology in Old and New England, 1570–1720* (New Haven, 1974); Charles E. Hambrick-Stowe, *The Practice of Piety: Puritan Devotional Disciplines in Seventeenth-Century New England* (Chapel Hill, 1982); Harry S. Stout, *The New England Soul: Preaching and Religious Culture in Colonial New England* (New York, 1986); and Edmund S. Morgan, *The Puritan Dilemma* (Boston, 1958). On the interplay between magic and religion, between clergy and ordinary folk, see especially David D. Hall's fine study, *Worlds of Wonder, Days of Judgment: Popular Religious Belief in Early New England* (New York, 1989), and also Richard Godbeer, *The Devil's Dominion: Magic and Religion in Early New England* (Cambridge, MA, 1992). On the much-studied witchcraft controversies, see, for example, Elizabeth Reis, *Damned Women: Sinners and Witches in Puritan New England* (Ithaca, 1997), and John Demos, *Entertaining Satan: Witchcraft and the Culture of Early New England* (New York, 1982).

As Rhode Island's Baptist history especially makes apparent, even in New England religion was not all of a single Puritan piece. On the prominence of dissent, see Philip F. Gura, *A Glimpse of Sion's Glory: Puritan Radicalism in New England, 1620–1660* (Middletown, CT, 1984), and William G. McLoughlin's monumental study, *New England Dissent, 1630–1833,* 2 vols. (Cambridge, MA, 1971), which traces in remarkable detail the Baptist interaction with society throughout all New England. For good analysis of Roger Williams's religious ideas, see Edmund S. Morgan, *Roger Williams: The Church and the State* (New York, 1967), and Edwin S. Gaustad, *Liberty of Conscience: Roger Williams in America* (Grand Rapids, 1991). On one of the major episodes of theological dissent and conflict, see David D. Hall, ed., *The Antinomian Controversy, 1636–1638: A Documentary History,* 2nd ed. (Durham, 1990).

On the cultural and religious interaction between the Dutch and the English in the middle colonies, see Randall H. Balmer, *A Perfect Babel of Confusion: Dutch Religion and English Culture in the Middle Colonies* (New York, 1989), and David G. Hackett, *The Rude Hand of Innovation: Religion and Social Order in Albany, New York, 1652–1836* (New York, 1991). Also see James Tanis, *Dutch Calvinist Pietism in the Middle Colonies* (The Hague, 1967). On the Scots, Ulster Scots, and the Presbyterians, see Ned C. Landsman, *Scotland and Its First American Colony, 1683–1765* (Princeton, 1985); Marilyn J. Westerkamp, *Triumph of the Laity: Scots-Irish Piety and the Great Awakening, 1625–1760* (New York, 1988); and Leigh Eric Schmidt, *Holy Fairs: Scotland and the Making of American Revivalism,* rev. ed. (Grand Rapids, 2001). On the Lutherans, see A. G. Roeber, *Palatines, Liberty, and Property: German Lutherans in Colonial British America* (Baltimore, 1993). For the early Jewish experience, see Eli Faber, *A Time for Planting: The First Migration, 1654–1820* (Baltimore, 1992).

One may profitably begin the examination of both Quakerism and Penn in the documentary history edited by Jean R. Soderlund, *William*

Penn and the Founding of Pennsylvania, 1680–1684 (Philadelphia, 1983). Both Melvin Endy and Mary Maples Dunn give major attention to the colony's founder, the former in *William Penn and Early Quakerism* (Princeton, 1973) and the latter in *William Penn: Politics and Conscience* (Princeton, 1967). Quaker preaching women have received particular attention in recent years; see, for example, Rebecca Larson, *Daughters of Light: Quaker Women Preaching and Prophesying in the Colonies and Abroad, 1700–1775* (New York, 1999), and Margaret Hope Bacon, ed., *Wilt Thou Go on My Errand? Journals of Three Eighteenth-Century Quaker Women Ministers* (Wallingford, PA, 1994). On Baptist conflicts over the speech of women, see Susan Juster, *Disorderly Women: Sexual Politics and Evangelicalism in Revolutionary New England* (Ithaca, 1994). On the French Protestant refugees, see Jon Butler, *The Huguenots in America: A Refugee People in New World Society* (Cambridge, MA, 1983). On the Moravians, see Jon F. Sensbach, *A Separate Canaan: The Making of an Afro-Moravian World in North Carolina, 1763–1840* (Chapel Hill, 1998), and Katherine M. Faull, ed., *Moravian Women's Memoirs: Their Related Lives, 1750–1820* (Syracuse, 1997).

For the sweep of the evangelical movement across the colonies, the career of evangelist George Whitefield is a good entry. See Harry S. Stout, *The Divine Dramatist: George Whitefield and the Rise of Modern Evangelicalism* (Grand Rapids, 1991), and Frank Lambert, *"Pedlar in Divinity": George Whitefield and the Transatlantic Revivals, 1737–1770* (Princeton, 1994). On the preludes to the revival, see Michael J. Crawford, *Seasons of Grace: Colonial New England's Revival Tradition in its British Context* (New York, 1991), and on its postludes, see Frank Lambert, *Inventing the "Great Awakening"* (Princeton, 1999). The rise of early Methodism receives fine treatment in Dee E. Andrews, *The Methodists and Revolutionary America, 1760–1800: The Shaping of an Evangelical Culture* (Princeton, 2000).

Part 2

RELIGIOUS FERMENT FROM THE REVOLUTION TO THE CIVIL WAR

CHAPTER 6

Liberty and Enlightenment

A long War of Independence, successfully concluded with a surprisingly generous peace treaty in 1783, set the thirteen colonies—now sovereign states—upon an uncharted course. Much uncertainty lay before them, as they grappled with the question of federal and national authority and as they struggled for some security or at least recognition as a nation among nations. One common thread bound the states together in peace even as it held them together in war: the fear of tyranny, of all tyranny, civil and ecclesiastic.

Americans in the eighteenth century understood tyrannical authority to be all of one piece. Lordly bishops like lordly princes paid little attention to ordinary folk, made few if any concessions to "majority will," and spoke seldom if at all of natural or inalienable rights bestowed upon humankind. For fourteen hundred years, by this line of revolutionary thinking, church and state had joined in a powerful alliance designed to cramp or suppress those rights and liberties. For fourteen hundred years, tyranny presented a united front, thereby forcing those who would declare their independence to fight a revolution to resist all tyranny, whether of church or of state, for in the final analysis all tyranny was one. Such at least was the pervasive assumption of those Americans who had won a revolution and signed a treaty of peace. And because of that common conviction, the American Revolution must be seen as a struggle for religious no less than civil liberty.

NO LORDS TEMPORAL OR SPIRITUAL

Resistance to "spiritual lords," more specifically, to the very idea of bishops being sent from England to America, grew especially strong in the 1760s just when the mother country tightened its control over the colonies and tried to gain a firmer grip. On their part, many Anglican clergy in the

23. Showing how biblical imagery intermingled with the cause of the Revolution, the Liberty Bell in Philadelphia's Independence Mall carries this inscription from the book of Leviticus: "Proclaim liberty through all the land." *Library of Congress*

Middle Colonies and New England raised their voices even higher in pleas that bishops be sent before it was too late, before the colonists turned not only away from the Anglican Church but against England itself. Even as late as the fall of 1776, the rector of Trinity Church in New York City, Charles Inglis (1734–1816), argued that England's cause could be rescued if only a bishop were quickly dispatched to America. "Upon the whole, the Church of England has lost none of its members by the Rebellion as yet," Inglis wrote, "none, I mean, whose departure from it can be deemed a loss." Like many other observers, Inglis saw the colonists' chances for a military victory as quite slim: "I have not a doubt but, with the Blessing of Providence, His Majesty's Arms will be successful, and finally crush this unnatural Rebellion." When that happens, England's "Church will indubitably increase, & these confusions will terminate in a large accession to its members."

If the hopes of Charles Inglis were real, so were the fears of those who saw religious liberty as well as civil liberty hanging upon the outcome of the "rebellion." As Presbyterian William Livingston (1723–1790) argued in 1768, the concerted effort to impose an Anglican bishop upon Americans posed a threat to liberty, property, and conscience even greater than the "deservedly obnoxious Stamp Act itself." That act, which had rallied the colonists against taxation without consent or representation, had been repealed in 1766, but the pressure for bishops continued, even increased. So Americans who loved their liberty had to be ever watchful, for as Boston minister Jonathan Mayhew (1720–1766) pointed out, "People are not usually deprived of their liberties all at once, but gradually, by one encroachment after another, as it is found they are disposed to bear them." Those who remembered the harsh religious persecutions carried forward by England's bishops (and who had not read Foxe's *Book of Martyrs?*) could never consent to "lords spiritual" of that stripe and heritage ever coming to America. Many of the colonists had fled England to escape such imperious bishops, and they would never allow them to land upon their own shores.

No bishops arrived, and thus the Revolution did not require a direct assault on such leaders, forcing them into exile or worse. What the Revolution did require was a swift abandonment of those privileges that the Church of England enjoyed wherever it had been legally established. In Virginia the legislature moved quickly to relieve all non-Anglicans from any further taxation for the support of Anglicanism. Laws that tried to enforce orthodoxy of belief were dropped, as toleration became the norm. But did not the Revolution require more than toleration? Did not its spirit call for a full liberty in religion, for those of all religious persuasions and even for those of none?

Here the events in Virginia must be followed closely, for they determined the course that the nation itself chose to follow. Here dissenters and deists, pietists and rationalists worked together to abolish all vestiges of an established church, substituting in its place a full and free liberty. Thomas Jefferson (1743–1826) in 1777 wrote a Bill for Establishing Religious Freedom that, as governor, he sent forward to the legislature. The latter body, dominated by members from the older Tidewater region of Virginia, was not yet ready to move away from all governmental alliance with or encouragement of religion. After all, Virginia had known more than a century and a half of close connection between the church and the state. Should this tie be totally severed? Should the Anglican Church be reduced to one more struggling sect, competing with all the other newer religious groups? Or could some compromise be found that would honor the Revolution without at the same time turning all history and society upside down?

One compromise proved particularly tempting to the legislature in Virginia: to establish not any single church or sect but Christianity itself as the official religion. Patrick Henry made several efforts to have his Bill Establishing a Provision for Teachers of the Christian Religion approved by his fellow legislators. His proposal, supported by several leading Anglicans, seemed a happy solution, for it would not discriminate against dissenters, yet it would help safeguard the social and moral order that a new state needed even more than before. It would be more broadly tolerant than previous laws had been, but at the same time it would not act as though the church and the state should have nothing whatsoever to do with each other. Christianity, if Henry's Bill should pass, would be officially declared "the established Religion of this Commonwealth; and all Denominations of Christians demeaning themselves peaceably and faithfully shall enjoy equal privileges."

Dissenters in the backcountry of Virginia suspected that this bill might be just a trick to restore the Church of England to its old favored position. Many of them also firmly believed that the confounding of civil and ecclesiastical authority, no matter how well intended, was both a bad and a dangerous idea. Baptists urged the legislature to continue in its push for a full religious liberty until "every grievous yoke be broken." Presbyterians, though often more sympathetic to the idea of an establishment than Baptists, were as wary as anyone of Anglican power and its abuses. They questioned whether Virginia legislators had the authority to make laws in the field of religion, urging such mere mortals not to presume their "Supremacy in Spirituals." Dissenters had been too long discriminated against, too long persecuted and jailed, to trust a legislature that for so many decades had been the instrument of that persecution and maltreatment. But dissenters alone could not have successfully countered Patrick Henry's moving oratory and considerable prestige.

James Madison, also a member of that Virginia legislature, assumed the task of ensuring Henry's defeat. He did so by gathering many signatures to a "Memorial and Remonstrance" against the bill and, even more, by gathering many arguments from history and from logic that could prevail against Henry's oratory and age-old habits of establishment. Religion, Madison had argued since he was twenty-two years of age, is a matter for reason to decide, not for a legislature to promote or an army to enforce. Now in 1785, a thirty-four-year-old Madison believed even more strongly in keeping civil power far removed from matters of worship and belief. Legislators simply do not have the right, much less the wisdom, to set themselves up as judges of religious truth, Madison argued. Beyond that, however, if today Virginia can lawfully establish Christianity to the exclusion of all other religions, what then will prevent Virginia tomorrow from lawfully establishing a particular denomination of Christians to the exclusion of all others? And if we do that, Madison pointed out, then we are right back where we started from before we fought a revolution to rid us of all tyranny, civil or ecclesiastic. Let us, Madison urged, leave all laws pertaining to religion to the only truly qualified authority in this area, namely, "the Supreme Lawgiver of the Universe."

James Madison prevailed; Patrick Henry lost. Thomas Jefferson (far away in Paris at the time) also prevailed, as now the Virginia legislature at last prepared itself to pass the bill that Jefferson had written long ago. In January of 1786 Jefferson's language, somewhat modified, became the Statute for Religious Freedom, making Virginia's disestablishment complete and Virginia's contribution to the nation's religious liberty crucial. Jefferson began with the fundamental premise that "Almighty God hath made the mind free." It follows then that humanity should do all it can to keep minds unshackled and uncoerced. Let us consider, Jefferson noted, that if an all-wise and all-powerful God restrained from coercing either the bodies or the minds of men and women, how utterly absurd it must be for "fallible, and uninspired men" to arrogate to themselves the right to exercise "dominion over the faith of others." But, someone will say, without the authority of the state all sorts of errors and heresies will spread. Jefferson responded that error can be conquered only by truth and that "truth is great and will prevail if left to herself."

With these presuppositions and affirmations, Jefferson's statute elevated rhetoric into law. "Be it enacted," therefore, "that no man shall be compelled to frequent or support any religious worship, place, or ministry whatsoever, nor shall be enforced, restrained, molested, or burthened in his body or goods, nor shall otherwise suffer on account of his religious opinions or beliefs." The first part of the statute defined religious freedom negatively—what citizens will not be required to do—and then, in the next breath, the statute added the positive constructions. All people "shall be free to profess, and by argument to maintain, their opinions in matters of religion." And whatever their opinions, this in no way will affect their citizenship or their rights. The statute, in short, provided for the freedom of religion but also the freedom from religion. What Jefferson had sought for so long in his "country" of Virginia was now assured; quite soon he and Madison would concern themselves with the even larger country and its liberties.

When delegates gathered in Philadelphia the very next year, 1787, to draft an entirely new outline of government, religion was not their most pressing concern. An effective union of the several states took highest priority. Nonetheless, the Constitution did not entirely ignore religion, paying attention to it only long enough to reduce potential sources of friction or division. Article Six provided that no religious test would ever be required of those holding federal office. The Constitution also allowed those taking the oath of office to "affirm" rather than "swear" their allegiance, this concession being a kindly gesture to Quakers and others who believed that biblical injunctions forbade such swearing of oaths. Other than that, the Constitution proper made no reference to religion, failing to offer even a token recognition of God's sovereignty over the people.

In a mere three months the delegates, led to a considerable degree by the astute and skillful Madison, managed to write a document that has proved remarkably resilient and enduring. When their work was done in the early fall, Madison quickly dispatched a copy to Jefferson, still in Paris. Jefferson complimented his younger colleague on a job well done but then wrote, "I will now add what I do not like." And the very first item on that list was the Constitution's failure to provide explicit guarantees for human liberties, the one Jefferson noted at the beginning being freedom of religion. The United States, no less than Virginia, must build liberty into its foundation, must not leave to chance or caprice or politics the security of those natural rights for which so many had died.

In the process of winning approval, state by state, of that Constitution written in Philadelphia, Madison discovered that many others shared Jefferson's passionate concern. He therefore promised that if the Constitution were ratified, he would make the framing of a Bill of Rights the very first order of business in the newly elected Congress. As good as his word, Madison helped guide such a bill through Congress in 1789. Ratified by a sufficient number of states by 1791, these first ten amendments to the Constitution gave liberty its solid base. The first phrase of the First Amendment spoke to the freedom uppermost in Jefferson's mind when it provided that "Congress shall make no law respecting an establishment of religion, or prohibiting the free exercise thereof." Here a double guarantee could be found: first, that government would do nothing to give official endorsement to a religion or to set one faith above another; second, that government would do nothing to inhibit the freedom of religion. In this sensitive area of the soul, government would keep its hands off. And for the first time in Western civilization, citizens of a nation could claim as their fundamental right their religious beliefs to be nobody's business but their very own.

So novel was this daring experiment in religious freedom, so unprecedented in European history, that none could be entirely sure just what it meant. Did the promise of "free exercise" extend to everyone, even to those who were not Protestants? To Roman Catholics? To Jews, Muslims, and Native Americans? Did the prohibition against "establishment" rule out federally promoted days of fasting or feasting? Did it rule out Congressional and military chaplains? Did it require a rigid neutrality that might at times appear to be even a hostility? And did it determine what the states might or might not do in the religious arena? These questions were not readily answered in the 1790s, and many of them remained just as open to debate more than two centuries later. For Jefferson himself, the language of the First Amendment seemed explicit enough. Those words, he wrote early in 1802, erected "a wall of separation between Church and State." This phrase, written during his first term as president, guided his own actions in that high office, even as to some degree it guided the nation after his death. Jefferson understood the American Revolution to have been a struggle equally against all "Lords Temporal or Spiritual."

"TO BIGOTRY NO SANCTION, TO PERSECUTION NO ASSISTANCE"

When George Washington (1732–1799) assumed the office of president in 1789, all eyes fastened upon him in order to learn whether the untried nation had merely exchanged a foreign tyranny for a domestic one. Since the history of religious persecution had been such a long and cruel one, many could hardly believe that the promises of freedom could survive the realities of politics. Those Americans who had been viewed with particular suspicion or unease had the most to fear. Roman Catholics, for example, knew firsthand the force of laws against "popery," against receiving immigrants from Catholic countries, against "divers Jesuit priests and popish missionaries." With understandable concern, they wrote to President Washington, first, to congratulate him upon his election and, second,

24. The apotheosis of George Washington was near complete in the new nation, making him the leading saint of civic duty, religious liberty, and republican virtue. *American Antiquarian Society*

to inquire concerning their status under a new form of government. With sensitivity and assurances, Washington replied (March 12, 1790) that he hoped to see "America among the foremost nations in examples of justice and liberality." With reference to the Catholics in particular, Washington added, "I presume that your fellow-citizens will not forget the patriotic part which you took in the accomplishment of their Revolution, and the establishment of their government." He also noted the critical assistance that France, "a nation in which the Roman Catholic religion is professed," had rendered to the nation in its struggle with Britain. Catholics, still a beleaguered minority confined mainly to Maryland and Pennsylvania, found hope in such promises of justice and liberality.

An even tinier minority, America's Jews, wondered if this still-vulnerable nation would continue on its Madisonian course of "offering an asylum to the persecuted and oppressed of every Nation and Religion." Newport's Hebrew congregation expressed its concern to the country's first president and received from him equally comforting words. Liberty of conscience, Washington noted (August 17, 1790), applied to all Americans alike, without distinction or discrimination. We no longer speak of "toleration," he wrote, but rather of "inherent natural rights." Then picking up an apt phrasing that the Newport congregation had used in its letter, Washington replied that "happily the Government of the United States . . . gives to bigotry no sanction, to persecution no assistance." He concluded with the wish that "the Children of the Stock of Abraham who dwell in this land [will] continue to merit and enjoy the good will of the other Inhabitants." The president envisioned a future in which "every one shall sit in safety under his own vine and fig tree, and there shall be none to make him afraid." For Jews, this post-Revolution framework of religious freedom was an extraordinary moment of emancipation, ushering in a triumphant experiment in modern citizenship yet raising vexing questions about how traditional community structures and regulations would adapt themselves to that new polity.

To many other religious groups as well, Washington affirmed that liberty was what this country was all about, that none should fear, none should waver. To the Quakers he declared that liberty in religion was not only among the nation's choicest "blessings," it was among its citizens' most certain "rights." To the Baptists he avowed that none would be more vigorous than he would be "against the horrors of spiritual tyranny, and every species of religious persecution." An old age had passed away; a new order was at hand.

That new order of the ages did not look so new, of course, to many Americans, for whom liberty to all appeared a hollow slogan. African Americans continued to labor under the harsh burdens of slavery and indignity. Even though the air rang with cries of liberty in the latter decades of the eighteenth century, few concluded that this liberty extended absolutely and unequivocally to all. In 1772 in Philadelphia, the Quaker Anthony Benezet (1713–1784) called for an end to the slave trade, "this unnatural and barbarous Traffic" and "the destruction & intolerable suffering it entails" both in the slave's country of origin as well as in the country of importation. That same year in Boston, Baptist John Allen (c. 1741–1774) argued that just as white Americans had scorned to be slaves to Britain, so black Americans should be emancipated from their bondage. "Every sensation of humanity, every bowel of pity, every compassion as a Christian" demanded that liberty be granted to "the most distressed of all human beings, the natives of Africa." Slavery in any land or nation is unforgivable, but for "those who love the Gospel of Christ" to engage in and even encourage "this bloody and inhuman Trade of Man-stealing and Slave-making" staggers the imagination and shocks all sensibility. The Declaration of Independence suffered from major deletions; the Constitution made major compromises; and the nation later confronted major consequences inflicting incalculable costs for failing to deliver on the promises of liberty for all. As abolitionist Sojourner Truth (d. 1883) would subsequently observe, "I take hold of this Constitution and it looks mighty big, and I feel for my rights, but there ain't any there."

Sojourner Truth also knew all too well that the failure to press the freedoms of democratic revolution to their full conclusion was similarly evident with the legal and political rights of women. Abigail Adams (1744–1818) had warned her husband, John, in 1776 in no uncertain terms: "In the new Code of Laws which I suppose it will be necessary for you to make, I desire you would Remember the Ladies, and be more generous and favourable to them than your ancestors. Do not put such unlimited power in the hands of Husbands. Remember all men would be tyrants if they could." Yet only a far-seeing few kept the liberties of women clearly in view. Deist Elihu Palmer (1764–1806) was among them, writing in 1797 on the unfinished work of this Age of Reason: "Among those causes of human improvement, that are of most importance to the general welfare, must be included, the total annihilation of the prejudices which have established between the sexes an inequality of rights, fatal even to the party which it favors. In vain might we search for motives by which to justify this principle, in difference of physical organization, of intellect, or of moral sensibility." While the limitations of the Revolution and the Enlightenment were many, they did hold within them a grand vision of humankind progressively advancing the causes of freedom, equality, justice, and material welfare. It was a vision amenable to the development of feminism and accordingly helped sustain America's first wave of suffragist reformers, including Elizabeth Cady Stanton (1815–1902) and Lucretia Mott (1793–1880). And the whole project of disestablishment, of throwing open the religious sphere to free competition, provided women with one of their richest domains for leadership, innovation, and social reform. The grand experiment in religious liberty was one that white American women, along with African Americans, especially seized and exploited.

If the federal government moved timidly with respect to the liberties of slaves and women, the states moved timidly with respect to a full religious freedom or failed to perceive the implications of a liberty that they generally embraced. Few states took steps as unambiguous as those taken by Virginia in 1786. Delaware's 1776 constitution required all public officials to swear their belief "in God the Father, in Jesus Christ His only Son, and in the Holy Ghost." Maryland, which stipulated that its officeholders be of the Christian religion, extended its benefits of religious liberty to Christians alone. Pennsylvania in 1790 vowed to deny state offices to any atheist as well as to anyone who did not believe in "a future state of rewards and punishments." Only Protestants could be elected in New Hampshire, Massachusetts, New Jersey, South Carolina, and Georgia—according to their constitutions of the 1770s and 1780s. Though all states supported the idea of religious liberty, their application of the concept was both uneven and gradual.

This was conspicuously so in both Connecticut and Massachusetts, where a measure of establishment continued well into the nineteenth century. Unlike the Church of England, which suffered great unpopularity during the Revolution and therefore experienced swift disestablishment, Congregationalism in New England was "locally owned and operated" and wholly committed to the revolutionary cause. No popular wave of resentment or suspicion washed over the Congregationalists, who continued to encourage local governments "to make suitable provision . . . for the institution of the public worship of God, and for the support and maintenance of public Protestant teachers of piety, religion, and morality" (to quote from the 1780 Massachusetts Constitution). In Connecticut Baptists, Quakers, and Episcopalians joined with Jeffersonian Republicans in a long struggle to sever the last remaining ties between Congregationalism and the state. In 1818 the knot was finally cut, with Jefferson writing happily to John Adams (1735–1826) that he rejoiced to see that "this den of priesthood is at length broken up, and that a protestant popedom is no longer to disgrace American history and character." Several more years passed before Massachusetts managed, after considerable involved litigation, to remove from its constitution all vestiges of an alliance between church and state that had endured for two hundred years. Step by faltering step, the sentiment responsible for the First Amendment filtered down to state and county, parish and town.

"A GOVERNMENT OF THE UNIVERSE"

If the founding fathers had much to say about liberty in religion, they also regularly acknowledged the overseeing Providence that directed all affairs of people and of nations. In 1789 George Washington called for the country to express its gratitude to "that great and glorious Being who is the beneficent Author of all the good that was, that is, or that will be." In his First Inaugural Address, the Anglican-reared president sounded the same theme: "No people can be bound to acknowledge and adore the invisible hand which conducts the affairs of men more than the people of the United States. Every step by which they have been advanced to the character of an independent nation seems to have been distinguished by some token of providential agency." Terms such as "the Grand Architect," the "superintending Power," the "Governor of the Universe," the "Great Ruler of Events"—terms both vaguely impersonal and broadly rational— were the ones used by Washington to speak of God. He rarely cited the Bible and never spoke of Jesus Christ, but he hardly needed to. For Washington had himself become a kind of Moses, leading his people from submission and captivity to a rich and bountiful Promised Land.

Washington's successor, John Adams, grew up in the Congregationalist milieu of colonial New England. He shared in the liberalism that eventually resulted in the separation of Unitarianism from its more orthodox ancestry; he also shared fully in the European Enlightenment, which sought its religious ideas more in Nature and Reason (both words being regularly capitalized by these thinkers) than in biblical revelation or Christian tradition. From Adams's youth to his old age, the subject of religion fascinated him: he could never quite let it go.

Adams had little patience with creeds and less patience with those who tried to impose them upon others. "Let the mind loose," he urged in a letter to his son in 1816; "it must be loose," uncramped by dogmatism, unfettered by superstition. The Christian religion is good—indeed, "as I understand it," the very best. But Adams understood Christianity to be primarily the sturdy ally of morality. Conduct rather than creed was the true measure of one's faith. At its best Christianity introduced millions to "the great Principle of the Law of Nature and Nations: Love your Neighbour as yourself, and do to others as you would that others should do to you." Where Christianity had gone astray was in its endless and barren disputing about theological issues, which did not alter the way in which women and men lived. Every church acted as though it had a complete monopoly on truth, Adams wrote, as though it had "the Holy Ghost in a Phial." Every church thinks only its members have guaranteed tickets of admission into heaven. In 1821 Adams noted that he simply refused to believe that "millions and millions of men are to be miserable and only a little handful of Elect Calvinists happy forever." Like Washington, Adams preferred to honor "the Power that moves, the Wisdom that directs, and the Benevolence that sanctifies" this grand and mysterious universe.

If Adams spent much time indicating what he rejected from the old orthodoxies, he also spent much time and effort emphasizing why religion was essential to the welfare of humanity in general and of the United States in particular. Adams wrote to a cousin in the early years of the American Revolution that all must remember, amid the excited cries for liberty, that "it is religion and morality alone which can establish the principles upon which freedom can securely stand." People will be free, he added, only so long as they are virtuous. "Without virtue, people may change governments, but in so doing they only trade one tyranny for another." If nations cannot survive without religion, neither can individuals. It is religion that teaches duty, that makes us responsible and honorable. Without religion, the Adamses themselves would have been "rakes, fops, sots, gamblers, starved with hunger, frozen with cold, scalped by Indians." Let us not talk about original sin, Adams cautioned, or about the absence of free will; rather, let us talk about our own responsibility and our own free choice to be "good husbands and good wives, good parents and good children, good masters and good servants." This is what religion calls us, and helps us, to be.

Thomas Jefferson, who succeeded Adams in the presidency, shared the view that religion often got off its proper track by getting lost in a wasteland of doctrinal absurdity and dogmatic perversity. Even more strongly than Adams, Jefferson condemned those who buried the "genuine precepts" of Jesus under a pile of priestly jargon and philosophical subtleties. In his retirement at Monticello, Jefferson spent many hours compiling the

Life and Morals of Jesus from a careful examination of the New Testament in Greek, Latin, French, and English. Extracting verses that emphasized the ethical content of Jesus' teaching, Jefferson hoped to make Christianity appear less the abstruse metaphysical system and more the clear moral code by which all people could live. "The sum of all religion," Jefferson noted, was proclaimed by "its best preacher: fear God and love thy neighbor." That's all there was to it: no mystery to be unraveled, no elaborate catechism to be memorized, no initiatory rite to be administered.

Why has religion, once so simple and pure, been changed into something all too complex? Jefferson's answer to that question was to blame the Platonists, who turned the pure morality of the Sermon on the Mount into "unintelligible jargon" and nonsensical whimsy. And the clergy from the fourth century down to the eighteenth have preserved their power only by preferring mystery over clarity, Jefferson argued. Jefferson, who had little sympathy for religious institutions and their "priests," declared that the paid ministry had been far more interested in profit and power than in the moral nature of humanity or the universe. Endlessly spinning out their theological formulas and defending their entrenched positions, the priests have kept their followers in ignorance and servility. But, Jefferson wrote, I wish it to be known to all that "our Saviour did not come into the world to save metaphysicians only." We have given up, he lamented, "morals for mysteries, Jesus for Plato."

The Jeffersonian theme was just this: keep Christianity simple, but also keep it moral. Like Adams, Jefferson thought morality was essential to the well-being of the country and Christianity—a purified, reasonable Christianity—was the best instrument for instructing and enforcing the moral duties. No system of morality would work, Jefferson believed, "without the sanction of divine authority stampt upon it." But this was where the emphasis of religion must lie: upon our deeds more than our words, upon our good works more than our declarations of belief. If I were to found a new sect, Jefferson observed in 1819, my fundamental principle "would be the reverse of Calvin's: that we are saved by our good works which are within our power, and not by our faith which is not within our power." Such an ethical emphasis on the practice of virtue was a cardinal tenet of deism. As Jefferson's revolutionary companion Thomas Paine said, "I believe that religious duties consist in doing justice, loving mercy, and endeavoring to make our fellow-creatures happy." Enlightenment religion bequeathed a liberal, humanistic faith, committed to virtue and benevolence: deeds not creeds; charity not ghost stories; practical technologies not airy theologies.

25. While Washington was divinized, many deists, including Thomas Jefferson and Tom Paine, were repeatedly charged with encouraging unbelief and all the sins that were thought a consequence of such infidelity. *Library of Congress*

Often called an infidel, atheist, or arch demon, Jefferson sincerely believed that he had not rejected Christianity, only purified it. He was more attached to the "pure wheat" of Jesus' teaching than were many others, who accepted the wheat all mixed up with the chaff. "I am a real Christian," Jefferson explained in 1803, in that I am "sincerely attached" to the instructions of Jesus, preferring Jesus' teaching to that of all others. Jesus taught a morality broader than that of the Greeks, who concentrated largely on the self, and more compassionate than that of the ancient Hebrews, whose ethics were "often irreconcilable with the sound dictates of reason." Jesus returned us to the Jewish idea of one God (away from all the polytheism of Greece and Rome) but gave us "juster notions of his attributes and government." Jesus, moreover, corrected the defects of ancient moral systems by "gathering all into one family, under the bonds of love, charity, peace, common wants, and common aids."

Like both of his presidential predecessors, Jefferson had no difficulty affirming "a government of the Universe." And like other deists of his time, Jefferson found the argument from design compelling. To explain a world of pattern and order and causation, one must assume a Creator and "Grand Architect." Trusting to our senses and our reason (not to biblical revelation), we know that God exists. He creates, regulates, preserves. Our reason tells us that God is One, not many; Jefferson rejected what he called "the incomprehensible jargon of Trinitarian arithmetic." And eventually, in a newly enlightened age, all will come to recognize the unity of God. "The religion of Jesus," Jefferson declared, "is founded on the Unity of God, and this principle, chiefly, gave it triumph over the rabble of heathen gods" so widely believed to exist in the Graeco-Roman world. "I have little doubt," Jefferson wrote in 1822, that "the whole of our country will soon be rallied to the Unity of the Creator."

That pure Unitarian view of God was the religion of the earliest Christians, Jefferson argued, and it would have remained the religion of all later Christians had not conniving priests so muffled the doctrines of Jesus in "mysticisms, fancies, and falsehoods." The anticlericalism of the Enlightenment went deep and thrived on images of priests as impostors, seducers, and power-hungry manipulators of the people. Jefferson and other American deists deeply shared in that disdainful perspective. There would never have been an infidel, Jefferson concluded, if there had never been a priest. This rhetoric against "priestcraft," in turn, would feed one religious insurgency after another in the new nation as democratic levelers repeatedly denounced the pretensions of learned clerics. In the words of one revival hymn from 1811,

Why are we in slavery, to men of that degree;
Bound to support their knavery when we might all be free;
They're nothing but a canker, we can with boldness say;
So let us hoist the anchor, let Priest-craft float away.

Anticlericalism thus often had a bite that deists did not fully anticipate, as it could be turned on the gentlemanly habits of learning that Enlightenment leaders so valued.

In the minds of the nation's founders, freedom from priestly control was critically important for the worldly welfare of humankind, but equally important was some continuing sense of transcendent value and immortality. Washington, Adams, and Jefferson all agreed and in various public addresses asserted that ours was a universe of morality and reason and a universe in which right would ultimately prevail—if not in this life, then in the life beyond. "A future state," John Adams affirmed in 1823, "will set all aright; without the supposition of a future state I can make nothing of this Universe but a Chaos." The whole world, without a sense of ultimate divine justice, would be nothing but "a boyish Fire Work." At the same time, though, American Enlightenment figures from Benjamin Franklin to Thomas Jefferson lacked any Puritan or evangelical urgency about the afterlife. There was simply no fear of hell, and Franklin especially could be downright cavalier about such beliefs: "You that are for no more Damnation than is proportioned to your Offences, have my Consent that it may be so: And you that are for being damned eternally, God eternally damn you all, and let me hear no more of your disputes." Still, none of America's great literati dispensed outright with ideas of ultimate reward and punishment or the immortality of the soul, holding to such beliefs to maintain a transcendent significance for human lives and to add "an important incentive" to moral conduct. For deists, as much as their orthodox Christian counterparts, the beneficence, providence, and architectural brilliance of an "All Wise Creator" abided.

In so many ways, the Enlightenment convictions about religious freedom held by the nation's founders shaped the course of religion in the United States. But what was that course? Were deists, like Jefferson and Madison, as public minded in their views of religion as they seemed to be? Or did they manage to make religion so much a private affair as to reduce it to individual commitment or even personal whimsy? When Jefferson was asked about his religion, he responded simply that "it is known to my god and myself alone." What he was willing to say, however, only underlined the private, individualistic thrust of his deistic religion: "I am of a sect by myself as far as I know," Jefferson concluded. Or as Thomas Paine said, "I do not believe in the creed professed by the Jewish church, by the Roman church, by the Greek church, by the Turkish church, by the Protestant church, nor by any church that I know of. My own mind is my own church." In a paradoxical way, Enlightenment intellectuals talked of creating a public religion, of orienting religion toward civic virtue, but equally they turned religion inward against institutions and organizations. This was a religion, at least at its logical extreme, without churches or communities or collective liturgies, constituted instead by individual believers all believing their own thing by the light of their own reason. "My own mind is my own church." If that sounded full of potential for an anarchic individualism, religious developments in the new republic would soon do much to confirm that potential.

CHAPTER 7

Freedom and Revival

At the end of the eighteenth century freedom of religion was no tired cliché but a prize of independence. In the early decades of the nineteenth century that principle would slowly suffuse daily life and the nation's development. Lyman Beecher (1775–1863), who passionately resisted the disestablishment of the Congregational Church in Connecticut, confessed after the event that severing the ties between church and state was "the best thing that ever happened to the State of Connecticut." He discovered that churches cut "loose from dependence on state support" found a renewed vigor and forcefulness. Relying "wholly on their own resources and on God," they moved forward with swift and astonishing speed to meet the challenges of a rapidly moving frontier and a rapidly expanding population.

Relying on their own resources, the churches and synagogues of America engaged in a voluntary effort of unprecedented magnitude. "Voluntarism," that is, action unaided by the state and undirected by any supreme ecclesiastical authority, came to be the distinguishing feature of religion in America, and at no time more conspicuously so than in the early decades of the nineteenth century. Robert Baird (1798–1863), one of the first historians of America's religious experiment, explained to Europeans that what was happening in the United States was different from anything they had known, and the difference lay chiefly in "the voluntary principle." For this principle, Baird noted, represented an energy and self-reliance that extended itself "in every direction with an all-powerful influence." By means of voluntary religious associations, men and women became instruments of this new force "wherever the Gospel is to be preached, wherever vice is to be attacked, wherever suffering humanity is to be relieved."

A SECOND GREAT AWAKENING

The challenge seemed enormous, perhaps well beyond the resources and will of the religious institutions themselves. First, the American Revolution had removed government from any significant role in religion. Second, the French Revolution, sending shock waves across the Atlantic, had attacked the churches and their clergy with a force and virulence that threatened the very fabric of society. Third, Enlightenment rationalism, personified in such men as Thomas Paine, Ethan Allen (1738–1789), and Elihu Palmer (1764–1806), sought to undermine the very foundations of the Christian religion, attacking biblical revelation and characterizing traditional religion as "an empire of superstition" (to quote Palmer). Fourth, the nation daily received new immigrants, who, taken together, would inexorably alter the eighteenth-century patterns of belief and behavior. Fifth, the new democratic air provided a heady atmosphere for religious innovation and schism in which there seemed to be a dearth of any reliable religious authority to referee the scriptural debates and homegrown theologies. Could any voluntary associations be strong and flexible enough to meet such challenges and address such social and intellectual changes?

What has come to be called the "benevolent empire" of the Second Great Awakening was the most robust effort to answer that question in the affirmative. Through the creation of many new agencies and organizations, through the founding of academies and schools, through the development of new techniques for recruitment and commitment, Protestant religious forces mounted a powerful counteroffensive against indifference, hostility, and fragmentation. The radical deists were routed (Thomas Paine died a lonely death, spurned by the very nation that he had rallied to revolution), and the larger rationalism of the Enlightenment was tamed for Christian purposes of progress and civilization. Immigrants were made the objects of reform and harassed by nativist organizations, and churches found new ways to assert authority and exercise power, putting a brake on some of the rambunctious sectarian energies of the period.

In the early decades of the nineteenth century new agencies sprang into existence with a bewildering profusion. In 1816 the American Bible Society arose out of individual and voluntary concern that the scriptures be widely and inexpensively distributed all across the country and even beyond. Such printing and circulation would help counter that false philosophy, masquerading "under the imposing names of liberality and reason," that would "seduce mankind" away from the truths of the Christian

26. In the first half of the nineteenth century many American Protestants were supremely hopeful that through the successes of cooperative voluntary associations the Christian millennium of peace and salvation was about to dawn. *Library of Congress*

religion and away "from all which can bless the life that is, or shed a cheering radiance on the life that is to come." Like most of the voluntary agencies springing up in the early nineteenth century, the Bible society saw itself as rising above denominational differences and sectarian jealousies to present a "united evangelical front" in the conquest of "the prodigious territory of the United States" and its rapidly increasing population.

Similarly, the American Sunday School Union, formed in 1824, would help to organize this new movement so that it might defeat or diminish all ignorance or faithlessness. The Sunday school at this time was really a school, often the only school on the frontier, where reading and writing could be taught. Because it did not require an ordained clergy to operate, the Sunday school frequently preceded the organization of a church and could exist for years independent of any church. The laity, male and female, took charge of such schools, with women playing an especially active and determinative role in their development. Sunday schools did exist, of course, prior to and apart from a "union" that attempted to coordinate and strengthen their efforts. But the union, in the words of its founders, represented "a combination of talent, of energy, and of means, and of the most approved plans of instruction." With this supervision, the schools would "become more successful, and their influence more extensive."

The very next year, the American Tract Society dedicated itself to the printing and distributing of "short, plain, striking, entertaining, and instructive Tracts" that would assist in the spread of good morals and sound religion. Noting that a ten-page tract could be produced for a single penny, the society saw such inexpensive printing as a boon particularly to the poor, most surely the "poor of an extended population." If necessary, such tracts could be given away, with the probable result that they would be used over and over, read and reread. "The traveler may scatter them along the roads and throughout the inns and cottages. . . . Merchants may distribute them to ship-masters, and ship-masters to seamen; men of business may transmit them, with every bale of goods, to the remote corners of the land and globe." In this fashion, so much good could be achieved at so little expense. "Next to the Bible and the living Ministry," nothing else could be so useful as the pervasive sprinkling of the land with booklets expressing "some of great and glorious truths of the Gospel."

Agencies such as the American Bible Society, the American Sunday School Union, and the American Tract Society reveal a strong commitment to and confidence in education. That commitment became even clearer in the establishment in the East and all along the frontier of academies and colleges that would operate under denominational influence if not control. In the early years of the young nation, states moved to support and supervise their own colleges and universities, the creation of the University of Virginia in 1816 being a conspicuous symbol of this effort. Under the sway of the Second Great Awakening, however, religious forces continued to dominate even most state institutions until well after the Civil War. When the state of New Hampshire sought in 1816 to take over Dartmouth College, then still under Congregational control, the stage was set for a major contest between religious and secular interests in higher education. When this famous case finally reached the U.S. Supreme Court in 1819, Chief Justice John Marshall's decision—to the dismay of Thomas Jefferson—upheld the right of the religious and private trustees to continue their control of the school without interference from the state.

Such a decision provided strong encouragement for denominations to launch their own colleges and maintain their long-standing dominance of higher education in America. So Congregationalists and Presbyterians

27. Among the voluntary associations proliferating in the antebellum period were those dedicated to home missions, and such efforts even included the building of floating churches to evangelize sailors and others thought to be imperiled by the transient life in port cities. *Library of Congress*

together founded such schools as Western Reserve (1826) in Ohio, Knox (1837) in Illinois, Grinnell (1847) in Iowa, and Ripon (1851) in Wisconsin. Methodists were responsible for such early frontier schools as McKendree (1835) and DePauw (1837) in Indiana, and Ohio Wesleyan (1842). Before the Civil War, Baptists brought these schools into existence: Denison (1832) in Ohio, Shurtleff (1835) in Illinois, and Baylor (1845) in Texas.

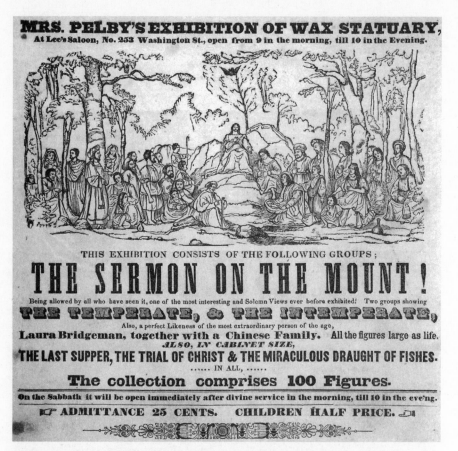

28. The entrepreneurial religious energies spawned by the Second Great Awakening took shape in new forms of religious education and entertainment, which included everything from mountains of cheap tracts to exhibitions of wax figures. *American Antiquarian Society*

These four denominations accounted for about half of all institutions of higher learning begun before 1860. By that latter date, Roman Catholics had started St. Louis University in 1832, St. Xavier in Illinois a decade later, and Indiana's Notre Dame in 1844. Episcopal schools included Ohio's Kenyon (1826) as well as Tennessee's University of the South (1858). Even such smaller groups as German Reformed, Quakers, and German Lutherans moved westward in sufficient force to create colleges in Ohio and Indiana. Religion, declared the Society for the Promotion of Collegiate and Theological Education in 1847, must be prepared to do for the frontier "what Yale, and Dartmouth, and Williams, and Amherst have done for New England: to call forth . . . a learned and pious ministry; to send life, and health, and vigor through the whole system of popular education; and, to . . . found society on the lasting basis of religious freedom and evangelical truth." Nowhere else, the society concluded, were the opportunities greater at that time than in "the valley of the Mississippi."

Finally, the Second Great Awakening rode on the waves of revivalism, a revivalism planned and promoted most effectively by Charles Grandison Finney (1792–1875). Professor of theology and sometime president of Oberlin College (founded in 1833), Finney led revivals not only in the growing towns of westward migration but also, and with equal if not greater effectiveness, in the major cities of the East. Revivals stressed the importance of individual response to Christian proclamations just as they gave the churches a renewed and enlarged membership. Under the pressures of voluntarism, churches could not live by the law of inertia alone, nor could they count on long-standing traditions to maintain their community status. To exist, churches had to persuade and recruit, win and enlist vast multitudes to their own fellowships and budgets. Revivalism proved a most valued technique for accomplishing these life-sustaining tasks, and Finney proved the most expert practitioner in the first half of the nineteenth century.

More than just a practitioner, however, Finney also defended conscious effort in promoting revivals. Some said that since revivals were given of God, one should sit back and wait until God sent a revival down to earth. Well, Finney responded, it's true that revivals, like all blessings, like harvests of corn, are ultimately the gift of God. But that did not mean that we as human beings have nothing to do but wait. Suppose one simply waited for a harvest without ever tilling the earth and planting the seed and clearing the weeds. That would make no sense at all. Neither does it make sense to suppose that we can make no preparation for the harvest of souls. "In the Bible, the word of God is compared to grain, and preaching is compared to sowing seed, and the results to the springing up and growth of the crop," Finney wrote in 1835. And just as we will reap a natural crop if we have done all our work properly, so we will reap a supernatural crop of converts only if we have done our work properly. One is as scientifically and philosophically certain as the other: proper means lead to worthy ends. Because the churches have lost sight of that simple connection between cause and effect, Finney wrote, "more than five thousand million have gone down to hell, while the church has been dreaming, and waiting for God to save them without the use of means." Now was the time, and America was the place to demonstrate the willingness of Christians, the eagerness of Christians, to gather as many lost sheep as possible into the churchly fold.

Roman Catholics had an answer to all this Protestant revivalism, and that was the parish mission. Though its roots lay in European Catholicism, the parish mission was effectively adapted as a revivalistic means for recruitment and renewal in the voluntaristic American context, including on the frontier. The bishop of the first frontier diocese, centered in Bardstown, Kentucky, Joseph Flaget (1763–1850), made his see an instrument of vigorous evangelistic activity. Prompted by the declaration of Pope Leo XII that 1825 would mark the opening of a Jubilee Year for Roman Catholicism everywhere, Bishop Flaget encouraged his own followers to celebrate not for one, but for two years in order to cover his vast territory with preaching and calls to greater repentance and dedication. Flaget "put himself at the head of his missionaries," an account written a few years later reported, "and despite the fatigue inseparable from long journeys, he wished to share with them in all the labours as well as in all the consolations." Even in the middle of winter people crowded to the churches, coming from miles around to attend Mass, to offer their confessions, and to "share in the graces flowing from the Sacrament of Penance." Evidences of repentance abounded, as even "sinners of the most inveterate habits were seen weeping over their past wanderings."

Such descriptions of Catholic parish missions paralleled the more familiar accounts of the frontier camp meeting, where members of many denominations or of none gathered for days on end to hear sermons delivered with unusual power, offer prayers, sing hymns, and find new strength in the fellowship of so many earnest Christians. Bishop Francis Asbury, one of the leading Methodist advocates of the camp meeting, estimated in 1811 that 3 to 4 million Americans were attending such events each summer; that was about a third of the entire population of the country! The drama and passion of such meetings greatly impressed the frontier observer Timothy Flint (1780–1840), who found it nearly impossible to portray the eager anticipation and the unrestrained excitement that characterized these great gatherings. Speaking of the Cumberland Valley of Tennessee in the late 1820s, Flint explained how publicity had been circulated for two or three months in advance of the actual time appointed for the meeting to begin. Then, as the day approached, "coaches, chaises, wagons, carts, people on horseback, and multitudes traveling from a distance on foot" hurried from every direction to the grove of trees selected for the encampment. There tents were pitched "and the religious city grows up in a few hours under the trees, beside the stream," which offered the necessary supply of water.

People of all ages and classes and backgrounds congregated: those run-

29. Revivalism was the great engine of Protestant growth in the new republic, and no form was more important or extensive than the camp meeting. *Library of Congress*

ning for office, those who wished merely to enjoy the spectacle, the young and beautiful "with mixed motives which it were best not severely to scrutinize," the middle-aged parents with their families, and the "men and women of hoary hairs . . . with such thoughts, it may be hoped, as their years invite." Such was the congregation "consisting of thousands," Flint reported. When lamps were hung on all the trees, when preachers of rough-hewn eloquence began to speak upon the "awful themes" of eternity, when all assembled in solemn excitement, then one beheld "the most brilliant theatre in the world," "a temple worthy of the grandeur of God."

Testimony from these camp meetings demonstrates their potency and their capacity to change the direction of lives and the intensity of loyalties. One black convert to Methodism, Zilpha Elaw (c. 1790–1846), told of first attending such a meeting in 1817 where she observed that "the hardest hearts are melted into tenderness; the driest eyes overflow with tears, and the loftiest spirits bow down." All sensed the presence of God, she added, in the midst of the "magnificently solemn scene." Worship began before sunrise, with a blowing of trumpets "to awaken every inhabitant of the City of the Lord." After devotions and breakfast in the family tents, trumpets announced the beginning of public prayer, followed at ten o'clock by the first round of public preaching, which lasted until nearly noon. Then

30. At camp meetings people not only thronged the preaching stands but also gathered in intimate groups for fervent prayer. *Billy Graham Center Museum*

after lunch in the tents, another period of prayer and preaching followed in the afternoon.

Evening brought little rest from devotion, and the night itself often became another prayer vigil. "At six o'clock in the evening, the public services commence again, as before," this continuing until around ten or so, when some stalwarts retired for further prayer and pleading. Religious services of this intensity might go on for a week or more, concluding with a "solemn love feast" after which all tents were struck as the thousands prepared to depart. The ministers, Zilpha Elaw wrote, "form themselves in procession and march round the camp, the people falling into rank and following them." After this formal processing, everyone stood still while a farewell hymn was sung. "This farewell scene is a most moving and affecting occasion," Elaw related. "Hundreds of Christians, dear to each other and beloved in the Spirit, embrace each other for the last time, and part to meet no more, until the morning of the resurrection." The camp meeting was part carnival and county fair, but it was also a time of spiritual regeneration, sustaining hope, and tearful joy. In all the topsy-turvy energies and reform-minded impulses of the camp meeting, one glimpses

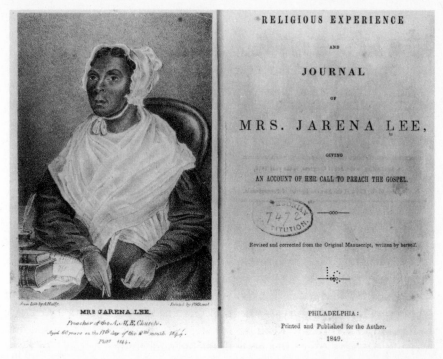

31. Despite considerable opposition, many women, both black and white, seized the opportunity to preach and exhort that the topsy-turvy world of the revivals cracked open. Jarena Lee was among the prominent African Methodist preaching women; she related in print the story of her extraordinary call to preach. *Library of Congress*

some of the central ambiguities of this Second Great Awakening—at once visionary and structured, rife with sectarian potential and yet devoted to denomination building.

UTOPIAN EXPERIMENTATION

While the Second Great Awakening sought to save the whole country, some smaller groups of believers sought to save themselves from the country. Or at least they, like the seventeenth-century Puritans, wished first to save themselves and then, perhaps by example, to save others. In the first half of the nineteenth century hopes were high, land was cheap, and experimental visions abounded. As Ralph Waldo Emerson commented to Thomas Carlyle in 1840, "Not a reading man but has a draft of a new community in his waistcoat pocket."

An early utopian community, the United Society of Believers in Christ's Second Appearing, known more familiarly as the Shakers, arrived in

America from England in 1774 under the direction of Mother Ann Lee (1736–1784). Ann Lee taught that procreation was unnecessary since the Kingdom of God was near at hand; this being so, Shaker men and women should live apart, leading celibate lives. If a married couple joined the Shaker community, the marital relationship ended as the common life began. Shaker theological reflection also developed a novel understanding of the ultimate significance of the founder: God had first appeared incarnate in a male, Jesus of Nazareth; now, the divine essence had its second incarnation in a female, Mother Ann Lee. The movement initially took hold in New England and New York, scandalizing the Congregationalist defender and avid geographer, Jedidiah Morse, by its mode of worship. Shaker worship, "if such extravagant conduct may be so called," Morse reported, included "dancing, singing, leaping, clapping their hands, falling on their knees, and uttering themselves in groans and sighs." Behavior of this sort, far removed from the sober decorum of the New England meetinghouse, led Morse to hope that Shakerism would swiftly disappear.

Rather than disappear, Shaker communities multiplied in the first half of the nineteenth century as these ascetic visionaries moved into Ohio, Indiana, and Kentucky. Reaping some of the harvest of the spreading revivals, Shakers grew to about 6,000 by midcentury. Typical of most utopian groups of the day, Shakers held all property in common, thus offering a dramatic reformulation of the economic principle of private property. Like the early Christians at Pentecost, Shakers did "not call the least thing their own." Also, first-century Christians "took no part in the heathen government, either in being officers or electing officers. They would not swear, or take oaths. They would not fight, or engage in war." Shakers saw themselves as reviving "The Pentecost Church" in their own time, one feature of that church being the commitment "to live a virgin life." Celibacy, the most distinctive doctrine of the Shakers, doomed this society to slow decline and ultimately near extinction. When revivalism and utopian experimentation waned, so did the growth of the Shakers. A single century after their peak membership of 6,000, only a handful of Shakers remained. Now the outside world remembers the Shakers chiefly for their style of furniture, even honoring them with on-line shopping sites where Shaker plainness can be purchased with a credit card. The Shakers are also sometimes remembered for their songs, including "'Tis a Gift to Be Simple."

John Humphrey Noyes (1811–1886) of Putney, Vermont, led his small band of followers in 1847 from that New England locale to the town of Oneida in western New York. True, this was an age of hope, Noyes

32. Shakers were known for a number of innovations, among them the use of dance in Christian worship. *Library of Congress*

observed, but so much of people's hope was misplaced, being centered on an idealization of the past or on expectations of some divine fulfillment in the future. We, on the other hand, said Noyes, believe in a spiritual revolution now at hand: "an outburst of spiritual knowledge and power—a conversion of the world from sensuality, from carnal morality, and from brain-philosophy, to spiritual wisdom and life." To bring about a spiritual revolution, a sexual revolution was required as well.

Rejecting the celibacy of the Shakers ("they virtually castrate themselves"), Noyes advocated what he called "complex marriage." Under his utopian system, the community itself would determine who should mate with whom, that decision being guided by the best principles of eugenics or "scientific propagation." Monogamy "is an absolute bar to scientific propagation." Consider, Noyes wrote, "how much progress would the horse-breeders expect to make if they were only at liberty to bring their animals together in exclusive pairs." No, monogamy made no more sense than celibacy did. What did make sense was bringing together the best specimens of the human race to procreate and thereby to lift all humankind up to the level where a truly spiritual revolution could occur. Surely, Noyes argued, this was better than the present system, which "restricts each man, whatever may be his potency and his value, to the amount of production of which one woman, chosen blindly, may be capable." What we have in effect done, he added, was choose the worst over the best, for "the good man will be limited by his conscience . . . while the bad man, free from moral check, will distribute his seed beyond the legal limits as widely as he dares."

It all made sense—except to the neighbors. Suffering from every harassment and ridicule, the Oneida Community limped along without recruiting many new members, gaining only in the number and intensity of its enemies. By 1880 this utopian experiment turned to economics for its salvation, so that the Oneida Community is remembered now less for its religious vision, social engineering, "Bible communism," and transformed sexuality than for its silverware.

GREAT EXPECTATIONS AND BITTER DISAPPOINTMENTS

Other visions depended not so much on questions of private property and marital proprieties but on God's plan for the future or revelation in the past. Millennialism wrestled with the book of Revelation (and other prophecies) in order to determine just when Christ would come again to usher in the thousand years of peace and virtue, when the devil would be chained and the earth cleansed of all unrighteousness. So much that was promising and good seemed to be happening in and to America in the early decades of the nineteenth century: Could it be that the Kingdom of God was just around the corner? Many thought so, including Charles G. Finney, who in 1835 announced that "the millennium may come in this country in three years."

An even more fervent and convinced proclaimer, William Miller (1782–1849) of upstate New York, predicted that Christ would come again sometime between March 21, 1843, and the following twenty-first of March. Basing his prophecy on Daniel 8:14, Miller argued that the "two thousand and three hundred evenings and mornings" spoken of there really meant a time period of twenty-three hundred years. That period began, Miller calculated, with the command of the Persian king Artaxerxes in 457 B.C.E. to rebuild Jerusalem. If one subtracted 457 from 2,300, the mathematical remainder pointed unmistakably to 1843—the year when the New Jerusalem would be established as Christ descended from the heavens. Attracting wide audiences from among the Baptists, Methodists, Presbyterians, and Congregationalists, Miller drew many into his net of great expectations. "If I have erred" in my calculations, he wrote, we shall all soon know. If, on the other hand, I have announced the truth, then "how

33. As is evident in this wall chart from the 1860s, the millennial interests of William Miller continued to enliven the Adventist movement long after the disappointment of the early 1840s. *Adventist Heritage Center, Andrews University*

important the era in which we live! What vast and important changes must soon be realized! And how necessary that every individual be prepared, that [this] day may not come upon them unawares."

Miller did err, with the consequence that all those great hopes led to the Great Disappointment, as this period came to be known. One expectant follower, Hiram Edson, recalled his dashed hopes when Jesus failed to return on October 22, 1844, the day that had come to be the final focus of Miller's speculations: "Our fondest hopes and expectations were blasted, and such a spirit of weeping came over us as I never experienced before. It seemed that the loss of all earthly friends could have been no comparison. We wept and wept until the day dawned." Baffled by the prophecy that failed, many returned to their former denominational homes while others, disenchanted, turned away from biblical religion altogether. Still others, convinced that the expectation was right and only the dating wrong, regrouped to await a later (and not so clearly specified) Second Coming of Christ. Among the most significant survivors of the Millerite disappointment were Seventh-day Adventists, following the visions of their new leader, Ellen G. White (1827–1915), who drew her disciples from dismay and disintegration to renewed confidence in God's sovereignty over human history and the urgency of Christ's Second Coming.

These Adventists (the word *advent* means coming or arrival) moved from their initial New England base to Michigan in 1855. By 1863 they could claim over 100 churches and more than 3,000 members, numbers that would grow dramatically during the following century. In addition to their emphasis upon the "advent," White's followers believed that the ancient Jewish commandment to "keep the Sabbath day holy" had not been canceled or revoked; therefore, one must keep the Sabbath, the seventh day of the week, and not Sunday as the day set aside by divine law. Moreover, one must keep one's body free of the defilement that comes from eating meat; drinking alcohol, coffee, or tea; smoking tobacco; or indulging in anything that works against a pure mind in a sound body. Their most conspicuous dietary success came from Battle Creek, Michigan, where Adventist W. K. Kellogg (1860–1951) created a whole new cereal empire. Health reform, an impulse that Adventists promoted but that extended far beyond them, led to popularizing diets of cereals, grains, and water but also to offering retreats and setting up hospitals and the medical staffs to go with them. Adventists and other mid-nineteenth-century health reformers helped pioneer the strong and ongoing link in American culture between the Christian gospel and bodily regimens for vigorous health.

Another kind of expectant Christian looked not so much forward to a millennial age yet to come but backward to an apostolic age now to be revived. *Restorationism* is the term applied to those earnest Christians who wished to bring back, to restore, the New Testament church in its purity and power. In western Pennsylvania Alexander Campbell (1788–1866) bemoaned the many divisions within Christendom, most of these (in his view) having no essential reason for being in the nineteenth century. Denominations arose because of special historical conditions or through the influence of powerful personalities. Now, was it not time to rise above these largely meaningless or accidental separations and return to the fount from which all had come and to which all owed their ultimate loyalty? In the 1820s Campbell, traveling throughout Ohio, Indiana, Kentucky, and Tennessee, observed that the "different regimentals" and the "different standards" did not mean all that much: "one is heroic and daring, another dastardly and timid under any insignia." "The flag"—that is, the denominational label—simply did not make that much difference. It was time, Campbell concluded, for all churches to become simply "Christians," simply followers or disciples of Christ.

The Christian world has seen too much of bickering and warfare, Campbell argued, too much of a family "torn by factions." Consider, Campbell wrote, that Protestants around the world are about 40 million strong, except that being so divided they were not strong at all. "How do they muster?" Campbell asked and then answered, "Under forty ensigns? Under forty antagonist leaders? Would to God there were but forty!" Geneva alone, Campbell added, could provide that many. Protestant divisions were beyond calculating: "I will not attempt to name the antagonizing creeds, feuds, and parties that are in eternal war, under the banners of the Prince of Peace. And yet they talk of love and charity, and of the conversion of the Jews, the Turks, and pagans!!!" It was enough to make a restorationist like Campbell weep over the supposedly seamless robe of Christ, now ripped to shreds and scattered across the globe.

What could be done? Alexander Campbell, along with a leader in Kentucky's enormous Cane Ridge revival of 1801, Barton Stone (1772–1844), preached the gospel of restorationism with energy and expectation. "There is but one Body, and one Spirit, even as we are called in one hope of our calling," Stone wrote. We will "pray more and dispute less," looking not to men's words but only to the Bible. We will trust not in churches or denominations, presbyteries or synods, but build only on "the Rock of Ages, and follow Jesus for the future." By 1833 most of the followers of Stone and Campbell merged into a single movement known variously as the Christian Church or Disciples of Christ or the "Campbellites." A church born of the revivals in the South and West, this new institution enjoyed its earliest successes in Ohio, Indiana, Illinois, Kentucky, Tennessee, and Missouri. By the end of the century, these disciples had passed the half-million mark. In growth, they flourished; in unity, they failed. For not only did the Disciples of Christ fail to heal the divisions within Christendom, they added to them by becoming a springboard to new denominations, dividing over such issues as the use of musical instruments in worship. That irony aside, it is a denominational family that has taken much of its identity from ecumenical projects of restored union.

THE POST-REVOLUTIONARY SOUTH

In the early decades of the nineteenth century, southern religion presented a dramatically new face. Wholly changed from the Anglican-dominated region it had been for so long, by 1820 the South had been transformed into a bastion of evangelical religion. Presbyterians, Baptists, and Methodists created a kind of cultural and religious unity that eluded Campbell and Stone. Not that denominational differences disappeared; rather, they were subsumed into a larger culture of southern evangelicalism. Baptists with their farmer-preachers, Methodists with their youthful circuit riders, Presbyterians with their local presbyteries managed to move across boundaries of class and race, of gender and political power. The aristocracy of an older Anglicanism fell before a revivalistic tide of emotional fervor and pietist conviction. Yet surging across boundaries as deeply etched as those of race, gender, age, and social standing is not the same thing as erasing those boundaries. This new democracy of the spirit retained many of the same social limits of the order it was replacing.

Denied formal ordination, women were by and large kept out of the ministerial ranks. That denial did not keep them, though, from taking a lead in the spread of evangelicalism. Women testified to their faith, served as deaconesses, raised funds for the support of missionaries both at home and abroad, and sometimes undertook themselves the roles of missionary teachers and evangelists. Women helped promote revivals, even as many had experienced their own conversions within that context. Women became missionaries in their own communities, even among those in the South that suffered the most serious neglect: the slaves. In Virginia, Ann Randolph Page (1781–1838) wrote in 1825 of her anxious concern for those "who inhabit the smoky huts and till our fields" but remained untouched by the Christian message. In her diary Page confessed her fears that some terrible divine wrath awaited those who "neglect to labor for souls committed to their charge," souls that were as dear to God as those of the masters. "Awake us—arouse us—strike an alarm from the vast ocean of eternity which rolls so near!" It was our solemn duty, she concluded, to care for both the bodies and souls of our slaves, "knowing that we must give an account of our stewardship."

Evangelical religion provided a bridge between the religious world of the slaves and that of white southerners. Often it was a bridge crossed by whites to exhort slave obedience or to offer paternalistic advice on moral improvement, but it was also one crossed by blacks to find stories of exodus, liberation, and apocalyptic reordering and to make those narratives their own. Slaves in growing numbers turned to a religion that spoke of an unchained freedom in Christ, of a God who was no respecter of color or social standing, of an eternal life without sorrow and separation. In hush harbors, set up on the sly to worship away from suspicious or hostile masters, and in their own churches (a number of black Baptist churches had come into being by 1790), slaves crafted an African American Christianity of revival, song, prayer, and resistance.

Taking his text from Romans 8:37, the black preacher John Jasper (1812–1901) explicated the meaning of the words "Nay, in all these things we are more than conquerors through him that loved us." Biblical history was filled with examples of how God had taken the lowly and despised and turned them into conquerors: Moses, Joshua, David, and many more. God's power had even been made manifest in a lowly Jewish carpenter, executed on a cross like a common criminal. The gospel made its promises not to the rich and mighty but to the poor and lowly, the oppressed and imprisoned, Jasper explained. Christianity was not the monopoly of the white master, and the Bible did not provide ideological justifications for slavery (even though scripture was often made to operate that way). God would judge all men and women, and the powerful would be subject to God's wrath and the powerless to God's mercy. With faith and fervor, Jasper proclaimed that one day the valley would be exalted and the mountains laid low; one day the mighty would fall and the weak be lifted up. One day, the evangelically committed slaves affirmed, we shall be more than conquerors.

THEOLOGY IN NEW ENGLAND

Theological variety in New England matched the ecclesiastical variety of the frontier. The Calvinism revived most forcefully in the writings of Jonathan Edwards continued into the nineteenth century where it bore the label of *the* New England theology. But as it turned out, it was only one theology among many. Reactions against the prevailing Calvinism first took the form of an entering Arminian wedge, which emphasized free will and the significance of good works. Charles Chauncy (1705–1787), Edwards's opponent in the first round of evangelical awakenings, moved from Arminianism to Universalism, which proclaimed the "Salvation of All Men" to be "the Grand Thing aimed at in the Scheme of God." God's love was such, in Chauncy's view, that the doctrine of eternal damnation no longer made sense.

Elhanan Winchester (1751–1797), native of Massachusetts, moved from a Baptist ministry to a Universalist one by the end of the 1780s. A careful study of the scriptures, Winchester declared, convinced him that a moral and loving God would not rest until all his creatures had been gathered to his bosom. We are told, Winchester said, that in the fullness of time every knee shall bow and every tongue confess that Christ is Lord. Winchester took these words seriously, amazed and shaken to discover "that any danger could have arisen from my expressing a hope that the Scriptures were true." But dangers there were, as former friends forsook him and condemned him as a heretic for having embraced the doctrine of "Universal Restoration." The new convert, however, stood firm, for "the truth appeared to me more valuable than all things and . . . I was determined never to part with it." By 1850 Universalism had spread throughout New England and across New York but displayed little strength elsewhere in America.

Unitarianism, far more than Universalism, shook Congregational orthodoxy to its very foundations. Rejecting the Calvinists' low view of unredeemed humans, wormlike creatures without the capacity either to do good or think well, the Unitarians spoke of the human moral nature, our rational capacity, our freedom to choose or to reject the doctrines taught and the promises offered by the Christian religion. In an important sermon delivered in 1819, Boston Unitarian William Ellery Channing (1780–1842) laid down the basic presuppositions of New England's new-found liberal faith. We accept that which is "clearly taught in the Scriptures," Channing said, though we do not "attach equal importance to all the books in this collection." In Channing's view, the general rule was that the New Testament supersedes and supplants the Old. When it comes to understanding what the New Testament says about God, Channing concluded that it taught the oneness not the threeness of God, a Unity, not a Trinity. We do "with all earnestness, though without reproaching our brethren, protest against the irrational and unscriptural doctrine of the Trinity."

Christ's mediation and mission were of great historical moment since "we believe that he was sent by the Father to effect a moral or spiritual deliverance of mankind." This did not mean, however, that Unitarians accepted the prevailing orthodox notion that human sin has in some way been paid for by a sacrifice on the cross, "that man, having sinned against an infinite Being, has contracted infinite guilt, and is consequently exposed to an infinite penalty." This and all the other complexities of the Calvinist teachings regarding salvation are, said Channing, both "unscriptural and absurd." We ask our adversaries, he added, "to point to some plain passage [in the Bible] where it is taught." Since they could not do so, it followed that such teachings were "the fictions of theologians," and Unitarians would dismiss them out of hand.

New England Unitarianism emerged not so much as a new denomination, with a charismatic founder or a supplementary revelation, but as a movement within Congregationalism, especially in eastern Massachusetts. It rejected an ancestral orthodoxy in favor of "a larger intellectual and religious life, free of the restraints imposed by a doctrinal system." For the first fifty years of its corporate life, Unitarianism scarcely moved beyond the bounds of the Congregational churches that gave it birth. Only in and around Boston did the church, as a church, exercise any real authority. But as a system of ideas and as a set of liberal attitudes, its influence grew out of all proportion to its numbers.

Among the famous names associated with Unitarianism, none is better known than that of Ralph Waldo Emerson (1803–1882). Ordained a minister of Boston's Second Church in 1829, Emerson resigned that position three years later to continue a philosophical and religious search that became known as Transcendentalism. Reacting against the overemphasis on community, especially sectarian community, as well as against the overcommitment to material goods and worldly prosperity, Emerson called for a self-reliance that affirmed the wisdom found within one's own soul. Intuition was more reliable than a syllogism, even as an arid rationalism robbed humankind of its noblest passions and deepest truths. Imitation, consistency, and conformity were weights on spiritual insight and genius. "The materialist," Emerson wrote in 1843, "insists on facts, on history, on the force of circumstances, and, the animal wants of man; the idealist on the power of Thought and Will, on inspiration, on miracle, on individual culture." To embrace inspiration and miracle was to put great distance between himself and the Unitarians, but even greater distance separated Emerson from the Calvinists. Would New England continue to divide itself until, as Emerson predicted, every person became his or her own newborn bard and prophet?

In Hartford, Connecticut, the Congregationalist pastor Horace Bushnell (1802–1876) thought that New England had seen enough intellectual warfare to last several lifetimes. Enough of the quarrels between revivalists and antirevivalists, between Trinitarians and anti-Trinitarians, between moralists and rationalists, between literalists and symbolists. Bushnell would if he could gather together all the opposing forces, transcend their differences with a theology that rejected neither this nor that entrenched position but moved the argument to a higher ground. To accomplish this, Bushnell advanced his theory of language, in which he explained that a totally precise, totally accurate, totally "correct" theology was simply not possible. The reason that it was impossible lay in the severe limitations of theological language; such language, moving far beyond the data gathered by the five senses, employed metaphor and figure to suggest, to hint at, to provoke the imagination into a reflection on things of God. What? No science of theology? None whatsoever, Bushnell calmly replied. "Human language is a gift to the imagination so essentially metaphoric, warp and woof, that it has no exact blocks of meaning to build a science of." This was hardly reason for despair, however, since neither can we build a science out of Homer or Shakespeare or Milton. "And the Bible is not a whit less poetic, or a whit less metaphoric, or a particle less difficult to be propositionized in the terms of understanding."

Unitarians who rejected the literalism of Calvinism substituted a literalism of their own, and Transcendentalists swept away old metaphors only to introduce new ones. How dreary and how sad, Bushnell noted, for "Nothing makes infidels more surely than the spinning, splitting, nerveless refinements of theology." Never content with suggestive allegory, we demand absolute propositions. We never get them, of course, but what we do get is "a history of divisions, recriminations, famishings, vanishings, and general uncharitableness." The gospel, like language itself, Bushnell wrote, is above all else a "gift to the imagination," and we can say nothing more exalted of Christ than to regard him as "the metaphor of God." Theology must be kept alive like a beautiful flower, fragrant and fresh, ever growing, ever appealing. In New England, Bushnell concluded, we take that flower, pull it apart petal by petal, squeeze out all its juices, rob it of all vitality and allure. Then we pack it all away in a dry herbarium. The result of our labors—that tasteless, odorless, lifeless thing—we are pleased to call "theology."

The Romantic religious currents in which Bushnell swam reached their greatest swiftness outside New England in Walt Whitman (1819–1892), whose *Leaves of Grass* (1855) marked him out as both poet and prophet of religious democracy and spiritual seeking. A Quaker by background who drank deeply at the wells of Emerson's Transcendentalism and Emanuel Swedenborg's mysticism, Whitman exhorted Americans to "re-examine all you have been told at school or church or in any book" and to "dismiss whatever insults your own soul." "I, now, for one, promulge," Whitman wrote, "a sublime and serious Religious Democracy." Embarking on a long journey of religious awakening and sensuous discovery, Whitman enjoined a similar quest upon all: "Not I, not any one else can travel the road for you, / You must travel it for yourself." Whereas the voluntaristic associations of Protestant benevolence had tried to act as a centripetal force pulling people back to the "center" of church influence, Whitman taunted such enterprises, happily inviting any and all to join him out on the open road. "The ripeness of Religion," he affirmed, "is doubtless to be looked for in this field of individuality, and is a result that no organization or church can ever achieve." Much of nineteenth-century American religion remained torn between Protestant desires for an evangelical empire and Whitmanesque prophecies of an all-out religious democracy.

CHAPTER 8

Redeeming the West

In the early nineteenth century the American West both attracted and repelled. Yale president Timothy Dwight (1752–1817), who visited the West (not very far west, to be sure, but at least beyond the bounds of New England), was not favorably impressed. He found an independence bordering on anarchy, an egalitarianism bordering on comedy. The pioneers, Dwight noted, "cannot live in regular society. They are too idle, too talkative, too passionate, too prodigal, and too shiftless to acquire either property or character." By their own estimation, however, westward migrants, wrote Dwight, were possessed of "uncommon wisdom," knowing more about law, medicine, politics, and religion "than those who have studied them through life." President Dwight did not expect much from the West and the settlers there.

In sharp contrast, fellow Congregationalist Lyman Beecher, who brought his family to Cincinnati in 1832, thought the West would fulfill all the rich promise of America. People were moving all the way to the Mississippi River in tremendous numbers. From the Appalachian Mountains to the great river, new states sprang up almost overnight and population increased in a single generation from about 150,000 to "little short of five millions." Stretching his imagination to the limit, Beecher prophesied that by the end of the century perhaps as many as 100 million people would live in that region "half as large as all Europe, four times as large as the Atlantic states, and twenty times as large as New England." Without religion and morality, the West—it was true—would sink into barbarism, but with religion and morality, then the future of the West "will be glorious." In an optimism that would not be bridled, Beecher exulted that "the sun and rain of heaven are not more sure to call forth a bounteous vegetation" than would Bibles and Sunday schools, colleges and clergy, in this promised land. Listening to travelers return from New Orleans, St. Louis, and even the Pacific Ocean with their wondrous tales, only then, Beecher

34. As spokesman and apologist for the West, the Congregational minister Lyman Beecher exercised his prodigious energies on behalf of Christianizing and taming the frontier. *National Portrait Gallery, Smithsonian Institution/Art Resource, NY*

confessed, "did I perceive how God, who seeth the end from the beginning, had prepared the West to be mighty."

Not much common ground could be found between Timothy Dwight and Lyman Beecher with respect to the West. Interested Europeans similarly found it difficult to reconcile reports of visitors to interior America, some praising the openness of the people and the land, others speaking only of its barbarism and bad manners. All could agree on one point, however: in the first half of the nineteenth century the United States added to its domain an enormous amount of "west." The purchase of the Louisiana Territory in 1803 virtually doubled the territory of the nation, and this great gulp of land was augmented in 1846 by the spoils of the Mexican-American War, which included all of the Pacific Southwest, and by a treaty with Great Britain that ceded all of the Pacific Northwest. From ocean to ocean a single flag now flew, and the wonder and fury of it all left citizens breathless. It also left churches and synagogues staggered by the enormity of the tasks thereby spread before them.

PROTESTANTISM

Less than a decade after the Louisiana Purchase, the Missionary Societies of Massachusetts and Connecticut sent observers westward to report on the state of religion and morals in a territory that, for most easterners, remained unknown. What these observers found in Louisiana offered little encouragement but much challenge. "The state of society in this country is very deplorable," they wrote, their Protestantism preventing them from finding much solace in the French Catholicism that had managed to take root there despite the withdrawal of the Jesuits long before. "The people are entirely ignorant of divine things, and have been taught only to attend mass and count their beads." Intemperance prevailed, vice flourished, and Sunday was treated more as a "high holiday" than an occasion for sober reflection and worship. Probably, the travelers asserted, more actual sin was committed on Sunday "than during the whole week besides." Even the newly appointed Roman Catholic bishop, Louis William DuBourg (1766–1833), "mourns over the depravity and wickedness of [this] place," the itinerant missionaries noted. Surely, much had to be done before the rest of the country had reason to regret that Thomas Jefferson ever signed that treaty and made that purchase.

Another missionary tour, which followed a couple of years later (1814–15), showed little improvement, only more urgency. Not a single Bible in any language could be found anywhere in New Orleans, either to be bought or given away. Protestantism was virtually nonexistent, and what Protestant clergy could be located were seldom of the educated and responsible sort. "What shall be done? Shall we leave one of our fairest cities to be completely overwhelmed with vice and folly? The dreaded inundation of the Mississippi would not be half so ruinous." The solution proposed was to apply the proven Protestant instruments of the Second Great Awakening: send missionaries, distribute Bibles and tracts, teach people to read and write, promote revivals, and instill a sense of duty, character, and right. Protestants would try to incorporate Louisiana within the voluntaristic empire of benevolence, and it was a strategy they would resort to, with varying degrees of success, in one place after another from Louisiana to California and Hawaii.

One of the missionary observers, John F. Schermerhorn (1786–1851), reported back east to the Society for Propagating the Gospel Among the Indians concerning the status of Native Americans in the newly added territories. The society, having originally ministered to Indians in New England, now determined to use its funds for "tribes in the remote parts of North America." Schermerhorn, like missionaries before him, expressed amazement at the diversity of tribes, the particularity of their cultures and languages, and their independence from or hostility toward one another. He also joined others in noting the negative effect that contact with Europeans wrought upon tribal life. In his 1814 report he suggested to the society that a mission might be most successful among the Chickasaws and the Choctaws, since they were relatively "uncontaminated by the vices of the whites." In Louisiana itself it was most difficult to find any Indians not adversely affected by contact with Spanish or French, British or American traders. With respect to Indians west of the Mississippi River, Schermerhorn confessed that he could only repeat the words of the few explorers, such as Lewis and Clark, who had actually made firsthand observations.

These missionary observers represented the new reconnaissance of Presbyterians and Congregationalists, who by a Plan of Union drawn up in 1801 determined to pool their resources in order better to meet the challenge of so much "west." Congregational missionaries even reached beyond California's shores to the Hawaiian Islands, with whom New England's whaling vessels had established contact. One native Hawaiian, Henry Obookiah (1792?–1818), made his way to Yale College, there to be brought into the Christian fold by Samuel J. Mills (1783–1818), another of those missionaries sent out to the trans-Appalachian West. In 1820 the first contingent of Connecticut missionaries and their wives arrived in the islands, establishing their mission on the largest island, Hawaii, in the village of Kailua. By 1837 over eighty missionaries had been dispatched to the Pacific outpost, with seventeen churches established there, and Hawaii had become the latest venue for the promotion of Protestant forms of revival and education. All this American missionary activity helped prepare the way for annexation of the islands before the end of the nineteenth century.

Also before the end of that century Protestantism set its eyes on another westernmost territory, Alaska, purchased by the United States in 1867. A Presbyterian missionary, Sheldon Jackson (1834–1909), moved from his labors among the Indians in Oklahoma, Minnesota, Wyoming, Montana, and elsewhere in the continental West to the land that Russian Orthodoxy had claimed as its mission field since 1792. Jackson, first visiting that northern land in 1877, saw the native Alaskans in much need of medicine, education, "republican government," and "industrial pursuits." Appointed U.S. General Agent for Education in 1885, Jackson pursued an assimilationist program of making Alaska an English-speaking Protestant land and minimizing the Russian Orthodox influences, even as he fought lawlessness, exploitation, and starvation. With respect to the last threat, he succeeded in introducing reindeer from Siberia to alleviate the Eskimo and Aleut dependence on seal herds, now depleted by the aggressive hunting techniques of traders. As a missionary Jackson was, in part, a buffer between native peoples and more hostile colonialist forces, but he was also a committed transformer of indigenous cultures—their economy, education, language, and religion. The American Protestant mission in Alaska showed all the ambiguities of missions elsewhere as it boldly sought to make "an English-speaking race of these Natives."

Presbyterians and Congregationalists reached into Oregon Territory, into California (added to the Union in 1850), and elsewhere in the West. One northwestern mission, identified with the labors of Marcus (1802–1847) and Narcissa (1808–1847) Whitman, was established in 1835 near Walla Walla, Washington, part of a string of missions spread out along the Columbia River. Among the first white women to cross the Rockies, Narcissa Whitman wrote often of her work in giving Bible instruction, in helping with the singing, in assisting in as many ways as her somewhat frail health would allow. She also wrote of her loneliness and dejection, far removed from family and friends back in Prattsburg, New York. All came to a tragic end for the Whitmans when in 1847 the Cayuse Indians, frustrated and angered by the growing pressure of white settlements, attacked the mission, killing Marcus and Narcissa Whitman along with a dozen other whites present at the time. It was a telling denouement, since both missionaries and Native Americans were caught up in a much larger web of imperial expansion, conflict, and violence.

Even more important for bringing Protestantism to the West were the Baptists and Methodists. A rapidly expanding nation, with mountains to be crossed and streams to be forded, seemed perfectly suited to circuit-rider Methodists and farmer-preacher Baptists. The former moved out on

35. Narcissa Whitman, who was among the pioneers of Christian missions in the West, met her death in the Oregon Territory in 1847. *Presbyterian Historical Society, Presbyterian Church (USA), Philadelphia*

the postroads leading westward just as soon as such roads were laid out, and if they were too impatient to wait for road builders, Methodist parsons simply mounted their horses and made their own trails to where any tiny knots of settlers or isolated families might be found. Whether a church could be built and sustained was not as important as bringing the ministrations of evangelical Christianity to Americans on the move. But churches were built, and one measure of Methodist success is that this denomination by 1850 had more churches than any other group in such western lands as Mississippi, Louisiana, Texas, Arkansas, Tennessee, Ohio, Indiana, Illinois, Michigan, Wisconsin, and Iowa.

By midcentury Methodists had also reached all the way to California and Oregon Territory. One of their number, Jason Lee (1803–1845), led the way into Oregon Territory even before it became American soil. Convinced that the Pacific Northwest was ripe for plucking by some nation or people, Lee argued that it should be part of the United States's domain. In an 1839 letter to a U.S. congressman, Lee wrote, "The country will be settled, and that speedily, from some quarter. . . . It may be thought that Oregon is of but little importance; but, rely upon it, there is the germ of a great state." Less than a decade later Oregon had been incorporated into the United States, and Lee's labors provided solid foundation on which not only Methodists but many others could build.

Baptists also followed, or sometimes led, the western migrations, racing with the Methodists toward a membership mark of 1 million by 1850. Like the Methodists, the Baptists by that year had reached all the way to the Pacific Ocean, and like the Methodists, too, they endeavored to evangelize both the new settlers and the Indians those very settlers were displacing. One missionary to the Indians, Isaac McCoy (1784–1846), argued for the creation of an Indian Territory in the West, which would offer some insulation from greedy and corrupting white traders. Cherokees, Creeks, Choctaws, and Chickasaws all gathered well before midcentury in what became Oklahoma. Indicative of the often-cozy relationship between missionary educators and the state, McCoy himself worked with and for the federal government, seeking ways to avoid the tragedy of Indian extermination and to reduce the bloody conflicts between the tribes and the U.S. government. In 1849 the Bureau of Indian Affairs was transferred from the War Department to the newly created Department of Interior, symbolizing a significant alteration in Indian policy that was not yet a reality.

In working with settlers in the West, Baptists leaned heavily upon local preachers, who were most likely also themselves new pioneers and hard-working farmers. Fully employed like their neighbors in clearing land and raising food, some in addition responded to what they believed to be a divine call to preach. No hierarchy was needed to approve such a ministry; no college or advanced education was required to enter upon such a ministry. While farmer-preachers may have lacked qualifications or degrees, they possessed one attribute that outweighed most others: they were there, on the scene, ready to preach as the Spirit prompted. But Baptists also sent missionaries from the East, including John Mason Peck (1789–1858), who arrived in St. Louis in 1817 and worked both sides of the river thereafter. Founding schools, distributing tracts, organizing denominational life, preaching countless sermons, and traveling thousands of miles, Peck saw the American West as God's new Zion. The prodigious labors of innumerable missionaries gave some substance to that millennial vision of the West redeemed.

ROMAN CATHOLICISM

Alone among the denominations moving from the East out to the West, Roman Catholicism entered lands that had already known the presence of the Catholic missionary. In the Louisiana Territory itself, French Catholics (notably the Jesuits but also others) had labored since the seventeenth century. When that territory came under United States control in 1803, French Catholicism continued to flavor the land. When Louis William DuBourg was appointed bishop of "Louisiana and the Floridas" in 1815, the area had been without any effective episcopal supervision for many years, being, in Archbishop John Carroll's gentle words, in a "relaxed state of civil and ecclesiastical authority." Since DuBourg had been appointed by the American archbishop, the French in New Orleans would have little to do with him, while the Spanish in East and West Florida calmly continued to take their orders from the bishop of Havana. Four years after DuBourg's elevation to the episcopate, the last portion of foreign soil east of the Mississippi, Florida, passed from Spain to the United States. DuBourg endured great difficulty with his remaining charges in Louisiana, being so unwelcome in New Orleans that he initially resided far to the north in St. Louis.

Though distracted by the internal quarrels and defiance of his authority, Bishop DuBourg nonetheless recognized those major religious needs, especially among the Indians, that required attention. He appealed to the Jesuits (their order having now been restored) of Belgium to come to his aid, one such man doing so with unusual effectiveness. Pierre Jean DeSmet, S.J. (1801–1873), left St. Louis in 1840 for the first of many trips to visit Indians in the West, notably among the Flatheads, whose advocate he became. Unlike many who served as missionaries to the Indians, DeSmet was neither scandalized nor offended by their culture. The Flatheads, he wrote in 1841, "are scrupulously honest in their buying and selling; they have never been accused of committing a theft . . . lying is hateful to them beyond anything else. . . . They are polite, always of a jovial humor, very hospitable, and helpful to one another in their duties." Incredulously, DeSmet asked, How do we dare to call such people "savages"? And he explained the high culture that he found among the Flatheads by noting that they had not yet "learned the vices of the whites."

Like a few other missionaries in colonial times and beyond, Father DeSmet found his trust in the Indians matched by a corresponding Indian trust in him. At the request of the Secretary of the Interior, DeSmet in 1868 persuaded the Sioux to accept a treaty of peace, accomplishing the delicate negotiations with skill and maintaining the respect of both sides. Admiring the Osage and the Sioux, the black-robed Jesuit also admired and entertained high hopes for the nation in which he labored for over fifty years. America, he wrote his brother in 1849, has within it the possibility, "the germ and the sinew, to raise a greater people than many of the proud, now tottering, principalities of Europe." This confidence, shared by so many who loaded wagons and set out on the Oregon Trail, prevented the West from being a mere appendage to the nation; it was imagined instead as a fulfillment of the nation.

By 1850 the Roman Catholic Church had become the largest denomination in the country, a status never thereafter surrendered to any other church. Its magnitude came chiefly as the result of massive emigration from Ireland, the potato famine encouraging hundreds of thousands to leave their poor and inhospitable land. Of the 5 million immigrants who settled in America from 1815 to 1860, 2 million came from Ireland. "Antipopery," the bread and butter of Protestantism, had reared its head regularly in early America, but now it raised itself to new heights. Nativist organizations, Know-Nothing political parties, and a host of scandalmongers challenged the right of Catholics to live freely in the United States. In Massachusetts in 1834 an angry mob burned an Ursuline convent to the ground, and in Philadelphia a decade later riots broke out, looters directing their wrath against Catholic churches in that city. Thomas Nast cartoons warned repeatedly against popish conspiracies to take over the United States, while Protestant publications involving pornographic fantasies of the sexual practices of priests and nuns proliferated. The *Awful Disclosures of the Hotel Dieu Nunnery* (1836), with its sensational tales of infanticide and priestly violence, was a runaway best-seller, and it had a host of competitors throughout the antebellum period. Voluntary associations designed to combat Catholicism were among the most visible organizations of the era and certainly suggested that not all the crusades of Protestantism's "benevolent empire" were particularly benevolent.

36. The fears of Protestant nativists centered on the impact of Catholic immigration on the public school system, but as this cartoon makes clears, xenophobia took many forms and extended to suspicions of Asian religions. Fears of Chinese immigrants would prove especially intense in the West. *Library of Congress*

In 1835 Samuel F. B. Morse (1791–1872) published a tract, typical in its assumptions, entitled *Imminent Dangers to the Free Institutions of the United States Through Foreign Immigration*. The imminent danger uppermost in his mind was that of a rapidly increasing Irish Catholic presence. "It is a fact," he patiently explained, "that Popery is opposed in its very nature to Democratic Republicanism; and it is, therefore, as a political system, as well as religious [system], opposed to civil and religious liberty, and consequently to our form of government." Catholicism was inseparably joined in the popular Protestant mind to priestly tyranny, and it was invariably seen as posing a double threat to republican government and the purified Christianity of Protestantism.

On the contrary, argued Orestes Brownson (1803–1876), a New England convert to the Catholic Church in 1844, Roman Catholicism "is necessary to sustain popular liberty because popular liberty can be sustained only by a religion free from popular control, above the people, speaking from above and able to command them." Even the Catholic bishops themselves could not ignore the many clamorous voices raised against their church. Lamenting the outbreaks of religious discrimination, the bishops in 1833 encouraged the faithful to stand firm against all the "vituperation and offense," against the misrepresentations of Catholic beliefs and the vilification of Catholic practices. We urge you, the bishops wrote, to ignore all of this and continue "to discharge honestly, faithfully, and with affectionate attachment your duties to the government under which you live." And in 1841 Bishop John England (1786–1842) of Charleston, South Carolina, called for an end to all attempts to divide the country along religious lines. "Men are beginning to perceive," he declared in a Boston address, "that the greatest curse which could befall our country would be the encouragement of any spirit of sectarian persecution."

While fending off both the quiet suspicions and active hostilities of other Americans, Roman Catholics were also busy trying to cope with the enormous ethnic diversity that confronted their own church in America. German Catholics were not happy when placed under the supervision of Irish brothers, sisters, and priests. Irish Catholics were not happy to find themselves saddled with French fathers who understood little of Irish feasts or Irish saints and sometimes less of the English language. Making matters even worse, some Catholic laity, observing the practices of their Protestant neighbors, decided that they, too, should have the right to hire or fire their own pastors, to own their own church property, and to control the parish finances. All of these immigrant difficulties, manifesting themselves with intensity east of the Mississippi, had their parallels in the West, where they were given a different complexity by the abiding presence of Hispanic Catholicism.

Spain's labors in North America left a lasting mark in the Southwest, notably in New Mexico, Arizona, California, and much of Texas (it also left an enduring imprint on Florida). Spanish missions constituted one of the most obvious features of the built environment, standing high above the sagebrush and chapparal. From the famed Alamo (formerly the San Antonio de Valero Mission) of Texas history to the even more famed chain of missions in California, Hispanic Catholicism shaped the prevailing image of an entire geographical region. The Jesuit Eusebio Kino labored in southern Arizona in the final years of the seventeenth and the first years of the eighteenth centuries, drawing maps, learning Indian languages, building chapels, and teaching farming. The San Xavier del Bac Church near Tucson, though a product of the 1790s, was erected on the site of Kino's first mission in that region. In California the Franciscan Junípero Serra (1713–1784) established missions from San Diego (1769) to Ventura (1782), with his successors continuing his work until a total of twenty-one

37. San Xavier del Bac Mission, located near Tucson, Arizona, is associated with the labors of Jesuit Eusebio Kino and is indicative of the established Hispanic Catholic presence that migrating Anglo-Americans encountered in the Southwest. *Keystone-Mast Collection, University of California, Riverside*

missions extended from San Diego in the south to San Francisco de Solano (Sonoma, 1823) in the north.

Mexico won its independence from Spain in 1821 and a dozen years later passed an act of secularization that turned over the abundant California mission lands to secular hands, reserving in each area only a single parish church to ecclesiastical authority. Monks and nuns were released from their vows, and an anticlerical Mexico encouraged many of the religious to leave for Spain. The government even agreed to pay the traveling expenses for those who had not sworn to uphold Mexico's independence. Then, as a result of the Mexican-American War of 1846 to 1847, all of the vast Southwest was seized for the United States. None could know just what that shift in sovereignty would mean in religious terms, though the military governor, General S. W. Kearney (1794–1848), assured Californians that their religious rights would be secured "in the most ample manner." What threatened Catholic rights was not so much the American flag as it was the American "invasion" of those easterners who came for gold or trade or Protestantizing.

A growing number of Protestant easterners left behind their familiar religious culture to face the predominantly Mexican, Spanish, and Indian Southwest. Protestant missionaries in northern New Mexico, confronted

38. Hispanic Catholic practices that became the object of recurring Protestant criticism (and fascination) included the Holy Week practices of the Penitentes, which centered on carrying heavy crosses in a reenactment of Christ's sufferings. *Library of Congress*

by late medieval Spanish Catholic practices that included severe self-mortification (notably among the Penitentes), denounced the "barbarities" and "ignorant superstitions" of what seemed to them a particularly odious example of foreign fanaticism. No sane or civilized Christian would go to such austere lengths of carrying huge crosses or lashing the body, the missionaries reasoned. French Catholic prelates in Santa Fe also objected to the Penitentes, trying as early as 1833 to bring them into greater conformity with Catholic practices as found in eastern America or northern Europe. Both Catholic and Protestant reformers failed, and the Penitentes continued in their self-abnegating practices.

In California, as elsewhere in the Southwest, easterners generally regarded themselves as superior in both education and religion to the Hispanics they encountered there. An English Catholic, Herbert Vaughan (1832–1903), visiting that state in 1864, thought otherwise, however. The "Yankee came, straining every nerve and energy in the pursuit of wealth," while the Spanish missionaries had sought to consecrate the land. The names that Anglos and Hispanics give to their respective towns and villages were proof to Vaughan that the higher culture belonged to the Catholics. The latter, he said, bestow such dignified titles as Jesus María, Buena Vista, and Nuestra Señora de Soledad, while the former afflict their settlements with such labels as Bloody Run, Rat-Trap Slide, and Jackass

Gulch. Let any fair-minded person decide which civilization truly endeavored to give a genuinely Christian flavor to all it discovered, explored, colonized, and missionized.

Vaughan was one among many visitors and settlers to find a certain "romance" in Spanish Catholic origins, and even many Protestants began to fantasize about making that "exotic" past their own. Slowly but surely, as historian Roberto Lint Sagarena has shown, Victorian Protestants (and their successors) gradually appropriated the missions and their architectural forms for their own cultural, religious, historical, and commercial purposes. From the Mission Inn (1876) in Riverside, California, to Henry Flagler's "Spanish Renaissance" hotels in St. Augustine, Florida, in the same era, Anglo-Americans displayed a striking desire to identify themselves with the Spanish Catholic heritage. In the process, the missions themselves became tourist attractions and civic landmarks as much as, and sometimes more than, living Catholic parishes.

If the missions of Hispanic Catholicism came to enjoy a good number of romantic admirers—those who doted on their architecture and their "colorful" history—flesh-and-blood Mexican American Catholics found it harder to muster defenders, sometimes even within their own ecclesiastical institution. Catholicism would continue to be directed from the East not the West, which meant its hierarchy would continue to be heavily Irish, French, and German. Through the exigencies of war and redrawn borders, a large portion of the American Catholic population was now Hispanic, but Mexican Americans had to wait until the second half of the twentieth century before making inroads into the upper clerical ranks of the Roman Catholic Church. The challenges of ethnic diversity and nativist hostility (now in the West aimed specifically at Mexican Americans) continued to prove difficult for the church to meet or resolve. Nonetheless, Catholicism could and did claim the American West as uniquely its own, with Catholics dominating the Southwest from the seventeenth century right into the twenty-first century.

JUDAISM

Though far smaller in membership than either Catholicism or Protestantism in the early nineteenth century, Judaism managed to move well beyond its early centers of worship along the Atlantic Coast. With a significant number of emigrants from Germany arriving in this period, Judaism found its fortunes rising from that of a tiny and scarcely visible colonial minority. German Jews, many of whom achieved a large degree of emancipation in their homeland, saw America in general, the West in particular, as a place where that freedom could find even fuller expression. Rabbi Isaac Mayer Wise (1819–1900), moving to the Ohio frontier at mid-century, urged his fellows to discard old European ways for new American ones. He also pushed for Judaism itself to reform its archaic rituals and presuppositions, recognizing that modern times have "revolutionized" how people think and feel. This age of the railroad and steamboat called for something more than the ideas and practices appropriate to the age of oxcart and mule. "The Jew must be Americanized, I said to myself, . . . in order to gain the proud self-consciousness of the free-born man." Once fired by this vision, Wise began "to Americanize with all my might." Hebrew Union College, founded in Cincinnati in 1875, helped keep alive Wise's vision and give substance to his hopes for a "reformed Judaism."

Traveling even more widely throughout the West, Rabbi Isaac Leeser (1806–1868) tried to help isolated Jewish communities hold together in obedience to the Torah and to their ancestral traditions. The greatest danger for Jews, numbering so few, was to become lost in an America so vast. That danger was accentuated in California, Leeser thought, where many went not to "settle" but to "acquire all the wealth possible in the least imaginable space of time." Under such circumstances, Jews were reluctant, Leeser reported, to contribute much money to erect a "suitable house of prayer" or to hire "ministers of the mental capacity and moral qualifications" demanded in a new and lawless country. Isaac Leeser nonetheless remained optimistic, looking forward to that day when he would hear of many synagogues being consecrated in the West and of many thousands faithfully keeping the Sabbath.

Judaism before the Civil War remained of modest size, with probably fewer than fifty synagogues to be found in the United States, coast to coast. Partly because of its restricted numbers, Judaism at this time also remained largely free of overt denominational divisions. When Jewish immigration sharply accelerated after the Civil War, bringing millions of East European Jews to the nation, then differences did arise regarding just what living in America required of or offered to the religiously observant Jew. Was a free nation an invitation to amend one's loyalty to the Torah, or was it instead an opportunity to observe it more faithfully than was possible elsewhere? As Roman Catholic immigrants had found, it was necessary to confront the relationship between religion and ethnicity. The issue was to determine what principles remained unchanging, what constituted "essential" beliefs and practices, and what traditions might be usefully adapted or even abandoned in confronting a new society.

THE WEST AS RELIGIOUS REGION

Nearly everyone recognizes that religion in the South demonstrates features peculiar to that area of the country. The uniqueness of the West is not so widely recognized, yet it, too, contains elements that set it apart from American religion at large. Three such elements will be noted here: (1) the "kingdom of the saints," that is, Mormonism; (2) the considerable presence of Hispanics and Indians; and (3) the harbinger of growing pluralism.

The Mormons managed to give utopianism a good name by refusing to wither away. The group's prophet, Joseph Smith (1805–1844), found no solace in the existing churches, and after a vision of the Angel Moroni in 1820 he embarked on a religious quest to restore the true church, the Church of Jesus Christ of Latter-day Saints. Though originating in the East (Fayette, New York) and dwelling for a time in Ohio, Missouri, and Illinois, the Latter-day Saints made the Far West their very own. Forced by the hostility of neighbors to move again and again, Mormons in Nauvoo, Illinois, thought that perhaps their last ejection notice had been served. Arriving there in 1839, they built a temple (one had already been abandoned in Ohio), established a government, and readied themselves against "Gentile" attack, if such should come. Gentiles in Mormon terminology included all those not of the inner community, all those rejecting the revelations and the authority of the founder, Joseph Smith. The "outside world" objected to Mormons holding property in common, objected to their adding to the Bible revelations of their own, objected to their zealous determination to be a "peculiar people," and certainly objected to the endorsement and practice of polygamy. When in 1844 Joseph Smith, arrested on a charge of destroying property, was placed in jail, a Gentile mob seized its opportunity: armed men stormed the jail, broke in, and assassinated both Joseph and his brother, Hyrum. At such a critical and difficult juncture, utopian colonies are supposed to fade away. But Mormonism refused to die. The prophet's death became a martyrdom, and his blood only furthered the church's growth.

Under the strong leadership of Brigham Young (1801–1877), these saints determined to take one more step, this one a giant step, away from states that would not welcome them and from neighbors who would not tolerate them. This time they would move where there were no states and where the only neighbors would be their own brothers and sisters. "The exodus of the nation of the only true Israel from these United States," said Brigham Young in 1845, "to a far distant region of the west where bigotry,

39. Joseph Smith's foundational encounter with the Angel Moroni became a standard part of Utah Mormon iconography. *Library of Congress*

intolerance, and insatiable oppression lose their power over them, forms a new epoch, not only in the history of the church, but of this nation." In 1847 the long and painful march began, from Nauvoo, Illinois, to Omaha

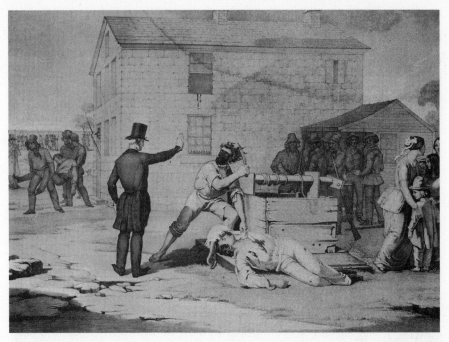

40. Martyred prophet of the Church of Jesus Christ of Latter-day Saints, Joseph Smith, fell along with his brother before a "gentile" mob in 1844. *Library of Congress*

("Winter Quarters"), Nebraska, until at last a great Salt Lake Basin received them. To that barren land—a land they could make blossom and flourish by imitating the diligence of the honeybee ("Deseret" in the Book of Mormon)—converts flocked as to a New Jerusalem. They came not just from the East but also from England, Scotland, Wales, Germany, and Scandinavia, many arriving in ships sent out from Liverpool, their passage paid for by the church, their trek from New Orleans arranged by the church, their welcome in Utah Territory (by 1850) assured by the church. Why did the recruitment of new members succeed on such a scale?

Mormon historians Leonard Arrington and Davis Bitton explain the many-sided appeal of this new and remarkably successful church. First, like the Disciples of Christ movement, the Mormons promised a return to the pure and primitive church of the New Testament, thus tapping into a yearning among many Americans for such a restoration. Second, though Joseph Smith stressed the importance of the Bible, he provided his followers with their own additional scriptural base: the Book of Mormon, first published in 1830. This book brought the New World and its native peoples into the whole divine plan, acclaiming America as a "land choice above all other lands." Third, successive revelations to the prophet created more distinctiveness, making this church not just another frontier variant of Christianity but a vast renovation of Christianity as a whole. Mormons added, for example, the practice of baptism for the dead (which created an entire genealogical industry) and the teaching of an eternal progression of humankind even beyond death (which gave the nineteenth-century doctrine of progress its most ambitious expression). Fourth, like the Millerites of upstate New York, Mormons also looked forward to an imminent end of the world, a Second Coming of Christ that Mormons were called to prepare for and thereby help bring about. The New Jerusalem, moreover, would be in America, not Palestine. Finally, Mormonism with its certain answers and strong central authority created a sustaining, enveloping community. This community would defend and protect, feed and house, make clear the difference between the saints and all the rest of a hostile, indifferent, and godless world. Like the seventeenth-century Puritans, the saints had founded a new kingdom, the new Israel.

If numbers can measure success, then this Mormon claim cannot be denied. As Brigham Young declared in 1849, "We have been kicked out of the frying pan into the fire, out of fire into the middle of the floor, and here we are and here we will stay." In the Great Basin of the Salt Lake Valley, the saints would irrigate and plant, harvest and prosper, knowing that God "will rebuke the frost and the sterility of the soil, and the land shall become fruitful." A century after Young's prophecy, all had been fulfilled, as Mormons dominated not only all of Utah but much of the land on all sides of Deseret. At that point Mormonism had become a fixed feature, often a determinative feature, of the western landscape.

Hispanics and Indians also shaped the culture of the southern deserts, the Great Plains, and the Pacific slopes. The former remained in those regions that had once been Spain's, then Mexico's, declining to surrender their culture when a United States, once confined to the lands east of the Mississippi, moved westward with dizzying speed. Neither did Hispanics surrender their religion to Anglo-Protestant missionaries or for that matter to Irish and French Catholics. Catholic authorities in the East, burdened by the large number of nineteenth-century immigrants arriving on the Atlantic shores, had few resources remaining to expend on the immense Southwest. A population predominantly agricultural and rural and even anticlerical would largely have to fend for itself, supervised lightly (if at all) by a hierarchy not yet prepared to elevate priests and bishops out of its own Hispanic ranks. That official slight notwithstanding, Mexican Americans remained crucial in the making of the region, rising to ever-increasing visibility across the West (and eventually, of course, across the whole nation).

Indians remained in the West because that was as far as they could be "removed" from the more settled areas of the East. Beginning with the removal of the Cherokees in the 1830s from northwest Georgia to "the West" (that is, Oklahoma "Indian Territory"), through the notorious "Trail of Tears," one solution to the Indian "problem" was simply to keep them as many steps as possible ahead of westward expansion. When that did not work, extermination and war (the two at times being virtually synonymous) were the major alternatives. As early as 1828 Congressman Edward Everett (1794–1865) found official policy with respect to Indians empty of all integrity and good faith. We have violated treaty after treaty, he noted, until the Indian has no reason to trust us and no security living among us. "We shall sign and seal, but we shall not perform. Let them go to Texas; let them join the Comanches, for their sakes, and for ours." That way, we may be spared further shame, Everett concluded. But further shame descended, in the Battle of Wounded Knee in South Dakota at the end of 1890 as well as in many other forms. Under such pressures, Indian population declined steadily throughout the nineteenth century, but in its comeback in the twentieth, the Indian presence in the West could be neither gainsaid nor ignored.

Finally, the West entered early into a pluralistic age that much of the rest of the nation would not know until decades later. The West was Protestant, Catholic, Jewish, and Russian Orthodox; the West was experimental in ways that went far beyond historic Christianity or Judaism (for starters, one might recall John Muir's sacramental devotion to nature, so stoked by the beauties of Yosemite and the sequoias); the West was more secular than the East (certainly, it had a lower percentage of formal affiliates with religious institutions). And the West was not only the West, but also a Hispanic North, a product of migrations northward out of Mexico. And the West was part as well of a larger Pacific Rim through which the cultures of Asia first entered the United States. In this region especially, as historian Laurie Maffly-Kipp has suggested, American religion is "a world history."

While most of the country did not encounter Asian religions until the World's Parliament of Religions met in Chicago in 1893, California knew Chinese immigrants before the Civil War. Migrating Anglo-Americans grew not only to know these other immigrants but also to fear them as foreign to the United States and foreign to the nation's familiar religious patterns. When as many as 3 million Chinese reached western shores by

41. Part of the West's distinctiveness as a religious region included the missions of the Russian Orthodox Church in Alaska and farther down the Pacific Coast. Sitka, Alaska, the location of this church, was an especially prominent center. *Keystone-Mast Collection, University of California, Riverside*

the early 1880s, political leaders decided the time had come to halt all further immigration of Chinese laborers and did so through the Chinese Exclusion Act of 1882. Similarly, the influx of Japanese along the West Coast, even more into Hawaii, led to sharp restriction of those who would introduce Buddhism and Shinto, even as the Chinese had brought with them Confucian, Taoist, Buddhist, and folk beliefs. Nonetheless, despite the intensity of anti-Chinese and anti-Japanese prejudices, Asian religions established their points of entry all along the Pacific shores. And no nativist organization, no racist rioting, and no reorganized immigration policy ever succeeded in erasing that presence once established. Also, with Alaska as its base, Russian Orthodoxy infiltrated the West all the way down to northern California, establishing an outpost and a church at Fort Ross in the early decades of the nineteenth century.

The American West, therefore, revealed a rich variety that gave to its religious life a character sharply different from that of any other region in the country. If in Boston or Philadelphia or Charleston or Nashville men and women might continue to think in terms of a "Protestant Empire" or a "Christian America," the cultural and religious diversity of the West subjected such concepts to serious question. Protestants set out to extend the institutions and programs of the Second Great Awakening across the land, but their grand plan of redemption foundered across the Mississippi, where Mormons, Mexicans, Chinese, Japanese, Russians, and native peoples met them and drew lines of resistance or made their own appropriations. The vanishing of a recognizable Protestant norm had become, in the West, the norm.

CHAPTER 9

A House of Faith Divided

In the first half of the nineteenth century the voluntaristic energies of the Second Great Awakening, along with the military and diplomatic successes of the nation, created for many Americans a sense of invincibility, assurance, and destiny. Nothing could halt the progress; nothing could stem the tide of reform; nothing could tarnish the moral sheen of this redeemer nation. Except slavery. Even for the most triumphalist and complacent, slavery was a fire bell ringing in the night, a dark cloud that grew ever more ominous and menacing.

For a time early in the nineteenth century, one could almost believe that the nation would reach a consensus that slavery was wrong, that it was only a matter of time—and not too much time at that—before slavery would be eliminated from the land. Church members of both North and South condemned the institution: Presbyterians at their General Assembly in 1818 unanimously declared, "We consider the voluntary enslaving of one part of the human race by another as a gross violation of the most precious and sacred rights of human nature; as utterly inconsistent with the law of God ... and as totally irreconcilable with the spirit and principles of the Gospel of Christ." By constitutional provision, the slave trade had come to an end in 1808, and "if we have no right to enslave an African," Angelina Grimké (1805–1879) pointed out, "surely we can have none to enslave an American." Yet ending the slave trade did nothing to undermine the continued indigenization of slavery in the United States—that is, the growing number of African Americans born into enslavement. So if slavery would not wither away for lack of importation, perhaps at least its territorial spread at home could be contained. Above all else, Americans would agree—would they not?—that slavery must not be expanded into other territories, into Missouri, for example, where it had not existed before. Yet little or no agreement could be found even on that point. The costly Missouri Compromise of 1820 preserved the Union—Maine entered as a free state, while Missouri entered as a slave state—but it left wide open the question of how much longer the republic could survive half slave and half free.

It was soon clear that no consensus was forthcoming and that only greater conflict lay ahead. As some pressed for immediate emancipation of all slaves, others expounded a ringing defense of the institution of slavery. As some concentrated on the moral issue, others spoke only of the political issue. As some cried out regarding human rights, others passionately defended their property rights. As abolitionists and apologists arrayed themselves in opposing stances, the rhetoric grew steadily harsher, the positions ever firmer and unyielding.

THE ABOLITIONISTS

With the founding of William Lloyd Garrison's radical newspaper, *The Liberator,* in 1831, antislavery voices grew noticeably louder, and to some they sounded increasingly strident. The New England Anti-Slavery Society was formed the very next year and was followed two years later by the creation in Philadelphia of the American Anti-Slavery Society. Calling for complete and immediate emancipation of slaves, the abolitionists offered no hint of compromise or concession. Slavery must go; it must go now. The Unitarian clergyman William Ellery Channing (1780–1842) in 1835 composed a powerful treatise against slavery, arguing from every philosophical, moral, and religious perspective that slavery was intrinsically, tragically wrong. "An institution so founded in wrong, so imbued with injustice, cannot be made a good." The essence of Christianity, Channing argued, is the spiritual kinship, the brotherhood of all humankind. This is the test set before those already privileged with freedom: to be able "to recognize our own spiritual nature and God's image in these humble forms, to recognize as brethren those who want all outward distinction." If we fail in this test, Channing concluded, then we fail "him who came to raise the fallen and to save the lost."

Two years after Channing published his addresses in Boston, the Reverend Elijah P. Lovejoy (1802–1837) affirmed his right to speak and to publish in Alton, Illinois. A Presbyterian clergyman and newspaper editor, Lovejoy defended the abolitionists for rejecting the view that black men and women were mere chattel or "an article of personal property" or "a piece of merchandise." Slaves were human beings, possessed therefore of natural and inalienable rights, created by and responsible to the same God as their white brethren. The only master of human beings was Almighty

42. Presbyterian clergyman Elijah P. Lovejoy died for both the freedom of the press and the freedom of the slave. *Library of Congress*

God, declared Lovejoy, and slavery usurped his prerogative "as the rightful owner of all human beings." And "whatever is morally wrong can never be politically right." Slavery, Lovejoy added, "is a political evil of unspeakable magnitude and one which, if not removed, will speedily work the downfall of our free institutions, both civil and religious."

Such sentiments were not popular in the South or in the North or on the frontier. In the process of printing and proclaiming his abolitionist views, Lovejoy had one printing press after another destroyed and dumped into the Mississippi River. Determined to defend a fourth press from similar attack, Lovejoy appealed to his fellow citizens in Alton to assist him. Not asking that they agree with him, Lovejoy pleaded only that his own right to life, liberty, and property be respected, that he be allowed to go home safely at night to his family "without being assailed," that his wife not be driven night after night "from a sick bed into the garret to save her life from the brickbats and violence of the mobs." He could flee from Alton, as he had fled from other places, Lovejoy added, but sometime, somewhere, one must take his stand. "I have concluded . . . to remain at Alton, and here to insist on protection in the exercise of my rights. If the civil authorities refuse to protect me, I must look to God; and if I die, I have determined to make my grave in Alton." On November 7, 1837, this Presbyterian abolitionist was shot and killed, the issue of slavery having long since ceased to be a matter for civil or rational debate.

African Americans likewise became active in arousing public opinion against slavery. The most famous black abolitionist of all, exslave Frederick Douglass (1817?–1895), spoke not only throughout much of America but abroad as well, contending that slavery was "a system of such gigantic evil, so strong, so overwhelming in its power, that no one nation is equal to its removal." Speaking before a packed house in London in 1846, Douglass attacked slavery, of course, but in addition he attacked a Christianity that seemed content to permit, even encourage, its continuance. "There has not been any war," he said, "between the religion and the slavery of the south." Indeed, the two seemed as partners. "The church and the slave prison stand next to each other. . . . The church-going bell and the auctioneer's bell chime in with each other; the pulpit and the auctioneer's block stand in the same neighbourhood." Beyond all that, the profits from slave buying and selling go to build more churches that will defend more masters. "We have men sold to build churches, women sold to support missionaries, and babies sold to buy Bibles and communion services." "Between the Christianity of this land and the Christianity of Christ," Douglass wrote in his autobiography, "I recognize the widest possible difference."

Daniel Payne (1811–1893), ordained as a Lutheran clergyman in 1839, then for a time a Presbyterian minister, found his lasting home as a leader (becoming a bishop by 1852) in the African Methodist Episcopal Church. Dedicated to the cause of black churches and a major figure in improving their institutional fortunes, Payne joined Douglass and other African Americans in the call for slavery's abolition. He condemned slavery, he said in 1839, "not because it enslaves the black man, but because it enslaves *man*." The unnatural and immoral relationship corrupts master as surely as it does slave, destroying the will of the latter and all moral restraint in the former. And of course it corrupts or destroys the allegiance of men and women to the Bible, which is turned into a proslavery tract by those whose only text is "Servants, obey your masters."

43. Crucial to the antislavery movement was the institutional infrastructure of the African Methodist Episcopal Church, the leading independent black denomination, as well as the moral vision and leadership of its bishops, including Daniel Payne. *Library of Congress*

So abolitionists, black and white, rushed across the land. Pulpits rang with calls for slavery's swift and sudden end; newspapers editorialized on the necessity of action now; books, such as Theodore Weld's *The Bible Against Slavery* (1837) and *Slavery as It Is* (1839) and even more Harriet Beecher Stowe's *Uncle Tom's Cabin* (1852) reached a wide and increasingly agitated audience. Addresses were delivered, public protest meetings held, revival meetings (such as those of Charles Finney) turned into antislavery crusades. Wendell Phillips (1811–1884), addressing the Massachusetts Anti-Slavery Society in 1853, declared that every means at the disposal of the abolitionist must be used in a cause that for the slave grew increasingly dire. "We dare not, in so desperate a case," Phillips said, "throw away any weapon which ever broke up the crust of an ignorant prejudice, roused a slumbering conscience, shamed a proud sinner, or changed in any way the conduct of a human being. Our aim is to alter public opinion." And on that battlefield opposing forces drew themselves up in ever-increasing numbers.

THE APOLOGISTS

As the rhetoric of abolitionism grew more uncompromising, so did the language of those now prepared to defend slavery on political or moral or religious grounds. The frontier Methodist preacher Peter Cartwright (1785–1872) described the insidious process by which many came to see slavery as something to praise rather than condemn. Methodist preachers, Cartwright said, started out poor, unable to afford any slaves and unready to participate in the institution of slavery. In that circumstance "they preached loudly against it." But then, said Cartwright, their economic circumstances improved, as many of them even married into slaveholding families. "Then, they began to apologize for the evil; then to justify it on legal principles; then on Bible principles—till lo and behold! it is not an evil but a good! it is not a curse but a blessing!" With rich sarcasm, Cartwright concluded that Methodist preachers in this last stage of their "education" about slavery even implied that "you would go to the Devil for not enjoying the labor, toil, sweat of this degraded race—and all this without rendering them any equivalent whatever!"

Just as abolitionism was not limited to the North, so apologies for slavery came not exclusively from the South. From New Jersey a Dutch Reformed minister, Samuel B. How (1790–1868), argued in 1855 that the biblical record demonstrated that slavery was no sin. The New Testament and the Old, How stated, "entirely agree" on the legitimacy of slavery as a social institution. The Bible teaches us "that there are rights of property; that there are masters and that there are slaves, and bids us to respect the right of the master, and not to covet his man-servant or his maid-servant" (Exodus 20:17). Samuel How emphasized the significance of property rights in the intensifying dispute, affirming that "the desire and the attempt to deprive others of property which the law of God and the law of the land have made it lawful for them to hold, is to strike a blow at the very existence of civilization and Christianity."

In Charleston, South Carolina, the Roman Catholic bishop, John England (1786–1842), also defended slavery as an institution approved by both God and man. Natural law does not prohibit, England explained, "a state in which one man has the dominion over the labour and the ingenuity of another to the end of his life." Natural law may not establish slavery, since in "pure nature all men are equal," but natural law does not prohibit slavery. Slaves voluntarily surrendered their freedom in order to receive protection and care from their human masters. This situation "insures to him food, raiment, and dwelling, together with a variety of little comforts;

it relieves him from the apprehensions of neglect in sickness, from all solicitude for the support of his family; and, in return, all that is required is fidelity and moderate labour." Many slaves, England concluded, are neither interested in nor would they accept their freedom. The arrangement is one of mutual benefit.

Similarly, the Baptist spokesman Richard Furman (1755–1825) explained that the "right of holding slaves is clearly established in the Holy Scriptures, both by precept and example." Furthermore, the golden rule, so often cited by the abolitionists as the ultimate argument against slavery, cannot be applied as though in a social vacuum. One must always consider the context, Furman pointed out, having "a due regard to justice, propriety, and the general good." For example, he asked, "A father may very naturally desire that his son be obedient to his orders; is he, therefore, to obey the orders of the son?" Social relationships as well as family ones require ordinary reason to be applied when implementing the rule to "do unto others as you would have them do unto you."

The problem with abolitionists, some apologists argued, was that they had left their religion and their Bibles far behind as they embraced foreign philosophies and radical thinkers. Such people could never be persuaded that they were reading back into scripture what simply was not there. Abolitionists, they said, act as though "Moses and Paul were moved by the Holy Ghost to sanction the philosophy of Thomas Jefferson!" Or, said Presbyterian Frederick A. Ross (1796–1883) in 1857, they leave the Bible in disgust because they cannot "torture" it any further into support of their cause; they then go off in search somewhere else of "an abolition Bible, an abolition Constitution for the United States, and an abolition God." Meanwhile, those who see slavery as totally "in harmony with the Bible" will cling even more faithfully to their holy writings and to their holy religion. The slaveholder, Ross wrote, "with the Bible in his heart and hand . . . will do justice and love mercy in higher and higher rule. Every evil will be removed, and the negro will be elevated to the highest attainments he can make, and be prepared for whatever destiny God intends."

If slavery could not be defended as a good, it could perhaps be justified as a political and economic given with which the churches should not interfere. South Carolina Lutherans in 1836 protested the "impropriety and injustice of the interference or intermeddling of any religious or deliberative body with the subject of slavery or slaveholding, emancipation or abolitionism." For themselves, they would henceforth have nothing to do with the subject or "at any time enter into a discussion of slavery." Others were willing to discuss it but only in terms of their own choosing: Christianity against atheism. On one side, said Presbyterian James H. Thornwell (1812–1862), we find "Atheists, Socialists, Communists, Red Republicans, [and] Jacobins." On the other, the "friends of order and regulated freedom" who see the workings of society not as the creation of man but the ordinance of God. Our task, said Thornwell, is to maintain "the principles upon which the security of social order and the development of humanity depend." Abolitionists think that "the duties of all men are specifically the same," while their opponents understand that men's duties "are as various as the circumstances in which men are placed." "Some are tried in one way, some in another," Thornwell explained, "but the spirit of true obedience is universally the same."

Like a rag doll, the Bible was tossed back and forth, now quoted to support slavery, now to attack it. The Christian religion was now the slaves' dearest friend, now their betrayer and deceiver. The church could be a station in the underground railroad, helping to spirit runaway slaves to freedom, or the church could be the gathering place from which to send out patrols to recapture slaves or to break up their religious meetings. Both sides, as Abraham Lincoln later and sorrowfully observed, "read the same Bible, and pray to the same God." The prayers of both, he added, could not be answered.

THE CHURCHES

While some churches managed to avoid bitter recrimination and lasting schism, churches with the largest following in the South could not escape being torn apart. Refusing to talk about the issue did not resolve it; praying about the matter did not alleviate it; creedal loyalty did not help; and a common denominational bond did not prove strong enough to hold. In the two decades immediately prior to the Civil War, the Methodist, Baptist, and Presbyterian fellowships all fell apart. If Christian love had proven not to be the tie that binds, what of civil law and national loyalty? Could either the nation or its churches long endure, half slave and half free?

In 1844 the youngest of the three denominations, the Methodist, was the first to suffer schism. Such painful parting of the ways could be readily anticipated in the sharply contrasting statements regarding slavery that came from the North and the South. In 1836 Bishop William Capers (1790–1855) of South Carolina took aim at the abolitionists, charging them with loyalty to "a false philosophy, overreaching and setting aside the Scriptures." Whatever may be the motives of these northern radicals, the conclusions reached "are utterly erroneous and altogether harmful." Bishop Capers held out no olive branch, allowed for no "good faith" on the part of those determined to eradicate slavery and to do it now.

A Methodist Anti-Slavery Convention, meeting in Boston in 1843, proclaimed views wholly unacceptable to brothers and sisters in the South. Holding slaves, treating human beings as property rather than persons, was, said the convention members, "a flagrant violation of the law of God: it is sin itself; a sin in the abstract and in the concrete; a sin under all circumstances." Not much room for negotiation there either. Then, addressing specifically the denominational issue, the Boston Methodists declared that neither unanimity nor harmony could exist within their church as long as slavery continued to flourish there. "We feel it our imperative duty," they concluded, "to use all such means as become Christians in seeking an immediate and entire abolition from the church of which we are members."

The very next year, therefore, the Methodist church in America, founded only sixty years before but already the largest Protestant body in the nation, ceased to be a single church. Splitting into two branches closely following sectional north-south lines, these two churches were predominantly white in membership. Two predominantly black Methodist bodies, the African Methodist Episcopal (formed in 1816) and the African Methodist Episcopal Zion (formed in 1821), continued their independent existence, operating initially in the North but eventually throughout the country. Active Methodist abolitionists, impatient for their whole church to act with respect to slavery, had formed the Wesleyan Methodist Church in 1843, but that separation involved only about 25,000 members as contrasted with the 1 million members caught up in the schism of 1844.

The immediate cause of that separation was the question of whether a slaveholding clergyman could be appointed a bishop in the national Methodist Episcopal Church. As early as 1836, when the General Conference of the church met in Cincinnati, that issue was raised, with southern delegates arguing that it was wholly inappropriate to make holding slaves a bar to the elevation to the episcopate. Northern delegates, on the other hand, contended that the Methodist Book of Discipline, following the lead of founder John Wesley, had taken a strong stand against slavery from the beginning, condemning it as a "great evil." Gradually, the church relaxed its position to the extent that it did not expel members who held slaves, but never did the church (so the northerners held) approve of slavery. "What, then, has been done to force the South to separation? What *new* grievance or injury has been inflicted by church action upon our brethren of the South? We are compelled to answer," a northern editor wrote in 1844, "none—absolutely none!" Southerners reasoned, on the other side, that if a Methodist member could hold slaves, then why not a Methodist bishop? Why make that the sticking point? Neither side would yield; the Methodist bond could not hold.

If, however, slavery were to be outlawed by presidential proclamation (as it was in 1863), then nothing would prevent northern and southern Methodists from reuniting—or so it seemed. By that time, however, twenty years of bitter recrimination and mutual accusation had only widened the chasm between the two branches. Southern bishops in 1865 indicated that a majority of their northern brethren had "become incurably radical." They had substituted politics for theology, social dogmas for churchly creeds. "Their pulpits," the bishops continued, "are perverted to agitations and questions not healthful to personal piety, but promotive of political and ecclesiastical discord." "Preach Christ and Him crucified," the bishops advised; "Do not preach politics." Earlier the U.S. Supreme Court had even had to settle property disputes between the two great divisions of Methodism, this further aggravating the wounds and postponing reconciliation. Not until nearly one hundred years later, in 1939, did northern and southern branches come together again.

In 1845 the Baptists, operating as a national entity only since 1814, similarly separated into northern and southern bodies, though in this instance the Southern Baptist Convention far outdistanced its northern counterpart in membership and expansion. Slavery once again served as the fulcrum upon which opposing sentiments teetered, with the appointment of a slaveholding missionary bringing the issue to the fore as among the Methodists it had been the appointment of a slaveholding bishop. In 1844 Alabama Baptists had put to the Boston-based board of missions a question concerning its willingness to appoint a missionary who held slaves. The board indicated that the question had never come up, but if it should the board could not appoint anyone who insisted upon retaining slaves. "We never can be a party to any arrangement which would imply approbation of slavery." Southerners felt excluded by such a pronouncement, since they contributed to missionary support but had no effective voice in missionary appointments. Shall the South "participate in all the burdens of the Convention," one writer inquired in 1845, "and be excluded from all its privileges?" Slavery is part of our land, our culture, and our economy: "We do not choose the place of our birth." We only claim the right, this author asserted, to act "according to the dictates of our own consciences without foreign control or interference."

Although denominational structures among black Baptists developed after the Civil War rather than before, many African American Baptists took active roles in resisting and condemning slavery long before the war. Baptist churches provided opportunities for such leadership and audiences for such sentiments, as Nathaniel Paul (1775?–1839) demonstrated in the Hamilton Baptist Church of Albany, New York. Celebrating that state's own Emancipation Day (July 4, 1827), Paul denounced slavery as blocking the path to salvation and to God's otherwise freely available mercies. "It stands," he declared, "as a barrier . . . to ward off the influence of divine grace; it shuts up the avenues of the soul, and prevents its receiving divine instruction; and scarce does it permit its miserable captives to know that there is a God, a Heaven or a Hell!"

In even more compelling and pointed rhetoric, another black Christian activist, David Walker (1785–1830) of Boston, issued an *Appeal* in 1829 that warned that the continued toleration of slavery would spell doom and ruin to the entire country: "For Almighty God will tear up the very face of the earth!!!" Anxieties that Walker aroused seemed totally fulfilled two years later when a black Baptist preacher and visionary, Nat Turner (1800–1831) of Southampton County, Virginia, led a slave rebellion that resulted in hundreds of deaths, black and white. Seeing himself as an instrument of God's long-delayed justice at last made manifest on earth, Turner reported in his *Confessions* that "it was plain to me that the Savior was about to lay down the yoke he had borne for the sins of man, and the great day of judgment was at hand."

Apocalyptic judgments came in sermons, in rebellions, and at last in a long and costly war. Despite all that and despite all separations and schisms, Baptists both black and white continued to grow before, during, and after the Civil War. Black Baptists passed the million mark before 1890, one of their number rejoicing in an increase "without precedent in the history of mankind. Truly we were once weak; but out of weakness we are made strong." African Americans turned to the Baptist denomination in greater force than to any other church, attracted by a relaxed polity that allowed them full independence in their own institutions and by an informal worship that permitted their own free and full expression. Meanwhile, the white branches of the denomination, with over 9,000 churches in 1850, increased fourfold in the subsequent century. Yet for those branches no reconciliation came, as the Baptist house of faith remained divided long after the issue of slavery had finally been laid to rest.

Presbyterians, the last of the three major denominations to divide, took its fateful step in 1857. Decades before, however, church members of

North and South found their disagreements over slavery firmly set. In 1835 South Carolina Presbyterians affirmed that slavery was "far from being a sin in the sight of God." On the contrary, it was nowhere condemned in scripture. In fact, slavery accorded with the example set by "patriarchs, prophets, and apostles" and was wholly consistent with "the most fraternal regard to the best good of those servants whom God may have committed to our charge." But in that very same year, Michigan Presbyterians avowed that slavery was most certainly "A Sin Before God and Man." It was an evil from every conceivable point of view, the synod declared—"moral, political, physical, and social." We are obliged, these Presbyterians of the North stated, "to endeavor to hasten the happy day of universal emancipation." If Presbyterians felt that strongly and that differently in 1835, none of the fast-moving events of the next twenty years would soften their disagreements or reveal any common ground.

Presbyterian abolitionists believed that to use the Bible to defend slavery was the surest way to bring calamity down upon that repository of religion as well as to defame and possibly even destroy all effectiveness of the Christian religion in America. Apologists for slavery, by contrast, argued that the Bible had little to do with the matter: abolitionists drew their ammunition from radical French philosophy or acted as though all Jefferson's assertions had been divinely inspired. The argument, southern Presbyterians believed, was not between Christian and Christian but between orthodox believer and foreign radical. Northerners believed time and history to be on their side: the idea that slavery was wrong, everywhere and always wrong, "is becoming as fixed as the everlasting hills."

Not as strong in the South as Methodists and Baptists had been, Presbyterians after the separation grew more rapidly in the North and West, the southern church limiting itself largely to the confines of the Confederacy. Approximately four times the size of the southern branch of Presbyterianism, the northern branch grew from about 500,000 in 1870 to around 3 million a century later. By that time overtures for reunion between the two sections grew more serious, and a merger was finally consummated in 1983.

The cost to American Protestantism of these major denominational divisions can hardly be overestimated. The crusading spirit of voluntaristic reform suffered enormously, as clerical leadership now spoke for regional bodies more than for national ones and reflected sectional differences more obviously than ever before. With the three major Protestant denominations ruptured, the evangelical hope for a Christian republic that rallied together around revivals, missions, and benevolence would never be quite the same. And then "all the horrors of civil war," which Methodist Peter Cartwright (1785-1872) had seen portended in the disunion of the churches, left still deeper scars.

THE NATION

Harriet Beecher Stowe (1811–1896) concluded her famous novel, *Uncle Tom's Cabin* (1852), with a plea to both North and South to repent of their respective injustices and cruelties while there was yet time. "A day of grace is yet held out to us," she wrote, and "the Christian church has a heavy account to answer." She hoped even in the decade of the 1850s to turn aside "the wrath of Almighty God," a wrath visited upon all the unjust and a wrath not to be escaped except through "repentance, justice, and mercy."

Revivalism had proved before to be a powerful instrument for healing differences and solving critical social or moral problems. Could revivalism rise to the challenges posed in the United States in the 1850s? Some thought that it just might work, as in 1858, a year of miracle and wonder, revivalism swiftly ignited city after city. Starting out in Boston and New York, the revival moved quickly beyond those centers to other towns and villages that anticipated another Great Awakening. "It swept over the land with such power," Charles G. Finney reported, that an estimated 50,000 or more conversions occurred in a single week. Reasonable estimates of conversions were hard to make, since the number of meetings increased so rapidly and since "all classes of people were inquiring everywhere." But then Finney added ominously, "Slavery seemed to shut it out from the South. The people there were in such a state of irritation, of vexation, and of committal to their peculiar institution . . . that the Spirit of God seemed to be grieved away from them."

Harriet Beecher Stowe continued to hope that the "great revival" of 1858 would become the "great reformation" of 1858, wherein men and women would resolve to draw closer to God and to become more Christlike in all their ways. "The great turning of the public mind to religion" raises our hopes, the novelist noted, that the nation can avoid tragic bloodshed. Northerners need to repent of the "profitable wickedness" of the slave trade; southerners need to repent of the continuing exploitation of the slave. What we so desperately need as a people are real revivals, Stowe concluded, which will "make men like Christ; or, if they do not make them like Him, at least set them on the road of trying to be like Him."

44. Author of *Uncle Tom's Cabin*, Harriet Beecher Stowe hoped for a great religious and moral revival that would forestall the Civil War. *National Portrait Gallery, Smithsonian Institution/Art Resource, NY*

However powerful this revival and however numerous the weekly conversions, it failed to bring North and South together. Animosities turned into violence and violence became war, a war that tried the national soul more than any event in American history. Early in the course of that struggle President Lincoln, meditating on the mind of God, declined to wrap the cause of either side in the mantle of righteousness and truth. "It is quite possible," he wrote, "that God's purpose is something different from the purpose of either party." Americans as a people have grown too accustomed to success, Lincoln observed in 1863, too self-sufficient, "too proud to pray to the God that made us." It is time, therefore, for humility and confession and earnest pleas for divine forgiveness.

The moral as opposed to the military climax of the Civil War came on the first of January, 1863, when Lincoln issued the Emancipation Proclamation freeing all slaves wherever federal authority could make that possible. This was a beginning, of course, rather than a conclusion in the march toward racial justice, but it was a necessary and crucial beginning. In the District of Columbia where emancipation was immediate, black Methodist Daniel Payne preached a sermon entitled "Welcome to the Ransomed." There he urged that a responsible and disciplined freedom be pursued by those now set free: "As you are now free in body, so now seek to be free in soul and spirit, from sin and Satan." That person is freest of all, Payne declared in the diction of the New Testament, who is free in Christ.

When the war itself ended in 1865, the losses in both body and spirit defied the imagination. Lincoln earlier that year in his Second Inaugural Address had called for all "to bind up the nation's wounds." Many wounds there were, and Lincoln, struck down by an assassin's bullet on Good Friday in 1865, could not assist in the binding up of those wounds. Neither would he be on hand to help assure that his own vision of reconciliation was actually pursued with "malice toward none, with charity for all, with firmness in the right, as God gives us to see the right." In that same year Horace Bushnell, delivering the commencement address at Yale, placed the awesome costs of the war in further theological perspective. As Christians, Bushnell said, we have been taught that without the shedding of blood there is no remission of sins. So it is, he added, that "without shedding of blood, there is almost nothing great in the world . . . for the life is in the blood, all life." Great has been the sacrifice, and great the suffering. But what has been given to us thereby is a nation reborn: "In this blood our unity is cemented and forever sanctified."

ABRAHAM LINCOLN'S JOURNEY

One historian has called Abraham Lincoln "the spiritual center of American history," and the estimation is apt. So many of the era's religious currents flowed through him that a closer look at his pilgrimage stands as a good capstone to the period's vast ferment. Lincoln grew up in a separatistic Baptist family in Kentucky, so austere in their predestinarian beliefs that missions were thought a presumption against God's inscrutable sovereignty. God saves who God saves, and before such divine decrees the actions of frail humanity paled into inconsequence. In Lincoln's speeches, filled with scriptural echoes, one can hear clearly the resonances of an older Calvinist piety: "The judgments of the Lord are true and righteous altogether" or "The Almighty has his own purposes."

Like Jefferson before him, Lincoln, though, remained aloof from institu-

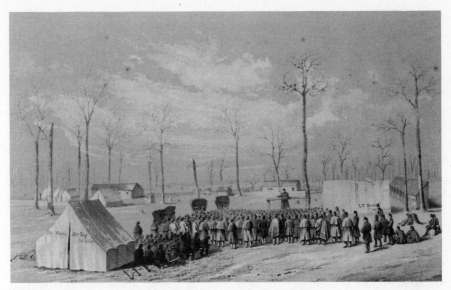

45. The armies of the Civil War, North and South, included a full complement of religious services and chaplains, and news of revivals in the camps spread widely on both sides. *Library of Congress*

tional Christianity and displayed a restorationist sense of the impurity of all existing churches. "When any church will inscribe over its altar as its sole qualification for membership," Lincoln related, "the Savior's condensed statement of the substance of both the law and Gospel, Thou shalt love the Lord thy God with all thy heart, and with all thy soul, and with all thy mind, and thy neighbor as thyself,—that Church will I join with all my heart and soul." As a young man, Lincoln had read with keen interest Tom Paine's *Age of Reason*, along with other deistic works, and throughout his life Lincoln often seemed to inhabit "a twilight" of belief and doubt somewhere between evangelical Protestantism and Enlightenment skepticism. As a freethinking questioner of standard creeds and institutional traditions, Lincoln carried forward the Jeffersonian side of American religious life. At the same time, as an orator and storyteller, he had learned much from the biblical cadences of Methodist itinerants and Baptist preachers.

Lincoln was also, as he said, "a seeking spirit," open to the religious experimentation that characterized the period's effervescent religious democracy. That was particularly evident in the interest that he and his wife, Mary Todd Lincoln (1818–1882), took in spiritualism. That movement, in which mediums sought to communicate with the spirits of the

46. National interest in spirits and angels had percolated throughout the 1850s, and the overwhelming casualties of the Civil War fed the growing numbers who sought consolation through the spirit world. *Swedenborg Library, Bryn Athyn College*

47. Not all were happy with this "occult" turn in American religious life, evident in this broadside equating the medium not with social reform and visionary power but with witchcraft (facing page). *Library of Congress*

VOL. I.---PICTORIAL HISTORY OF THE CAUSE OF THE GREAT REBELLION.

WITCHCRAFT.

WITCH OF ENDOR.   SATAN REPRESENTING SAMUEL.   SAUL.

These Pictures are intended to show that Modern Spiritualism of A. D. 1865, as practised in the United States, was described and practised thousands of years since under the names of Witchcraft. That the Spiritualism of 1865 is the Witchcraft described in the Bible.

[For a description of Witchcraft see 1st Samuel, Chap. 28th, Verses 7th, 8th, 11th, 13th, 14th, 15th, 16th, 17th, 18th, and 19th.] And if by Modern Spiritualism true communications can sometimes be obtained from the spirit world by calling on the spirits of the departed.

The same was done by Witchcraft, (for the proof of which see 1st Samuel, Chap. xxxi, verses 1st, 3d, and 6th, and 1st Chronicles, chap. 10th, verses 13th and 14th.

Modern Spiritualism was condemned as an abomination thousands of years since, under the name of Witchcraft by the Inspired Prophets who lived at the time it was practised. [See Deuteronomy, Chap. 18th, verses 9th, 10th, 11th, 12th; and first Samuel, Chap. 15th, verse 23d.

For the Bible tells us that "the dead know not any thing,"

The Witchcraft described in the bible consisted in calling up the spirits of the dead. Modern Spiritualism also consists in calling up the spirits of the departed.

These pictures show them to be one and the same thing—only a change of name.

SPIRITUALISM.

SPIRITUALIST.   SATAN REPRESENTING DECEASED FRIEND.   MEDIUM.

Copy Right Secured by ALFRED GALE, Asbury, New Jersey.

dead, began humbly enough in Hydesville, New York, in the late 1840s with a series of mysterious knockings and rappings that many interpreted to be ghostly communications. Through the 1850s and 1860s it became a mass movement, attracting innumerable followers and inquirers. The active investment of the Lincolns in spiritualism was initially at Mary's prompting. Grief-stricken over the death of her eleven-year-old son, Willie, in 1862 and still haunted by the death of her three-year-old son, Eddie, in 1850, she turned, as so many others did, to various mediums for some tangible consolation, for some way to reconnect with her sons who "had gone before." During Lincoln's presidency, mediums visited the White House at least eight times to hold séances, and the president, at once skeptical and yet open to prophetic signs and dreams, attended several of these meetings. The carnage of the Civil War only deepened the American fascination with spiritualism as the number of the bereaved multiplied with each new casualty. Sorrowing widows, parents, and children sought comfort in spirit messages, spirit songs, and even spirit photographs.

Spiritualism was more than a movement bridging the visible and invisible worlds. It was also another reform movement in which female mediums received messages about the causes of women's rights and abolition. Not surprisingly, one of the mediums who ministered to the Lincolns in the White House, Nettie Colburn (1841–1892), later claimed that messages from the spirit world had urged the president fearlessly to pursue emancipation for the slaves. So in that occult connection, too, Lincoln represented another dimension of the religious life of the period, the ways in which religious innovation and social reform mapped onto each other.

Above all, it was Lincoln's theological grappling with the Civil War and with slavery that made his journey so characteristic of the age. As he speculated in his Second Inaugural Address, "If we shall suppose that American slavery is one of those offenses which, in the providence of God, must needs come, but which, having continued through his appointed time, he now wills to remove, and that he gives to both North and South this terrible war, as the woe due to those by whom the offense came, shall we discern therein any departure from those divine attributes which the believers in a living God always ascribe to him?" The "mighty scourge of war" became, in Lincoln's exegesis, a national atonement for the offense of slavery.

Suggested Reading for Part 2: Religious Ferment from the Revolution to the Civil War

On the broader Enlightenment frameworks of the revolutionary era and beyond, see Henry F. May, *The Enlightenment in America* (New York, 1976); Mark A. Noll, *Princeton and the Republic, 1768–1822: The Search for a Christian Enlightenment in the Era of Samuel Stanhope Smith* (Princeton, 1989); and Mark Valeri, *Law and Providence in Joseph Bellamy's New England: The Origins of the New Divinity in Revolutionary America* (New York, 1994). For the religion of the political founders of the new nation, see Edwin S. Gaustad, *Faith of Our Fathers: Religion and the New Nation* (San Francisco, 1987). For particular attention to the origins and implications for religion of the First Amendment, one may turn to Thomas J. Curry, *The First Freedoms: Church and State in America to the Passage of the First Amendment* (New York, 1986), and also to Leonard W. Levy, *The Establishment Clause: Religion and the First Amendment* (New York, 1994). The role of Unitarianism is outlined in Sydney E. Ahlstrom and Jonathan S. Carey, eds., *An American Reformation: A Documentary History of Unitarian Christianity* (Middletown, CT, 1985).

The religious ferment of the early republic has received much attention. The book that has set much of the agenda for recent discussions is Nathan O. Hatch, *The Democratization of American Christianity* (New Haven, 1989). For a good overview of the reform-minded side of the period, see Robert H. Abzug, *Cosmos Crumbling: American Reform and the Religious Imagination* (New York, 1994). Stephen J. Stein has written the standard work on the Shakers with *The Shaker Experience in America: A History of the United Society of Believers* (New Haven, 1992). Lawrence Foster explores the Shakers, the Mormons, and the Oneida Community in *Religion and Sexuality: Three*

American Communal Experiments of the Nineteenth Century (New York, 1981) as does Louis J. Kern in *An Ordered Love: Sex Roles and Sexuality in Victorian Utopias* (Chapel Hill, 1981). William Miller is the focal point of the important work edited by Ronald L. Numbers and Jonathan M. Butler, *The Disappointed: Millerism and Millenarianism in the Nineteenth Century* (Bloomington, 1987). Nineteenth-century Protestants relied heavily on popular visual images for the building of their educational, cultural, and devotional enterprises—a phenomenon that David M. Morgan explores fully in *Protestants and Pictures: Religion, Visual Culture, and the Age of American Mass Production* (New York, 1999).

On that most successful of the utopian colonies, the Mormons, one may consult Leonard J. Arrington and Davis Bitton, *The Mormon Experience: A History of the Latter-day Saints* (New York, 1992). The reader may also turn to Jan Shipps's influential interpretive work, *Mormonism: The Story of a New Religious Tradition* (Urbana, 1985). Two biographical studies by able historians should also be noted: Richard L. Bushman, *Joseph Smith and the Beginnings of Mormonism* (Urbana, 1984), and Leonard J. Arrington, *Brigham Young: American Moses* (New York, 1985). For the wilder reaches of the ferment among new religious groups, see Paul E. Johnson and Sean Wilentz, *The Kingdom of Matthias* (New York, 1994). For highbrow variants of that religious innovation and seeking in New England Transcendentalism, see Arthur Versluis, *American Transcendentalism and Asian Religions* (New York, 1993), and Catherine L. Albanese, ed., *The Spirituality of the American Transcendentalists: Selected Writings of Ralph Waldo Emerson, Amos Bronson Alcott, Theodore Parker, and Henry David Thoreau* (Macon, GA, 1988). On Judaism in the period, see Lance J. Sussman, *Isaac Leeser and the Making of American Judaism* (Detroit, 1995).

The force of revivalism can be reckoned with through various sources, including Nathan Hatch's work mentioned above. See as well William G. McLoughlin, *Modern Revivalism: Charles Grandison Finney to Billy Graham* (New York, 1959), and Charles A. Johnson, *Frontier Camp Meeting: Religion's Harvest Time* (Dallas, 1955). In these revivalistic currents, women often flourished as preachers, despite widespread suspicion and hostility, a story that is compellingly told in Catherine A. Brekus, *Strangers & Pilgrims: Female Preaching in America, 1740–1845* (Chapel Hill, 1998). That revivalism was not a Protestant monopoly is made evident by Jay P. Dolan in his *Catholic Revivalism: The American Experience, 1830–1900* (Notre Dame, 1978). For particularly insightful studies of evangelical religion in the South, including its racial and social dimensions, see Donald G. Mathews, *Religion in the Old South* (Chicago, 1977), and Christine Leigh Heyrman,

Southern Cross: The Beginnings of the Bible Belt (New York, 1997). On religion in the West, see especially Laurie F. Maffly-Kipp, *Religion and Society in Frontier California* (New Haven, 1994); Sandra Sizer Frankiel, *California's Spiritual Frontiers: Religious Alternatives in Anglo-Protestantism, 1850–1910* (Berkeley, 1988); and Roberto Lint Sagarena, "Inheriting the Land: Defining Place in Southern California from the Mexican American War to the Plan Espiritual de Aztlan," Ph. D. diss., Princeton University, 2000.

C. C. Goen's *Broken Churches, Broken Nation: Denominational Schisms and the Coming of the American Civil War* (Macon, GA, 1985) spells out how the denominational separations ominously foretold the political events to follow. For a broad range of recent scholarship on religion's role in the war, see Randall M. Miller, Harry S. Stout, and Charles Reagan Wilson, eds., *Religion and the American Civil War* (New York, 1998). The lasting religious consequences of the Civil War for the South are illuminated in Charles R. Wilson, *Baptized in Blood: The Religion of the Lost Cause, 1865–1920* (Athens, GA, 1980). Albert J. Raboteau's *Slave Religion: The Invisible Institution in the Antebellum South* (New York, 1978) remains the anchoring work on its topic, but see as well Sylvia R. Frey and Betty Wood, *Come Shouting to Zion: African American Protestantism in the American South and British Caribbean to 1830* (Chapel Hill, 1998). William L. Andrews offers an excellent group of primary texts on the evangelicalism of black women in *Sisters of the Spirit: Three Black Women's Autobiographies of the Nineteenth Century* (Bloomington, 1986). Black Baptist developments, both before and after the war, are charted in James M. Washington, *Frustrated Fellowship: The Black Baptist Quest for Social Power* (Macon, GA, 1986). On Lincoln's religion, see Allen C. Guelzo, *Abraham Lincoln: Redeemer President* (Grand Rapids, 1999), and William J. Wolf, *The Almost Chosen People: A Study of the Religion of Abraham Lincoln* (Garden City, NY, 1959).

Gerda Lerner's *The Grimké Sisters from South Carolina: Pioneers for Woman's Rights and Abolition* (New York, 1998) nicely demonstrates the interrelationships between women's rights in particular and human rights in general. The wider connections between the era's religious ferment and women's rights are highlighted in Ann Braude's *Radical Spirits: Spiritualism and Women's Rights in Nineteenth-Century America* (Boston, 1989). On the connections within nineteenth-century Judaism, see Karla Goldman, *Beyond the Synagogue Gallery: Finding a Place for Women in American Judaism* (Cambridge, MA, 2000).

Part 3

MODERN PROSPECTS FROM CITYSCAPES TO BIBLE BATTLES

CHAPTER 10

Immigration and Diversity

Although the history of the United States is indeed a history of immigration, the period after the Civil War symbolizes that fact in a uniquely powerful way. Between 1860 (when the population of the whole country was 31 million) and 1890, newly arrived immigrants numbered some 10 million. In the briefer period from 1890 to 1914, the number soared to 15 million. This mighty movement of peoples, largely from southern and eastern Europe, was augmented by migrations across the Mexico-U.S. border and by an influx of Chinese and Japanese along the Pacific Coast. The multiplicity of cultural patterns gave religion new opportunities for colorful display, even as it heightened anxieties regarding national unity and religious direction.

In the tumult of transplanting, religion often provided both personal security and ethnic cohesion. In a new land and generally faced with a new language, far removed from ancestral homes and former national identities, uncertain immigrants turned hungrily toward synagogue, church, temple, and shrine for the comfort of the familiar. When so much had been so abruptly interrupted, religion stood ready to offer the assurance of some continuity. In the communities of faith the uprooted still found roots from which they could grow in new directions.

ETHNICITY AND RELIGION

While religion often reinforced ethnic cohesiveness, ethnicity sometimes challenged the unifying dimensions of religion. Ethnic loyalty created social community at the same time that it threatened or shattered theological and ecclesiastical community. Nowhere were the challenges more dramatic than among America's rapidly expanding Roman Catholics. The Irish immigration before the Civil War was so great that it gave the American Church a Hibernian stamp and flavor that would last for at least one hundred years. Among the bishops and archbishops of the Roman Catholic Church in late-nineteenth-century America, the Irish exercised a virtual monopoly. Like all monopolists, they jealously guarded their preserve, only reluctantly and tardily agreeing to share their power.

German Catholics who in many cases had arrived long before the Irish newcomers especially resented the domination exercised by the spiritual heirs of Saint Patrick. In 1886 a Milwaukee priest, P. M. Abbelen (1843–1917), protested to the Vatican on behalf of his German brothers and sisters, asking that German parishes "be entirely independent of Irish parishes" and that "the rectors of Irish parishes . . . not be able to exercise any parochial jurisdiction over Germans enrolled in any German church." What was at stake, Father Abbelen pointed out, was more than merely the German language; the whole character of worship differed between Irish and German. The Irish "love simplicity" and "do not care much for pomp and splendor," while the Germans "love the beauty of the church edifice and the pomp of ceremonies, belfries and bells, organs and sacred music, procession, feast days, socialities, and the most solemn celebration of First Communion and weddings."

Moreover, German laity, he said, tend to exercise much more control of the administrative structure of the parish, while the Irish seem inclined to leave everything in the hands of the priests. "Finally, even manners and social customs of the two nationalities differ exceedingly," the most obvious example of this being that rarely do Irish boys marry German girls or German boys Irish girls. This is not said, the Milwaukee priest and vicar-general carefully noted, in order to argue that one group is superior to the other, only that they are different and that the Catholic church will be a healthier institution if it respects that difference rather than trying to suppress or obliterate it.

Similarly, the Italians and Portuguese, the Austrians and Czechs found themselves ruled over by Irish unfamiliar with their customs and their language, sometimes unsympathetic to their difficulties and concerns. An Italian Catholic, recalling his boyhood in New York early in the twentieth century, indicated that the Irish leadership was often responsible for driving Italians away from institutional Catholicism. Italian men, he pointed out, had never been too fond of Italian clergy, but the American clergy they despised. In the Church of Our Lady of Mount Carmel in New York, built in 1884, Italian Catholics were consigned by Irish and German Catholics to the basement for worship, despite their growing numerical dominance of the parish. The devotions of the new Italian immigrants— from their grand street festivals dedicated to the Madonna right down to

48. Ethnic parishes dominated Roman Catholic life in the late nineteenth and early twentieth centuries as in the Polish community in Buffalo, New York, gathered here for an Easter mass at Corpus Christi Church. *Library of Congress*

their way of collecting church offerings—were the objects of scorn and condescension from Catholic neighbors who thought they knew better.

Polish Catholics, too, found the adjustment to the United States extraordinarily difficult to make. To some, it even appeared so difficult that schism from the church of their birth turned out to be the only possible path. In Scranton, Pennsylvania, in the 1880s and 1890s Polish Catholics found themselves ruled not by a Polish bishop but an Irish one, governed not by a Polish mayor but an Irish one, outvoted even in their own parish by what they described as a "foreign priestly power." True catholicity was one thing, but too much Irishness quite another. When riots erupted, concerned laymen looked for assistance somewhere, anywhere. A Polish priest and former rector in Scranton came to the rescue, advising all those "who are dissatisfied and feel wronged" to set about organizing and building a new church of their own. In Buffalo, Chicago, and other cities where large Polish communities could be found, similar sentiments led to ecclesiastical independence. Mass was celebrated in Polish, religious journals were published in Polish, and Polish saint days and festivals were celebrated; by 1904 the Polish National Catholic Church in America had become a reality. Although the vast majority of Poles remained in the Roman Catholic Church, the ethnic church continued to survive and prosper as one symbol of ethnicity's tenacious power.

On the whole, however, the Catholic Church successfully resisted the natural tendency of ethnic enclaves to run their own ecclesiastical affairs and to establish competing hierarchies. In this respect Catholicism remained "catholic." On the other hand, the failure to assure some kind of proportional representation in the American hierarchy to the several ethnic groups led to continued tensions and struggles within a church striving, against great odds, to prove its universality and its inclusiveness. In the twentieth century Hispanic Catholics would have to make many of the same arguments about representation that had been made by German, Italian, and Polish parishioners before them.

In the post–Civil War period, the ethnic composition of Judaism underwent radical transformation. Largely German dominated before that war, Judaism in the succeeding decades acquired a decidedly Eastern European cast. Especially from Russia and especially in response to the bloody massacres or pogroms of 1881, 1891, and 1905, Jews by the hundreds of thousands left a hostile Europe for a beckoning America. The most famous words of welcome to immigrants, written by the Jewish poet Emma Lazarus (1849–1887) in 1883, found their way onto the Statue of Liberty:

> Give me your tired, your poor,
> Your huddled masses yearning to be free,
> The wretched refuse of your teeming shore,
> Send these, the homeless, tempest-tost to me,
> I lift my lamp beside the golden door.

That golden door did not stay open indefinitely, but it did stand wide long enough for the United States to become the major center of Jewish population in the world.

More was changed than mere ethnicity, however, for the ethnic shift (from Jews of the German Enlightenment to Jews of the Russian persecutions)

49. One of the innovations of Reform Jews, marking an accommodation with the wider religious culture, was the development of confirmation ceremonies for both boys and girls. *Library of Congress*

also led to a religious shift. German Jews, typified by Rabbi Isaac Mayer Wise, saw the reforming and the Americanizing of Judaism as a coordinated task. Here in America Judaism did not need to hunker down behind ghettoed walls or live in isolation from or in terror of the prevailing culture. Jews were free to worship as they chose, but more than that Jews were free to modernize their religion if they chose. Wise believed that Judaism should free itself of ancient legislation and ethnic limitation to become a universal and ethically focused monotheism with appeal to all humanity. To do this Jews had to become totally and proudly American, shorn of all foreignness. If the Jew continues "under German influences," Wise wrote, "he must become either a bigot or an atheist, a satellite or a tyrant. He will never be aroused to self-consciousness and independent thought." In short, Wise concluded, the Jew must become unambiguously an American rather than merely an ethnic or religious refugee.

Many Eastern European Jews, however, sought nothing so much as the opportunity to practice their ancient religion without hindrance or limitation. Arriving in New York City or other eastern ports, they hurried from the ship to create a synagogue: intimate, free, and above all orthodox. These Jews did not wish to reform the ancient law (or Torah); they wished only to obey it. Being or becoming Americans was not nearly so pressing or important as being or becoming faithful Jews. For decades they had been harassed or hindered, beaten or robbed, jailed or slain. Every obstacle that could be thrown in the path of ritual purity and communal worship had been thrown; every burden that could be thrust upon observant Jews had been pressed upon them, their families, their children. Now that they had come to a land where they could worship without fear, and they wanted do just that. They did not wish to hear of reform; they wished rather for the freedom to be observant.

Among America's newly arriving Jews, ethnicity represented, therefore, more than just the competing allegiances found among America's newly arriving Catholics. Here one found a sharply contrasting psychology, a pointedly different stance with regard to culture. Reform Judaism argued for change and transformation as an organizing principle within Judaism; Orthodox Judaism argued against change across the board: "All change is forbidden by Torah," the architects of modern Orthodoxy claimed. In between these two groups, Conservative Judaism arose as yet another alternative, arguing for a limited openness to change amid a steadfast traditionalism. Solomon Schechter (1847–1915), who arrived in America in 1902 to become president of the Jewish Theological Seminary in New York City, defended the Conservative approach. "There is nothing in American

50. Maintaining or even enlarging the traditional Jewish holidays to compete with the American Christmas, New Year's, and Easter was one way to hold assimilationist pressures at bay and to keep Jewish identity intact. One of the Jewish holidays, Purim, was celebrated as part carnival masquerade, part charity ball. *Library of Congress*

citizenship," he wrote, "which is incompatible with our observing the dietary laws, our sanctifying the Sabbath, our fixing a Mezuzah [small portion of Hebrew scripture] on our doorposts, our refraining from unleavened bread on Passover, or our perpetuating any other law essential to the preservation of Judaism." In Europe compromises were forced upon us, said Schechter. In America, they are not. "In this great, glorious and free country we Jews need not sacrifice a single iota of our Torah; and, in the enjoyment of absolute equality with our fellow citizens, we can live to carry out those ideals for which our ancestors so often had to die."

Ethnicity, together with the vagaries of historical circumstance, introduced sectarian or denominational differences among America's religious Jews. Many of the new immigrants, however, found their interests to be more political or economic than religious, with the result that only about half of the nation's Jews belong now to the synagogues or temples of the Reform, Orthodox, and Conservative branches. No hierarchy from abroad had directed the development of Judaism in America; thus no schism

51. The degree to which dietary laws were maintained was one of the tests of ritual observance that often distinguished Orthodox from Conservative from Reform Jews; here kosher
wine is inspected in New York City in 1942. *Library of Congress*

from or rebellion against external authority has ever been necessary. Synagogue government is local and democratic, a fact that enables ethnicity in
the large urban centers to survive with its own leadership and traditions,
its own enduring, sustaining sense of community.

Protestantism also enjoyed ethnic enriching in the period following the
Civil War. Lutheranism in particular revealed a pattern of development in
which ethnic loyalties prevented the creation of any single Lutheran
church. The large Scandinavian immigrations (Swedish, Danish, Norwegian, Finnish, Icelandic) of the second half of the nineteenth century led to
separate ecclesiastical entities whose reason for being was neither doctrinal nor geographical but ethnic. Affiliation with German Lutherans who
had arrived in the eighteenth century was out of the question, but so also
was affiliation with fellow Scandinavians. Each group wanted its own language, its own festivals, and its own familiar patterns of life. In Minnesota, for example, as one Lutheran later recalled, "the Swedes and
Danes and Finns kept to themselves in communities that had names like

Swedish Grove and Dane Prairie and Finlandia. The groups could have made themselves understood to one another," he added, "and might have found they had much in common. But these exchanges did not occur." The twentieth century opened with twenty-four separate Lutheran groups in America, but the peak had been reached. Gradually the process began to reverse itself, as Old World ethnic distinctions gave way to a new Lutheran identity that was more specifically American.

Ethnicity did not always conquer theology and ecclesiology. In the case of the Dutch Reformed, for example, Dutchness itself was not enough to maintain unity between Dutch who arrived in the nineteenth century and those who had arrived two centuries earlier. The newer immigrants found their compatriots who had been in America for half a dozen generations or so already too Americanized; their theology, moreover, had lost some of its Calvinist precision, some of its careful fidelity to the Heidelberg Confession. Thus the Christian Reformed Church in North America, organized in 1857, declined to be identified with the older Reformed church. Less than a hundred years later, the Christian Reformed itself suffered a separation, the charge again being one of doctrinal or theological inexactitude. In each instance, while ethnicity mattered, theology mattered more.

In the twentieth century, the close tie between ethnicity and religion was nowhere better illustrated than in the several branches of Eastern Orthodoxy. Russian, Greek, Albanian, Armenian, Bulgarian, Romanian, Syrian, Serbian, Ukrainian, and more ethnic labels defined not just parish boundaries but all social relationships and family alliances as well. Part of Eastern Orthodoxy's relatively low profile in American public life results directly from the persisting power of ethnicity to fragment Orthodoxy into small, self-governing national or ethnic bodies. Ecumenical efforts, especially as articulated by the Orthodox Church of America (which carries a strongly Russian heritage), have long foundered on the rocks of ethnic difference and discord. Of course, the very tenacity with which Orthodox Christianity is interwoven with distinct cultures—different branches having different foodways, calendars, celebrations, languages, or iconic representations—has made these churches such anchors of both social and religious life. As one immigrant said, "There couldn't be any Greek life without the church."

RELIGION AND RACE

The deep scars from the Civil War made it wholly unnecessary to demonstrate the power of race. None dared question its might. And what could divide a nation could certainly divide the churches not only before the war but long thereafter. Black Methodists in the North already had created their separate institutions (African Methodist Episcopal in 1816, African Methodist Episcopal Zion in 1821), but black Methodists in the South did not create a denomination of their own until 1870. At that time about 100,000 blacks withdrew from the Methodist Episcopal Church, South, to form what was then called the Colored Methodist Episcopal Church. After nearly a century of growth the name "Christian" was substituted for "Colored." Growth among black Baptists following the war was even more impressive than among Methodists.

As early as 1880 black Baptists had formed their own missionary organization; a decade and a half later a fully developed denomination, the National Baptist Convention, came into being, its creation in part the result of African Americans feeling unwelcome in the white-dominated parent bodies. As one black pastor, E. K. Love (1850–1900) of Savannah, Georgia, noted in 1896, "It never was true anywhere, and perhaps never will be, that a Negro can enjoy every right in an institution controlled by white men that a white man can enjoy." Like many others, Love also believed that a "bright and glorious future" awaited America's blacks in religious institutions of their own creation and their own direction. In this way, noted another pastor from Helena, Arkansas, blacks could identify and develop "a host of intelligent, self-reliant practical leaders among us."

This is precisely how it turned out, as black Baptists created their own publishing house in 1898, their own mechanisms for educating missionaries to Africa, and their own lobbying machinery designed to improve the condition and future of the nation's black population. With about 2 million members by 1900, these Baptists felt strong enough to take the gospel message back to Africa, to "be a power as a missionary force for the evangelization of the world," as one of their number proclaimed in 1903. While all the world should receive missionaries, Africa in particular, "the original home of the race," called out for evangelists to come among them. "A great work remains to be done for the race in this and other lands," the spokesman concluded, "and every Baptist should therefore be intensely a missionary Baptist." The National Baptist Convention itself suffered a schism in 1915, yet now two major denominations pressed forward in growth and influence across the continent.

Though black Christians could frequently be found in such prevailing white institutions as the Episcopal and the Roman Catholic Churches, the majority belonged to denominations where the leadership was wholly theirs, where the worship more faithfully reflected their own musical and sermonic practices, and where their contribution to the total Christian

52. The number of independent black churches, especially Baptist churches, increased dramatically after the Civil War, and worship life continued to center on prayer meetings, revival preaching, and song. *Library of Congress*

community could be more freely rendered. The tragedy of involuntary segregation remained, but as E. K. Love noted at the close of the nineteenth century, black denominations could have this mitigating effect: "We can more thoroughly fill our people with race pride, denominational enthusiasm and activity, by presenting to them for support enterprises that are wholly ours." The religious life of African Americans in the second half of the nineteenth century turned out to be another way of echoing Bishop Daniel Payne's "Welcome to the Ransomed."

In the generation or two following the Civil War, prejudice in the United States was directed at many convenient targets. As immigration increased, those who were so inclined could find looming threats in the growing number of Catholics and Jews and in the growing "foreignness" in general. Blacks, of course, though not part of the immigration surge, encountered prejudice and violence on many other grounds. Then into the West came Asians, creating even more unease, who found the path to acceptance either exceedingly difficult or totally blocked. Bringing with them such "foreign" religions as Confucianism and Buddhism, Chinese and Japanese emigrants also posed an economic threat as they bartered their labor at the cheapest rates. With over 3 million emigrants from China by 1882, public pressure led to the adoption of the Chinese Exclusion Act, which suspended all immigration from China for ten years. The act was renewed ten years later, and a decade after that Chinese immigration was suspended indefinitely. By that time public feeling against the increased Japanese influx led to similar anxieties about the "Yellow Peril" and the racial dilution or "mongrelization" (to use a term popular with the Ku Klux Klan) of the nation. The so-called Gentlemen's Agreement of 1907 and 1908 between Japan and the United States effectively halted the flow of the Japanese into the West Coast states.

The nation's religious forces were no more effective in promoting a blindness to race with respect to Asian immigrants than they had been with respect to African Americans. Missionaries and schools were charged with the responsibility of Christianizing and Americanizing these immigrants, but initial successes were limited. Converts, moreover, tended to be placed in ethnically restricted churches: the Korean Baptist Church, the Chinese Methodist Church, the Japanese Presbyterian Church. Ethnicity, sometimes seen as enriching and brightening the whole fabric of American society, could also be regarded as detrimental to social cohesion and religious destiny. The growing Asian presence, especially in the West, was a major factor in the nation's choosing to restrict immigration more severely in the early decades of the twentieth century, to close that "golden door" of which Emma Lazarus had written.

RELIGION AND GENDER

In the wake of the Emancipation Proclamation and the gradual extension of voting rights to a wider segment of the population, women began to participate more broadly in public affairs. In religion, leadership by women (as in the case of the Shakers and in Christian Science) drew comment and attention, as it did in the rapidly multiplying Holiness and Pentecostal bodies, where female ministers were common. In more traditional religious settings, however, the drive for true equality, especially in ministerial roles, was both difficult and uneven. The long shadow of tradition, along with the selective support of biblical injunction, combined to keep women from sharing in leadership and authority. Emancipation came with much reluctance, and in many cases it did not come at all.

Antoinette Brown Blackwell (1825–1921) had no trouble being admitted to Oberlin College, a school founded under the joint auspices of the Congregationalists and the Presbyterians and a school that early on had taken a firm stand in favor of coeducation. But then, after her undergraduate studies, Blackwell did what no female student had done before: she applied for admission to the theological department, where advanced study normally resulted in ordination to the ministry. After much discussion the faculty decided that Blackwell would be admitted to advanced study but would not be granted a degree and presumably therefore would not be ordained. Somehow, it seemed the perfect academic compromise. Nonetheless, the determined woman finally won her ordination in 1853, being the first woman set apart for ministry by one of the major denominations (Congregational). She spent the remainder of her long life raising the consciousness of her fellow citizens on the questions of equity with respect to women's rights in general and on women's ministry in particular.

Among those not persuaded by Blackwell's argument or example was Professor Robert L. Dabney (1820–1898), a Presbyterian minister and theologian in Virginia. Writing in 1879, he explained that not all social novelties were healthy, not all "progressive" developments were biblical. Ordaining women to the ministry was, according to Dabney, an example of innovation without scriptural foundation and without any socially redeeming quality. The Old Testament, he argued, "allowed no regular church office to any woman." "No woman ever ministered at the altar as either priest or Levite." And the Old Testament pattern was very much followed in the New. Moreover, Dabney added, woman really was the "weaker vessel," not designed by God for all the responsibilities or all "the franchises in society to which the male is entitled." We hear much of "women's rights" these days, Dabney observed; this is a "common movement," not supported by scripture. It is a movement that threatens biblical authority at large and undermines the foundation of Christian marriage in particular; it is, in short, "simply infidel," and good Presbyterians will have nothing to do with that general trend and certainly not with the specific effort to create women preachers.

Dabney based his argument heavily on the Bible, and just there, said Elizabeth Cady Stanton (1815–1902), lies much of the difficulty besetting American women. "The Bible teaches that woman brought sin and death into the world," Stanton wrote in 1895, "that she precipitated the fall of the race, that she was arraigned before the judgment seat of Heaven, tried, condemned and sentenced." Marriage was to be her bondage, childbearing her curse, and intellectual dependence her earthly fate. "Here is the Bible position of woman briefly summed up." On that foundation, Stanton believed, little real emancipation for women can ever be based. What is required is a new critical understanding of those scriptures that have been used to justify centuries of patriarchy and female submission. This new foundation Stanton sought to provide in *The Woman's Bible*, issued in two volumes in 1895 and 1898. To those shocked by the thought that liturgies and scriptures might be thus revised and criticized, Stanton offered this counsel: "Come, come, my conservative friend, wipe the dew off your spectacles, and see that the world is moving." So it did move as equality in education, in political participation, and in career opportunity all advanced, however incrementally. But to Stanton's distress, the religious world still moved very slowly when it moved at all.

NATIONAL UNITY AND MOUNTING DIVERSITY

With millions of new immigrants, with dozens of new ethnic tensions, with concerns about both race and gender, many worried in the late nineteenth century about the oneness of the nation. All this difference made Americanization the great cause of many native-born whites: to take all that "foreignness" in language, custom, dress, and religion and somehow to melt it all down into a familiar, domesticated, English-speaking "American." The religion of such an American would preferably be Protestant—at least Bible believing and informed by a moral code that could be seen as essentially biblical. Temperance (if not abstinence) would be required so far as alcoholic beverages were concerned. Sunday as a day of rest, worship, and moral uplift (not riotous recreation) would be encouraged, often with the force of law. Public schools would serve as a major instrument of the Americanization process, celebrating a whole calendar of flag days, and private or parochial schools would often be regarded with considerable suspicion as divisive and even un-American.

These uneasy anxieties informed and gave momentum to the broad-gauged revivalism identified with Dwight L. Moody (1837–1899). A Boston shoe clerk, Moody was impressed by the earnestness of his Sunday school teacher and joined the Congregational Church when he was eighteen years old. Later that same year, 1856, he left for Chicago to make his own way in the world of business but soon he decided that money-making should take second place to gospel preaching. Moody spent his after-business hours organizing Sunday schools, distributing tracts, raising money for the building of churches, and ministering in a dozen ways to Chicago's poor and distressed. By 1860 he emerged from "the hardest struggle I ever had in my life" with the decision to give himself totally to the cause of religion.

During the Civil War he worked in army camps, offering aid to the wounded and counsel to those uprooted from family and home. After that conflict he returned to the slums of Chicago to direct relief, establish mis-

53. Dwight L. Moody dominated Anglo-American revivalism in the second half of the nineteenth century as Charles G. Finney had before him and Billy Graham would after him. *Library of Congress*

sions, and acquire a reputation as a Christian leader who repeatedly managed to get things done. He won his greatest fame, however, as a revivalist, and he won that fame far from Chicago. His earliest evangelistic successes came in Great Britain, and from his victories there he returned to America in 1875 to become as much the popular hero at home as he had been abroad. When he joined forces with the song leader and hymn writer, Ira D. Sankey (1840–1908), his revivals gained even greater acceptance.

Unordained and uneducated (he never finished the seventh grade), Moody preached simple sermons. Stressing the need for personal redemption, he called upon his hearers to respond to clear and compelling divine initiatives. "Now, let me say, my friends," he declared from the pulpits, "if you want the love of God in your hearts, all you have to do is to open the door and let it shine in. It will shine in as the sun shines in a dark room. Let him have full possession of your hearts." Such straightforward sentences were spoken earnestly, quietly, without theatrics or bombast. He encouraged no great emotional display on the part of the congregation and countenanced no histrionics, and ushers were instructed to remove those who became overly demonstrative. A simple gospel, simply presented: that was the heart of Dwight L. Moody.

And it so obviously worked in the final quarter of the nineteenth century. In New York City's Madison Avenue Hall in 1875 crowds gathered in such abundance that hundreds had to stand outside, straining to hear what went on within. A reporter covering the meeting could not help but note the great air of expectancy, the eagerness with which the 5,000 people crowded inside joined in the singing of hymns taken from the *Moody and Sankey Hymnbook,* their rapt attention during the sober sermon. "The quiet of the audience during Moody's preaching and Sankey's singing," the reporter noted, was remarkable. "Even the rough fellows who crowd the gallery passages make no sound." And in city after city the scene was repeated in hippodromes and auditoriums, in churches if they were large enough and in public parks if they were not. Once again, as in the First Great Awakening and the Second, revivalism swept over much of the land, and it warmed the civic hearts of those Protestants who saw revivals as integral to the cohesion of the republic.

But revivalism is notoriously fleeting, a surge of heightened excitement inevitably followed by a decline and a lull. Moody himself, recognizing the ephemeral nature of such excitement, turned much of his attention to creating longer-lasting institutions, especially in the area of education. Moody pleaded for "teachers who shall teach and show what the gospel is." In 1879 he founded a school for girls near his old home in Northfield, Massachusetts; the Mount Hermon school for boys opened two years later. In 1889 he transformed Chicago's Evangelization Society into a coeducational religious school, later to be known as the Moody Bible Institute. From these centers, aided by wealthy and powerful supporters (Cyrus McCormick, John Wanamaker, Anson G. Phelps, T. DeWitt Talmadge, Phillips Brooks, James McCosh, and Henry Ward Beecher, among others), Moody's name and fame spread throughout North America and far beyond.

With respect to the larger social and political issues of his day, Moody was no radical, no zealous reformer prepared to turn tables upside down or drive moneychangers from the temple and marketplace. Reform was possible, said Moody, only when "the reformer gets into [people's] hearts." The principal business of religion, he argued, was to change those hearts, to see that Christianity met the personal, private needs of the individual. His clerical supporters generally pursued a similar path, the persuasive Phillips Brooks (1835–93), rector of Boston's Trinity (Episcopal) Church, maintaining that the only way to a better world was through patience, prayer, Bible reading, and churchgoing. In an address to the working men of Boston in 1882 Brooks spoke not of capital and labor, not of municipal corruption or the widening inequalities of wealth. The great enemies of the working man, Brooks pointed out, were "intemperance, slothfulness, unskillfulness, and the rest." The salvation of the working man, on the other hand, lay "in sobriety, in intelligence, in industry, in skill, in thrift." "Until the heart is made right," said Dwight L. Moody, "all else will be wrong."

A fellow Congregationalist, Josiah Strong (1847–1916), saw more reason for social reform but, like Moody, worried about the increasing diversity in America, the growing variety in religion, and the luxuriant secularism in the culture. In *Our Country: Its Possible Future and Its Present Crisis*, a widely read book published in 1885, Josiah Strong was not content with a simple call to repentance or a generalized homily about changing one's heart. He presented hard data about the economic woes of capitalism, the exploitation of labor, the growing self-indulgence in money making and pleasure seeking, the delusions of a socialism that acted as though a brotherhood of man could be achieved without a fatherhood of God being recognized. But along with all his social statistics and his sense of promise for America, Strong did find a "present crisis." That crisis, in short, was the threat to Anglo-Saxon civilization and pure Christian religion. The Greeks brought beauty to the world, the Romans, law; the Egyptians brought the "seminal idea of life," while the Hebrews stressed purity. Now in the modern age the torch has been passed to the Anglo-Saxons, who have made two great contributions: the love of liberty and a "pure spiritual Christianity."

Emigration to America, however, threatened to divide "our country" into "little Germanies here, little Scandinavias there, and little Irelands yonder." Foreigners profane the Sabbath, Strong asserted, and foreigners promote intemperance. Politically, we now have an Irish vote, a German vote, a Roman Catholic vote, a Mormon vote, a liquor vote, and, Strong asked, who knows where all this will end? Religiously, the Protestant consensus is challenged, especially by the great surge of Catholic immigrants and by the rapid rise of the Mormons. Catholicism, declared Strong, threatens America's free speech, free press, and free public education. Wherever the Catholic Church has full sway, as in Italy or in Spain, Strong warned, the church totally dominates the educational system and generally limits educational opportunity to an elite minority of the population. Revealing his Protestant biases fully, Strong raised the question of the dual loyalty of Catholics in America: loyalty to the United States, but above that, loyalty to an infallible pope and foreign prince. "Manifestly," Strong concluded, "there is an irreconcilable difference between papal principles and the fundamental principles of our free institutions." Strong particularly worried about the American West, where Jesuits have "empires in their brains."

He also worried about the American West because Mormonism was strongest there. Many Americans, he said, think of the Mormon empire as more a disgrace than a danger; it is both. Polygamy was not the problem, for in 1885 that was already on its way out. No, said Strong, despotism was the problem. The real strength and the real threat of this new church lay not in its sexual ethics but in its political power. According to Strong, Mormonism was not a church but a state, exercising total control over the moral, industrial, social, political, and religious life of its people. Much of Mormon growth, like Catholic growth, resulted directly from immigration. Sending out between 200 and 400 missionaries a year, Strong calculated, this church imported a steadily increasing number of converts from abroad. This threatened the destiny not only of pure Christianity but of America as well, and in Strong's view of Western history, the destiny of America would to a large degree shape the destiny of the world. We speak of the immigrant being "Americanized," Strong observed; instead, the country is being "foreignized," and that, in a nutshell, was the "present crisis."

Within a few decades the foes of unlimited immigration won their point, but the proponents of a religious uniformity lost theirs. Diversity in religion increased, not only because of large-scale immigration, but also because of repeated innovation. In 1872 a small Bible study group led by Charles Taze Russell (1852–1916) planted the seeds of what became the Jehovah's Witnesses. Russell guided his group in a close study of those passages of scripture relating to the Second Coming of Christ. Convinced that a great cosmic contest between Satan and Jehovah would end with a physical, visible return of Christ to earth and further convinced that this

54. Millennial expectancy continued to fuel religious innovation at the end of the nineteenth century as it had in the first half of the century. This was evident in the birth of the Jehovah's Witnesses, led by Charles Taze Russell. *Library of Congress*

event was near at hand, Witnesses proclaimed that "millions now living shall never die." By 1879 Witnesses had their own publication (the *Watch Tower*), by 1893 their first national assembly (Chicago), and by 1909 their world headquarters (in Brooklyn, initially taking over the former parsonage of Henry Ward Beecher, Congregational pastor there from 1847 to 1887). Beecher's bowing out in favor of Witnesses typified for Josiah Strong and many others the "perils" confronting American religion. Numbering

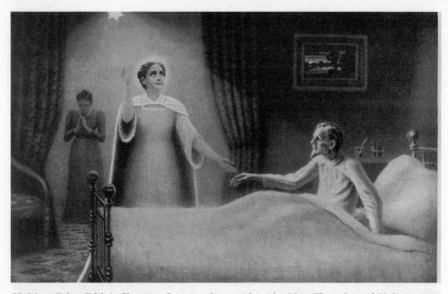

55. Mary Baker Eddy's Christian Science, along with wider New Thought and Holiness currents, made faith healing a common religious practice at the end of the nineteenth century. *Princeton Theological Seminary*

only a few hundred in the 1870s, Witnesses in America and beyond grew to millions a mere century later.

Also in the 1870s Christian Science arose in Massachusetts under the leadership of Mary Baker Eddy (1821–1910). A native of New Hampshire, Eddy as a young woman suffered much ill health, and traditional remedies offered little relief. Led to the discovery of a "science of health" through association with Phineas P. Quimby (1802–1866) in the 1860s, Eddy was ready a decade later to strike out on her own. Her important book, *Science and Health*, first appeared in 1875, and the first Church of Christ, Scientist, was chartered four years later. The founder explained that healing could not be accomplished by science alone; it required a specific religious understanding as well. The correlation between false belief and ill health was direct and inescapable. Disease had no independent reality of its own: it was mental error, error that could be corrected through appropriate metaphysical comprehension. Mind controls matter and much more besides, she wrote. It controls and conquers "sin, sickness, and death." Jesus was the first Scientist, for he recognized that only God was real; all else was illusion and error. And the Bible, properly understood, gives "all our recipes for healing," but it must be properly understood. In 1883, therefore, Mary Baker Eddy provided a "Key to the

Scriptures," which would thereafter be a fixed part of *Science and Health*. By the time of the founder's death in 1910, Christian Science was firmly established with more than 1,000 churches spread from the Atlantic to the Pacific. Christian Science reading rooms, public lectures, and carefully centralized organization kept its message before the American public.

In 1875 Madame H. P. Blavatsky (1831–1891) organized the Theosophical Society, dedicated to blending the ancient wisdom of India with the occultist traditions of the West, all for the sake of religious reawakening and enlightenment. In the 1880s and 1890s mind-cure institutes, metaphysical clubs, and New Thought exponents multiplied the religious options in ways that both Moody and Strong found dismaying. Getting in tune with the infinite and tapping into a cosmic spirit of plenty became a pressing pursuit for innumerable American seekers, and in that seeking they found a multiplying number of guides and gurus, from Blavatsky herself to Ralph Waldo Trine (1866–1958) and Horatio Dresser (1866–1954). New Thought proponents Trine and Dresser provided Americans with an open, optimistic gospel of self-affirmation to guide them in their search for emotional repose and religious harmony. While such spiritual quests resonated greatly with Transcendentalist musings, they had far less affinity with evangelical Protestant hopes for a Christian America and thus only added to the religious medley. The purchase of Alaska in 1867, with its Russian Orthodox and native populations, as well as the annexation of Hawaii in 1898, with its mix of Asian and indigenous communities, only widened the American religious alternatives.

The most dramatic staging of religion's variety in the final quarter of the nineteenth century came in Chicago in 1893 with the opening of the

56. The World's Parliament of Religions in Chicago in 1893 was a critical event in heightening American awareness of religions beyond Christianity, as this relatively diverse platform of speakers suggests. *Presbyterian Historical Society, Presbyterian Church (USA), Philadelphia*

World's Parliament of Religions. Now, for the first time on such scale, Americans saw and heard about the religions of the world from the actual devotees of those religions. Buddhist, Hindu, and Baha'i representatives, breaking down some of the distorting stereotypes and easy dismissals, arrived with earnest testimony and persuasive power. Brainchild of Congregationalist John Henry Barrows (1847–1902), the parliament provided not only a hearing for Asian religions but also a common platform for the rival siblings of Judaism, Christianity, and Islam. The parliament preached a comforting universalism—that out of all these religious differences a recognizable core of common truths would clearly emerge. That assurance notwithstanding, the World's Parliament also provided incontrovertible evidence of the direction the United States was headed. Religious diversity, made ever more palpable through ongoing immigration and innovation, was the nation's course, but whether to embrace, assimilate, fear, or repudiate that variety remained a wide open question at the end of the nineteenth century.

CHAPTER 11

Cities and Social Gospels

The face of the United States altered radically between 1850 and 1900. Two forces especially drove that alteration: first, the massive growth of cities; second, the increasing industrialization of the economy and the workplace, epitomized in the mushrooming of factories. Such transformations, hallmarks of the modern order, were made rough, even jagged, by mounting antagonism between capitalist owners and wage laborers and by profound cultural ambivalence toward both urbanization and industrialization. Symptoms of the social stress came in the form of strikes, financial panics, riots, slums, sweatshops, poverty, bribery, and graft. Rural America, Jefferson's land of the yeoman farmer, was rapidly disappearing. Many were uneasy about its passing and quite unsure about its successors, the modern city and the factory system.

Immigration doubled or tripled the population of the coastal cities, but urbanization was by no means a coastal phenomenon alone. Americans in the Midwest and elsewhere left hamlet and homestead for the city—any city. By 1900 Chicago had become the nation's second largest city; it had grown from a mere 29,963 people in 1850 to 1.7 million at the end of the century. Similarly sharp growth was also evident in Detroit, Milwaukee, Minneapolis, St. Paul, St. Louis, Indianapolis, Cleveland, Columbus, Toledo, Kansas City, Denver, and Omaha. The city lured newcomers with promises of economic opportunity and unabashed freedom, with the bright colors of department stores and the carnivalesque pageantry of the streets, with grand churches and still grander hotels, with the latest entertainment and night life. And the city let them down, too, with scams, poverty, exploitation, race hatred, and ill-developed public services.

In this same half century, from 1850 to 1900, the Industrial Revolution reshaped the nation, especially in the North. The word *revolution* is no exaggeration, for changes transformed many areas of life: transportation (steam engine, combustion engine, and electric engine); communication (telegraph, telephone, transatlantic cable, typewriter, and linotype press); agriculture (binders, threshers, cutters, and improved harvesters); and domestic life (electric lights, sewing machines, phonographs, and gas stoves). The greatest revolution, however, occurred in the labor market itself, where thousands of propertyless men and women had nothing to barter but their toil and their sweat. They became workers in an economy of grinding hours and brutal sweatshop conditions.

To all the ills and pains of social dislocation and change, institutional religion could not long remain indifferent. Though many continued to believe that changing the individual heart was sufficient cure for all troubles, others found disease in the very character of the city itself, in the routinized and impersonal nature of the factory itself, or perhaps even in the greed and indifference of the capitalist order itself. Could religion offer any cure for diseases of this deep-seated sort? For some the question went like this: Should religion allow itself to become involved in political, economic, and social questions far beyond its own area of expertise and competence? Salvation of souls had been the traditional business of American Christianity. Did it now have any business going beyond that domain, venturing into the deep waters of a social gospel?

THE CITY

In health, housing, and education, the metropolis presented both church and synagogue with a wide array of pressing problems. The immigrant journalist Jacob Riis (1849–1914), looking at the poorer neighborhoods in New York City, was shocked at what he found. He soon shocked the nation by reporting in 1890 on *How the Other Half Lives*. The tenements in which the poor live, Riis wrote, evoking all the fears (and stereotypes) that haunted American imaginings of the city, were "dark and deadly dens" where the home lost all sanctity, where character went undeveloped, where children were "damned rather than born" into the world. And where were the churches in the poor neighborhoods? Saloons outnumbered churches ten to one or more. "Either the devil was on the ground first, or he has been doing a good deal more in the way of building." The congregation in the saloons was also larger than that in the churches, Riis reported, "and the contributions more liberal the week round."

Roman Catholic bishop of Peoria, Illinois, John Lancaster Spalding (1840–1916) worried most about the city's effect upon the family, the social unit that most Americans then (and now) regarded as fundamental to all human relationships and moral development. What Bishop Spalding

found in the city, however, was not moral development but moral degra-
dation. "The conditions of life are not favorable to purity," he wrote, "and
the grossest sensuality prevails." In the city "where people have no settled
home and no local traditions, the loss of good name is often looked upon
as a mere trifle." Even the simplest kinds of moral education, such as the
teaching of courtesy and good manners, "cease to be handed down as
sacred heirlooms." Victorian Americans carried around a kind of romanticized ideal of the American home: as Spalding pictured it, the vine-cov-
ered cottage, the fireside gatherings, the mother and father bringing up
healthy, happy children in "love and religion . . . nurtured by traditions of
honor and virtue." So far as the city is concerned, that rural ideal is hope-
lessly shattered, said the Peoria bishop. "Lodging-houses where people
sleep and eat are not homes. Hired rooms which are changed from year to
year, and often from month to month, are not homes." What one finds in
these urban dwellings "is the grave of the family, not its home."

Such pessimistic assessments would certainly seize the attention of the
city fathers (would they not?) so that they could correct the terrible housing, the intolerable levels of sanitation, the high rate of infant mortality,
the explosion of prostitution, drunkenness, and major crime. Unfortunately, the city fathers were often part of, even agents of, the problem.
Municipal corruption was widespread and seemingly built into the very
structure of city government itself. Graft, greed, and partnership with
crime afflicted local political organizations and their agencies, and these
realities drove religious leaders to assert whatever moral authority they
could.

Washington Gladden (1836–1918), a Congregationalist pastor in Columbus, Ohio, realized that a voice crying in the wilderness (or even from the
pulpit) might not be nearly so effective as a voice on the city council itself.
Thus with "no special fitness" for the office, he announced that he would
run in 1900. He was elected and served for two years, educating himself,
to be sure, but also bringing some measure of his own moral commitment
to bear on the many problems that Columbus, like so many other American cities, confronted. He argued for public ownership of such utilities
as water, lights, and gas, pointing out that these monopolies "furnish us
with the necessaries of life; and monopolies of that nature must belong to
the people." If we grant such power to a private corporation, Gladden
noted, then we might as well give a private corporation the right to tax us
as well.

Gladden identified two fundamental problems at the base of municipal
corruption. First, responsible citizens "think it bad form" to get involved

57. Congregationalist minister Washington Gladden was one of the founders of the theology of the social gospel with its mission of urban and economic reform. *Library of Congress*

in local politics, and "so long as anything resembling this is true, we shall, of course, have bad government in our cities." Second, city authorities were not so much corrupt as they were simply incompetent, and this to some degree prevailed at the level of state government as well. Major policy decisions "are generally in the hands of men who have no fitness to deal with them; and this is mainly because the men who have the necessary equipment for such work almost uniformly refuse to undertake it." Gladden not only set an example by serving on the city council, he also wrote widely and well of the necessity of what he called *Applied Christianity: Moral Aspects of Social Questions* (1886). In that book and some thirty-eight others, Gladden helped create a new style of Christian witness, an expressly social gospel aimed at confronting modern social and economic ills at an institutional, systemic level.

In Kansas City, Missouri, machine politics, under the direction of Thomas J. Pendergast, helped to give city government a bad name. Rabbi Samuel S. Mayerberg (1892–1964), on the other hand, tried to give the forces of religion a good name as he urged his own members as well as other religiously motivated people into organized battle against the Pendergast machine and all its flagrant violation of every principle of dignity, equity, and honesty. "The tyrants," Mayerberg reported, not only dominated all municipal life but had invaded private life as well. "People were actually told what physicians they might use, what lawyers might practice, what merchants might do business." All this was carried on in close alliance between the affairs of the city and the bosses of the underworld. Every attempt was made to turn the rabbi aside in his reforming crusade. As he noted in his autobiography, "The racketeers began to fight back in their vicious ways": they tapped his telephone "in my Temple study"; they ransacked his files, stole the records of the resistant organization that Mayerberg had helped form, and tried to get members of his congregation to bring pressure upon him to quit the crusade. The racketeers "threatened me and attempted to bribe me." Like Gladden, Mayerberg found the entire experience difficult but educational, concluding that the only solution to such problems across the country was for honorable people, driven by "conscience and the power of religious conviction," to enlist in the battle against all forms of municipal corruption and greed.

In the neighboring state of Kansas, a Congregationalist pastor in Topeka tackled the problem of the city's sins in yet another way. In the place of sermons or civic service or crusading leagues, Charles M. Sheldon (1857–1946) wrote a novel, *In His Steps,* first published in 1897 and reprinted or serialized innumerable times thereafter. An all-time bestseller, this fairly simple story encouraged the modern Christian to ask repeatedly, "What would Jesus do?" (Sheldon's refrain has now been repopularized in contemporary Christian circles, cropping up in abbreviated form—WWJD—on bracelets and pendants.) While Sheldon's approach could have led to a mere repetition of the calls to private piety, he demonstrated a full awareness of the growing gap between rich and poor, the irrelevance of the usual fare of American Christianity for those whose basic needs remained unmet, and the unwillingness of most religious folks to confront forthrightly the problems in their own neighborhoods. "Every day I have more and more confidence," Sheldon told his congregation in 1895, "in the wonderful results which I believe God is going to bring about in the social and political life of the world." Such results will come, he added, as God "uses us who are Christians as instruments to do his great will."

In Chicago Jane Addams (1860–1935) founded her famous Hull House in 1889, this institution becoming the centerpiece of the settlement house movement. Being a missionary to the city slum, she argued, was not nearly so helpful as being a steady presence in that slum. As one reformer put it, "Suppose that the Lord, when he came on the earth, had come one day at a time and brought his lunch with him, and then gone home to heaven nights." To put the issue that way was to invite the answer: neighbor love can come only from a neighbor. So the settlement house arose in the midst of the tenements, among the neediest; there it became a school, a church, a library, a theater, an art gallery, a bank, a hospital, and a refuge. By 1910 hundreds of settlement houses dotted America's city-scapes.

In Hull House Jane Addams, in harmony with the Quaker principles of her father, determined to recognize the good in all persons, "even the meanest." One must be filled with "the overmastering belief that all that is noblest in life is common to men as men." Addams threw herself into the battle for social justice on a wide front, for women's rights and civil liberties, for child labor laws and for international peace. But the settlement house movement in general and Hull House in particular remained her most influential commitment, a commitment that, as she wrote in *Philanthropy and Social Progress* in 1893, "will not waver when [the human] race happens to be represented by a drunken woman or an idiot boy." Those who reside in a settlement house "must be emptied of all conceit of opinion and all self-assertion. . . . They must be content to live quietly side by side with their neighbors until they grow into a sense of relationship and mutual interest." With a firm belief in the oneness of all humankind, Jane Addams argued that improved and fulfilled lives must be a vision not only for the affluent but for all.

If for some the city was primarily an object of reform, a place in desperate need of an applied social Christianity, for many others it was an object of consuming desire. That allure was embodied especially in the new department stores—Macy's, Wanamaker's, Lord & Taylor—that were born and grew to maturity in the half century or so after 1850. One side of the new industrial economy was the transformed means of production, and the other side was a proliferation of goods made possible by that transformation. By 1900 an urban consumer culture had arisen in which advertising, show windows, and colorful displays multiplied and in which satisfying desire through shopping and buying became a primary pursuit. That piece of city culture, too, would have a notable impact on religion, and religious leaders found it just as hard to resist and confront as urban corruption and poverty. As one merchant explained in 1912, the growing consumerism "speaks to us only of ourselves, our pleasures, our

58. The cities of the late nineteenth and early twentieth centuries became renowned for their bustling marketplace and wondrous department stores. Often Christianity was visibly joined to (and juxtaposed with) the expanding consumer culture, expecially at Christmas, but also at more mundane times. *Library of Congress*

life. It does not say, 'Pray, obey, sacrifice thyself, respect the King, fear thy master.' It whispers, 'amuse thyself, take care of yourself.'"

While some religious figures, including Gladden, offered critiques of this new consumerist ethos, many others offered new gospels of wealth and material well-being to bless the growing abundance of the urban marketplace. One such spokesman was Bruce Barton (1886–1967), the son of a Congregationalist minister, who decided against the pastorate in favor of the corporate world of advertising in New York City. In his leisure he still dabbled in religious writing, offering such inspirational works as *More Power to You* (1917) and *Better Days* (1924). His most popular work was a biographical study of Jesus called *The Man Nobody Knows* (1925), in which Christ is recast as both a virile outdoorsman and a hustling, shrewd businessman. Jesus is a leader with great personality and go-getter energy, one who is able to motivate others (notably a ragtag band of apostles) and to achieve success where others would have failed for lack of confidence. As a storyteller Jesus also has, so Barton related, a profound intuitive grasp of

59. The spirit of abundance was also on display at Easter as a parade of spring fashions in dress and millinery became one of the holiday's great cultural expressions on city streets. *Library of Congress*

modern advertising principles, including the arts of simplicity and repetition. Jesus, in other words, is able to create a demand for his religious message in the same way that modern advertising agents, like Barton, were able to create new needs and desires.

In this heady atmosphere of advertising and consumer plenty, religion often became one more blessing upon this great American abundance. Daily prayers or affirmations were available for the aspiring to offer up in order to align themselves with "the Spirit of Infinite Plenty." The faithful were encouraged to reiterate to themselves such encouraging sayings as the following: "I think of myself as a child of God, heir to all the riches of the Kingdom. This is the truth about me. I know that I am worthy of abundance. My prosperity is assured." Or "God, my opulent Father, has poured out to me all resources, and I am a mighty river of affluence and abundance." Such affirmative pieties grew up and flourished in the expansive commercial culture at the turn of the twentieth century. Figures such as Russell Conwell, Bruce Barton, and Charles Fillmore pioneered the gospel of prosperity, and that message long continued to find expression. This is

60. One popular embodiment of the new affirmative, optimistic pieties of the age was the rage for the Billiken doll, the God of Happiness, who promised its owner a sunny disposition. *Private collection*

61. The city was an object of social reform and consumer longing, but it was also at a primary level a place to practice one's religious life, as is evident in this woman's home altar on a dresser in Washington, D.C. *Library of Congress*

evident, for example, in Bruce Wilkinson, whose *The Prayer of Jabez* (2000) and *The Secrets of the Vine: Breaking through to Abundance* (2001) were recent best-sellers.

The city was not only—indeed was not primarily—an object of social reform or a place of consumer longing. It was a place to live. It was a place to build families and home altars, to celebrate Passover, to hold street festivals for the Virgin Mary or Christ's Passion, and to parade in fine Easter bonnets and carry holiday flowers to the homebound. It was a place to set up monasteries and convents, to open storefront chapels and healing shrines, as well as to create giant institutional church complexes with gyms, libraries, Sunday schools, and even hospitals. It was a place of interracial encounter and closely kept boundaries, where migrant African Americans from the rural South, primarily Protestant, took up precarious residence alongside Polish Catholics and Russian Jews. Social reformers and advertising dreamers were, to be sure, crucial for imagining the religious significance of the new cities, but such visions were only two facets of the multifaceted urban worlds that immigrants from abroad and migrants from villages hammered out for themselves.

THE FACTORY

In the turmoil of the Industrial Revolution, class struggle and class consciousness were born. Karl Marx's *Das Kapital*, written over the long period from 1867 to 1895, was one kind of response to the revolution. The social gospel or social action of American religious institutions was another kind of response. Theologians and religiously motivated reformers—Protestants, Catholics, and Jews—joined in the effort to bring justice into the marketplace and the mill, to soften the antagonisms between capital and labor, to mitigate the cruelties of unemployment and grinding poverty. In the year of the Haymarket Riots (1886), Episcopal bishop Frederic D. Huntington (1819–1904) noted that "Man has killed or maimed his fellow-man" only because he did not recognize the common humanity that bound them all. Brotherhood was more than a nice idea: it had become a necessary condition for survival in an industrialized world. In the contest between the rich and poor, the New York bishop observed, the duty of the church toward the latter is compellingly clear. In the New Testament itself, one must concede that "it is the rich and prosperous, not the less successful and disfavored, who are most severely denounced, most in danger of ruin, and most in need of a changed and watchful mind, and of a quickened conscience."

With so many of the nation's Roman Catholics recently arrived at the Atlantic shores, it is not surprising that Catholics constituted a large proportion of the laboring class. James Cardinal Gibbons (1834–1921) came to labor's defense, not only against the managerial and capitalist classes in America, but against European Catholic and Vatican attitudes as well. Laborers, especially when organized and potentially powerful, struck the conservative Catholic community abroad as a seedbed of radicalism and revolution, of socialism or communism. When the Knights of Labor (predominantly Catholic in membership) organized in 1869, Gibbons was forced to come to the defense of the very notion of a labor union. The exploitation of not only the laboring man but the laboring woman and child as well is evident to all, the cardinal noted. In some airless, sunless tenement an entire family might have to work fourteen to sixteen hours a day, seven days a week, rolling cigars or sewing clothes or whatever, just to earn, as a group, one barely living wage. Unsafe working conditions went uninspected, unrestrained. No insurance covered the worker injured on the job; no compensation came to him or her when unemployed; no independent arbitrator helped to determine a just or living wage.

Under such deplorable conditions, did not laborers, particularly Catholic laborers, have a right to organize, to unite? After all, Gibbons pointed out, association and organization are recognized as the most natural, the most just, the "most efficacious means" by which to attain any worthy public end. In the Knights of Labor, Catholics may be associated with Protestants, perhaps even with atheists or Communists (as its enemies had charged). But, said Gibbons, this fact cannot be allowed to discredit the Knights of Labor, for Catholics in this country must at almost all times associate with those not of their own faith. "In a mixed people like ours, the separation of religious creeds in civil affairs is an impossibility." Even were it possible, it might not be desirable, for citizens need to work with and understand one another, not insulate themselves from all others. But most of all, Cardinal Gibbons pointed out to the Vatican in 1887, to condemn the Knights of Labor would be to risk "losing the love of the children of the Church, and of pushing them into an attitude of resistance against their Mother." The Catholic worker is obedient to the Church but not blindly so. Condemnation of the union would "be considered both false and unjust." Catholic laborers "love the Church, and they wish to save their souls, but they must also earn their living." For this just end, affiliation with a labor union is the appropriate means.

In Rochester, New York, a Baptist seminary professor, Walter Rauschenbusch (1861–1918), agreed that such unions were legitimate and necessary for the worker to achieve any measure of economic justice. True, labor unions exist to serve the interests of their members, but, he argued, few people manage to pursue interests that transcend all limits of race or class, country or creed. "Why should we demand of one of the lowest classes, fighting on the borderland of poverty," Rauschenbusch inquired, "an unselfish devotion to all society which the upper classes have never shown?" The unions stand "for human life against profits," while capitalism "makes the margin of life narrow in order to make the margin of profit wide." It is time, the Baptist reformer wrote in 1907, to turn the spiritual force of Christianity "against the materialism and mammonism of our industrial and social order." It is time to stop treating human beings as "things," things put to the dreary task of only producing more things. Jesus had asked, "Is not a man more than a sheep?" Rauschenbusch responded, "Our industry says 'No.' It is careful of its live stock and machinery, and careless of its human working force."

62. Roman Catholic James Cardinal Gibbons defended labor's right to organize and to receive fair compensation for a day's work. *Library of Congress*

Rauschenbusch was not encouraged by what appeared to him to be the indifference of many in the religious community to the fundamental problem. Modern-day revivalists, he scornfully observed, produce only "skin deep changes. Things have simmered down to signing a card, shaking hands, or being introduced to the evangelist." A torn and bleeding society needed more than that; a hungry and exploited working class needed more than that. "It is the function of religion," Rauschenbusch wrote, "to teach the individual to value his soul more than his body, and his moral integrity more than his income." At the same time, however, it is equally the function of religion "to teach society to value human life more than property, and to value property only insofar as it forms the material basis for the higher development of human life." The Industrial Revolution, he argued, is in danger of killing the goose that laid the golden egg, and "humanity is that goose." We have been taught that "man does not live by bread alone." Let us then have the courage of our religious faith, urged Rauschenbusch, to stand by that claim and to assert it boldly, to help our nation understand that its true life consists not in the abundance of the things that it produces "but in the way men live justly with one another and humbly with their God."

From Baltimore's Catholic Gibbons to Rochester's Baptist Rauschenbusch and across an entire spectrum of denominational life in between, advocates of social and economic justice dedicated themselves to shaming a whole nation—if that's what it took—into a greater faithfulness to both its religious heritage and its democratic promises. These advocates also dedicated themselves to speaking, insofar as possible, with a united voice, not allowing themselves to be lost or drowned out in the noise of an industrial boom. American religion did not have a unified voice either then or a hundred years later, but early in the twentieth century it had begun to move away from ever-increasing schism and separation. In 1908 some 12 million Protestants came together to form the Federal Council of Churches, this group taking as one of its first orders of business the adoption of a "Social Creed" that would emphasize "the mighty task of putting conscience and justice and love into a Christian civilization." The creed took stands that might have been radical in the first decade of the twentieth century but would be thought of as tame and commonplace a century later. The Federal Council followed Methodists, who had often assumed the lead in such matters, in calling for the abolition of child labor, the careful regulation of "toil for women" in order to "safeguard the physical and moral health of the community," the "release from employment one day in seven," and for "the principle of conciliation and arbitration in industrial dissensions." Radical then, commonplace now.

In 1918 the Central Conference of American Rabbis (Reform Judaism) also confronted that same "mighty task" of implementing conscience, justice, and love. Declaring that "the dignity of the individual soul before God cannot be lost sight of before men," the conference argued for a "fundamental reconstruction of our economic organization." But the rabbis, not content with generalities, proceeded to be specific in their call for reform, also advocating the abolition of child labor "and raising the standard of age wherever the legal age limit is lower than is consistent with moral and physical health." Workmen's compensation—a new phrase as well as a new idea—should be granted in the case of all "industrial accidents and occupational diseases." Labor's right "to organize and to bargain collectively" must be recognized, and a "minimum wage" must be established that would "insure for all workers a fair standard of living." The government should concern itself with proper housing, with "constructive care" of dependents, with some method of "social insurance" for "meeting the contingencies of unemployment and old age." Radical then, commonplace now.

World War I had helped to encourage united and responsible social responses on the part of Roman Catholics, just as it had among all the nation's religious communities. A National Catholic War Council had been formed in 1917 in response to the urgencies of war, but it proved too useful an entity to be allowed to fade away once that war was over. Renamed the National Catholic Welfare Conference a few years later, this organization gave Catholicism a unity and a public voice that hitherto it had lacked in America. In 1919 the conference adopted the Bishop's Program of Social Reconstruction, which called for "a reform in the spirit of both labor and capital." Under the guiding hand of Monsignor John A. Ryan (1869–1945), the bishops opposed child labor, advocated a minimum wage and vocational training, urged controls upon the rapidly rising cost of living, and declared that a "Christian view of work and wealth" would do much to ameliorate the industrial ills. There is such a thing, the bishops concluded, as a "human and Christian" ethics of industry; this rather than commercialism run wild must regulate as well as enrich our common life.

Because these socially sensitive, forward-looking statements were perceived as radical, they aroused strong opposition among people of all religious persuasions or of none. Preach the gospel, stick to the Bible, obey the powers that be—many brakes were applied in the effort to keep religion from being applied where it hurt the pocketbooks of some, the politics of others, and the theology or ecclesiology of still others. But Protestants, Jews, and Catholics dedicated to reform were not readily turned aside or easily silenced. Their collective and courageous voices continued to be heard so that what was radical then has become the commonplace now.

WOMEN AND REFORM

After the Civil War women played an increasingly public role in social reform. Much of their efforts were understandably aimed at increasing voting privileges for women, but often joined to the suffrage movement (the Nineteenth Amendment finally passed in 1919) were such reformist matters as temperance, world peace, and civil liberties. The Woman's Christian Temperance Union (WCTU), organized in Ohio in 1874, endures as one of the best-known manifestations of public reform directed by women. Frances E. Willard (1839–1898) gave the union its impetus and for nearly twenty years served as its president. The religious motivation was made evident in its very name, and its official purposes also emphasized the necessity of following scriptural injunctions to make one's body the "temple of the Holy Ghost." The WCTU, moreover, would "help forward the coming of Christ into all departments of life," correlating "New Testament religion with philanthropy" and the "church with civilization." Both nicotine and alcohol were identified as enemies to a purer and nobler spirituality.

By the second half of the nineteenth century more and more Americans had concluded that the key to any successful social reform lay in organization. The WCTU, therefore, represented much more than a sentiment in favor of prohibition: it offered a "Plan of Work," which could "focus scattered influence and effort." Public sentiment would be reshaped by such techniques as mass meetings, wide circulation of temperance literature, school prizes for essays on the evil effects of alcoholic indulgence, and "organizing temperance glee clubs of young people to sing temperance doctrines into the people's hearts as well as heads." Much attention has been paid to attacking saloons with ax in hand, Carry Nation–style, but members of the WCTU wisely recognized that the real problem lay with the consumer, not the distributor. "If nobody would drink, then nobody would sell." "Dear sisters," warned the WCTU officers in 1874, "we have laid before you the plan of the long campaign." Hard realism not soft sentiment guided the effort; careful organization not insular protests made the effort count.

In the Salvation Army women assumed major leadership roles early on. They were as much in evidence as men, often more so, as the "hallelujah lasses" and "Sally Anns" played tambourine and trumpet, collected coins in their kettles, and "exhorted" as freely and frequently as the males. Organized in England in 1865 by William and Catherine Booth as a movement of both evangelical revival and social witness, the army marched quickly across that island and soon set sail for North America. Evangeline Booth (1865–1950), daughter of the founders, served as field commissioner in the United States from 1904 to 1934 and as general of the whole international movement for some years thereafter. During her thirty-year leadership role in America, Booth helped the army win a reputation for social service that knew no limits, especially in serving "the lowest fallen,

63. An 1874 Currier & Ives engraving emphasized the prominent role that women played in moral reform, especially with respect to temperance. *Library of Congress*

depraved, and the most neglected." Soldiers visited the sick, fed the hungry, clothed the naked, employing charity—organized and vigilant—to alleviate the hardships that industrialization and urbanization brought.

Slum brigades fought filth and disease, while rescue homes for prostitutes sprang up all across the nation. Services then provided by no other

64. The temperance campaign was always also a campaign to save the family and to inculcate the domestic piety so dear to the Victorian middle classes. *Library of Congress*

agency—legal advice, first aid, life insurance, even a missing persons department—were extended to all and often seized with desperate eagerness. Men roused at night from freight cars and empty wagons found their way to a Salvation Army shelter, where "for ten cents a night, or its equivalent in work," the destitute could find sleep. The typical church

65. In the period of World War I, Evangeline Booth directed the Salvation Army in the United States. *Library of Congress*

revival was fine, one army leader pointed out, but such carefully managed events appealed more to the middle-class churchgoer, while "the godless multitudes drifted past their doors." For those multitudes, other methods were required, and the Salvation Army demonstrated its capacity to develop those methods. The effective ministry of women, as Frederick Booth Tucker readily acknowledged in 1899, was a vital ingredient in those new methods. Both the deeds and the words of these hallelujah lasses often went "straight to the hearts of their hearers" and resulted in "wonderful reformations."

In the Roman Catholic community, emphasis upon women's domestic role and submission to male authority made participation in public social reform more difficult. The many orders of sisters, to be sure, practiced great social service to the ill, the poor, the illiterate, and the orphaned. Even there, however, the demands of teaching in the parish schools absorbed an increasing amount of the sisters' energies and commitment. Nuns labored in the nearly 4,000 parochial schools that had been established by 1900 and to a lesser extent in private academies attended by both Catholic and non-Catholic children. They also served in over 200 hospitals, frequently bearing the full administrative responsibility. In times of epidemic, as of cholera or yellow fever, as well as in times of war, the work of the women religious helped enormously not only the immediate objects of their solicitude but also the reputation of the Catholic Church for charity and social commitment.

The path to public service for Catholic laywomen was harder to establish. Writing in the *Catholic World* in 1893, Alice T. Toomy declared that there was a legitimate public sphere for Catholic women. A Catholic Women's Congress held that year in Chicago would permit a genuinely organized effort on behalf of "day nurseries and free kindergartens, protective and employment agencies for women, and clubs and homes for working girls." We are behind in these respects, Toomy noted, as "tens of thousands of our ablest Catholic women are working with the WCTU and other non-Catholic philanthropies, because they find no organization in their own church as a field for their activities." But in the very same issue of the *Catholic World* Toomy was answered by another Catholic woman, who asserted that it was settled "beyond question" that women, as women, can have no vocation in public life.

Also in 1893 as part of the World's Parliament of Religions, a Congress of Jewish Women was formed, this group permitting a more collaborative participation of Jewish women in social and public reforms. Though largely attended by German American Jews and largely identified with Reform Judaism, the congress (and its successor, the National Council of Jewish Women) identified many social services needed by Russian and largely Orthodox Jewry. As one speaker noted at the congress, the history of Judaism is filled with women who rendered great service, both in the home and beyond. America's Jewish women, therefore, should not hesitate to play significant public roles now. As Hannah Solomon (1858–1942) noted in 1897, the persecution that any woman may receive who places herself before the public is only a "sting" and lasts but a moment. Woman, she added with a touch of humor, must bear major burdens because instead of being created in the beginning out of dust, "the Lord waited until he could build her out of a strong, healthy, germproof bone." And so the women in the National Council established schools, provided for manual and vocational training, established summer camps, encouraged philanthropy, and in a host of other ways left their mark on the public sphere. Solving the problems of city and factory was everyone's task: male and female, religious and secular, new arrival and already established. But the magnitude of the problems became apparent at the same time that women were finding their voice and were about to find their vote. Thus a deep partnership between women and reform accelerated a process that, even so, often seemed to move with frustrating deliberation.

EXTENDING RELIGION'S REACH

Since the earliest years of the nineteenth century, religion in America had made a virtue out of voluntarism, that is, out of the necessity for the churches and synagogues themselves, not the government, to advance the related causes of religion and morality and human help. Ecclesiastical institutions did much more than just look after their own survival, pay their own bills, and care for their own members. Churches saw themselves as supply depots for—not cozy retreats from—the needs of all those passing hurriedly by their doors. To serve those needs, ever more organization and initiative were required.

A distinctly American enterprise, the Knights of Columbus, began in 1882 as a kind of group insurance venture and soon turned its attention also to education, charity, and social service. Under the leadership of Patrick H. Callahan (1865–1940), the knights during World War I operated over 300 recreational centers for servicemen in the States and a like number abroad. But this was only a single dimension of the far-flung enterprises in which the Roman Catholic knights were engaged. A layman himself, Callahan encouraged other laymen to experiment with profit sharing between management and labor. He served on the National Child Labor Commission and worked for greater racial understanding and for better relationships between Catholics and the nation's other religious groups. Meanwhile, the Knights of Columbus grew to over 300,000 members by the time of World War I, even spinning off a parallel women's society, the Daughters of Isabella.

The Catholic Young Men's National Union, formed in 1875, offered acceptable recreations, night school education, and vocational training, arguing that it made more sense to assist the young before problems developed, not waiting until afterward. Similar ministries to young women were provided by the Sisters of Charity, the Sisters of Mercy, and the Sisters of St. Joseph, among others. Finally, a National Conference of Catholic Charities, founded in 1910, coordinated many of the scattered efforts on behalf of bettering society and improving the lot of those trapped by its impersonal cruelties. That conference, whose formation had been encouraged by a Catholic University sociologist, also represented a growing professionalism, as opposed to casual happenstance, in the area of religious philanthropy. Charity, too, could be made systematic and efficient.

That professionalism had been encouraged when, soon after the Civil War, the Catholic hierarchy issued a pastoral letter commending "the great increase among us of Societies and Associations"; from these newly formed groups the bishops anticipated "the most beneficial results to the cause of morality and religion." They commended in particular the Society of St. Vincent de Paul, a lay organization that began in France but moved to the United States in 1845. By 1865 the organization had seventy-five chapters or conferences in this country, indicating the strength of motivation as well as the size of society's needs. Industrial schools and boarding homes gave youth the security, training, and religious discipline that would enable them to live productive and fulfilling lives. But the society also, like the Salvation Army, gathered donations wherever it could in order to offer help wherever possible.

Protestant agencies also sometimes originated abroad, frequently finding in America the greatest reception for their work. The Young Men's and Young Women's Christian Associations (popularly, the "Y") had their beginnings in England before the Civil War but enjoyed their most dramatic development later in the United States. Working first among the very poor, the Ys offered housing and job training, help in finding employment, recreation, and reading material for the lonely and bored. Evangelism was very much a part of early Y activity, as efforts to win converts were made in jails, hospitals, poorhouses, rescue missions, and even among the sailors temporarily in port. Religious tracts, printed inexpensively, were scattered like seed in the hope of reaping a harvest of newly enlisted young people. But evangelism was never interpreted in narrow terms. Young people simply had to be helped, whatever the problem, whatever the means for its solution. One enterprising YMCA director, James Naismith (1861–1939), in desperation even invented the game of basketball in order to provide some indoor activity for his youth during the long winter months.

Similarly, Young Men's and Young Women's Hebrew Associations arose in the nineteenth century, working at first with German Jewish youth but soon called upon to meet mushrooming needs as immigrant numbers swelled. The YMHA and the YWHA assisted newcomers in adjusting and assimilating but always showed special concern for the young. Just as World War I prompted the Roman Catholic community to "get organized" in order to respond more systematically to the nation's needs, so the Jewish Welfare Board was created to help advise the govern-

66. Nurturing the religious lives of children and young people was the focus of a raft of organizations from Sunday schools to the YMCA. The loss of "childlike" faith increasingly became the object of modern concern and nostalgia, and here in this scene of evening prayer from 1906 even the dog cooperates in supporting the religious life of the child. *Library of Congress*

ment on the choice of Jewish chaplains for the army. The very word *welfare*, however, suggested the utility of a group that might be able to speak for all of American Jewry in certain matters of public interest.

The temperance issue, highlighted by the WCTU but shared by many others beyond its ranks, reached a political climax with the passage of the Eighteenth Amendment in 1917. That amendment was made possible, once again, only by organization, in this instance of the Anti-Saloon League in 1895. For over twenty years the league supported politicians who would vote "dry," vigorously opposing all "wets" who ran for office. For decades individual churches had been engaged in gathering pledges from those who would forswear the drinking of all alcohol. The attempt had been made to shut down the saloons, but none of this had really worked, a league superintendent explained. Moral suasion had had its turn; now it was time for political compulsion. The league was formed in the conviction that "in most communities there were more anti-saloon than there were pro-saloon votes, and if the great mass of anti-saloon votes could be organized, the power of the saloon in politics would be broken." The league began its recruitment with the churches, especially the Methodists, arguing that the church must conquer the saloon or else be conquered by it. Passed at the end of 1917, the Eighteenth Amendment won ratification by early 1919. Fourteen years later, the Twenty-First Amendment brought the "noble experiment" to an end.

But by that time religion was heavily involved in many other experiments of more enduring effect. Municipal corruptions had been cleaned up in city after city, many a reformer recognizing the critical assistance rendered by priests, ministers, and rabbis; by laymen and laywomen from many communities of faith. Also by that time, many of the grossest excesses of the Industrial Revolution had been curbed and a legitimate role for government recognized. Ecclesiastical bodies, moreover, now routinely had their Departments of Social Justice or their Social Action Committees or their Welfare Councils and Conferences. Many problems defied solution, of course, or arose in a somewhat altered form in later years. War did not vanish; racism and sexism did not disappear; equitable distribution of wealth proved elusive; and moral progress became harder and harder to demonstrate or even define. Churches and synagogues climbed each hill only to find a higher one still in the road ahead.

CHAPTER 12

The Church and the World

In the last two decades of the nineteenth century and the first four of the twentieth, the United States of America entered upon the world stage in a way that had not been true in the first century of its history as a nation. The country engaged in war well beyond its own borders, participated in international congresses and conferences, acquired territories and new responsibilities in the Pacific Ocean, and rediscovered and reaffirmed the Monroe Doctrine, which in effect declared the entire Western Hemisphere to be uniquely an American concern. The United States had come of age as a global power.

So had its churches and synagogues. The boundaries of the parish now extended to the whole world, as missionary movements stretched around the globe and religious destiny often merged with Manifest Destiny. Municipal reform and factory safety continued as legitimate concerns, but religious institutions raised their sights beyond the local and near at hand to take in the whole continent, still being explored and settled, as well as the whole world, now being embraced and evangelized. The command to "Go ye therefore unto all the world" had enjoyed a special standing in Christian history for eighteen centuries or more. In the closing years of the nineteenth century those words acquired a special force.

EMPIRE OR REPUBLIC?

In 1898 the United States annexed the Hawaiian Islands, for the first time adding to its domain territory far removed from the North American continent. That annexation resulted from a combination of national and commercial interests, but it also represented a culmination of religious and cultural ties dating back to the 1820s, when New England dispatched Congregational missionaries to this Pacific outpost. Once drawn into the American orbit, Hawaii contributed dramatically to a religious pluralism

255

that moved well beyond the familiar contours of Judaism and Christianity. As the country established a foothold in the Pacific, so Buddhism, Confucianism, and Shinto established a significant port of embarkation for the mainland of America.

Even more dramatic was the Spanish-American War of that same year, a war entered into at least in part to rescue Cuba from the inhumanitarian treatment at the hands of a harsh Spanish regime. Of course, imperialism joined with loftier motivations to create a public mood that seemed ready for war. If social gospel advocates could resist cruelty and exploitation at home, many of them saw no reason to ignore cruelty and exploitation abroad, especially when that "abroad" lay only ninety miles off the coast of Florida. America had both a duty and a destiny, it was argued, to grant Cubans the same right of self-governance that Americans themselves had won more than a hundred years earlier. Understandably, Spain felt otherwise and declared war in April of 1898. Responding swiftly with its own declaration of war, the United States moved its navy with surprising effectiveness against Spain, not only in Cuba but also in the far distant Philippine Islands. In a few months the "splendid little war" (as Secretary of State John Hay called it) was over; in those few months the United States entered a new phase of its existence.

What was that phase to be called? More important, was this young nation about to follow the unhappy model of ancient Rome, leaving behind the virtues and restraints of its years as a republic to become now a greedy, grasping, and ultimately unvirtuous empire? This haunting question inspired heated public debate, and in this debate religious leaders were vocal and visible participants. In addition to the general question of whether America should now become a conquering power imposing its will on other peoples, a more narrow question was raised with respect to the Philippines: Should this territory, essentially Roman Catholic, be subject to Protestant as well as American conquest? Should Protestant missionaries be allowed or even encouraged by the government to turn the Filipino people away from their old religious loyalty at the same time they were being encouraged to abandon their old political loyalty to Spain?

President William McKinley (1843–1901), an earnest Methodist, gave a religious spin to the public debate when he declared that through prayer he came to see that it was the nation's duty "to uplift and civilize and Christianize [the Filipinos], and by God's grace, do the very best we could by them, as our fellow men for whom Christ also died." But many church leaders needed little encouragement to see the American victory as an opportunity to spread American Protestantism to an ignorant and deluded

67. Key figures in the Spanish-American War of 1898 gathered in Washington, D.C., soon after the war ended: President William McKinley, James Cardinal Gibbons, Admiral George Dewey. *Keystone-Mast Collection, University of California, Riverside*

people, whether in the Pacific or in the Atlantic. Congregational editor and clergyman Lyman Abbott (1835–1922) viewed the Spanish-American War as altogether noble, a war that required neither apology nor defense. "We fought the American Revolution to free ourselves," Abbott explained, "the Civil War to free a people whom we had helped to enslave." This latest war, he concluded, was waged "to free a people to whom we owed no other duty than that of a big nation to an oppressed neighbor."

Well, perhaps, there was one other duty: to rescue these poor people from the oppressions of Catholicism at the same time that they were rescued from the cruelties of Spain. Presbyterian missionary executive Arthur J. Brown (1856–1963) argued that the old regime of the Philippines was of a single piece: the government, the educational system, the imposed national religion of Spain. To overthrow one was to overthrow all. Besides, Brown noted, Protestant missionaries did not thrust Protestantism upon the native population, and they did not depend on taxation or on the civil arm of government to enforce their doctrines. All was voluntary. "The Protestant Churches of the United States rely wholly upon moral suasion and the intrinsic power of the truths which they inculcate." Surely, no one could object to that.

Roman Catholics, however, could and did object, both on the grounds of the nation's moral posture in the war itself and on the grounds of a genuine religious liberty for the Filipinos. Arguing the first point, Bishop John Lancaster Spalding (1840–1916) of Peoria, Illinois, cautioned against allowing an unquenchable thirst for expansion and empire to alter the fundamental character of the nation. We have stood for liberty, he explained, and by the power of our example may encourage others to seek liberty for themselves. Yet "we have never looked upon ourselves as predestined to subdue the earth," the bishop declared, nor are we obliged "to compel other nations, with sword and shell, to accept our rule." Our own articles of faith, derived from the Declaration of Independence and the Constitution, have bestowed great blessings upon the American people, "but we have never dreamed that they were articles to be exported and thrust down unwilling throats at the point of the bayonet."

Beyond the question of empire or republic, other Catholics rejected the notion that the Philippine Islands were now proper missionary fields for American Protestants. In St. Paul, Minnesota, Archbishop John Ireland (1838–1918) took issue with action that seemed to him contrary to the spirit of the nation's commitment to freedom of religion. "As a Catholic," Ireland pointed out in 1899, "I cannot approve of any efforts of Protestants to affect the religious duties of the inhabitants of the islands." Imagine the Protestant reaction were the situation reversed, Ireland suggested. Would Protestants rejoice to see Catholic missionaries sent en masse to a solidly Protestant land? "Now, as an American I will no less object to efforts to implant Protestantism in those islands." Besides, Ireland added, it is not prudent policy from the nation's point of view. Spain will say to its former subjects that they have lost more than their civil government: "They are also taking away your religion." In fact, "if I were America's enemy today, I would say to American Protestants," Archbishop Ireland observed, "hurry your missionaries to Cuba, to Puerto Rico, and the Philippines, and have them tell the inhabitants of those islands that their historic faith is wrong." No swifter or surer way could be found, he concluded, to turn these populations against the United States and make its very flag a symbol of cruel oppression and religious tyranny.

Like the mythical Paul Bunyan, the United States had taken giant steps across the earth. But, asked religious and political leaders, how steady and sure were those steps? And did they represent points of no return in the

68. Archbishop John Ireland of St. Paul defended the right of Philippine Catholics to continue undisturbed in the practice of their religion. *Library of Congress*

transformation of an agrarian republic into a military-industrial imperial power? In less than a generation the nation was plunged into another war, this time far more consuming in scale. And if it was a case of Western civilization's ethnocentricity to call it a "world war," it was for the United States another bold step onto a far wider stage. In that brutal struggle, what role would religion in America be called upon to play?

A WORLD AT WAR

In August of 1914 England and France along with their allies declared war against Germany and the Austro-Hungarian Empire and their allies.

Americans, forgetting they had stepped halfway across the globe, initially took comfort in the fact, or the feeling, that this war was so very far away. They also, under the leadership of President Woodrow Wilson (1856–1924), a steadfast Presbyterian, took comfort in the promise of a neutrality that would give the United States a special role in helping to negotiate a lasting peace once the cannons stopped their deafening roar and the submarines ceased their menacing prowl. The United States was enough of an ethnic medley that partisans on both sides of the conflict had their American supporters. Gradually, however, public sentiment—with Wilson again in the lead—shifted to the side of Great Britain. By 1917 World War I was neither far away nor of purely theoretical interest to Americans.

As in the case of the Spanish-American War, religious leaders in 1917 were divided in the manner and degree of their support for the war effort. Lines this time, however, were drawn not between Protestant and Catholic but between those who believed in the moral worth of war and those who recoiled from its long-term consequences. Does war make "the world safe for democracy," or does war by its very nature make men and women more barbaric, more inhumane, more prone to tyranny or revenge? Some religious leaders, especially those involved in the moral crusades of the social gospel movement, could be persuaded that war was an even greater, more glorious crusade. Wilson helped build this sentiment by declaring that the United States had no selfish interest in going to war: it sought no territory, it sought no compensation for losses already suffered or to be suffered. We go to war, Wilson said, to fight for the rights of mankind. "We shall be satisfied when those rights have been made as secure as the faith and freedom of nations can make them." A high purpose of this sort made it necessary to abandon neutrality, to surrender for the moment one's dedication to pacifist principles.

The abandonment of a religious pacifism did not come easily. Unitarian minister John Haynes Holmes (1879–1964) in 1915 denounced all war as a "foul business." "From the standpoint of things spiritual as well as of things material," Holmes declared, "war is the antithesis of life. Its one end is to destroy." We talk of noble purposes and high ideals, but, said Holmes, "No man is wise enough, no nation is important enough, no human interest is precious enough, to justify the wholesale destruction and murder which constitutes the essence of war." A good friend of Holmes's and fellow religious leader in New York City, Rabbi Stephen Wise (1874–1949), shared these strong views. In 1915 Wise wrote to President Wilson to condemn what seemed a steady buildup of a war mentality. We need to prepare for peace, not for war, Wise advised, adding, "I should not, my dear President, have written in this way nor would I burden you with my thought on this question if I did not feel conscience bound to dissent in pulpit and on platform from your position."

John Haynes Holmes had spoken of "the wholesale destruction" that modern warfare entailed. So indeed it did, as those closest to the conflict quickly discovered. Submarine warfare had indiscriminately murdered men, women, and children—combatant and noncombatant alike. Poison gas introduced new levels of horror; where it did not destroy, it maimed for life. Trench warfare, incredibly costly in the number of lives lost, reduced war from a theater of heroic glamor to a ditch of filth, stench, disease, terror, and death. Yet another New York clergyman, Harry Emerson Fosdick (1878–1969), by 1917 had heard as much about the "glory of war" as he was prepared to endure. Anyone who speaks of war that way, Fosdick asserted, "is morally unsound." We paint war in bright colors, Fosdick said, along with "rhythmic movement" and the "thrilling music of the military parade." But that is not war. "War now is dropping bombs from aeroplanes and killing women and children in their beds; it is shooting, by telephonic orders, at an unseen place miles away and slaughtering invisible men; it is murdering innocent travelers on merchant ships with torpedoes from unknown submarines." Who can dare call this kind of war a "crusade"—literally, a bearing of the cross?

But even greater numbers of clergy, like the public at large, did lend voice and energy to America's participation in the nation's first "world" war. Some abandoned any dedication to Wilsonian idealism, shifting to a demonization of the enemy, especially the German one. Lyman Abbott despaired of any reform on the part of the German people, despaired of any solution except extermination. The German is my enemy, said another Protestant clergyman, because he "is a robber, a murderer, a destroyer of homes, a pillager of churches, a violator of women. I do well," this minister added, to hate an enemy like that. With a mixture of motives and with varying degrees of restraint, the majority of church members, like the majority of their leaders, fell into the ranks of those marching on to war.

Historic peace churches, that is, churches who throughout their history had made pacifism an article of faith, continued to stand strong, though their numbers were small. The Church of the Brethren, the Moravian Church in America, Adventists, Quakers, Mennonites, and others were chiefly responsible for the over 60,000 young men who, on the grounds of conscience, claimed exemption from the Selective Service Act of 1917. Not all of these were granted conscientious objector status, of course, and many of those who did receive such status were encouraged nonetheless to accept some position in the armed services that did not require their taking or threatening human life. Many served in such auxiliary efforts as the medical or engineering or quartermaster agencies. In 1917 the leading Quaker philosopher, historian, and devotional writer, Rufus Jones (1863–1948), helped to form the American Friends Service Committee, a group that helped Quakers (and many others) to stand firm in their testimonies for peace. The organization also encouraged active humanitarian relief efforts both in the United States and abroad.

A large-scale modern war requires planning to be organized and centralized. Likewise, American religious groups, more than at any previous time, found it necessary during the First World War to speak and act with some degree of unity. Roman Catholics, for example, gathered in Washington, D.C., in 1917 in a general convention, the immediate consequence of which was the creation of a National Catholic War Council. Such a council could supervise the recruitment and training of Catholic chaplains as well as oversee the less formal ministries to young Catholics in military uniform. After the war was over, the newly named National Catholic Welfare Council (later Conference) took on far broader tasks: supervising Catholic education, "improving social conditions in accordance with the spirit of the Church," developing additional agencies among the laity, and promoting a more vigorous missionary program. As the Catholic bishops made clear in their pastoral letter of 1919, the overall purpose now far exceeded the narrow ones of the war; the new council would "promote more effectually the glory of God, the interests of His Church, and the welfare of the country."

Similarly, American Judaism, divided into varying theological orientations and among hundreds of largely self-ruled congregations, moved toward closer cooperation during World War I. Formal organization, however, did not come until 1926, when the Synagogue Council of America was born. Its purposes were explicitly announced in the preamble to the council's constitution: "That a Council composed of representatives of national congregational and rabbinical organizations of America be formed, for the purpose of speaking and acting unitedly in furthering such religious interests as the constituent organizations in the council have in common." Within a few years, the Synagogue Council estimated that its membership contained about 65 percent of all Jewish ministers in America and that (as the council declared in 1931) "religious Israel had found a voice." Just as Catholics could speak with some degree of unity on matters of public policy and social welfare, so now could religious Jewry.

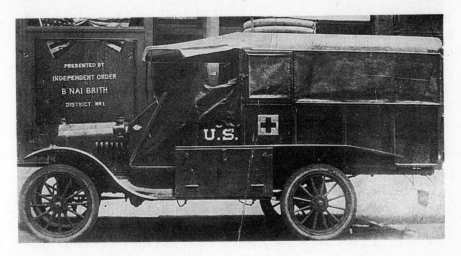

69. American members of B'nai B'rith donated this World War I ambulance to the allied forces. *B'nai B'rith International, Washington, D.C.*

Protestants, at least a large number of them, had found their public voice a decade or two earlier. In 1908 thirty Protestant denominations created the Federal Council of Churches in order to "bring the Christian bodies in America into united service for Christ and the world." Protestants, of course, had the largest task of all, for by the beginning of the twentieth century schism and separation had seemed to be the most obvious feature of their tradition. With pressures for unity increasing on the political level, it was time, or well past time, for larger unity at the ecclesiastical level. Over 12 million Protestants coming together for common tasks in 1908 represented an important first step toward unity; at the very least it represented a reversal of a trend toward proliferation. This Protestant organization, moreover, like its Catholic and Jewish counterparts, saw its role not so much as influencing the affairs of the local congregation as confronting the challenges before the nation as a whole: war and peace, labor and capital, rich and poor, "equal rights and complete justice for all men in all stations of life," to quote from the council's 1908 "Social Creed of the Churches."

National life, especially during wartime, dramatized the need for greater unity among the many scattered synagogues and churches. Once that unity was achieved in ecclesiastical terms, it managed to endure well beyond the war that gave it impetus. What did not endure was the idealism that Woodrow Wilson and others had bestowed upon World War I itself. The decade of the 1920s constituted, in many respects, a time of discouragement and disillusionment so far as grand dreams were concerned.

A major element in the Wilsonian dream as early as 1916, the League of Nations, came into being in 1919 as part of the treaty that brought the war to a formal end. The league was designed, above all else, to preserve peace. This it ultimately was unable to do, but where it (and Wilson) failed immediately was in winning the support of the U.S. Congress and the American public. Both remained skeptical, even though the influential Church Peace Union (founded in 1914) favored the league by a proportion of twenty to one and even though the Federal Council of Churches cabled Wilson when he was in Paris that the league was the "political expression of the Kingdom of God on earth." Many others, however, saw the league as a way of perpetuating American involvement in those entangling alliances against which George Washington had warned. And so Wilson suffered the bitter disappointment of seeing even his own country turn its back on his last, best hope. The league, he had told the Senate on July 10, 1919, inspires the United States "to yet higher levels of service and achievement." Destiny calls us, he added, "by no plan of our conceiving, but by the hand of God who has led us into this way." But it was not to be. If it could be called a crusade at all, this world war, like those great crusades centuries earlier to retake Jerusalem and other holy places, would be remembered mainly for what it failed to accomplish.

Among other things, it failed to burnish the moral reputation of war. In the years that followed the Treaty of Versailles, pacifism won a new respectability and popularity—and not just among those smaller peace churches. Now large numbers of mainline Protestants along with many Catholics and Jews saw war as an unacceptable means for settling the conflicts and competition among nations. A Disciples of Christ minister, Kirby Page (1890–1957), in 1921 helped create the Fellowship for a Christian Social Order, which took as its cardinal principle that men and women (in the words of the old spiritual) "ain't gonna study war no more." More than 20,000 clergy in America petitioned President Warren Harding (1865–1923) to call a conference on international disarmament, with the result that such a conference convened in Washington on November 12, 1921. Promptly, churches and synagogues named November 6 as a day of prayer for peace and for all the delegates chosen for the disarmament conference.

Under the leadership of Secretary of State Charles Evans Hughes (1862–1948), a Baptist layman of note, the conference did not content itself with passing idle resolutions or appointing commissions for further study. It proposed actual disarmament according to a specific schedule, with the destruction of specific weapons and the sinking of a stated number of naval ships. Having learned their lesson from the rejection of the League of Nations, the nation's religious membership prayed, preached, lobbied, and maintained a keen public interest until the U.S. Senate ratified the resolutions of the conference. Hopes rose even higher in 1928 when the Briand-Kellogg peace treaty (Pact of Paris) resulted in fifteen nations renouncing war as an instrument of national policy. The agreement, Southern Methodists asserted, was illumined by "the light that shone in Bethlehem." Everywhere it seemed that peace was about to break out, and everywhere religious forces gave hand and heart to the pacifist effort.

In 1936 the General Conference of the Methodist Church officially pronounced war as "the greatest social sin of modern times." Even more strongly, the conference declared that "the Methodist Episcopal Church as an institution does not endorse, support, or purpose to participate in war." The Northern Baptist Convention agreed that war was "the supreme social sin," adding that as long as nations resort to war "there can be no safety for our homes or for our civilization and no realization of the kingdom of heaven on earth." A conference in London, representing worldwide Anglicanism, including this nation's Episcopalians, pointed out that just as "Christian conscience has condemned infanticide and slavery and torture, it is now called to condemn war as an outrage on the fatherhood of God and the brotherhood of all mankind." Congregationalists proclaimed, "The church is through with war!" Universalists declared that the Quakers had been right all along and it was now time for all other churches to join them in "conscientious objection to all war." Disciples of Christ members, at their convention, pronounced war to be "destructive of the spiritual values for which the churches of Christ stand," and—like the Methodists—they would "serve notice to whom it may concern that we never again expect to bless or sanction war."

Without question the First World War had done little or nothing to redeem the notion of war, even as a sometimes sadly necessary instrument for warding off an unjust political order. Quite the contrary, it had given new intellectual scope and organizational range to the peace movement. Pacifism, explained Quaker Rufus Jones, is not passivity but activism and nonviolent engagement with the world. Pacifism, he wrote, "is not a theory; it is a way of life. It is something you are and do." So what would the churches do? What would they become? The answer to those questions rested, to a great degree, upon the energies and undertakings of the missionary movement.

MISSIONS ABROAD

Even with all their pursuits on the home front, Protestants in the nineteenth century found energy and resources to send missionaries abroad. The Student Volunteer Movement (SVM), for example, originating in 1886 as a device for recruiting missionary volunteers on college campuses, grew to prominence and surprising strength by the early decades of the twentieth century. Assuming leadership of the SVM soon after its founding, John R. Mott (1865–1955), a tireless Methodist layman, in 1895 created the World's Student Christian Federation and helped prepare for a World Missionary Conference held in Edinburgh in 1910. The organizational bustle was more than mere bureaucratic busywork: it pointed to a vision that was indeed worldwide, to an intention to scale all walls—linguistic, cultural, political—in the name of the Christian cause.

Mott had the pleasure of seeing some of his organizational structure duplicated in Britain, Holland, Germany, Norway, Sweden, Denmark, Finland, Switzerland, and South Africa. By the time of World War I, the SVM had sent out more than 5,000 volunteers; in 1920 alone the number reached 2,700. Mott also had the pleasure of seeing that his optimism, neatly capsuled in the title of his book *The Evangelization of the World in This Generation* (1900), was shared widely in the Western world. Noting the growing hostility between nations and races in 1914, Mott declared, "The only program which can meet all the alarming facts of the situation is the worldwide spread of Christianity in its purest form." It was more important to change inner motivations, Mott argued, than external structures. "The springs of conduct must be touched. A new spirit must be imparted." Mott harnessed an enormous reservoir of youthful energy and goodwill toward all humankind in a way that President John F. Kennedy would do in establishing the Peace Corps a half century later.

Protestant missions were, of course, broader than the inspired labors of a single man like John Mott. Protestant women, in fact, had been active in this realm for at least as long as the SVM itself. In the second half of the nineteenth century Congregationalist, Presbyterian, Baptist, and Methodist women had organized their own foreign missionary societies, with women's involvement steadily increasing so that by 1914 more than 3 million American women were actively supporting the worldwide enterprise. As historian Patricia Hill has noted, the woman's foreign missionary activity was, in fact, "the largest of the great nineteenth-century women's movements." Women raised money and raised consciousness at home about the world's needs. Women's mission boards also dispatched women "to foreign fields" as doctors, nurses, teachers, and spouses of ordained clergy who labored side by side with their husbands, rendering service of virtually every sort.

Organizational unity both before and after World War I gave even greater efficiency to a logistical effort of mammoth proportion. Writing of *The New Opportunity of the Church* in 1919, Presbyterian Robert E. Speer (1867–1947) found one of the few justifications for the war to be that moral ideals prevailed over material struggles. That war, he wrote, "has clarified and confirmed our fundamental religious ideas and revealed the power of their appeal to the present day mind." Given that confident assurance, Speer contended that missionaries should now go forward in greater numbers and with greater boldness to help heal the wounds of war and to counteract the political imperialism of the time. Speer acknowledged that Christians had done great damage to non-Christians in such matters as "commercial exploitation, the liquor traffic, the slave trade, . . . the opium traffic." But, he argued, the one element in the West that has protested against these and many other abuses has been the missionary enterprise. Year after year, he wrote, "it has joined with that wholesome moral senti-ment existing among the people in a death struggle against the great iniq-uities that Western civilization [has] spread over the world."

In the 1920s China especially received a major share of Protestant atten-tion and monies. In 1922, for example, about 750,000 dollars in voluntary offerings left the United States for China. At that time Protestants oper-ated 219 kindergartens, 700 elementary schools, over 300 high schools, and more than 40 teacher-training institutes in this one country alone. But that was only a beginning: colleges, seminaries, medical schools, orphan-ages, leper colonies, and a dozen institutions for the deaf and blind all resulted directly from Protestant endeavors. The American Bible Society by 1923 had sent nearly 20,000 Bibles to China along with more than 2 million publications containing some portion of the Bible. This tremen-dous outlay could find its counterpart in Korea, Japan, Burma, Thailand, much of Africa, and throughout the South Pacific, though the numbers were not quite so impressive,

Roman Catholics in America, meanwhile, had not been idle, though special circumstances prevented their taking up an active missionary effort before the twentieth century. The Catholic Church in America was itself regarded by the Vatican as a missionary field until 1908; to be sure, the nineteenth-century American church, growing so rapidly and in such vari-ety, needed all the help it could get. But in the very year that the Vatican declared the church in the United States no longer a missionary dependent, some 15 million Roman Catholics were called upon to assume their proper responsibilities around the world. Opening a Missionary Conference in Chicago in November 1908, Archbishop James Edward Quigley (1854–1915) of Chicago summarized the purposes of the conference this way: "to crystallize the missionary sentiment now being awakened in the Catholic clergy and people, to the end that all may realize their common duty of preserving and extending the Church of Christ." And in closing the meeting, Archbishop William H. O'Connell (1859–1944) of Boston sounded a similar note. "It is time," he said, "for the Church in America to be vigilant in preserving the unselfishness and generosity of spirit which animated the pioneer Catholic missionaries who planted on this continent the seed of faith." Once France and the French language had been the major power behind or vehicle of Catholic missions. Now, declared the archbishop, it was the turn of the United States and of the English language. "The providential hour of opportunity has struck," he noted, sounding so very much like John R. Mott. "We must be up and doing. All indications point to our vocation as a great missionary nation."

O'Connell's words found their most visible response in the creation of the Catholic Foreign Missionary Society of America in 1911 with headquarters in Maryknoll, New York. Maryknoll fathers and Maryknoll nuns carried on especially effective work in the Roman Catholic countries of Central and South America. After World War I the National Catholic Welfare Conference coordinated the sporadic missionary efforts of the nation's dioceses, giving them greater effectiveness and wider visibility. As with Protestants, Catholic missions saw their task as meeting whatever human need they encountered. The more narrowly defined roles of offering spiritual counsel and conducting Mass were often accompanied by building and operating schools, hospitals, and orphanages. And like Protestants, Catholics gave much attention to recruiting and developing a native clergy so that the necessity to import ecclesiastical leadership from abroad would gradually fade away. It was a matter of making Christianity indigenous, and that endeavor often proved so successful that eventually the missionary flow would reverse itself, with pastors and missionaries arriving from Korea or Brazil or Kenya to reclaim secular America.

Other and newer groups in America, notably Mormons, Seventh-day Adventists, and Jehovah's Witnesses, carried on so vigorous a missionary effort that they attracted almost as much attention as the far larger religious bodies. Mormons made missionary activity an obligation resting upon every young male Mormon (and eventually young women would have that option of service as well). This duty led to a large commitment in language training and to a broad cosmopolitanism in this church's membership. Adventists, putting great emphasis upon health and education both at home and abroad, created a missionary program in which doctors, dentists, nurses, and teachers played an even larger role than the clergy. And Jehovah's Witnesses, who expected all their members to be vigorously engaged in missions around the world, soon found their membership abroad equaling, then surpassing, the membership at home. That shift in membership balance became common for many groups, from Mormons to Pentecostals, by the end of the twentieth century. American faiths so successfully exported themselves that they eclipsed their Americanness in larger global identities.

That very success often occasioned sharp resistance. Hostility of host nations to the entire missionary enterprise sometimes led to a sharp

70. This Seventh-day Adventist medical mission on the Amazon River suggests the global social commitments of American Christian missions. *General Conference of the Seventh-day Adventists*

downturn of activity in specific geographical areas. In China, for example, the very foreignness of foreign missions became an argument against encouraging or tolerating these emissaries from abroad. In the 1930s waves of anti-Christian, antiforeign, anti-Western sentiment spread across China. When Japan invaded in 1937, the position of Western missionaries worsened, a deterioration that continued for the next decade or more until hardly a foreign missionary was permitted to stay in China. Meanwhile, the Great Depression in the United States during the 1930s undermined the financial base that had supported so much of the worldwide effort. Even more damaging to some aspects of Protestant missions, however, was the growing tension in America between conservative and liberal forces within Protestantism.

Those tensions took many forms, and we will explore most of them in the following chapter. But on the mission field in particular, tensions appeared in the form of a contest between how much the missionary movement should be allowed to drift off in the direction of general social service and how much it should remain focused on evangelism and conversion. Early in the twentieth century mission boards and commissions defended both approaches: to the body as well as to the soul, to concern about life here on earth as well as life hereafter. By the early 1930s, however, following the bruising battles of the 1920s between fundamentalists and modernists, much mainstream Protestantism came under attack from the more evangelically minded. Around the same time, many of those Protestants under siege themselves began questioning some of the culturally imperialist assumptions that often lay behind the missionary movement. E. Stanley Jones (1884–1973), Methodist missionary to India, startled many in 1925 when he suggested that American Christians had as much to learn from Indian Hindus as the other way around. "The religious genius of India," Jones affirmed, "is the richest in the world." Should the citizens of India adopt Christianity, it will be ultimately a very different sort of Christianity, Jones noted, than that familiar to most Americans: it "will be essentially Eastern and not Western."

Others questioned the effect of asking people to forsake cultural and tribal patterns, the effect of isolating them from centuries of tradition or bonds of communal affection. Still others wondered if the primary purpose of missions had not now become something quite different. "Starting with the purpose of saving souls, [missionaries] have been drawn on by necessity into efforts to build up the minds, and the bodies, and to improve the social life in which these souls are engaged. The educational and other associated interests have grown until in volume and variety they now outrank the parent activity." Those two sentences come from a 1932 report titled *Re-thinking Missions: A Layman's Inquiry After One Hundred Years*. Leading the inquiry was Congregational churchman and professor of philosophy at Harvard William Ernest Hocking (1873–1966). As a result of widespread second thoughts about missions in general, Hocking had been asked to undertake a major assessment of Protestant missions around the world, the point being to determine if the missionary enterprise should continue and, if so, in what revised or altered form.

71. Increasingly American Protestants were divided over liberal, modernist theological views that stressed reevaluating the commitment to foreign missions out of greater respect for indigenous cultures and religions. *Billy Graham Center Museum*

The very fact of such an inquiry pointed to the pervasive doubts about Christianity's proper relationship to other religions of the world, about America's role in imposing its culture and often its will upon less powerful peoples. If missions had become largely social service, then was it not time to let other agencies, probably governmental, carry on that service? On the other hand, if Christian missions had ceased their primary business of saving souls, then was it not time for other Christian bodies to assume that task?

In the 1930s, therefore, conservative evangelical forces, including many Pentecostal and Holiness bodies, began to take up the slack so evident in the missionary resolve and purpose of liberal Protestants. The Federal Council of Churches represented much of Protestantism but certainly not all. This was made clear in 1942 with the creation of the National Association of Evangelicals, with the introduction in America a few years earlier of the Intervarsity Christian Fellowship—conservative religion's answer to or revival of the Student Volunteer Movement. Protestant missions did not so much decline in the 1930s and 1940s as take on a different coloration and develop a different cadre of denominational supporters. In this later period foreign missions became less a feature of establishment concern or public policy and more a subculture of zealous evangelization, riding the waves of technological advances and strong religious passion. Meanwhile, many Americans, liberal and conservative, Protestant, Catholic, and Jew, found themselves challenged to solve pressing problems closer at hand.

MISSIONS AT HOME

In the two decades between the great wars, social ills and dislocations commanded the attention of organized religion. Immigration had effectively halted in 1924, but the task of Americanizing and Christianizing recent arrivals continued to preoccupy many religious leaders. Before immigration ceased, a Lutheran church paper in 1920 addressed the momentous task of reaching the "seventeen million foreign-born in our midst, and the aliens arriving in our ports, now at the rate of five thousand daily." This concern found its echo in many other church groups, as missions to immigrants (preferably in their own language, preferably with a Bible already printed in that language) occupied many who saw the tasks at home as every bit as pressing as those abroad. With "melting-pot" imagery still enjoying high favor in the 1920s, churches tended to see themselves as major partners in the process of assimilation.

If some viewed aggressive evangelical efforts among the immigrants in an unfavorable light, others adopted attitudes toward the new arrivals that won even less approval. Catholics and Jews found many Americans already turned against them, as a revived Ku Klux Klan tried repeatedly—and with some success—to make its case for an America that would be ruled by white Protestants only. America "must remain Protestant," declared the Klan's Imperial Wizard in 1926; the nation's destiny would be fatally damaged, he added, "if we became priest-ridden, if we had to submit our consciences and limit our activities and suppress our thoughts at the command of any man, much less of a man sitting upon Seven Hills thousands of miles away." Other religious voices protested this myopic view of what America or what being an American was all about. The rabbi of Temple Emanu-El in New York City asked, also in

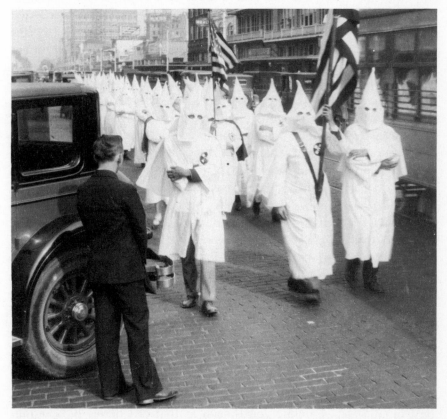

72. Ku Klux Klan members, who represented nativist Protestant hatred of immigrants, Catholics, Jews, and blacks at its most glaring, marched in St. Petersburg, Florida, in 1926. *Keystone-Mast Collection, University of California, Riverside*

1926, "What justification is there for this twentieth-century religious persecution on American soil?" The rabbi found none; indeed, what he found was that the "Americanism" of the Klan was the most un-American feature to be seen in all the land.

The presidential election of 1928 gave a sudden surge to anti-Catholicism in the country. For the first time, one of the major political parties had nominated a Roman Catholic to be president of the United States. Alfred E. Smith (1873–1944) had been a member of the New York legislature for many years and had been the state's governor for four terms, but to a large number of Americans the only biographical bit worth mentioning was that he was a Roman Catholic. All of the older nativism of the nineteenth century was reborn in an instant as broadsides and sermons, newspaper articles and editorials explained the great danger to American liberty if a Catholic were to be elected president. Smith himself found this attitude tragically un-American, noting how closely it reflected the mentality and bigotry of the Klan. "Nothing could be so out of line with the spirit of America," he pointed out during the campaign. Nor could anything be so out of line with the spirit of Christianity, Smith added. "The world knows no greater mockery than the use of the blazing cross, the cross upon which Christ died, as a symbol to install into the hearts of men hatred of their brethren, while Christ preached and died for the love and brotherhood of man." Smith was defeated, and though, to be sure, other issues were at stake besides his Catholicism, the campaign dramatized in an unforgettable way that the "mission at home" had much work to do in eradicating religion-based prejudice.

Similar prejudice was aimed at Jews, whose numbers grew rapidly in the closing years of the nineteenth century and the early years of the twentieth. By 1913 Jews had created the Anti-Defamation League, whose overriding purpose was to identify the sources of religious and racial prejudice and then through a program of education and persuasion try to alter attitudes so deeply ingrained. In the 1920s the situation worsened, as quota systems were applied to limit enrollment of Jews in major universities, housing covenants excluded Jews from many neighborhoods, and "gentlemen's agreements" regularized harassment of and discrimination against Jews. Even Henry Ford added his public weight to rumors of conspiracy by international Jewry. Jews were thought to resist assimilation or, if assimilated, to subvert both the economic and the political systems of the United States. Catholic voices such as that of Charles E. Coughlin (1891–1979) and Protestant voices such as that of Gerald B. Winrod (1899?–1957) sullied the 1930s with strident expressions of anti-Semitism, this at the very time when in Germany much more powerful voices were being raised against Jews.

African Americans likewise suffered in this same period, not merely from petty persecution and humiliating segregation but from repeated instances of public murder. It was called lynching, and these ritualized hangings disgraced America over and over again. From 1882 to 1927 nearly 5,000 lynchings took place, not all of the victims being black, though African Americans constituted the vast majority. Lynchings were not limited to the South; indeed, only four New England states wholly escaped this tragic blight. Racial discrimination was so blatant, so widespread, so much the norm that church bodies could neither ignore it nor dispute its omnipresence. For the most part, however, church leaders spent more time discussing the problem than taking concrete steps to solve it. Public revulsion against lynchings, nonetheless, did result in a steady decline in the 1920s and 1930s, so that by the 1940s lynchings had virtually ceased. Other forms of racial injustice, however, continued apace, with the total immersion of the churches into the questions of racial injustice and human rights awaiting a later day.

The Great Depression of the 1930s galvanized the forces of religion in a way that nothing had done since the First World War. In 1931 the Federal Council of Churches, the National Catholic Welfare Conference, and the Central Conference of American Rabbis gathered together in an effort to find "Permanent Preventives of Unemployment." In that same year Pope Pius XI issued an important encyclical, *Quadragesimo Anno* ("Fortieth Year," commemorating the socially progressive encyclical issued by Pope Leo XIII in 1891), which addressed depression-related problems that by that time had spread worldwide. Urging men and women to avoid the extremes of individualism on the one hand and of collectivism on the other, the pope called upon the cooperation of governments "to make all human society conform to the needs of the common good; that is, to the norm of social justice."

Pronouncements, however, often failed to satisfy urgent human needs. As Roman Catholic activist Dorothy Day (1898–1980) said with respect to African Americans, "We just went out and *did* things. We didn't form a Committee to Promote Interracial Relations. We took Negroes in our homes and lived with them." So also her Catholic Worker movement, founded in 1933, did not issue manifestos on poverty or hunger; the movement, with its Hospitality Houses and farm communes, simply fed the hungry and clothed and sheltered the poor. With its radical economic critique of American society, the Catholic Worker movement embraced

Marxist forms of class analysis while continuing to see religion as the source of salvation, both social and spiritual: "Religion is not the dope of the people. Religion is the hope of the people." In the 1930s the Society of St. Vincent de Paul, along with other already-established groups such as the Salvation Army, the YMCA and YWCA, and the Jewish Welfare Board, encountered more demands for the bare necessities of life than they could meet.

The election of Franklin D. Roosevelt (1882–1945), an Episcopalian, in 1932 seemed to offer hope, though his New Deal took many years to rescue large numbers from their grinding poverty. For some church people, Roosevelt began on the wrong foot by repealing the noble experiment known as prohibition. The brevity of the experiment as well as the widespread flouting of the law suggested that constitutional amendments were less than satisfactory solutions for religiously specific moral reforms. Roosevelt won back some of his detractors, however, by using the power of government more actively and aggressively to deal with fundamental dislocations and prolonged human suffering. He, too, had a "mission at home," with it becoming increasingly clear as the 1940s approached that America and the wider world were mutually interdependent. America's religious enterprises in all of their many expressions, like its political ones, no longer stopped at the water's edge.

For a half century or more, from the end of the 1880s to the beginning of the 1940s, the churches and synagogues recognized that they had mighty tasks to perform: in war and peace, in domestic matters as well as international ones. These were busy years for American religious groups. But the institutions of religion could not ignore even more immediate and anxiety-raising concerns. While aggressively pursuing crowded agendas both at home and abroad, the churches suffered great inner turmoil and dissension. Some of the vitality of the period found expression not in service but in schism. How healthy, how whole, were the nation's households of faith?

CHAPTER 13

Growth and Schism

In the final decade of the nineteenth century Christianity still dominated the religious life of the United States. The eight leading denominational families, in order of membership, were these: Roman Catholic, Methodist, Baptist, Presbyterian, Lutheran, Disciples of Christ, Episcopalian, and Congregational. These familiar, "mainstream" varieties were accorded a great deal of cultural recognition, from the statehouse to the marketplace, from the print media to the military. Yet their hold on the American religious world was far from complete, and the status of each of these groups on the eve of the twentieth century requires some comment.

American Catholicism, with about 8 million members, had survived the resentments of Protestant neighbors, the tensions of the Civil War, the strains of ethnic jealousy, the suspicions of European Catholics—all with organizational unity somehow still intact. A remarkable achievement this was, considering the stupendous stresses the church was subjected to in nineteenth-century America: wave after wave of immigration, wave after wave of nativist attack, wave after wave of territorial assimilation. No other church confronted so great a challenge; no other church emerged so conspicuously strong and so well positioned for further growth in the twentieth century.

Methodism, unlike Catholicism, emerged from the nineteenth century with no conspicuous unity in organization. The Methodist family of about 5.5 million members was often quarrelsome: divided by race, by sectional sentiment, by argument over the authority of their bishops or superintendents, and by disagreement over the pursuit of John Wesley's "Christian perfection." Yet the family as a whole continued to flourish with such zest that it more than offset the internal dividing and extravagant spinning off of new religious bodies.

Like the Methodists, the Baptists enjoyed no structural oneness. They, too, had been divided by the Civil War; they, too, had watched the creation

277

of separate entities for their black members; they, too, had found still other grounds for repeated separation. Baptists could not even agree on their own history or on the uniqueness of their mode of baptism or on the terms by which one might be invited to share in the Lord's Supper or on the authority of the congregation or, for that matter, on the precise wording of the Lord's Prayer. Yet, despite the range of differences and the tenacity of localism, Baptists did constitute a "family" of about 4 million strong in the closing years of the nineteenth century.

Presbyterians, nearly as successful on the frontier as Baptists and Methodists had proved to be, elevated quarrelsomeness to a higher juridical level. With a more closely knit system of church governance, based on a pyramid structure of sessions, presbyteries, synods, and ultimately a General Assembly, Presbyterians tried heroically to maintain unity in doctrine, in practice, and certainly in organization itself. But in the freewheeling environment of an open-ended American experiment, this effort often failed. Divided over the "new measures" of revivalism, Presbyterians, like Baptists and Methodists, split up just prior to the Civil War. And like their fellow evangelists in the movement westward, they also saw black members create their own organization, even as they struggled with the question of proper ordination and educational requirements for all Presbyterian clergy. With about 1.5 million members in 1895, this family moved with some ease into all sections of the country, north and south, east and west.

Immigration in the second half of the nineteenth century gave Lutheranism significant numerical standing by 1895: nearly as numerous as the Presbyterians and fifth in ranking according to membership. But Lutherans did not have to wait until they arrived in America to find reasons for division and separation; they brought their reasons with them. As noted already in Chapter 10, ethnic and national distinctions were numerous. Thus Lutherans who were simply Lutheran in Sweden, for example, found it necessary in America to be identified as Swedish Lutherans. Separate organizations existed for Norwegian Lutherans, Finnish Lutherans, Danish Lutherans, German Lutherans, and so on. This only began to account for the divisions, however, as quarrels broke out about theology, creedal loyalty, personal piety, and many other matters. At the beginning of the twentieth century Lutheranism in America was separated into some two dozen distinct ecclesiastical bodies.

Alone among the top eight mainstream churches, the Disciples of Christ bore no European stamp. Its origin, described in an earlier chapter, belonged to the American frontier of the pre–Civil War period. The youngest of these eight nevertheless grew vigorously enough to claim nearly a million members by 1895, thus overtaking groups such as Dutch Reformed and Quakers, who had enjoyed a far earlier planting on American soil. The movement's youth, however, as we shall see later in this chapter, did not prevent it from suffering internal tension and ultimate division.

Ranking seventh and eighth in this census of the 1890s were the two churches that in the colonial period had been at the very top: the Episcopalians and the Congregationalists. Once it had seemed that they virtually divided the country between them, but by 1900, if not long before, this was obviously no longer the case. Still powers to be reckoned with, Episcopalians and Congregationalists had fallen far behind their competitors, neither group proving to be all that effective on the frontier, neither group adjusting all that readily to the new realities of a totally open market in religion. With around 600,000 members apiece, these two churches brought into the twentieth century the assurance that earlier privilege and prestige had bestowed. However, their numbers suggested already some narrowing of both these historic streams.

In 1900 the population of the country stood at 76 million and church membership at around 26 million. More than four-fifths of those church members could be found in the eight families noted above, and that is a crucial demographic detail. No other religious body had as many as a half million members, at least so far as the official census takers were able to determine. Much American religion then and now, however, eludes the census taker and escapes wide public notice. Religious, linguistic, and ethnic enclaves often lead an existence on the edges of the wider society—a social space that sometimes conceals their numbers and regularly reduces their public voices. At the turn of the twentieth century religious diversity was growing, and new religious movements that would gradually shake up this "mainstream" religious profile continued to thrive. In the first half of the twentieth century, the prevailing religious denominations would find their channels neither so clear nor so deep as they had earlier been perceived to be.

ERA OF CHURCH GROWTH

At the beginning of the twentieth century about one-third of the nation's population could be found on the membership rolls of the churches and synagogues. By the middle of that century, membership had increased to well over 50 percent. In that same fifty-year period, the population as a whole doubled, from around 76 million to over 150 million. As a consequence, church membership grew in absolute numbers as well as in percentage of the total population. The eight "mainstream" denominations all participated dramatically in that growth: Catholics from 8 million to over 25 million; Methodists from 5.5 million to twice that; Baptists from 4 million to more than 15 million (passing the Methodists); Presbyterians from 1.5 million to over 3 million; Lutherans from fewer than 1.5 million to more than 5 million; Disciples from fewer than 1 million to about 4 million (in the whole "family" derived from Barton Stone and Alexander Campbell); Episcopalians and Congregationalists from well under a million each to around 3 million and 2 million, respectively. But church growth was by no means a monopoly of these leading groups alone. Others were growing—and gaining fast.

Mormon growth was as sharp as it was surprising. Surprising because utopian communities in nineteenth-century America had a way of quietly shrinking from public consciousness if not altogether from existence. Surprising because groups once deprived of their original charismatic leadership regularly splintered into countless insignificant fragments. Surprising because Mormons had been exiled to a barren and (it was widely assumed) soon-to-be-forgotten wasteland. The Church of Jesus Christ of Latter-day Saints was not finished with surprises. The abandonment of polygamy in 1890 led to neither doctrinal nor communal decline; on the contrary, family loyalties intensified. The admission of Utah as a state in 1896 led not to greater conflict with the church's old enemy, namely the United States, but to a stronger embrace of the nation's pervading cultural values, indeed to patriotism distinguished by its unswerving passion. Perhaps most surprising of all, the slow acceptance of Mormonism into the wider currents of American culture led not to lassitude and complacency but to an increasingly fervent missionary enterprise abroad as well as at home.

One direct consequence of that last surprising feature of twentieth-century Mormonism has been a growth curve that older religious bodies in America could regard with only envy and wonder. With a membership of a mere quarter of a million in the 1890s, Mormons by 1950 had more than twice that number in the state of Utah alone. In the United States Mormonism stands as the best example of a large ecclesiastical institution whose power base is neither urban nor eastern but rural and western. The Utah branch is far larger than its cousin, the Reorganized Church of Jesus Christ of Latter Day Saints, renamed in 2001 the Community of Christ, whose strength lies mainly in and around Independence, Missouri. The

73. As social and religious upstarts, Holiness and Pentecostal groups often gathered in unpretentious structures such as this one near the New York–Pennsylvania border. *Library of Congress*

Utah group has spread across state boundaries into southern Idaho and Montana, northern Arizona and New Mexico, western Wyoming, and eastern Washington, Oregon, and California. Mormonism, once so commonly ridiculed and routinely dismissed by establishment religion, came of age in the twentieth century in ways hardly anticipated.

Methodism helped to spawn a host of new denominations that, in their newness, quickly overtook the parent group insofar as growth rates were concerned. John Wesley, founder of Methodism, had stressed the necessity for all Christians to press beyond the stage of mere justification by faith to a higher plateau, a loftier goal of entire sanctification, that is, of being made wholly holy. Taking his cue from the New Testament command to "be perfect, as your heavenly Father is perfect" (Matthew 5:48), Wesley and many of his followers pursued the ideal of Christian perfection in one's own life here on earth. Such striving for sanctification was quite individual or personal, but it also became characteristic of whole churches and eventually entire denominations.

After the Civil War a National Camp Meeting Association for the Promotion of Christian Holiness was formed to inspire greater commitment on the part of "brothers and sisters of the various denominations" to the steady pursuit of holiness. Though Methodists led in this early organization, the movement itself had too much vitality and lively spirit to be contained within a single ecclesiastical institution. In the 1880s and beyond, dozens of new denominations were born, all vying with one another to prove their restless passion as they pursued the high goal of Christian perfection. D. S. Warner's Church of God sprang into being in 1880, this quickly followed by A. B. Simpson's Christian and Missionary Alliance in 1887, then by J. H. King's Fire Baptized Holiness Church in 1895, then by the Pilgrim Holiness Church in 1897. Also in 1897 the Church of God in Christ was born, and it eventually towered over the rest of the Holiness and Pentecostal churches. A predominantly African American group, it was founded by a Baptist preacher named Charles H. Mason (1866–1961), who preached revival across Mississippi and Tennessee and who eventually led the body from its Holiness roots into the Pentecostal movement. In 1914 a half dozen smaller groups rested just long enough to agree on a new denominational name, the Church of the Nazarene, another body that exploded from a base of a few thousand to a quarter of a million by 1950.

Also thriving were distinct Pentecostal bodies, so named from the description in the book of Acts (2:1–4) of the Day of Pentecost when the Holy Spirit descended in power upon the apostolic worshipers. One manifestation of that power was that those present "began to speak in other tongues, as the Spirit gave them utterance." Speaking in tongues as well as practicing spiritual healing of physical infirmities became the chief distinguishing features of this array of rapidly growing denominations in America. The Azusa Street revival in Los Angeles, which began in 1906 and grew rapidly over the next several years, is often taken as the great launching pad for these new Pentecostal churches. Though in early years the Holiness and Pentecostal movements were closely associated (as was

74. The Church of God in Christ, a predominantly African American denomination, was among the most important religious bodies to emerge out of the ferment of the Holiness-Pentecostal movement. Its community life was built around Spirit-filled worship, as is suggested by this church service in 1942 in Washington, D.C. *Library of Congress*

evident in C. H. Mason's Church of God in Christ), the two gradually pulled further apart. Holiness folks considered speaking in tongues a delusion and concentrated on the experience of entire sanctification, while their Pentecostal brothers and sisters saw the spiritual gifts that surrounded the baptism of Holy Spirit as the hallmark of the Christian life. In 1914 in Hot Springs, Arkansas, the Assemblies of God denomination gathered many scattered and ever-splintering Pentecostal churches into a single fold. This group was destined, along with the Church of God in Christ, to become a leading representative of the whole Spirit-filled movement. It had fewer than 50,000 adherents in the 1920s, but by century's end it counted well over 2 million in the United States and far more abroad.

In general Pentecostal churches grew more rapidly in the South than did Holiness churches, in part because Holiness groups emphasized social reform, and to this the South, since slavery days, tended to be resistant. Pentecostal churches attracted both black and white members and, surprisingly, sometimes in the same church. In the early days of the movement, many of the revival meetings were interracial—most famously at Azusa Street, where the racial and ethnic complexity of Pentecostalism was especially pronounced. Many of the major leaders, moreover, were black, including C. H. Mason and also William J. Seymour (1870–1922), who was the key figure in the movement in Los Angeles. Clearly, the Pentecostal phenomenon was every bit as much a black movement as a white one. Gradually, however, the patterns of the surrounding culture led to mainly segregated churches for these denominational groups as they had for American religion at large. But in both segments of the nation's population, white and black, Pentecostalism proved to be enormously popular. And soon that popularity spread as Pentecostalism became a major force among Latinos as well. Among the early leaders of the movement was the evangelist Francisco Olazábal (1886–1937), who converted to Pentecostalism in 1917, preached its gospel across the country for the next two decades, and augured the rise of a strong Latino Protestant insurgency.

The Jewish population in America increased sharply from about 1 million in 1900 to 5 million a mere half century later. Most of that increase resulted, of course, from immigration, especially prior to World War I, though some augmentation came from European refugees in the 1930s and 1940s. Not all Jews emigrating to America were conspicuously religious in behavior or institutional affiliation, though it would be difficult to draw neat lines between the sacred and secular aspects of what it meant to be Jewish in America. Certainly the synagogue, especially among Eastern European Jews, provided the greatest sense of community as well as the strongest thread of continuity for the vast majority of newly arrived Jews. Particularly in New York City, many synagogues held together people from the same Old World towns, if not from the same ships that brought them to America.

Jews proved their Americanness by duplicating the tendency toward schism and separation that their non-Jewish neighbors had indulged in for years. Jews disagreed on the degree of accommodation to the wider culture that might be required or desired; they disagreed on the degree of loyalty demanded to ancient customs and ancient laws; they disagreed on the need for a single Jewish voice, in matters religious or otherwise, to speak for all; they disagreed on the meaning of chosenness as a people; they disagreed on the relative merits of home, of faith, of culture, of history, or of tradition in arriving at the defining essence of Jewishness; and they disagreed on the question of a Jewish homeland under Jewish rule as the one feature essential to a secure Jewish future.

A Hungarian Jew, Theodor Herzl (1860–1906), gave Zionism (the program for a Jewish homeland) powerful leadership through a book he published in 1896 called *The Jewish State*. Herzl, dismayed by the continued outbursts in Europe of violent anti-Semitism, argued that Jews would have no peace, no freedom from harassment and persecution, until they had a land of their own. Therefore, Herzl declared, "Let sovereignty be granted us over a portion of the globe adequate to meet our rightful national requirements; we will attend to the rest." Just where that homeland might be was not as urgent a question for Herzl as that there be one, so that the history of Jews in the twentieth century could differ sharply from their history in the preceding centuries, centuries that went all the way back to the Maccabees (a hundred or more years before the rise of Christianity) when Jews last enjoyed any political independence.

Soon after Herzl's book appeared, Jews in America began to organize on behalf of the Zionist idea—an idea that they were determined to turn into a reality. In 1912 Henrietta Szold (1860–1945) founded the Women's Zionist Organization of America, and six years later an even broader Zionist group was born. Conservative Judaism as represented by the Jewish Theological Seminary in New York City became a major recruiting center and training ground for American Zionists as the movement steadily gathered force in the 1920s and 1930s. Then in 1948, following World War II, the state of Israel at last came into being. It was seen as the culmination of countless dreams and as a haven for thousands of homeless Jews from all around the world. From that point on, the existence of a Jewish homeland would play a determinative role in America's large Jewish community, arousing its moral passion and in new ways calling upon that community's spiritual as well as financial resources. For an increasing number of American Jews, the pressing question was no longer one of accommodation to a Gentile culture but of dedication to a new Jewish political and religious reality.

Eastern Orthodoxy, despite its early presence in "Russian America" (that is, Alaska), is more a feature of twentieth-century America than of an earlier period. In the latter decades of the nineteenth century one group of Byzantine-rite worshipers from the region around the Hungarian-Russian borders emigrated to the United States in significant numbers. These Uniates (sometimes also called Carpatho-Rusyns), who had a married clergy, for a time enjoyed a special relationship with the Roman Catholic Church, but they ultimately found it more comfortable to renew and solidify their ancient ties with Orthodoxy—especially after a 1907 Roman bull that laid down conditions unacceptable to this group. Despite the fact that this body numbered perhaps as many as a quarter of a million by 1900, they remained little known beyond their own enclave of believers. And that has been the story of Eastern Orthodoxy over and over, as separate immigrations of closely knit ethnic peoples took up residence in America in enclaves that resisted acculturation and escaped widespread public attention.

The Russian Revolution in 1917 of course drew wide public notice, but the many emigrations resulting from it attracted little concern beyond the confines of the churches themselves. Even there, feuding and factionalism kept Russian Orthodoxy from becoming a recognizable force in American religion. In 1919 an "All-American Convention" meeting in Pittsburgh declared that Russian Orthodoxy in this country would be altogether independent of the Russian Orthodoxy in the Soviet Union. Such a proclamation was more easily announced than enforced, however, as the New York courts in 1925 and 1926 were called upon to settle the question of which group of Russian Orthodox in America held the legitimate title to Saint Nicholas Cathedral in New York City. Litigation and quarreling continued for another generation until in 1952 the United States Supreme Court (Kedroff v. Saint Nicholas) agreed that church law itself must determine the proper ownership. On that basis the cathedral was deemed to be the property not of the largest group of Russian Orthodox living in America but of the group legally tied to the Patriarchate of Moscow. It was not a popular decision in Cold War days, its unpopularity captured in part by the remark of dissenting justice Robert H. Jackson (1892–1954), who observed that he did not think "New York law must yield to the authority of a foreign and unfriendly state masquerading as a spiritual institution."

By 1952 and indeed long before, Orthodoxy in America had many more representatives than just those who had fled the Bolshevik Revolution. Syrians, Serbians, Rumanians, Albanians, and Bulgarians—among others—arrived in the interval between World Wars I and II. It was Greeks, however, who most conspicuously swelled the ranks of Orthodoxy, in this case, an ancient Orthodoxy in which allegiance was given not to the Roman papacy but to a national "patriarch." The patriarch, who usually resided in the capital city of the nation, was recognized, with

75. Eastern Orthodoxy had even more of an impact in the eastern half of the United States than it did in the western half. It made its presence known especially through the architectural distinctiveness and prominence of its churches, evident here from this cityscape in Pittsburgh, Pennsylvania, in 1938. *Library of Congress*

varying degrees of consistency and fervency, as the true spiritual father. But Orthodoxy's progeny in America, like all other American progeny, found loyalties torn and tested as they tried to balance Old World ties against New World realities. The Greeks, no less than others, faced this problem, especially as their numbers grew by World War I to around 100,000.

In 1918 the archbishop of Athens (historically under the patriarch who ruled from Constantinople) came to the United States to form an all-Greek church where unity and love would prevail. Disorder and factionalism prevailed, however, frustrating his plans, just as those of the All-American Convention of the Russian Orthodox had been frustrated. But Archbishop Meletios persisted, his authority increasing dramatically when in 1921 he was named Patriarch of Constantinople. On a second visit to the United States that year he created the Greek Orthodox Archdiocese of North and South America, an entity that now serves as the ecclesiastical home for some two million members. Factionalism did not disappear with one organizational stroke, however, as successive leaders struggled to make unity, at least among the Greeks if not among all the Orthodox in America, more nearly a reality. Archbishop Athenagoras (1886–1972), who held the highest American office from 1930 to 1949, was especially successful in this regard, though he, too, often found it necessary to resort to the civil courts to untangle many disputatious knots. When Athenagoras in his turn was named Patriarch of Constantinople in 1949, President Harry Truman provided his own plane to assist him in moving from America to Turkey. This presidential gesture indicated that Orthodoxy was at last emerging from its relative invisibility in American public life.

By 1950 most Americans still did not regularly acknowledge the significant presence of Orthodoxy in the nation. One continued too casually to speak of "Protestant-Catholic-Jew" as encompassing virtually all of American religion. *Catholic* was understood almost without exception to mean Roman Catholic, with that other church catholic and apostolic, the Eastern one, largely ignored. Given the antiquity of the Eastern church's history, the drama of its liturgy, the color of its iconography, and the richness of its cultural diversity, such lack of awareness became increasingly difficult to maintain, especially with respect to the two largest branches, Greek and Russian. Both national and world events also conspired to bring greater attention to Orthodoxy. First, the public embrace in 1965 between Rome's Pope Paul VI and Constantinople's Patriarch Athenagoras I represented a step toward healing a bitter schism some nine hundred years old; and second, the nomination of Michael Dukakis for president in 1988 was the first time a member of that ancient Orthodoxy had been thus honored.

So if "Protestant-Catholic-Jew" proved a label too narrow to cover all of American religion, stretching it to include Orthodoxy would help somewhat but clearly not enough. For the United States by 1950 had become better acquainted with traditions well beyond the confines of Judaism and Christianity. The World's Parliament of Religions, held in Chicago in 1893, had widened the cultural gate through which knowledge about Islam, Hinduism, Buddhism, Confucianism, and Shinto flowed. The annexation of Hawaii in 1898 opened that gate even more. Immigration to the mainland, especially to the West Coast, continued to widen those gates, both in the late nineteenth century and in the twentieth. Before 1900 Japanese Buddhism had become a major religion in Hawaii, and before that date the religious heritage of both China and Japan had long been represented in California. From that rich heritage, Buddhism emerged as the most vigorous, the most adaptable, the most "missionary minded" of the Asian religions, with the United States being seen in the twentieth century as an important mission field.

Formally established in San Francisco in 1899, the Buddhist Mission of North America grew out of the labors of two priests sent from Japan. By 1942 the mission was sufficiently well established to permit the name to be changed, more simply, to Buddhist Churches of America. Churches and temples had been established in the intervening years in large enough numbers to suggest that Japanese (and to a lesser extent Chinese) Buddhism had found a permanent home in America. Not easily, however. First, in 1924 acts to restrict immigration included one named the Japanese Immigration Exclusion Act, whose very name tells all. Then, with the outbreak of World War II, Japanese Americans by the thousands (about 100,000 in all) were relocated in internment camps, the government taking this action on the grounds that national security required it. This injustice, for which the nation later officially apologized and provided financial reparation, was based less on national security considerations than on deep resentment over Japan's attack on Pearl Harbor (December 7, 1941) and on the long-standing racism of which the exclusion act was but one indisputable sign.

Like Eastern Orthodoxy, Buddhism represents not a single strand or "denomination" but several liturgical and national traditions. Zen Buddhism, of Japanese origin, with its focus on meditation and artistic simplicity demonstrated an appeal as part of a philosophical and religious counterculture in the West. The Japanese Buddhist scholar D.T. Suzuki (1870–1966) moved from Japan to La Salle, Illinois, in 1897, becoming a leading translator and popularizer of Zen Buddhism in the English-speaking world over the next half century. While Zen gradually took on a bohemian cachet, many other schools of Japanese Buddhism flourished both in the Hawaiian Islands and along the West Coast of the United States. Buddhist traditions from China, Korea, Vietnam, Tibet, and other Asian countries also made their appearance in America, some more obviously in the decades after World War II.

Hinduism, closely identified with the culture of India, did not prove as exportable or missionary minded as Buddhism. Nevertheless, a kind of

76. Zen Buddhism, mediated through such intellectuals as D. T. Suzuki, was among the leading strands of Buddhism to garner converts and seekers in the United States. Here a Zen Buddhist teacher encourages proper posture and concentration. *Zen Center of Los Angeles*

universalistic or Westernized Hinduism did enter the United States following the World's Parliament of Religions in 1893. Swami Vivekananda (1863–1902) established a local chapter of the Vedanta Society in New York City in 1894, and in 1920 Swami Yogananda (1893–1952) moved to the United States and began a ministry that led to the establishment of Self-Realization Fellowships around the country. This kind of Hinduism, a hybrid of Indian philosophy and American self-help, appealed not so much to recent immigrants as to Euro-Americans intrigued by the wisdom of such Hindu literature as the Upanishads. On a smaller scale, Confucianism and Taoism from China as well as Shinto from Japan found footholds in the United States, with the West Coast again predominating. As racism somewhat diminished and as the claims to religious liberty were more assertively pressed by different Asian groups, the buds of an ever-broadening religious pluralism became evident to all, and these burst into full bloom after 1965.

Religious organizations of all kinds and from all countries generally enjoyed a period of steady growth from the end of the nineteenth century to the middle of the twentieth. That growth was a result of immigration, population increase throughout the nation, and a growing cultural readiness (even eagerness) to identify with a religious body. But total growth could be deceptive. For in the very midst of statistics that seemed to move ever upward and onward, recrimination and strife weakened religion's voice or, perhaps better, raised the noise level of many competing voices.

STRUGGLES AND SCHISMS

A dramatic heresy trial held in the final decade of the nineteenth century pointed to troubled decades ahead in the twentieth. Charles A. Briggs (1841–1912), appointed in 1891 as professor of biblical theology at Union Theological Seminary, New York City, was charged by the Presbyterian Church "with teaching that errors may have existed in the original text of the Holy Scripture." A Presbyterian himself, Briggs was brought to trial in 1893, where he was given an opportunity to defend himself. In his reply to the charges, Briggs explained, "The only errors I have found or ever recognized in Holy Scripture have been beyond the range of faith and practice, and therefore they do not impair the infallibility of Holy Scripture as a rule of faith and practice." This answer was judged to be unsatisfactory. It was enough that Briggs failed to declare scripture to be without error of any kind, "inerrant." Found guilty of violating the essential standards of the Presbyterian Church, he was dismissed from the New York Presbytery. He was not dismissed from the seminary, however, but continued to teach there until his death in 1912.

What happened in the 1890s in a single denomination was duplicated many times over in other denominations and, indeed, again within Presbyterianism itself. The struggle is commonly identified through such labels as *fundamentalism* on one side and *modernism* on the other. The intellectual and theological issues underlying these labels will be more fully discussed in the following chapter, but the ecclesiastical turmoil deserves consideration here. As in the Briggs trial, the issue often turned narrowly on attitudes toward the Bible, but the questions more broadly related to attitudes toward the modern world at large. And in this broader sense the controversy was reflected in Catholicism and Judaism no less than in Protestantism.

In the sixteenth-century Reformation, Martin Luther and other Protestant leaders regarded the role of tradition (the teachings and authority of the medieval Church) as being less significant than the voice of scripture. To reform the Church, they argued, one must take scripture most seriously, using it to correct tradition and to purify faith. *Sola scriptura*, that is, scripture alone and above all else, became the watchword of Protestantism. It is not surprising, therefore, that when scripture itself came under scrutiny (through new manuscript and archaeological discoveries and through new historical and literary techniques), Protestantism would suffer most severely. And so it did, as heresy trials multiplied, churches quarreled, seminaries struggled to survive, and denominations divided.

In the first third of the twentieth century, the three Protestant groups most severely torn by fundamentalist-modernist issues were the Presbyterians, the Northern Baptists, and the Disciples of Christ. Other bodies did not escape unscathed but did escape without enduring schism. Episcopalians, for example, had their heresy trial early in the twentieth century, as Algernon Crapsey (1847–1927) was charged with being unfaithful to that church's historic creeds; found guilty in 1906, he was deposed from the priesthood. Methodists, drained of many of their most ardent evangelicals through the Holiness churches, weathered the storm somewhat better, though not without charges and countercharges hurled by liberals and conservatives alike in the 1920s and 1930s. The Dutch Reformed suffered schism in the late nineteenth century, though this was related more to immigration patterns and disputes over the right of members to join secret organizations such as the Masons. In 1890 the Christian Reformed Church began its ecclesiastical life apart from the older parental body, the Reformed Church in America. Finally, Lutherans, still dispersed in many ethnic enclaves, escaped the harshest aspect of the quarrels until much later in the twentieth century.

Presbyterians found that the Briggs trial settled very little. Other trials followed, as did other attempts to define precisely the boundaries of Presbyterian orthodoxy. In 1910 the General Assembly emphasized five "fundamentals" that should not be compromised in any way: the inerrancy of

Scripture; the virgin birth of Christ; his vicarious atonement (that is, substituting his death for the eternal punishment of others); his bodily resurrection; and the reality of his biblically recorded miracles. Though leading liberals such as Arthur C. McGiffert (1861–1933) and Harry Emerson Fosdick (1878–1969) came under heavy attack, the denomination as a whole rejected the fundamentalist stance. In 1929, for example, leaders managed to pull Princeton Theological Seminary away from the control of the most conservative elements within the church. In the 1930s some conservatives, concluding that they no longer had a doctrinally comfortable home within the Presbyterian Church in the U.S.A. (a largely northern body), withdrew to create competing smaller denominations. Under the leadership of the scholarly J. Gresham Machen (1881–1937), conservative forces drew lines that said in effect: here we stand; we will concede not another inch; we will love the modern world less and the ancient truths more.

Northern Baptists were even more riddled by dissension and strife, as the opposing sides struggled for the soul of the denomination. (Baptists, like Presbyterians, were still divided at this time into northern and southern sections.) In the 1920s fundamentalists and conservatives sought to impose creedal uniformity upon all those identified with the Northern Baptist Convention, while modernists and liberals resisted such efforts as contrary to the Baptist tradition of having no creed other than the Bible. In one sense, the liberals won since they maintained control of the denominational boards, seminaries, and agencies. Yet in other senses they lost as schisms weakened the larger body and as evangelical energies were siphoned off into other causes. In 1933 fifty congregations withdrew from the parent group to form the General Association of Regular Baptists; fifteen years later more disaffected members separated to form the Conservative Baptist Association of America. Numbering about 1.5 million in 1925, Northern Baptists remained at roughly that level of membership for the next half century. This was an era of growth—but also of schism and separation.

The Disciples of Christ, a frontier church that dreamed of reducing denominational divisions, ironically added even more labels to an already confusing situation. Early in the twentieth century the conservatives, who resisted many aspects of the creeping liberalism (as they perceived it), withdrew to create a new denomination, the Churches of Christ. These churches maintained a fiercely independent congregational polity: no denominational headquarters, no ecumenical participation with other religious bodies, no national programs or institutions or boards. They also held to the authority of the Bible in such a way as to resist any of the new interpretations or modifications becoming familiar in the fundamentalist-modernist contest. This conservative separation, however, was distinct from those among Presbyterians and Baptists in one visible respect: it had a clear geographical component. The Churches of Christ found their centers of strength in Tennessee, Arkansas, and Texas, while the Disciples of Christ continued to be the major faction in Missouri, Illinois, Indiana, Ohio, and Kentucky. In 1927 yet another division afflicted Alexander Campbell's movement, this group taking the name of the North American Christian Connection. Neither southern nor border state in makeup, this third group challenged the parent group more directly in its own home territory. The older Disciples of Christ group, it charged, had grown too fond of scholarship associated with the University of Chicago, too ready to surrender its denominational distinctives to a kind of undifferentiated Protestantism. Once again the cry of the schismatic was heard across the land: "Come out from among them, and be ye separate, saith the Lord" (2 Corinthians 6:17).

Protestants, however, were not alone in their concern about where the modern world was leading traditional and historic religion. Roman Catholic authorities in the Vatican found much of European biblical scholarship worrisome in the extreme. In 1893 Pope Leo XIII condemned that biblical study "dignified by the name of 'higher criticism'" as an "inept method." It "pretends to judge the origin, integrity, and authority of each book from internal indications alone," without paying any attention to the views of the early church fathers or to the teaching authority of the Roman church itself. Then in 1907 Pope Pius X in a long letter used the very word *modernism* in order to make clear that it was heretical, dangerous, and beyond enduring. Modernists talk of progress, the pope said, even progress in doctrine and dogma, but what they call progress is, in fact, "corruption." "To the laws of evolution everything" for the modernists "is subject under penalty of death—dogma, church, worship, the books we revere as sacred, even faith itself." Modernists question everyone's wisdom but their own, the pope added; they understand scripture where all the doctors of the church have failed; they know "the needs of consciences better than anybody else"; they perceive the course of history where all others fail to do so. In fact, Pius X declared, though often rebuked and reprimanded, they continue undeterred, "masking an incredible audacity under a mock semblance of humility."

So sweeping was this 1907 condemnation that it left little room for maneuver or reinterpretation. Indeed, Pius X directed all bishops and archbishops to root out any hint or suggestion of modernism in their own jurisdictions, especially in the universities and seminaries. Some European scholars were disciplined, but in the American church no schismatic threat emerged. Yet while the Roman Catholic Church escaped the kind of external break that many Protestant bodies suffered, the former did not emerge unscathed. Catholic scholarship in general, but biblical scholarship in particular, for more than a generation found itself confined and thwarted by the severe prescriptions of this papal letter.

A later pope, however, in 1943 sounded a very different note as he promoted biblical scholarship of the most responsible sort. Pius XII specifically encouraged a study of the original biblical languages of Hebrew and Greek, along with closely associated ancient tongues, as well as a full attention to "the historical, archeological, philological, and other auxiliary sciences." It was quite wrong, the pope pointed out, to assume that all truth was already known so that "nothing remains to be added by the Catholic" scholar of today. "On the contrary, these our times have brought to light so many things, which call for a fresh investigation and new examination." What was "fresh" and "new" had won by the 1940s a place in Catholic circles that had been denied to it in the 1890s and early 1900s.

Judaism did its dividing, too, along similar though not identical lines. As with the Dutch Reformed, immigration patterns (country of origin, time period of emigration) shaped some of the disagreements. But many of the familiar issues were present as well: attitudes toward the Bible (specifically toward the Torah or Books of Moses), attitudes toward history and tradition, attitudes toward modern civilization and the notion of progress. A platform adopted by Reform Judaism in 1885 highlighted issues that in other contexts would be called modernist. The platform, for example, asserted that "modern discoveries of scientific researches . . . are not antagonistic to the doctrines of Judaism, the Bible reflecting the primitive ideas of its own age." The old Mosaic laws, moreover, were necessary as "a system of training" for Jews in ancient Palestine, but "today we accept as binding only the moral laws and maintain only such ceremonies as elevate and sanctify our lives." Judaism, like all religion that deserves to survive, must be "progressive," the platform declared, "ever striving to be in accord with the postulates of reason."

According to Orthodox Judaism and much Conservative Judaism as well in the early twentieth century, to embrace reason so readily, to be so willing to pick and choose among the demands of biblical law, was to love the modern world too much. Solomon Schechter (1850–1915), president of the Jewish Theological Seminary, argued in 1901 that Judaism was primarily not a progressive religion but "a revealed religion" that must continue to take the Bible very seriously. "Our great claim to the gratitude of mankind," Schechter asserted, "is that we gave to the world the word of God, the Bible. We have stormed heaven to snatch down this heavenly gift." And because that gift is so great, we have "allowed ourselves to be slain by the hundreds and thousands rather than become unfaithful to it." With passion and purpose, Schechter, speaking on behalf of many identified with Conservative Judaism, dedicated himself to drawing lines: this far and no further will we go in accommodating and compromising, in sacrificing hoary tradition upon the altar of trendy progress.

Most religious bodies in America suffered severe strain if not actual break during those decades, for the relative merits of the ancient and the recent seemed to demand daily evaluation or decision. Some groups escaped, such as the Eastern Orthodox communions, only because they had not yet absorbed enough of modernity's progressive assumptions to be challenged or threatened by them. Others, such as the Unitarians, escaped because they had long before made the critical cultural choices about embracing the changes of modernity. For the vast majority, however, not enough tranquillity prevailed to permit wild rejoicing over the growth in numbers that was taking place at the same time. To a society still troubled by racism, still unsure of the status of women, still anxious about assimilation and Americanization, religion in the first half of the twentieth century was forced to concentrate more and more on its own internal, badly bruised affairs. Faith, one might well have argued at such a time, led not to social stability and order but to social unrest and disorder.

ECCLESIASTICAL AFTERMATH

In 1922 Harry Emerson Fosdick preached a sermon that captured wide attention across the country. In "Shall the Fundamentalists Win?" Fosdick sharpened the terms of debate as well as tried to put those acrimonious decades into some kind of historical perspective. Fosdick explained that the modernists had collectively demonstrated the virgin birth to be "no longer accepted as historic fact, the literal inerrancy of the Scriptures [to be] incredible, the second coming of Christ from the skies [to be] an outmoded phrasing of hope." Such candid comment did little to lower the level of acrimony, Fosdick later noted, for while he pleaded for goodwill, what he received was "an explosion of ill will, for over two years making headline news of a controversy that went the limit of truculence." But did the fundamentalists win?

A token victory of sorts was theirs in 1925 when a young high school

77. William Jennings Bryan, three-time candidate for the U.S. presidency, won another kind of fame as the leading force against the teaching of evolution. *Library of Congress*

biology teacher, John Thomas Scopes (1900–1970), was brought to trial in Dayton, Tennessee. In what remains the most famous trial in the entire fundamentalist-modernist contest, the civil courts took up the question of whether Scopes had violated a Tennessee law that prohibited "the teaching of the evolution theory in all the universities, normals [teacher training institutions], and all the public schools of Tennessee which are supported in whole or in part by the public school funds of the state." The issue had drama, of course, but the courtroom provided even more since the attorney for the prosecution was none other than three-time candidate for the presidency of the United States, William Jennings Bryan (1860–1925). The defense attorney, Clarence Darrow (1857–1938), though not quite such a public figure, was nonetheless widely known as an outstanding trial lawyer from Chicago. In the battles of the giants, Bryan versus Darrow, young Scopes almost dropped from view.

The courtroom may seem an odd place to settle an issue of the science curriculum in the schools, and indeed it is. But of course the issue was far broader than that since for so many the question was not state law but the authority of the Bible and the authority, thereby, of the churches not just in Tennessee but across the nation. The national press was present in force, alongside the infant radio industry. Bryan identified with clarity the breadth of the issues at stake. "This case," he said aptly, "is no longer local; the defendant ceases to play an important part." Then Bryan said, "The case has assumed the proportion of a battle royal between unbelief that attempts to speak through so-called science and the defenders of the Christian faith, speaking through the legislators of Tennessee." If the jury votes to acquit Scopes, then, Bryan argued, Christ is crucified all over again. "If the law is nullified, there will be rejoicing where God is repudiated, the Saviour scoffed at, and the Bible ridiculed." But on the other hand, if the law is upheld, then "millions of Christians will call you blessed."

The law was upheld, Scopes was fined one hundred dollars, and the country went on with its business: a nominal victory for fundamentalism. Nominal, because in much of the national press the town of Dayton was portrayed as a rural backwater, fundamentalism as a know-nothing absurdity, and the trial itself as part carnival and part farce. In the cultural struggle for the hearts and minds of Americans, fundamentalism's victory in 1925 was far less clear-cut. Indeed, liberalism retained control of most denominational seminaries and colleges, most publishing boards, most prestigious pulpits, and most endowed funds. Perhaps the Scopes trial was only a hollow victory for fundamentalism, but it was certainly not a defeat (as it has been popularly presented). Locked in a much longer struggle with modernism, fundamentalist forces moved on from Dayton to fight the next battle for the Bible against scientific materialism and scoffing unbelief. While leaders in evangelical circles gathered together new institutional resources for renewed campaigns, it was religious liberalism that looked tired and far less self-assured in the 1930s and 1940s. Would the social gospelers and modernist pastors be able to hold the hearts and minds of their own faithful in an age of secular rationality and managerial efficiency?

CHAPTER 14

Faith and Reason

In the first half of the twentieth century broad cultural shifts gradually moved religion away from its princely position of intellectual and ethical leadership in the nation. Increasingly, cultural rewards went to artists, novelists, and journalists, while bureaucratic expertise was accorded politicians, engineers, and social planners. Religion, of course, was not immune to the growing professionalization of the time, but the clergy as a profession steadily lost status in favor of physicians, lawyers, and scientists, among others. One simple measure of that loss was financial: the salaries of clergy fell far behind those of other professionals, not even matching those of most business and labor leaders or of many civil servants and academicians. Such slippage in the professional standing of the clergy only symbolized far more significant losses in cultural authority at large. These losses resulted in part from the growing institutional power of many other intellectual disciplines, but they were also a product of internal crises within modern religious thought itself.

PHILOSOPHY AND RELIGION

Traditionally the closest of allies, philosophers and theologians found themselves drawing apart in the twentieth century as each group pursued its own agenda. Many philosophers turned away from the larger metaphysical questions in which religion had a keen interest to narrower ones of linguistic analysis or symbolic logic that, to the theologian, often seemed irrelevant. Many theologians, on the other hand, continued to be bound by creedal loyalties and biblical precedents in a way that made fruitful dialogue with philosophy increasingly unproductive if not impossible.

John Dewey (1859–1952), without question the most influential American philosopher in the first half of the twentieth century, deliberately took as his goal the reconstruction of American society. In art, logic, politics, science, and education he influenced and reshaped intellectual debates in ways that defy precise measure. And he accomplished this reconstruction without much reference to religion except to explain how irrelevant most ancient religious answers had become to the newer ways of investigation and discovery. "Anthropology, history, and literary criticism have furnished," Dewey wrote in 1934, "a radically different version of the historic events and personages upon which Christian religions have built." So also biology and psychology, geology and astronomy challenged traditional religious points of view. But the principal issue, Dewey argued, was a quarrel not about the truth of this or that particular dogma or article of faith but about the only valid method modern intellectuals had come to accept for arriving at truth. Not by consulting sacred writings or ancient oracles, he explained, but by rational investigation and observable experiment do we come to fresh and significant understanding. Dewey's program was the Enlightenment celebration of reason over revelation triumphantly extended.

As an exponent of pragmatism (which he also often called instrumentalism), Dewey saw the universe as open-ended, not closed; he saw truth as something not given but discovered, not fixed but ever unfolding and enlarging. "For the educated man today," Dewey observed, "the final arbiter of all questions of fact, existence, and intellectual assent" are these scientific methods of investigation and verification. This was so dramatic a shift from religious ways of looking at the world that it constituted, in Dewey's view, nothing less than a "revolution." Disputes about "this and that piecemeal item of belief" were irrelevant; the point, he said, is what methods one accepts as leading to new truths, which will, in turn, lead to even more truths. "In this revolution, every defeat is a stimulus to renewed inquiry; every victory won is the open door to more discoveries, and every discovery is a new seed planted in the soil of intelligence, from which grow fresh plants with new fruits." The universe bubbles over with possibilities. To realize those possibilities, all that was necessary, Dewey believed, was for men and women to leave their outworn shells and with vigorous optimism fashion a finer future for all the world.

Outworn shells were represented, more often than not, by institutional religion, which to Dewey seemed more interested in defending truths already known than in seeking truths yet to be found. In Dewey's world of the future, a place for religious language and religious experience could still be found but only as churches surrendered "the whole notion of special truths that are religious by nature, together with the idea of peculiar avenues to such truths." Somehow, one must be able to separate religion from the idea of intellectual assent to some special doctrine, "even that of the existence of the God of theism." To take the place of these old and outmoded ideas, religious people can dedicate themselves, with faith and devotion, to that "one sure road of access to truth—the road of patient, cooperative inquiry operating by means of observation, experiment, record, and controlled reflection." Dewey did not think he was asking religion to give up much that mattered. For most theologians, however, what he called for was a total capitulation of religion to the demands of modernity.

Even more popular writers than Dewey carried similar messages in this same period of time. Walter Lippmann (1889–1974), for example, as a remarkably influential journalist and widely read author, convinced much of the literate American public that traditional religion was all washed up and finished. In *A Preface to Morals*, published in 1929, Lippmann explained that the old cultural cohesion had been dissolved by "the acids of modernity." Modern men and women have now become "brave and brilliant atheists who have defied the Methodist God," Lippmann wrote. Religious certainty, like the ocean floor, had given way to some momentous tidal shift, and nothing had yet replaced it. "Insofar as men have now lost their belief in a heavenly king," Lippmann observed, "they have to find some other ground for their moral choices than the revelation of his will." What that ground should be Lippmann was not sure, since for him even science failed to guarantee human dignity or offer sure promise of human destiny. One may turn, perhaps, to stoicism or humanism or objective detachment, but in any case one could no longer find strength in "leaning on the everlasting arms" of familiar faith. In subsequent books and regular newspaper columns, Lippmann continued his search for better certainties or at least "civilities" that would guide the society of which he was a part, but he would henceforth find neither certainty nor civility in American religion.

Not all philosophers, to be sure, dismissed traditional religion so swiftly and surely. Harvard professor William James (1842–1910), though also a pragmatist, found religious questions—and religious answers—to be significant and relevant. Such questions and answers did have consequences for human behavior, and anything that had consequences the true pragmatist could not ignore. In many major areas of life, faith "is one of the indispensable preliminary conditions" for reaching some goal; "faith creates its own verification," James concluded. Alfred North Whitehead (1861–1947), also of Harvard, did not dismiss the idea of God though he altered it to emphasize "the tender elements in the world, which slowly and in quietness operate by love." For Whitehead God was neither Aristotle's unmoved mover nor some kind of "ruling Caesar, or ruthless moralist." God moved by persuasion rather than by coercion, which was one reason, Whitehead pointed out, that the mills of the gods ground so slowly.

Despite the notable countercurrents of Whitehead's process philosophy, professional philosophizing by midcentury had clearly distanced itself from any intimate or supportive alliance with theology. Liberal religious thinkers tried to keep the bridges between faith and reason in good repair, but often in the process yielded so much to modern measures of rationality and critical methods of inquiry that any uniqueness of perspective that religion might claim seemed minimal. For their part, conservative religious thinkers kept pointing to the idolatry of modern presuppositions, to the liberal debasement of religious authority, all but forfeiting the hope of exercising intellectual leadership in wider cultural arenas. The breach between faith and reason was a serious one, though it was not without its healers.

SCIENCE AND RELIGION

Far better known in this period were the contests and conflicts between scientists and theologians, the Scopes trial being only a single if highly public example. From the point of view of theologians, science kept invading their territory, answering questions about the origin and purpose of the world, about the nature and destiny of humanity—questions that were fundamentally religious rather than scientific. From the point of view of scientists, theology blocked the pathways to knowledge, ruling the experiments of the laboratory as off limits, improper, and even dangerous. Each side saw the other as rude, ambitious, imperious, and uncompromising. Each side, to a degree, was right.

In the closing years of the nineteenth century leading theologians searched for accommodations with the growing authority and prestige of science. But in this searching they were often limited not only by their own religious convictions but also by the authorities of the churches with which they were identified. Roman Catholics, for example, found their church's face set strongly against Darwin, as James Cardinal Gibbons (1834–1921) pointed out that crude theories not in accord with revelation must be rejected. This was false science, he added, not true science, for between true science and religion no conflict is possible. "There is as much difference between true and false science, as there is between authority and despotism, liberty and license," the cardinal noted, and it was the church's duty to support one and resist the other. When the church sees the scientist "raise his profane hands and attempt to touch the temple of faith, she cries out, 'Thus far shalt thou go and no farther!'"

A few years later a Roman Catholic professor of physics at Notre Dame tried to suggest that Darwinism was not irreconcilable with Catholic dogma. In a book published in 1896 called *Evolution and Dogma*, John Augustus Zahm (1851–1921) explained that there can be theistic evolutionists just as there can be atheistic or agnostic evolutionists. And to one who believed in God, everything within Darwinism "is a part of a grand unity betokening an omnipotent Creator." God's hand, Zahm argued, may be seen in all of creation, from the lowest to the highest, and God's handiwork can be found in all of nature. "His power and goodness are disclosed in the beauteous crystalline form of the snowflake, in the delicate texture, fragrance and color of the rose, in the marvellous pencilings of the butterfly's wing." All these and more, Zahm concluded, "are pregnant with truths of the highest order." But Catholicism was not yet ready for this synthesis of new biology with old theology, and Zahm's book was denounced and withdrawn from further publication or circulation.

Protestants likewise were not ready to fully embrace evolution, the popular Brooklyn preacher, T. DeWitt Talmage (1832–1902), denouncing the idea as both "atheistic and absurd." In arguing that man came from beast, man was made more bestial. In arguing against immortality, the evolutionist destroyed all foundation of morality and purpose. "We all die alike—the cow, the horse, the sheep, the man, the reptile. Annihilation is the heaven of the evolutionist," Talmage asserted. His advice followed immediately: "From such a stenchful and damnable doctrine, turn away." Talmage acknowledged that he believed in a kind of evolution but one far different from that put forward by Charles Darwin. He believed, he wrote, in a "gracious and divine and heavenly evolution—evolution out of sin into holiness, out of grief into gladness, out of mortality into immortality, out of earth into heaven!"

While Talmage was pronouncing against evolution, another Brooklyn Protestant, Henry Ward Beecher (1813–1887), contended that the whole history of Christianity was itself an instance of natural evolution. In a series of sermons preached in 1885 Beecher argued that evolution was but another example of "the diversified unfolding of God's plans on earth." Certainly, the idea of evolution affected religion in general, Christianity in particular, Beecher agreed. But the effect was for good rather than ill, for evolution weeded out the base and inferior, making room for the good and the strong. "Theology and the Church are undergoing a process of evolution, towards perfection," Beecher declared, "changing upwards and for the better."

Brooklyn could not contain the conflict that spread across the country and across the denominations. The popular revivalist Billy Sunday (1862–1935) continued well into the twentieth century to denounce and ridicule "the bastard theory of evolution," winning wide approval from his audiences and even from several state legislatures. His near contemporary Lyman Abbott (1835–1922), on the other hand, reached even wider audiences through his editorial labors and many books designed to reconcile the teachings of Christianity with those of Darwin. In evolutionary doctrine we find support, Abbott wrote in 1915, for the view that "man is gradually emerging from an animal nature into a spiritual manhood." The Genesis account of creation was not the issue, Abbott asserted. "For the question whether God made the animal man by a mechanical process in an hour or by a process of growth continuing through centuries is quite immaterial to one who believes that into man God breathes a divine life." Just how and when such "breathing" occurred was a detail Abbott was prepared to leave to others.

If biology provided the battleground for the late nineteenth and early twentieth century (and again later in the twentieth), psychology, sociology, and anthropology also kept the fires of intellectual and theological controversy burning. The theories of Sigmund Freud (1856–1939) challenged traditional doctrines of sin and salvation, guilt and repentance, innocence and depravity. For Freud religion was a wishful illusion, for Karl Marx (1818–1883) an opiate that numbed the suffering of the masses, and for neither was religion a legitimate or effective means for dealing with the ills of the individual or of society. Religion was, in fact, responsible for a good many of those ills, both men argued. The sociology of the time rested on a positivism that dismissed all ideas not immediately derived from sense experience, with theology often viewed as a stage that humankind would inevitably outgrow—the sooner, the better. Anthropology raised questions of cultural relativism and openness to religious difference—questions that seemed to threaten the very truth, goodness, and superiority of Christian civilization. Both sociology and anthropology were seen as suggesting that any and all gods were little more than social productions functioning to order and maintain communities.

Once again, those religious leaders who tried to keep open a dialogue between theologians on the one hand and scientists and social scientists on the other often appeared all too ready to surrender the distinctiveness of their own traditions. And those who, like Billy Sunday, declared that no reconciliation between science and religion was ever possible abandoned any claim to cultural authority and simply fed the ridicule of those who had come to see religion as a benighted domain. Certainly, all along one could find middle-ground institutions, such as the Conference on Science, Philosophy, and Religion, first convened in 1939, but the sounds of theological warfare regularly drowned out such voices. As one fundamentalist champion declared, "Above all things I love peace, but next to peace I love a fight, and I believe the next best thing to peace is a theological fight."

THEOLOGICAL BATTLE STATIONS

Modernists and fundamentalists quarreled about more than who would run what agency, who would control what college, who would preach from what pulpit. They also argued about ideas. In one form or another the contest over ideas affected Catholicism and Judaism no less than Protestantism, and in one form or another that contest continues to the present day. In part, the issue was a perennial of all human life: How much of the past does one hold on to and honor? How much of the future does one adapt to and welcome? But rarely did the partisan proposals or protests appear in such simplified form.

Protestants debated both the future and the past: the future with respect to the Second Coming of Christ, the past with respect to biblical history and command. In the nineteenth century large numbers of Protestants from time to time had been caught up in heady expectations that the world would soon come to an end and that Christ would dramatically, visibly reappear to establish a Kingdom of God on earth in a new (or the old) Jerusalem. In the early twentieth century such views seemed outmoded to many who believed that the future was one of peace and progress, not of Armageddon (Revelation 16:16) and catastrophe. For these modernists, the Kingdom of God might indeed come, but if so it would come through the efforts of enlightened and energetic women and men working together for the greater good of the social whole. The Kingdom of God, on these terms, would come not because God had given up on an evil, warring world, but because God looked with pleasure and satisfaction upon what his sometimes erring children had managed to accomplish.

As many backed away from the notion of a visible Second Coming of Christ, other Protestants defended that proposition even more vigorously and in sometimes bewildering detail. After William Miller's "Great Disappointment" of the 1840s, few were willing to name a specific time or day for the Second Coming, but the notion that it would be soon, very soon, filled the air. Premillennialists (those who believed that Christ's coming would precede the thousand years of peace and plenty foretold in the book of Revelation) did not agree on all the details. One of the more pervasive manifestations of this premillennial point of view, dispensationalism, was associated with the Plymouth Brethren in England and, in America, with the name of Cyrus I. Scofield (1843–1921) and his enormously popular Scofield Reference Bible, which first appeared in 1909. Dispensationalism divided the world's history into seven ages or "dispensations," and humankind was now living in the sixth age, known as "Man Under Grace." This age will soon end with "the descent of the Lord from Heaven, when sleeping saints will be raised and, together with the believers then living, caught up 'to meet the Lord in the air' (1 Thessalonians 4:16, 17)." Then the seventh and final dispensation will follow, "Man Under the Personal Reign of Christ," and this, said Scofield, "is the period commonly called the Millennium." Christ "will reign over restored Israel and over the earth for one thousand years.... The seat of his power," Scofield added, "will be Jerusalem."

Premillennialism, whether of the dispensationalist variety or some other, was enormously popular in much of American Protestantism. It was the particular emphasis of the Jehovah's Witnesses, the Seventh-day Adventists, the International Church of the Foursquare Gospel founded by Aimee Semple McPherson (1890–1944) in 1927, Plymouth Brethren, and many more. But it was also present in much of more mainstream Protestantism, and this is where contests about the future became most heated and disruptive.

Shailer Mathews (1863–1941), Baptist professor at the University of Chicago and a leading modernist spokesman, confronted the issue directly and forcefully in 1917 in a brief tract titled "Will Christ Come Again?" His answer was no, in the sense that the premillennialists expected Jesus physically to return. Such a view, Mathews argued, misread history, misused the Bible, and misunderstood the spiritual nature of God. Premillennialists, said Mathews, deny "that God is capable of bringing about His victory by spiritual means." The God of the premillennialists cannot "save the world by spiritual means. In order to succeed He has to revert to physical brutality ... [and] miraculous militarism." Neither did the premillennialists represent the essence of Christian orthodoxy. According to Mathews, nothing like their views could be found in the

78. Evangelist Aimee Semple McPherson, founder of the International Church of the Foursquare Gospel, was a leading proponent of premillennialism. *Library of Congress*

fathers of the early church or the leaders of the Reformation. The premillennialist, said Mathews, demanded that the "Christian should give up intelligence and education in order to live the life of faith ... [and] forces men to choose between the universally accepted results of modern culture and diagrams from the Book of Daniel." But in another and more significant sense, Mathews argued, Christ will come again as "a spiritual presence, leading us through the Holy Spirit into all truth, regenerating men and institutions." Here was the real Kingdom of God on earth and the true victory in spiritual battle: "The triumph of the ideals of Jesus will come when the spirit of Jesus comes into human hearts."

For many, Mathews's spiritualized millennium was wholly unacceptable. It was, said another Baptist, Isaac M. Haldeman (1845–1933) of New York City, a terrible joke. In a direct response to Mathews, Haldeman said that he read the professor's tract "with amazement, with pity and with indignation." Professor Mathews's view of the millennium was "nothing less than a burlesque, a grotesque and dishonoring caricature of one of the most sacred, immense and initial subjects of Holy Writ." Arguing carefully from the biblical text and sometimes returning to the original Greek, Haldeman declared that Mathews contradicted the plain sense of scripture. He apparently regarded the New Testament, said Haldeman, as "nothing better today than a bundle of pre-Christian error." And insofar as "orthodoxy" was concerned, Haldeman replied that Christian history was full of testimony, especially in its earliest and "purest" years, of expectation regarding the Second Coming. For those so misguided as to believe that without direct divine intervention the world was getting better and the Kingdom of God was just around the corner, Haldeman had nothing but pity. Evil triumphs, not good; infidelity wins, not orthodoxy; spiritual and moral character deteriorates, not "evolves." So Haldeman in the midst of World War I concluded, "I am hoping and intensely praying for the return of the Lord in my day and generation to put an end to this suicide of nations, this butchery and blasting, solace the hearts that are breaking, hush the lamentation, wipe away the tears of wives, of mothers and orphans."

Similarly, Presbyterians, Methodists, Disciples of Christ, and others held stridently opposing views about the Second Coming. The visible return of Christ became for some a kind of single-issue theology, a litmus test of one's faithfulness as a Christian, one's loyalty as a church member. It became a leading "fundamental" within fundamentalism, a question to be pressed at the time for ordaining new clergy, a matter to be settled before calling a new pastor or hiring a new professor. And by no means was passionate dedication to the doctrine of the visible, imminent Second Coming a phenomenon associated chiefly with the period of World War I. In many circles the concern has continued unabated, one measure of premillennial popularity being the issuing of a New Scofield Reference Bible by Oxford University Press in 1967. Copies sold numbered in the millions.

Underlying this apparently rather narrow or specifically limited item of belief was a far broader concern: the authority of the Bible for this and all other matters of faith and morals. The Bible might even be a book of history, telling us when the world was created, or a book of science, telling us of the origins of humanity and races and of supernatural suspensions of natural law. In the first century of Christian history the test of orthodoxy was "What think ye of Christ?" In the twentieth century the test was "What think ye of the Bible?"

This test clearly underlay the Mathews-Haldeman clash described above. Mathews said that premillennialists misused and misunderstood the Bible, regarding every recorded belief of early Christians "as the teaching of the Bible." Logically, this must mean, Mathews wrote, that contemporary Christians must believe "in a flat earth, the perpetuation of slavery, the submission to rulers like Nero." There was, however, another and better way to use the Bible, Mathews added, a way sometimes called "historical" but that "might better be called the common sense way." Christians using their Bibles in this way know that "inspiration was progressive, accumulative, dependent upon and fitted to successive periods of human intelligence." Beliefs of the early Christians, for example, "can be understood only as they are studied in the light of the habits of thought prevalent in their times." That's just common sense.

Or was it nonsense? Haldeman opted strongly for the latter. "The truth is," Haldeman wrote, that "Professor Mathews and his school accept only that part of the Bible ... which agrees with their theory of world progress, the march of humanity to higher and better things." Mathews clearly denied that the Bible was and is "the complete and perfect Word of God." And this, Haldeman just as clearly recognized, was the central issue. "Here is where Professor Mathews and premillennialists confront each other. This is the firing line. This is the 'front.'" Furthermore, this casual attitude toward biblical authority, this loving attitude toward modernity, has "given us a class of ministers who might as well preach in the name of Buddha or Confucius as Christ." It would be as impossible, Haldeman concluded, for premillennialists to question any statement in the Bible, no matter how insignificant, as it would be for Mathews to believe it.

79. Modernists and fundamentalists squared off especially over the authority of the Bible and the place of critical scholarship, associated with Germany, in its interpretation. *Billy Graham Center Museum*

Mathews and Haldeman, however, were only single protagonists. Each represented constituencies far broader than the University of Chicago on the one hand and premillennialists on the other. For Protestantism throughout the twentieth century, "What think ye of the Bible?" was the question above all questions, the battle station that both drew and gave the greatest fire. In 1924 Harry Emerson Fosdick published a book titled *The Modern Use of the Bible.* Here he tried to summarize the results of modern biblical scholarship (linguistic, historical, archaeological) in a way that

80. Many fundamentalists were sure that making peace with theological liberals would spell the undoing of Christianity itself. *Billy Graham Center Museum*

the average Protestant churchgoer could understand and perhaps even welcome. Fosdick's point was that the Bible became even more meaningful, not less, more uplifting, not less, when one understood its different periods of development, its gradually accumulated insights. Now, as a result of all the new learning, "we can," Fosdick wrote, "trace the great ideas of Scripture in their development from their simple and elementary forms, when they first appear in the earliest writings, until they come to their full maturity in the latest books." We can follow any single idea, such as the idea of God, or any ethical precept, such as honor or love, said Fosdick, from its rudimentary beginnings to rich fulfillment. Modern critics, Fosdick noted, are constantly accused of "tearing the Book to pieces, of cutting out this or that." But the precise opposite is true, he asserted. "The new approach to the Bible once more integrates the Scriptures, saves us from our piecemeal treatment of them, and restores to us the whole book seen as a unified development from early and simple beginnings to a great conclusion."

Fosdick had his admirers but also his detractors, who saw in this "modernity" just another sly attempt to evade clear biblical demands. These critics also considered the very foundation of Protestant Christianity to be undermined in any questioning of the Bible's sufficiency and validity. The Bible, Charles Hodge of Princeton had long ago written, was the storehouse of all theology. Just as the biologist studied nature to gather facts and arrive at truth, so the theologian studied the Bible in precisely the same way. Congregationalist Reuben A. Torrey (1856–1928) in a large book called *What the Bible Teaches* (1898) made thousands of biblical propositions perfectly plain, scientifically precise, authoritatively required. The modernists, said Torrey, set the Bible aside in order to substitute what they think is demanded "by the modern evolutionary method of thought." The modernist really does not believe in the Bible at all, Torrey declared, but he has neither the intellectual honesty nor the moral courage to say so.

As a successor to Hodge at Princeton, J. Gresham Machen (1881–1937) agreed that modernism, rather than a more sophisticated version of Christianity, was no Christianity at all. It was a point made evident in the sharp juxtaposition in the title of one of his classic works, *Christianity and Liberalism* (1923). "In trying to remove from Christianity everything that could possibly be objected to in the name of science, in trying to bribe off the enemy by those concessions which the enemy most desires," Machen wrote, "the apologist has really abandoned what he started out to defend." The biblical critics and the modern liberal church, thought Machen, were primarily interested in defending contemporary culture, doing so under the guise of reforming and refining New Testament religion. But what they were really doing, Machen firmly believed, was undermining and destroying that "faith once delivered unto the saints."

Protestants felt strongly about ideas; they differed widely and sharply in their expectations for the future and in their understandings of the past. But Protestants were not alone in being torn by the tensions and novelties that modern scholarship had introduced into institutional religion. Roman Catholics, both European and American, confronted similar though not identical crises. Not as engaged in debate about the details of a Second Coming, Catholics did also face questions of progress, history, dogma, the sacred authority of the Bible, and the teaching authority of the church. They were not only surrounded by these debates, they were besieged by them.

For a hundred years or more the Roman Catholic Church in Europe had been thrown on the defensive: attacked during the French Revolution, abused by Napoleon, forced to retreat wherever monarchy was dethroned or weakened, robbed of its papal states, and reduced in its temporal power over and over again. Modernity was no great gift from heaven. Modernity, in fact, was a major mistake, as Pope Pius IX made clear in 1864 in his famous "Syllabus of Errors." By the time the twentieth century arrived, the church was no more relaxed about the political sufferings it had endured. When, to all these indignities, modern scholarship added its challenges to the dogmatic theology of the church, patience wore thin. In 1907 Pope Pius X summarily dismissed *moderism* as repugnant, as horridly misplaced secular learning

The new scholarship left nothing exempt, not even the Bible. For the modernists, the Bible was but a summary of experiences, instructive, to be sure, but nonetheless human experiences. We may ask of the liberals, Pius X said, "what then becomes of inspiration? Inspiration, they reply, is in no wise distinguished from that impulse which stimulates the believer to reveal the faith that is in him by words or writings. . . . It is something like that which happens in poetical inspiration." And if the Bible is only a summary of experience, the church, in the view of modernists, is nothing more than "collective conscience." If, moreover, the church's authority ultimately rests upon individual conscience, then the church must be subject to the conscience; that is, it must become more democratic. But even here, said the pope, modernists are not through with scandalizing and horrifying. They even hold that the state must "be separated from the Church, and the Catholic from the citizen." In fact, the pope asserted, the modernists behave like liberal Protestants and can hardly be distinguished from them.

One difference between Catholics and Protestants, liberal or conservative, however, was the Vatican's powerful authority not only to scorn modernism but to condemn it officially and uproot it. This the pope did in language as stern as it was explicit: all bishops, all heads of religious orders, all directors of schools and seminaries were to exercise the greatest vigilance in seeing that modernism be blotted out. With respect to administrators and professors at Catholic universities, "anyone who in any way is found to be tainted with Modernism is to be excluded without compunction from these offices, whether of government or of teaching, and those who already occupy them are to be removed." Pius X urged special caution concerning "those who show a love of novelty in history, archaeology, biblical exegesis" or a tendency to abandon or criticize the teachings of St. Thomas Aquinas, the "Angelic Doctor" of the thirteenth century. Every diocese, the pope added, shall have its "Council of Vigilance" with its appointed clergy to "watch most carefully for every trace and sign of Modernism both in publication and in teaching." Modernism for the Vatican was no innocent novelty to be tolerated with mild amusement; it was heresy to be fought against with every resource at the church's command.

In his anti-modernist encyclical in 1907, the pope had his eye more on Europe than America, for in the American church a full-fledged modernist was hardly to be found. What could be found, of course, were liberal Catholics arguing against conservative Catholics, Americanizing bishops contending with bishops who saw America as more the problem than the solution, world-affirming Catholics opposed to world-fleeing Catholics, Catholics who rejoiced in development and progress baffled by Catholics who rejoiced in neither. Such Catholic bishops in America as John Ireland (1838–1918) of St. Paul, Minnesota, and John Lancaster Spalding (1840–1916) of Peoria, Illinois, led the liberal forces, while such bishops as Michael A. Corrigan (1839–1902) of New York City and Bernard J. McQuaid (1823–1909) of Rochester led the opposing conservative ranks. The effect of the 1907 encyclical, however, was to shift the odds for victory heavily to the side of the conservatives. In the words of one Catholic historian, "In one fatal blow the Pope destroyed the budding renewal of Catholic theology." Catholics avoided the Protestant path of schism, but an artificial and enforced unity against modernism also extracted a high cost.

Within Judaism, concerns were similar but again not identical. There was no obsession with the Second Coming of Christ, of course, and no anxiety about the final authority of a centralized hierarchy. But broader underlying questions about science, cultural evolution, revelation, tradition, and the uneasy relationship between sacred and secular disturbed or divided the religious community of Jews as it had those of Protestants and Catholics. The Torah or Laws of Moses occupied a unique place of honor, and that uniqueness for a long time prevented a hearty embrace of biblical criticism by observant Jews, especially in the Conservative and Orthodox branches. Jews argued instead about the interpretations of Mosaic law, the commentaries on that law—about the Talmud (Babylonian or Palestinian), about the schools of Rabbi Shammai or Rabbi Hillel, about the Halakah (legal portions of Talmudic literature) and the Haggadah (nonlegal portions, including the ritual readings for the Passover meal). But in all of this the biblical Torah itself stood largely untouched until the twentieth century.

Under the auspices of the Jewish Publication Society, and after many years of intensive labor, a new translation of Hebrew Scriptures appeared in 1917. Long dependent upon Christian translations into English (except for the early work of Isaac Leeser), the American Jewish community now had its own "official" Bible, one that testified to the growing importance of the Jewish presence in the United States as well as to the maturing biblical scholarship of many of the nation's Jews. As the preface to this translation declared, "We have grown under providence both in numbers and in importance, so that we constitute now the greatest section of Israel living in a single country outside of Russia." It was only fitting, therefore, the translators added, that "we have applied ourselves to the sacred task of preparing a new translation of the Bible into the English language, which, unless all signs fail, is to become the current speech of the majority of the children of Israel."

The next several decades, representing a period of great biblical activity among both Protestants (the Revised Standard Version appeared in 1952) and Roman Catholics (the New American Bible appeared in 1970), saw Jewish scholars also busy with yet another translation that would take advantage of the newest manuscript discoveries and other developments in biblical scholarship. In 1962 a fresh translation of the Books of Moses was published under the title *The Torah: A New Translation of the Holy Scriptures According to the Masoretic Text.* Twenty years later the whole of Hebrew Scriptures appeared in a precedent-setting translation that testified to the scholarly maturity of American Jewry, in which Reform, Conservative, and Orthodox scholars cooperated and also worked closely with biblical scholars in Israel. Biblical scholarship proved among America's Jews to be not so much an instance of division and bitter dispute as a matter of cooperation and a point of pride.

Of course, institutional divisions within Judaism persisted. Reform Judaism continued to be the group most comfortable with modernity, though the Columbus Platform of 1937 was less optimistic about progress and more sympathetic to tradition than the 1885 Pittsburgh Platform had been. Conservative Judaism, stressing the importance of a moderate traditionalism (for example, the continued importance of studying Hebrew or the embrace of dietary laws in the home), persisted as a kind of middle ground between Reform and Orthodoxy. (As one Jewish observer quipped, "On the one hand, you had Reform. On the other, you had

Orthodox. And on both hands—the Conservatives.") Orthodox Judaism, the official religion of the state of Israel, viewed itself in America not so much as an "American religion" but as the steady, uncompromising continuation of Jewish practice and belief across the centuries. To some degree, therefore, it intentionally isolated itself from the temptations of acculturation and the seductions of modernity. As a consequence it also remained far less visible outside such major centers of Jewish population as New York City and Los Angeles. The infusion of a strongly pietistic element among the Orthodox, known as Hasidism, drew greater public notice to it, especially as portrayed in the popular writings of the novelist Chaim Potok.

America in the twentieth century, moreover, introduced yet another stream into the Jewish landscape: Reconstructionism. The work chiefly of Mordecai Kaplan (1881–1983), whose great opus was *Judaism as a Civilization* (1934), Reconstructionism argued that Judaism was more a form of community than it was a revealed religion. The peoplehood of Israel was thus more important than the supernatural emphases of the Torah. The function of religion was more social than theological for Kaplan, more a matter of historical identity than beliefs about God. And he hoped his school of thought would have particular appeal for the many Jews in America who were not affiliated with any temple or synagogue yet who still found strength and support in their sense of belonging to an ancient tradition and to an identifiable people.

The peculiarly American character of Reconstructionism is evident in its very first platform issued in 1935, where this statement appears: "As American Jews we give first place in our lives to the American civilization which we share in common with our fellow Americans, and we seek to develop our Jewish heritage to the maximum degree consonant with the best in American life." If that sounded to some more like sociology than theology, Kaplan saw no reason for concern. The important issue, he argued, was "not what idea of God the individual Jew must hold," but to what common purpose "the Jews as a people are willing to be committed." Reconstructionism, while remaining a relatively small movement compared to the Reform-Conservative-Orthodox triumvirate, was a notable parallel to the modernism found among both Protestants and Catholics. Pragmatic and humanistic, Kaplan's Reconstructionism imagined a Judaism thoroughly at home in the scientific, pluralistic, and free society of the modern United States. Yet it was also a Judaism that continued to celebrate, in quite deliberate ways, the vibrancy of ethnic particularity and solidarity.

THEOLOGICAL AFTERMATH

One must keep in mind that the labels *modernist* and *fundamentalist* represent special types more than they do the full-orbed reality that is American religion. At no time in the twentieth century was it possible to classify the majority of church and synagogue members as belonging to either one or the other of these categories. Where did everyone else fit? Probably somewhere in the middle, attracted now to aspects of one position then to aspects of another but never wholly aligned with either party. The two movements themselves, moreover, did not remain static but underwent shifting emphases and even internal divisions. After the bitterest battles in the first third of the century, modernists gradually lost their confidence in progress and their uncritical fondness for the surrounding culture. Similarly, fundamentalists lost their belligerence with respect to other Christians and their hostility to all forms of "applied Christianity."

Within Protestantism a broad coalition of conservatives, preferring to call themselves evangelicals, joined together in 1942 to form the National Association of Evangelicals. As one of the leaders of the new coalition stated, we must "be wise and gracious enough to recognize that there are differences of doctrine among Bible-believing members of the Church of Jesus Christ upon which there is little hope that we will see eye to eye." Nonetheless, "profitless controversy over issues which are relatively unimportant" should not prevent a greater degree of cooperation and fellowship among the more than one million members entering into the association. In the following decade a leading evangelical scholar, Carl F. H. Henry, who served as the founding editor of *Christianity Today*, called for abandoning the old narrow legalism and at the same time embracing the social implications of Christianity. The Christian religion, Henry pointed out in 1957, "is by no means the social gospel of modernism." But neither was it the mere "personal abstinence from dubious social externals" so dear to the hearts of earlier fundamentalists. "Christian ethics probes deeper," Henry observed, and the new evangelicals must apply "the gospel message" to "marriage and the home, labor and economics, politics and the state, culture and the arts, in fact, [to] every sphere of life."

On the liberal side, theologian Reinhold Niebuhr (1892–1971) pulled sharply away from the naive optimism of an earlier generation. One cannot maintain, Niebuhr argued, that the progress of humankind is steadily upward or that, in the words of a popular cliché of the 1920s, "every day in every way we are getting better and better." One can hold such a

81. Reinhold Niebuhr, shown here in 1963, had retired by that time from Union Theological Seminary in New York City but not from the theological fray. *Religious News Service*

position, Niebuhr declared, only by ignoring reality. The reality is that human nature is perverse and that society tends toward evil. Science, sanitation, and education cannot, will not, produce a perfect world, Niebuhr asserted; neither will a sentimental Protestantism that refuses to confront the undeniable realities of war, greed, exploitation, prejudice, poverty, cruelty, injustice, and lust. We tell people to love and imitate Christ, assuring them, Niebuhr wrote, that all will be well. But Christ loved, and all was not well: he ended up on a cross. So a kind of "Christian realism" is called for, a realism that recognizes that the highest goal among nations is justice not love; that the means to achieve justice sometimes require force and violence. Niebuhr preferred to speak of human depravity, not nobility; of society's folly, not its promise of progress. By midcentury, neither modernism nor fundamentalism much resembled what each had been a generation before, the former having been chastened by a neoorthodox realism and the latter having readied itself for a neoevangelical rebirth.

Niebuhr, a member of a small Protestant denomination called the Evangelical and Reformed Church (which later merged into the United Church of Christ), transcended denominationalism, transcended Protestantism, transcended even the whole field of religion as he shaped the thinking of political scientists, statesmen, journalists, diplomats, and a host of others. Similarly, a Jewish refugee from Germany and Poland, Abraham Joshua Heschel (1907–1973), moved beyond the confines of organized Judaism to offer both comfort and rebuke to modern civilization as a whole. Arriving in the United States in 1940, Heschel became a professor at Jewish Theological Seminary in 1945 but soon found himself speaking to audiences extending well beyond his own students. Lecturing across the country, he contended, "The fate of mankind depends upon the realization that the distinction between good and evil, right and wrong, is superior to all other distinctions." Religion, particularly biblical religion, can assist humanity in making those critical distinctions. We move, wrote Heschel in 1951, like the heavenly bodies in ellipses, not circles. "We are attached to two centers: to the focus of our self and to the focus of God." The tragedy of modern civilization, said Heschel, is that "the vision of the sacred has all but died in the soul of man." Modernity's secular shortcomings had found another clear-eyed critic.

Heschel himself was an activist in the battle against evil: in Selma identifying with the cause of civil rights, in Washington decrying the folly of America's imperial ambitions. The soul of the individual as well as of the nation and of the world became Heschel's consuming concern. If we lose our sense of the sacred, he said, it is as though we have lost the light from the sun. The world stands or falls upon not its wealth or its power but its spiritual well-being. "All our life," he wrote, "hangs by a thread—the faithfulness of man to the concern of God." Moreover, everything worthwhile in what we call "civilization" as opposed to barbarism and chaos "depends upon man's sense for the sacredness of life, upon reverence for this spark of light in the darkness of selfishness." Once "we permit this spark to be quenched, the darkness falls upon us like thunder." Heschel liked to tell the story of the blacksmith who learned everything there was to know about his trade, all the skills, all the tools, all the techniques of the true artisan. Only one thing he failed to learn: how to kindle a spark.

Heschel kindled many sparks in his lifetime. One of them was the light he shed on the reuniting of theology and philosophy, religious practice and serious scholarship, in modern American society. "Judaism teaches

82. Rabbi Abraham J. Heschel addressed the problems of modern Judaism in particular and of modern civilization in general. *Library of the Jewish Theological Seminary of America*

that God can be found in books," he said, and he himself pursued that possibility with vigor. In the process he renewed the passion of many Americans for attaining a life of both learning and prayer.

If secular acids were eating away at religion's viability in the modern world, they did not appear to be eating very deeply into American culture as a whole. Even archcritics of religion, such as the acerbic journalist H. L. Mencken (1880–1956), had to admit that the modern crisis of belief did not affect that many Americans. For himself, he knew the dark, existentialist truth—that it was the fate of men and women "to live absurdly, flogged by categorical imperatives of their own shallow imagining, and to die insanely, grasping for hands that are not there." If religion's hold on modern society, as Mencken still avowed, was waning, "this lessening is to be seen only in relatively small minorities, admittedly damned." Sad to say, "the great masses of people," Mencken concluded, were doomed to religion's false hopes and clerical bamboozlements. The recurring tones of Enlightenment skepticism were sounded loudly in the early to mid–twentieth century, but to the chagrin of religion's critics, from Dewey to Mencken, religious bodies kept renewing and multiplying themselves. Indeed, after World War II the membership rolls of the churches and synagogues only hit new highs, giving those who dreamed of secularization further cause to shake their heads.

Suggested Reading for Part 3: Modern Prospects from Cityscapes to Bible Battles

Jay P. Dolan has provided an enduring account of immigration and its impact on American Catholicism in his *The Immigrant Church: New York's Irish and German Catholics, 1815–1865* (Baltimore, 1975); but also see his general survey, *The American Catholic Experience: A History from Colonial Times to the Present* (Garden City, NY, 1985). For an ethnographic feel of the texture of immigrant religious life in New York, see Robert Anthony Orsi, *The Madonna of 115th Street: Faith and Community in Italian Harlem, 1880–1950* (New Haven, 1985), and, on Boston, see Paula M. Kane, *Separatism and Subculture: Boston Catholicism, 1900–1920* (Chapel Hill, 1994). For an excellent examination of the relations between Catholics and African Americans in their mutual convergence in the cities, see John T. McGreevy, *Parish Boundaries: The Catholic Encounter with Race in the Twentieth-Century Urban North* (Chicago, 1996). Also of particular note is the varied essay collection edited by Robert Orsi, *Gods of the City: Religion and the American Urban Landscape* (Bloomington, IN, 1999). For an excellent and accessible survey on Eastern Orthodoxy, see John H. Erickson, *Orthodox Christians in America* (New York, 1999).

A highly lucid presentation of Judaism's major denominational groupings can be found in Marc Lee Raphael, *Profiles in American Judaism: The Reform, Conservative, Orthodox, and Reconstructionist Traditions in Historical Perspective* (San Francisco, 1984). Arnold M. Eisen's *The Chosen People in America: A Study in Jewish Religious Ideology* (Bloomington, IN, 1983) is excellent on developments in American Jewish thought, and Jenna Weisman Joselit's *The Wonders of America: Reinventing Jewish Culture, 1880–1950*

(New York, 1994) is richly rewarding on holidays, home life, food obser-
vances, rites of passage, and everyday religion.

The bigoted opposition that new immigrants so often faced is a story
told authoritatively in John Higham's *Strangers in the Land: Patterns of
American Nativism, 1860–1925* (New Brunswick, 1955). For wider exploration of how insider-outsider distinctions in religion were constructed
and used in American culture, see R. Laurence Moore, *Religious Outsiders
and the Making of Americans* (New York, 1986). See as well Robert N. Bellah
and Frederick E. Greenspahn, eds., *Uncivil Religion: Interreligious Hostility
in America* (New York, 1987).

On the social dimensions of Christianity in the modern period, many of
the older works remain standards. See, for example, Henry F. May, *Protestant Churches and Industrial America* (New York, 1949), Robert T. Handy,
ed., *The Social Gospel in America, 1870–1920* (New York, 1966), and Aaron I.
Abell, *American Catholicism and Social Action* (New York, 1960). Two more
recent works of note are Susan Curtis, *A Consuming Faith: The Social Gospel
and Modern American Culture* (Baltimore, 1991), and Eugene McCarraher,
Christian Critics: Religion and the Impasse in Modern American Social Thought
(Ithaca, 2000).

There are several good biographies of religious activists and politically
minded theologians, including Ruth Bordin's *Frances Willard* (Chapel Hill,
1986); Timothy Miller's *Following in His Steps: A Biography of Charles M.
Sheldon* (Knoxville, 1987); Fran Grace's *Carry A. Nation: Retelling the Life*
(Bloomington, IN, 2001); William D. Miller's *A Harsh and Dreadful Love:
Dorothy Day and the Catholic Worker Movement* (New York, 1973); and
Richard Wightman Fox's *Reinhold Niebuhr* (New York, 1985). For social
reform, politics, and gender in African American religious life, see Evelyn
Brooks Higginbotham, *Righteous Discontent: The Women's Movement in the
Black Baptist Church, 1880–1920* (Cambridge, MA, 1993); Judith Weisenfeld,
*African American Women and Christian Activism: New York's Black YWCA,
1905–1945* (Cambridge, MA, 1997); and Ralph E. Luker, *The Social Gospel in
Black and White: American Racial Reform, 1885–1912* (Chapel Hill, 1991).

A vibrant and compelling history of the Salvation Army is provided by
Diane Winston, *Red-Hot and Righteous: The Urban Religion of the Salvation
Army* (Cambridge, MA, 1999). Winston's attention to the impact of mod-
ern commercial culture on religion (and vice versa) is complemented by
William Leach, *Land of Desire: Merchants, Power and the Rise of a New Ameri-
can Culture* (New York, 1993); R. Laurence Moore, *Selling God: American
Religion in the Marketplace of Culture* (New York, 1994); Leigh Eric Schmidt,

Consumer Rites: The Buying and Selling of American Holidays (Princeton, 1995); and Alexis McCrossen, *Holy Day, Holiday: The American Sunday* (Ithaca, 2000). One of the most penetrating analyses of the religious and cultural discontents of the period remains T. J. Jackson Lears's *No Place of Grace: Antimodernism and the Transformation of American Culture, 1880–1920* (New York, 1981). For the twists and turns in Protestant missionary thought, the best treatment is that of William R. Hutchison, *Errand into the World: American Protestant Thought and Foreign Missions* (Chicago, 1987); and on millennialist turns of thought, see James H. Moorhead, *World Without End: Mainstream American Protestant Visions of the Last Things, 1880–1925* (Bloomington, IN, 1999).

The Protestant struggles early in the twentieth century may best be followed through the analytical efforts of two authors: William R. Hutchison, *The Modernist Impulse in American Protestantism* (Cambridge, MA, 1976; rev. ed., Durham, 1992), and George M. Marsden, *Fundamentalism and American Culture: The Shaping of Twentieth-Century Evangelicalism, 1870–1925* (New York, 1980). One of the major Bible brouhahas of the era is examined with particular clarity and insight in Peter J. Thuesen's *In Discordance with the Scriptures: American Protestant Battles over Translating the Bible* (New York, 1999). Between or beyond the fundamentalist-modernist divide were the Pentecostals, and their early history is handled with aplomb in Grant Wacker's *Heaven Below: Early Pentecostals and American Culture* (Cambridge, MA, 2001). See as well Edith L. Blumhofer, Russell P. Spittler, and Grant A. Wacker, eds., *Pentecostal Currents in American Protestantism* (Urbana, 1999). Catholic tensions in the same period are explicated in Robert Cross, *The Emergence of Liberal Catholicism in America* (Cambridge, MA, 1958), and R. Scott Appleby, *"Church and Age Unite!": The Modernist Impulse in American Catholicism* (Notre Dame, 1992).

The intellectual and theological climate responsible for modernity in its many manifestations has understandably received considerable attention. On the philosophical side, useful analyses include these studies: Bruce Kuklick, *The Rise of American Philosophy, Cambridge, Massachusetts, 1860–1930* (New Haven, 1977), as well as his later book, *Churchmen and Philosophers: From Jonathan Edwards to John Dewey* (New Haven, 1985); and John Edwin Smith, *The Spirit of American Philosophy* (New York, 1963). For broad historical perspective on the modern crisis of belief in American culture, see James Turner, *Without God, Without Creed: The Origins of Unbelief in America* (Baltimore, 1985). Also highly illuminating is David A. Hollinger, *Science, Jews, and Secular Culture: Studies in Mid-Twentieth-Century American Intellectual History* (Princeton, 1996).

The struggles between science and religion have attracted much attention. Recent examinations include David C. Lindberg and Ronald L. Numbers, eds., *God and Nature: Historical Essays on the Encounter Between Christianity and Science* (Berkeley, 1987); Ronald L. Numbers, *Darwinism Comes to America* (Cambridge, MA, 1998); Edward J. Larson, *Summer for the Gods: The Scopes Trial and America's Continuing Debate over Science and Religion* (New York, 1997); James Gilbert, *Redeeming Culture: American Religion in an Age of Science* (Chicago, 1997); Rick Ostrander, *The Life of Prayer in a World of Science: Protestants, Prayer, and American Culture, 1870–1930* (New York, 2000); David N. Livingstone, D. G. Hart, and Mark A. Noll, eds., *Evangelicals and Science in Historical Perspective* (New York, 1999); and Robert Bruce Mullin, *Miracles and the Modern Religious Imagination* (New Haven, 1996).

Part 4

RELIGIOUS TRANSFORMATION
FROM WORLD WAR II TO
THE NEW MILLENNIUM

CHAPTER 15

War, Peace, and Religious Renewal

In the 1940s and 1950s both the nation and its religious institutions endured the trials of war and the fears of fascism and communism. Churches, synagogues, and other religious organizations found themselves tested by brutal revelations of humanity's inhumanity, by awesome new technological powers of destruction, and by temptations to become instruments or pawns in the Cold War. Amid the darkness, however, signs of renewal and resurgence could be seen—from Billy Graham crusades to the feel-good gospels of postwar suburbia to innovative movements of liturgical reform. Renewal and transformation became especially powerful themes among America's Roman Catholics in the early 1960s.

WARS AROUND THE WORLD

Immediately following the surprise Japanese attack on Pearl Harbor on December 7, 1941, the United States entered a war that had already engaged most of Europe since 1939 and much of Asia since the Japanese invasion of Manchuria in 1931. In the midst of America's involvement in the war, organized religion followed two broad approaches. In the first, ministries of faith offered consolation, guidance, inspiration, and a wide variety of war-related services. Bandages wrapped, food and medical supplies sent, entertainment and housing provided, Bibles dispatched, chaplains appointed, plaques honoring the dead dedicated—these and countless other activities characterized a good part of religion's wartime mission.

More than 8,000 ministers, rabbis, and priests served as chaplains in World War II. Confessions were heard within earshot of the noise of battle, hymns were sung above the roar of the battleship's throbbing engines,

83. Pictured here is an army chaplain serving at Fort Bragg, North Carolina, during World War II, one of thousands of ministers, rabbis, and priests to serve in the military during that conflict. *Library of Congress*

sermons were preached in arctic snow and tropical heat, communion was offered in frontline hospitals and last rites within frontline trenches. Hasty services gave some dignity and limited solace to burials in often unmarked graves or in trackless seas. Chaplains lived in tents, trailers, troop ships, and open fields. Wherever combat soldiers and sailors moved, the uniformed clergy lived or died alongside. The often heroic sacrifice of military chaplains during the conduct of the war was personi- fied (and immortalized) by the four who died on the *Dorchester* when it was torpedoed by a German U-boat in 1943. Standing arm in arm as the ship slowly sank into the Atlantic Ocean, the four men—two Protestants, a Catholic, and a Jew—died, along with nearly 700 American soldiers, after giving up their own life jackets in an attempt to save others.

A second approach threw religion's weight on the side of softening war's inevitable cruelties and severe dislocations. Even before the United States entered the conflict, Quakers and others supported humanitarian efforts abroad in an endeavor to clothe the needy, feed the hungry, and minister to the sick. Quaker representatives in France in 1940 reported that it was "heartbreaking to be charged with the responsibilities of deciding who shall eat and who shall go hungry, who shall have clothing and who shall have none. Dispensing charity in France today means exercising the power of life or death over one's fellows." How, a person on the scene anxiously asked, "does one do it and retain his sanity?" But Quakers and others working with the American Friends Service Committee did do it before, during, and after the war. In 1947 the Nobel Peace Prize Committee agreed that the American Friends Service Committee itself should be honored for service rendered all over Europe and in China and India as well.

The global refugee problem was more severe than any had anticipated or than any could deal with satisfactorily. But the United States had its own refugee problem following Pearl Harbor. On the stated grounds of national security but the unstated grounds of persisting racism, the nation decided that most of the Japanese on the West Coast needed to be moved to "relocation centers" in Idaho or Arizona or elsewhere in the inland West. More than 100,000 Japanese, the majority of whom were American citizens, sat out the war behind barbed wire and under armed guard, wondering about the merits of their citizenship in a country that continued to see so much through race-colored glasses. The churches could provide some help during this long indignity but not much. Finally, over forty years later, the nation issued an official apology to all Japanese Americans for its wartime behavior, an apology that included financial reparation to those whose lives had been so abruptly interrupted, whose occupations and property had been so unnecessarily sacrificed.

Pacifism, too, had been sacrificed in the course of World War II. Although the 1930s had seen an unprecedented growth in pacifist sentiment among the churches, these views along with isolationist "Keep America Out of the War" campaigns quickly withered after 1941. Yet many religious groups were determined not to be as uncritically supportive of this (or any) war as they had been of World War I. War was evil, though sometimes a necessary evil. And "just war" theories had to contend with unprecedented saturation bombings of heavily populated areas, with propaganda machines of a larger magnitude than the world had ever known, with cruelties and tortures that could under no circumstances be justified. Many church members agreed that the war could be supported only on the grounds that such injustices might thereby be brought more quickly to an end.

Pacifism, of course, did not wholly disappear. Mennonites, Church of the Brethren, and Quakers helped to run Civilian Public Service camps where conscientious objectors could render alternative service, especially in forestry, agriculture, and environmental protection. The privilege of claiming "CO" status was at this time still limited to young men who "by religious training and belief" objected to all warfare. For most draft boards, this meant limitation to those who belonged to such historic peace churches as those named above. But even within these churches, the claims of conscience were by no means exercised uniformly, many choosing alternative service, others agreeing to serve in the armed forces. Seventh-day Adventists provided a significant number of objectors during this war, as did even some mainline Protestant denominations. Jehovah's Witnesses fell into a special category, creating consternation among draft board members and confusion or resentment in the broader public. Technically not pacifists (since they would participate in Jehovah's War of Armageddon), the witnesses nonetheless declined to participate in this war, since it was a human conflict, not God's final battle. Many witnesses ended up not in civilian camps but in prisons.

The vast majority of Catholics, Protestants, and Jews, however, joined in the war even as with steady vision they joined in an effort to see that a just and durable peace followed the end of that war. While the allies spoke chiefly in terms of unconditional surrender, many religious and political leaders argued for a moral plane higher than that. Prominent Presbyterian layman John Foster Dulles (1888–1959), later to become secretary of state, headed a group of church leaders in considering the proper grounds for an enduring peace. A World Council of Churches, organized in Amsterdam in 1948, gave most of its energies and monies to international relief for refugees and prisoners of war, along with assistance to European churches devastated by the bombings and military occupations. Church World Service, Catholic Relief Services, Lutheran World Relief, Jewish Joint Distribution Committee, Meals for Millions, and a host of other church-related entities worked tirelessly all around the world, trying to alleviate war's hurts as well as those conditions that made war more probable.

Sometimes the service rendered was personal and immediate: a cup of cold milk to a starving child at the edge of the Sahara Desert. Other times the service was more impersonal but more far-reaching: demonstrations to farmers in India of fertilizers that could increase food production by over 300 percent. Smallpox inoculations were administered in North Africa and penicillin protection provided in the Middle East. The creation of the United Nations in 1945 soon led to other worldwide humanitarian efforts such as the U.N. World Health Organization, the U.N. Children's Emergency Fund, and the U.N. Relief and Rehabilitation Administration.

All of these bodies, ecclesiastical and political alike, struggled to mitigate the effects of the modern world's deadliest plague.

Not all plagues, however, resulted from the military might of nations at war. The extermination in Germany of millions of Jews and others in such scenes of horror as Dachau and Auschwitz was the product of coldly calculated policies of state. During the war itself some warned of Adolf Hitler's genocidal pogroms; in 1942 Rabbi Stephen Wise called upon the United States and its allies "to serve notice upon the Nazi despots that the horror of Nazi mistreatment of civilians should cease, whether of Jews, Protestants, or Catholics, whether of Poles, Czechs or Greeks." Between 1936 and 1943 some 150,000 Jewish refugees were settled in the United States, a number that pales in comparison with the millions who endured suffering, experimentation, torture, and death in the concentration camps.

Only when allied troops liberated those camps did the full horror of gas chambers and mass burials become evident. The Holocaust sickened the souls of modern men and women, Jew and Gentile alike, even as it challenged the traditional efforts of theology to account for evil: evil magnified, evil intensified, evil that mocked the very concept of civilization itself. Of those who wrote movingly or despairingly of the Holocaust and its message, none displayed greater sensitivity than Elie Wiesel, a native of Romania who came to the United States in 1956. A childhood survivor of Auschwitz and other concentration camps, Wiesel saw dark implications for all humankind in what this tragic episode revealed to people about themselves, in what it revealed concerning "the silence of God." "Man's betrayal matches God's silence," Wiesel wrote in 1975. "If we are moved by the dehumanization of the victim," he added, "we must be shocked by the dehumanization of mankind." So is despair the answer? No, Wiesel responded, despair is the question: "It is the question, the question of questions. It is both man's way of questioning God and God's way of questioning man." And to this hardest of all questions, "there is no answer coming from either side."

Does this mean that all faith is lost? Again Wiesel responded in the negative. One continues to believe in God, and at the same time "go[es] on questioning Him *through* such belief." The whole rabbinical tradition is one of questioning, Wiesel observed, quoting an earlier rabbi who noted that "no heart is as whole as a broken heart." To which Wiesel added that "no faith is as pure as a broken faith." Other post-Holocaust questioners of God's silence insisted that Hitler's campaign against the Jews must not be allowed any postwar triumphs over Jewish practice, identity, and determination. After the genocidal policies of the Nazis, philosopher Emil

84. In the aftermath of Hiroshima and Nagasaki and with the onset of the Cold War, one of the most pervasive cultural concerns was finding security in an age of atomic war, an anxiety given clear expression in this simple devotional plaque. *Library of Congress*

Fackenheim said, a new commandment had been added to Jewish law: "Thou shalt grant Hitler no posthumous victories."

If the Holocaust strained people's faith to the breaking point, so Hiroshima and Nagasaki in 1945 tested faith and challenged humanity to somehow find a moral power equal to the awesome might of atomic power. In dropping a single bomb over Hiroshima on August 6, 1945, the United States wrought destruction on a scale hitherto beyond imagining: 100,000 Japanese killed instantly and another 100,000 mortally wounded. True, the unleashing of this power brought World War II quickly to an end, thereby saving an indeterminate number of lives. But it also put in the hands of fallible beings, and soon in the hands of many nations, a force that took on a life of its own. Some saw religion as the only possible restraining counterforce, the only power capable of checking willful pride, capable of instructing men and women in the art—now the necessity—of peacemaking and arms control.

Richard M. Fagley, a member in 1945 of the Federal Council of Churches' Commission on a Just and Durable Peace, wrote just two months after the bombs were dropped over Japan that the only alternative to total world disaster was "repentance and regeneration." Fear can take us only so far, he noted, for the "fear of destruction from atomic bombs in the present world of competing states would insure and hasten sudden, ruthless attacks" with those very bombs. "The fate of the world, therefore, in a literal sense," Fagley concluded, "depends upon the ability of the moral and religious forces . . . to call men effectively to repentance, worship, service." The oneness of all humankind, rather than the competitiveness among all, must become the guiding principle by which the world is safeguarded and civilization saved. Fagley's call for a religious solution came as the world entered the atomic age, but the questions of nuclear war, nuclear deterrence, nuclear disarmament, and nuclear proliferation would only become more pronounced in the decades ahead.

WARRING FOR THE HEARTS AND MINDS

In the Eisenhower era (1953–1961) of the postwar world, a measure of peace and prosperity settled upon the land. During those years Billy Graham came to prominence as the leading revivalist in the second half of the twentieth century. Emphasizing a gospel of individual repentance and conversion, Graham saw himself as an evangelist above all else, a "proclaimer of the good news" that Christ died for all and was prepared to redeem or save those that believed. The evangelist was not, Graham acknowledged, primarily a theologian or a social reformer, and the evangelist's message was not the whole message of religion to a modern world. The task and the message were, nonetheless, excellent places to begin in promoting the power of the spiritual to a more prominent place. First change the hearts of women and men, Graham argued (like Dwight L. Moody before him); then one may proceed to transform the world.

Over the years Graham grew in his understanding of how much responsibility individual Christians bore for applying religion to large social and political problems. In 1960 Graham reported, "My belief in the social implications of the gospel has deepened and broadened." Faith must express itself in action, he pointed out; otherwise, that faith is dead. "The evangelist must not hedge on social issues," Graham declared, and "the cost of discipleship must be made plain from the platform." The question for Graham was not whether religion was personal or social, for it was both; nevertheless, all reform necessarily began with the individual. "Social sins, after all, are merely a large-scale projection of individual sins and need to be repented of by the offending segment of society." The experience of conversion, Graham argued, is not one that takes men or women out of society; rather, it enables them to work as partners with God, more powerfully than ever before, to reform social ills.

As an adviser to presidents, notably Dwight Eisenhower, Lyndon Johnson, and Richard Nixon, Graham enjoyed an unusual degree of public visibility. His many big-city "crusades," drawing thousands of people to football stadiums and civic auditoriums, also won great attention, particularly when radio and television carried the revival meetings themselves into millions of homes across the country. But Graham was more than a public figure who represented in some vague way the presence of religion in the affairs of the nation. He was, in addition, the leader of a new religious conservatism or neoevangelicalism that was to play an increasingly conspicuous role in national life. With Graham's strong backing and with members of his family directly involved, the conservative journal *Christianity Today* was launched in 1956, this magazine giving his movement not only visibility but respectability as well. Neoevangelicals were no longer perceived as fringe critics of a culture they could neither understand nor embrace; now they were regarded as responsible defenders of the ability of revivalism and indeed of religion itself to enhance both personal and corporate life. Through a network of activities and agencies, Billy Graham helped create a real alternative between old-time fundamentalism and old-time liberalism.

No other revivalist enjoyed the popularity that Graham did in the

85. The Reverend Billy Graham joined with presidential candidate Richard M. Nixon in Pittsburgh, Pennsylvania, in the summer of 1968. *Religious News Service*

1950s and 1960s. But some preachers, holding forth more privately in their own churches or in television studios, won audiences of enormous dimension. They did so by proclaiming, not Graham's message of repentance and surrender, but a message of self-confidence and vibrancy. That optimistic message they elaborated by returning to and greatly extending the gospels of inner peace and outward plenty that had grown up at the turn of the twentieth century in such motivational writers as Ralph Waldo Trine and Bruce Barton. Norman Vincent Peale (1898–1993), Dutch Reformed pastor in New York City, astounded many, perhaps even himself, with the success of a book published in 1952: *The Power of Positive Thinking*. Breaking virtually all records in nonfiction sales, Peale's work opened with the simple but clearly winning advice to "believe in yourself!" One cannot succeed, Peale insisted, without great self-esteem, "a humble but reasonable confidence." The habits of self-affirmation, properly developed, lead "to self-realization and successful achievement," to health, wealth, and happiness. The goal of his book, Peale said, was to "help you believe in yourself and release your inner powers."

86. Monsignor Fulton J. Sheen, a Catholic proponent of the therapeutic and religious value of positive thinking, spoke in White Plains, New York, in 1948 with Francis Cardinal Spellman, archbishop of New York, at the left. *Religious News Service*

Similarly, Monsignor Fulton J. Sheen (1895–1979) in a volume called *Peace of Soul* declared that the conversion experience "makes somebodies out of nobodies by giving them a service of Divine Sonship." It also improves one's health "by curing the ills that sprang from a disordered, unhappy, and restless mind." It cures depression and "enables the soul to live in constant consciousness of God's presence." In his exceptionally popular television programs, Sheen inspired confidence by his mere presence and steady assurance, promising a kind of spiritual tranquillity and calm that only faith could bestow. "The true peace that follows conversion is deepened, not disturbed, by the crosses, checks, and disquietudes of the world, for they are all welcomed as coming from the hands of the Loving Father." Look within, not without, for strength. Claim those spiritual powers that are all around you (like radio waves), just waiting to be appropriated and put to use.

In a great deal of Peale's "positive thinking" and Sheen's "peace of soul" as well as in analogous inspirational writing such as that of Rabbi Joshua Liebman (1907–1948), whose *Peace of Mind* was another best-seller, the emphasis lay more on changing one's internal attitude than on changing the external world. Emphasis also often rested upon what religion can do for the individual; that is, religion was seen as more useful for comfort and healing than for spiritual combat, civic struggle, and social service. Other religious bodies in this same period approached religion much more in terms of political and social structures to be criticized and reshaped, much more in terms of dedication to causes that lay well beyond the limits of one's own body and mind and even beyond the limits of one's own community or country. There, too, lurked potential liabilities and vulnerabilities.

In the 1950s many liberal church members found themselves under attack as Communists or, at the very least, Communist sympathizers or "dupes" of the Communist conspiracy. Though some anti-Communists sincerely feared the overthrow of the American system, other anti-Communists used that fear to weaken the forces of political and religious liberalism. Especially during the early 1950s when Joseph R. McCarthy (1908–1957), U.S. senator from Wisconsin, held much of the country captive to exaggerated anxieties about a "communist takeover," headlines and television time were guaranteed to any who pointed a finger at suspected subversives, whoever and wherever they might be.

When, therefore, a relatively obscure congressional aide charged that liberal Protestant clergymen led the ranks of traitors in America, he could be assured a national stage upon which to play his role and speak his piece. In 1953 J. B. Matthews, chief investigator for the House of Representatives committee probing "un-American" activities, and author of such incendiary tracts as *Reds and our Churches*, publicly charged that since World War II "the Communist Party has enlisted the support of at least seven thousand Protestant clergymen" as either party members or "fellow-travelers, espionage agents, party-line adherents, and unwitting dupes." Without trying to prove the validity of his figure of seven thousand, Matthews proceeded to ask how such wholesale defection could possibly happen. He found his answer in the "social gospel" that "infected the Protestant theological seminaries more than a generation ago." "Could it be," Matthews asked, "that these pro-Communist clergymen have allowed their zeal for social justice to run away with their better judgment and patriotism?" That question, so slyly put, suggested that one had best rein in his or her passion for social justice, that one had best be concerned about patriotism above all else. Otherwise, the finger pointing and the name calling were almost certain to begin. (As a twenti-eth-century archbishop of Brazil commented, "When I fed the poor, they called me a saint. When I asked, 'Why are they poor?,' they called me a Communist.")

One whose name was frequently called, Methodist bishop G. Bromley Oxnam (1891–1963), was president of the Federal Council of Churches from 1944 to 1946 and president of the World Council of Churches for six years after that. Because he was so visible, a successful attack on Oxnam could seriously weaken if not destroy the socially active wing of Ameri-can Protestantism. The Un-American Activities Committee in the House of Representatives repeatedly implied that Oxnam was either a Commu-nist or else out of stupidity he allowed the Communists to use him for their own causes. Such implications flowed over and over from committee press releases, with the bishop given no opportunity to explain or defend or face his accusers. Finally, in July of 1953 Bishop Oxnam demanded to be heard, to be given some semblance of American justice before the House Un-American Activities Committee.

After first stating that his Christian faith was unwavering and his rejec-tion of both atheism and materialism complete, Oxnam severely rebuked the committee for its practice "of releasing unverified and unevaluated material" that the committee then accepted no responsibility for—and none either for the untold havoc that such material wreaked. Such action is irresponsible at best, deliberately malicious at worst, Oxnam charged. In either case, the result was the same: "to question loyalty, to pillory or to intimidate the individual, to damage reputation, and to turn attention from the Communist conspirator who pursues his nefarious work in the shadows, while a patriotic citizen is disgraced in public." Then, lecturing the committee sternly, the bishop affirmed that "the churches have done and are doing far more to destroy the Communist threat to faith and to freedom than all investigating committees put together."

When Senator McCarthy was formally censured by the U.S. Senate in 1954, his popularity and influence quickly waned, along with that of the many investigators, critics, and opportunists who rode on his coattails. The net effect on American religion, however, and especially upon liberal Protestantism, was to weaken its moral leadership in those very areas of social justice where such leadership was critically required. But in the Eisenhower era, peace and prosperity lulled all too many into a state of quietude so far as social injustices and inequities were concerned.

RELIGIOUS RENEWAL

For two decades following World War II, mainstream religion prospered. Church membership rose to nearly 65 percent of the national population, its highest proportion ever. Among Catholics weekly attendance at worship reached about 60 percent. Contributions to church and synagogue, measured in the billions of dollars, steadily increased. And in 1957 the U.S. Bureau of the Census conducted a poll that discovered that an astounding 96 percent of the nation's citizens identified themselves with some religious tradition, whether or not they were members or contributors or attendees. With an adult population of about 120 million in 1957, the U.S. Census Bureau estimated that about 70 million Americans thought of themselves as Protestant, about 30 million as Roman Catholic, and nearly 4 million as Jewish. Religious traditions other than the broad categories of Protestant, Catholic, or Jewish were also discovered by the census, while only about 4 percent of the population indicated no religious identification at all.

The two decades following the Second World War were growth years for the major denominations and many of the minor ones as well. Religion also enjoyed a good deal of public confidence, as measured by the regular Gallup polls that inquired about such things. So far as the American landscape was concerned, however, the most obvious sign of renewal was a burst of activity in ecclesiastical building, taking advantage of new technologies and new architectural forms. As Otto Spaeth, the founder of the Liturgical Arts Society, observed, "The first requirement of a church or temple today is that it be of today." The parishioner, Spaeth pointed out, "drives a streamlined car to work in an office or factory where everything has been designed for maximum efficiency and comfort." But then he "is asked to hurl himself back centuries to say his prayers in the pious gloom of a Gothic or Romanesque past." The obvious implication of all this, Spaeth concluded, is that "God does not exist today."

In the 1950s, therefore, the United States witnessed the designing and constructing of many sophisticated, contemporary church buildings. In Portsmouth, Rhode Island, for example, under the direction of the liturgy-conscious Benedictines, the Priory of St. Gregory the Great was erected. With sheet copper for the roofs, concrete slabs for the walls, and redwood board for much of the interior, the resulting octagonal church created a stunning image of innovation. The First Presbyterian Church of Cottage Grove, Oregon, on the other hand, avoided all traditional symbols of arch or steeple or stained glass. Dedicated in 1951, this church snuggled quietly

87. Religious architecture underwent renewal in the postwar period, as is shown in this modern synagogue in Jamaica, New York, with the Star of David built into its ceiling design. *Library of Congress*

into a residential neighborhood rather than rise majestically or pretentiously over all its surroundings. Built entirely of native fir, the church revealed the same severe simplicity in its interior design as it did externally. And between the two coasts, in Bloomington, Indiana, the First Baptist Church, dedicated in 1956, likewise intended its new structure to partake of modern materials and modern methods of construction. As members of a church committee declared, their building should provide a place of worship "so simple and meaningful and honest that no one will be made afraid by lavish appointments or pretensions of any kind." The committee also explicitly emphasized its desire to "provide in the stone and wood of the building a Christian symbol which will speak of man's search for God in the forms and with the materials of our time."

At the same time that American religious communities were exploring new architectural forms, they participated in a liturgical renewal as well. Liturgy, literally the "work of the people," gathers worshipers together in a collective ritual of celebration. Through liturgy, Jews honor the exodus from Egypt, the law given on Mount Sinai, the temples dedicated before and after the Babylonian Exile, the deliverance of the oppressed Jews by Judas Maccabees, and many other events in the Jewish past. Similarly, Christian liturgy centers on remembrances of things past, notably, the birth, death, and resurrection of Christ. In the 1950s and beyond, more conscious attention was given to the place of such remembrances, even among groups that thought of themselves as largely nonliturgical. And though denominational differences in liturgical expression could be found, one could also find Presbyterians singing Lutheran hymns, Episcopalians offering Catholic prayers, or Methodists and Baptists sharing in the congregational readings used on the occasion of the Lord's Supper. In this renewal as in many others, the Roman Catholic activity of the early 1960s was particularly conspicuous.

In 1960 the voting public of the country for the first time elected a Roman Catholic as its president: John F. Kennedy (1917–1963). Religion was prominently under discussion in this presidential campaign, as it had been some thirty years before when another Catholic, New York Govenor Alfred E. Smith (1873–1944) ran for this high office. But certain things had happened to the country and to religion in the intervening generation.

88. Chief Justice Earl Warren administered the oath of office to the nation's first Roman Catholic president, John F. Kennedy, in 1961. *Religious News Service*

Pluralism had become more acceptable or at the least more obvious; nativism and anti-Catholic bigotry had become less acceptable or at the least less blatant. Yet Kennedy found the "religious question" pressed upon him again and again during the course of the campaign. Clearly, it would not be enough to say that the U.S. Constitution prohibited the imposition of any religious test upon someone seeking federal office. Too many Americans were still unsure about papal claims in general and about papal influences in particular upon any Catholic presiding in the White House.

On three occasions, therefore, Kennedy dealt directly with the fact of his Catholicism: before the Society of American Newspaper Editors in Washington, D.C., in April of 1960; before the press in Los Angeles in July of that year after he had won the Democratic nomination; and in September, before the Ministerial Association in Houston, two months prior to the election. To each audience he made the point that should he become president he was committed to upholding and defending the U.S. Constitution, including its First Amendment guarantees regarding freedom of religion. He also argued, as had Alfred Smith before him, that he wished no votes cast for him just because he was a Catholic and no votes cast against him for that reason alone. And he noted that Roman Catholics had served in every other conceivable civil capacity without questions concerning their religion being raised. "Little or no attention was paid to my religion," Kennedy noted, "when I took the oath as senator in 1953—as a congressman in 1947—or as a naval officer in 1941. Members of my faith abound in public office at every level except the White House."

In the United States the presidency, Kennedy observed, was not an instance of one-man rule. No president could ignore Congress or the courts or the voters. But despite this fact, sheer bigotry might prevail. "If that bigotry is too great to permit the fair consideration of a Catholic who has made clear his complete independence and his complete dedication to separation of church and state," said candidate Kennedy, then "we ought to know it." While bigotry still could certainly be found, it had lessened sufficiently to permit the election in 1960 of the nation's first Roman Catholic president.

Two years before that election, another John was elevated to high office, a genial Italian churchman taking the papal title of John XXIII. His brief pontificate, from 1958 to 1963, was even more revolutionary than America's election of a Catholic president. In his late seventies when he was chosen as a presumably safe, compromise pope, John XXIII startled many, both in the church and beyond, by his own openness as well as by his intent to create a more open church. In sharp contrast to his austere and remote predecessor, Pius XII (whose long reign extended from 1939 to 1958), this short, round, smiling pope inspired affection and trust around the world. He escaped the Vatican "prison" as often as possible and labored during his four and a half years to help his church loosen the hold of the Vatican's entrenched bureaucracy. Of humble origin in northern Italy (farming, the pope said, was his father's way of staying poor), this John kept the common touch, refusing to allow himself to be isolated or arbitrarily elevated.

Two major encyclicals demonstrated the spirit of the man and of a pontificate that would embrace the modern world rather than fear or condemn it. In 1961 the letter *Mater et Magistra* ("Mother and Teacher") addressed itself to social, economic, and political questions in terms drawn not from medieval conditions and language but from twentieth-century concerns and demands. Pope John probed the standards for justice and equity in an industrialized world; he searched for ways to assure a family life that would be "decent and humane"; he defended social insurance and social security as appropriate means "whereby imbalances among various classes of citizens are reduced"; and he spoke on behalf of an improved rural life through governmental provision for such essentials as "pure drinking water," good housing, decent roads, and quality education. With great breadth of vision, John XXIII noted as well that "perhaps the most pressing question of our day concerns the relationship between economically advantaged commonwealths and those that are in process of development."

Attracting even more attention was the second encyclical, *Pacem in Terris* ("Peace on Earth"), issued in 1963. That attention came in part, of course, from the topic itself, but also because this pope went out of his way to address his letter to those beyond the Roman Catholic community, indeed to "all men of good will." Beginning with a recognition of basic human rights, including the right of all people "to honor God according to the sincere dictates" of their own consciences, John XXIII proceeded to urge that all governments provide a "charter of fundamental human rights . . . drawn up in clear and precise terms and that it be incorporated in its entirety in the constitution" of that nation. Only if there was justice at home could one begin to speak meaningfully of justice abroad. Only as "an equal natural dignity" was recognized as the fundamental right of all people could powerful nations begin to treat other nations in terms of their "equal natural dignity as well." When that happens, peace becomes a genuine option.

The pope urged a cessation of the arms race, an obliteration of all lingering traces of racism, and a limitation on the burgeoning power of individual nations. Problems that are worldwide required worldwide authority, he argued, perhaps even a world government or at least a greatly strengthened United Nations. "The moral order itself," the pope declared, "demands that such a form of public authority be established." An authority of this magnitude can then "tackle and solve problems of an economic, social, political, or cultural character which are posed by the universal common good." Years later, people of goodwill across a wide religious spectrum were still studying and evaluating this important encyclical and its vital subject of concern. "In no religious document of our time," Norman Cousins wrote in 1965, "is there a more profound awareness that peace is the one overriding issue and challenge of our age than in *Pacem in Terris*." And in no document was there a more determined effort to move nations beyond their nationalism, races beyond their racism, and churches beyond their parochialism.

John XXIII was remembered less for these two major letters, however, than for his calling of the modern world's most important church council: Vatican II, which met from 1962 to 1965. Not since the Council of Trent in the sixteenth century had so much been undertaken, had so much been at stake, as in this Herculean effort of the Roman Catholic Church to come to terms with the non-Catholic world, with the non-Christian world, with the complex, secular, pluralistic modern world. John XXIII did not live to see the council complete its work; he did live long enough to open that window in the Vatican that, as he said, would let in some fresh air. To some bureaucrats it must have seemed as though a wind of hurricane force blew through that single window. Before Vatican II was over, sixteen official documents had been drawn up, argued over, revised, debated, and finally voted upon by bishops assembled from all over the world. And before Vatican II was over, the Roman Catholic Church would be a much-altered, much-shaken institution.

Another John now enters the story, namely the Jesuit theologian and professor John Courtney Murray (1904–1967). Introducing into Vatican II what was generally called the "American document," the "Declaration on Religious Liberty," Murray watched over the precarious movement of this document through all the hazards of debate and dedicated resistance. Like a mother or father hovering over a sick child, Murray would not let his attention wander or his guard fall as he defended, pleaded, cajoled, and persuaded a majority that the time had at last come for the Catholic Church to recognize the reality of, indeed the desirability of, religious freedom. This document was, Murray wrote, clearly "the most controversial document of the whole Council," primarily because it implicitly recognized what had long been denied: that doctrine does develop, that dogma does change. "The notion of development, not the notion of religious freedom, was the real sticking-point," Murray commented, with the sharp differences between the "Syllabus of Errors" in 1864 and this document of a century later still waiting "to be explained by theologians." The declaration on religious freedom represented a tremendous breakthrough, Murray explained, as it brought "the Church at long last abreast of the consciousness of civilized mankind." It represented a "transition from the sacral society to the secular society," and at the same time it symbolized the church's acceptance of "historical consciousness."

If the document was symbolically important, its substantive value cannot be dismissed. For the church now recognized the utter inappropriateness of coercion in matters of conscience. "Truth cannot impose itself except by virtue of its own truth, as it makes its entrance into the mind at once quietly and with power." Sounding very much like Roger Williams or William Penn, the council agreed that "the exercise of religion, of its very nature, consists before all else in those internal, voluntary and free acts whereby man set the course of his life directly toward God. No merely human power can either command or prohibit acts of this kind." And sounding somewhat like the First Amendment, the council acknowledged that both human nature and the nature of religion require the right of free assembly and freedom of worship according to conscience. Somehow Murray also persuaded the authorities voting in Rome at the end of 1965 to concede that the church at times has acted in a manner "hardly in accord with the spirit of the Gospel or even opposed to it." The church at this point demands no special privilege, only "that full measure of freedom which her care for the salvation of men requires." John Courtney Murray could and did take as much pride in his authorship of this document as Thomas Jefferson had taken in his authorship of Virginia's Statute for Religious Freedom.

Vatican II, of course, did much more than issue a pronouncement in favor of religious freedom. It revised the liturgy so that a far wider use of the language of the people replaced the mandatory Latin. It called for revising the order of the Mass itself "in such a way that the intrinsic nature and purpose of its several parts, as also the connection between them, can be more clearly manifested." In addition, the council extended its hand to other Christians, now seen not as "erring schismatics" but as truly brothers and sisters in Christ. Special efforts were made to soften the antagonism between the Western and the Eastern churches, the pertinent document observing that "History, tradition, and numerous institutions manifest luminously how much the universal church is indebted to the Eastern Churches." And the council endeavored to remove the centuries-old burden that many Christians had heaped upon Jews in the twisted logic of Christian anti-Semitism, namely, that all Jews past and present were somehow collectively responsible for the crucifixion of Christ. That event, declared the council, cannot be blamed "upon all the Jews then living, without distinction, nor upon the Jews of today." Jews should not be regarded as under some enduring, reiterable curse; on the contrary, "God's all-embracing love" extends to them as to all people. The church, moreover, "deplores the hatred, persecutions, and displays of anti-Semitism directed against the Jews at any time and from any source."

Even in three years Vatican II could not address every issue that pressed hard upon the Roman Catholic Church or upon the Church universal. It could, however, reveal a new spirit of dialogue and mutual respect, a new freshness in perspective and interpretation, a new courage in confronting the problems of its own history and of the world's history. When Vatican II was under way, the key word heard nearly everywhere was *aggiornamento:* a bringing up to date, a modernizing of the Church, a making religion relevant to this day, this time. Vatican II set a model for religious renewal, its pattern imitated by some and scorned by others. A few Roman Catholics even broke away, preferring to keep the Latin rite unchanged, the traditions unmodified. Most churchgoers in America, however, as elsewhere, found that fresh air coming in through the Vatican window to be both invigorating and challenging. For a great many Americans, the three Johns of the early 1960s—John F. Kennedy, John XXIII, and John Courtney Murray—signaled the beginning of a new epoch.

CHAPTER 16

The Courts, the Schools,
the Streets

In the years following World War II, even the most secular Americans could not help but notice the powerful presence of religion in the nation. That presence made itself felt in a host of public places: the daily press, political campaigns, public schools, placard-waving protests in the streets, calls for constitutional amendments, and legal battles. Above all else, the courts—municipal, state, and federal—found their dockets crowded and their seating capacity strained as contentious religious partisans cried out for justice and fairness. From the perspective of litigation, at least, the nation had unmistakably entered upon a new era of conflict over the meaning of religious freedom and the separation of church and state.

For the first century and a half of national existence, religious issues rarely reached the Supreme Court. Beginning in the 1940s, however, religion cases came to be an almost daily diet, with those cases increasing in both frequency and difficulty in succeeding decades. The public divided sharply over one judicial decision after another, and the justices themselves were rarely much closer to agreement. More and more it appeared that religion in America was something that one took to court. By the 1980s, with local confrontations mounting over the public display of such Christian symbols as nativity scenes, even the baby Jesus, the three wise men, and the reindeer pulling Santa's sleigh had made it to the Supreme Court in the case of *Lynch v. Donnelly* in Pawtucket, Rhode Island.

The reasons for this dramatic burst in litigation are several. First, the Supreme Court in a 1940 case decided that the First Amendment was applicable to the states; that is, states no less than the federal government itself were bound to respect the free exercise of religion and to avoid any establishment of religion. Second, by World War II the ever-growing pluralism of the country had become so palpably evident that one could not pretend or suppose or act as though all citizens believed and behaved alike. Third, specific organizations such as Americans United for Separation of Church and State, the American Jewish Congress, and the American Civil Liberties Union helped bring religion cases to the highest court in order to test the protections and the limits of the First Amendment with respect to religion. Fourth, the federal Constitution itself became increasingly the great symbol of national unity as well as the source of both goodness and truth; citizens, therefore, turned more and more often to that sacred charter and its official interpreters in order to find their way in a bewildering, morally complex world. And fifth, liberal demands for a more thoroughly secular state, which had been brewing for over a century, reached a point of critical leverage by the 1960s. Freethinking concerns about everything from prayer in the public schools to tax exemptions for religious organizations were finally able to get a sustained hearing.

Whatever the combination of factors at work, the Supreme Court in the single decade of the 1970s or 1980s heard more church-state cases than it had in the years from 1790 to 1940 put together. Issues heard one day, moreover, could reappear the next in a slightly altered form, or issues heard one day were heard again later with surprisingly different results. Even as the Court was feeling its way through an entangling thicket, so American society was groping for some clear path that would yield a viable relationship between religion and public life.

CASES OF CONSCIENCE

The "free exercise" clause of the First Amendment has been called upon many times to protect behavior guided by conscience, shaped or determined by religion. No group in America's history has done more to enlarge the understanding of what free exercise really means than the Jehovah's Witnesses, who time and again have pressed their claims all the way through the legal system. Preaching in public parks, distributing religious literature, violating Sunday "blue laws," trespassing, and failing to obtain a municipal license—these and a host of other issues led to confrontations between the witnesses and the law enforcement or judicial agencies. But nothing attracted as much attention as the two cases concerning the requirement that the salute and Pledge of Allegiance to the American flag be offered as a daily exercise in the public school.

In 1940 the U.S. Supreme Court heard a case (*Minersville School District v. Gobitis*) that arose from the refusal of two Jehovah's Witnesses children,

89. The Jehovah's Witnesses, who were at the center of some of the most important "free exercise" cases of the twentieth century, gathered en masse at a convention in 1950. *Library of Congress*

William and Lilian Gobitis (ages ten and twelve, respectively), to salute the flag and join in the Pledge of Allegiance each school day. Their refusal was based upon the teaching of their denomination that such action constituted idolatry, for it violated the commandment in the book of Exodus to have no other gods before Jehovah: "You shall not make yourself a graven image. . . . You shall not bow down to them or serve them" (Exodus 20:3–5). Witnesses had gradually come to this position during the 1930s when they were being persecuted in Adolph Hitler's Germany, especially when they decided that the arm raised in a *Heil Hitler* salute was itself idolatry. State courts in America who had heard cases based on the refusal of Jehovah's Witnesses' children to salute the flag regularly decided against them or else threw the case out of court on the grounds that no substantial question of freedom of religion was involved.

So also in 1940 the Supreme Court, by a vote of eight to one, ruled that the requirement imposed by the small school district in Pennsylvania was a constitutional one. Justice Felix Frankfurter (1882–1965), speaking for the

Court, acknowledged that the dilemma long ago posed by Abraham Lincoln spoke to the issue then before the justices: "Must a government of necessity be too strong for the liberties of its people, or too weak to maintain its own existence?" Recognizing that the failure of the Gobitis children to salute the flag was indeed based upon religious scruple, Frankfurter nonetheless argued for the critical importance of the flag as "the symbol of our national unity." He declared, "The ultimate foundation of a free society is the binding tie of cohesive sentiment," adding that the flag was important for creating and maintaining "that unifying sentiment without which there can ultimately be no liberties, civil or religious." On the other hand, Justice Harlan Stone (1872–1946) dissented from the majority view, declaring that the very essence of civil and religious liberty was "the freedom of the individual from compulsion as to what he shall think and what he shall say, at least where the compulsion is to bear false witness to his religion." But in 1940 Frankfurter prevailed.

Two results of that decision against the Jehovah's Witnesses quickly surfaced. First, popular resentment against the group mounted as wartime patriotism increased in fervor. Witnesses were victims of mob violence all across the country, from Maine to Oregon; also, many communities that had no formal requirement for all schoolchildren to salute the flag now added one, making public school attendance increasingly problematic for all Jehovah's Witnesses. Second, legal scholars, religious leaders, editorial writers, and others joined in a general chorus condemning the 1940 decision as undemocratic in tone and effect, especially as the burden of the adverse decision fell upon a hapless and widely persecuted minority. It also soon became clear that several members of the Court itself were having second thoughts.

In 1943, therefore, the Court agreed to hear a similar case arising in this instance from West Virginia. But if the case was similar, the results were vastly different. Now, in *West Virginia State Board of Education v. Barnette* the Court reversed its earlier finding and did so in ringing, stirring language in an eight-to-one decision. Speaking for the Court, Justice Robert Jackson (1892–1954) agreed that national unity was vital and that such unity, fostered "by persuasion and example," was not questioned. "The problem," Jackson added, "is whether under our Constitution compulsion as here employed is a permissible means for its achievement." Then Jackson affirmed, "If there is any fixed star in our constitutional constellation, it is that no official, high or petty, can prescribe what shall be orthodox in politics, nationalism, religion, or other matters of opinion, or force citizens to confess by word or act their faith therein." If there were any exceptions at all to that fundamental and inalienable right of all Americans, Justice Jackson confessed that he could not think of them. As might be expected, Justice Frankfurter wrote a long and passionate dissent, but in 1943 he did not carry the day.

Religious minorities also helped broaden the understanding of free exercise with respect to the many Sunday laws on the books of nearly every village and town east of the Mississippi River. But in this instance, Orthodox Jews and Seventh-day Adventists rather than Jehovah's Witnesses led the judicial battles. For the two former groups, the Sabbath began at sundown on Friday evening, not at sunrise on Sunday morning. If an Orthodox Jew kept his shop closed on Saturday as a religious requirement, he found that he must also close his shop on Sunday as a legal requirement. As a consequence, he suffered economic penalties not imposed upon the majority who already accepted Sunday as the appointed day of rest and worship. In 1961 the Court heard two cases, one from Pennsylvania and one from Maryland, challenging the validity of the Sunday closing laws. Chief Justice Earl Warren (1891–1971) in both cases argued that the laws were more part of general welfare regulation than they were a sign of sectarian favoritism. He also stated that such laws, imposing "only an indirect burden upon the free exercise of religion," met the tests of constitutionality.

In the first case *(McGowan v. Maryland)*, Justice William O. Douglas (1898–1980) dissented sharply, pointing out that the state had no right to "make protesting citizens refrain from doing innocent acts on Sunday because the doing of those acts offends sentiments of their Christian neighbors." Imagine a situation, Douglas suggested, in which you have a state legislature composed chiefly of Orthodox Jews and Seventh-day Adventists. They pass a law, let us suppose, making it a crime to keep a business open on Saturday. "Would a Baptist, Catholic, Methodist, or Presbyterian," Douglas asked, "be compelled to obey that law or go to jail or pay a fine?" Constitutional rights were not to be decided by numerical dominance. And in the second case of 1961 *(Brownfield v. Brown)* Justice Potter Stewart (1915–1985) dissented in these succinct words: "Pennsylvania has passed a law which compels an Orthodox Jew to choose between his religious faith and his economic survival. This is a cruel choice." Moreover, Stewart added, "It is a choice which I think no State can constitutionally demand." What, after all, were the rights of the religious conscience?

This question had its clearest answer two years later in the case of *Sherbert v. Verner.* There the Court decided that a Seventh-day Adventist who had been denied unemployment benefits because she would not work on Saturday was, in fact, entitled to such benefits. For to hold otherwise, said Justice William Brennan (1906–1997), was to force this person "to choose between following the precepts of her religion and forfeiting benefits on the one hand, and abandoning one of the precepts of her religion in order to accept work on the other hand." This was equivalent, Brennan added, to imposing a special fine on anyone who chose to worship on Saturday rather than Sunday. Justice Stewart agreed with the Court's opinion in this instance, believing the crux of the matter to be that the Constitution "commands the positive protection by government of religious freedom—not only for a minority, however small—not only for the majority, however large, but for each of us." Brennan in an earlier dissent had also found what he believed to be the central issue in the remark of one of those debating the passage of the First Amendment in 1789: "The rights of conscience are, in their nature, of peculiar delicacy, and will little bear the gentlest touch of governmental hand."

In America's history, that delicacy of conscience has been most apparent in the many cases relating to military conscription and service. For as long as the nation has been involved in war, it has wrestled with the issue of conscientious objection to war and sometimes to any involvement, however indirect, in a war effort. In the 1960s, however, the problem was greatly aggravated by the duration and unpopularity of the Vietnam War and by the widespread refusal of young men either to register for the draft or to accept conscription into the armed forces. No longer was it enough to ask whether one were a Mennonite or a Moravian. Neither was it enough to ask what the First Amendment required. The Court now had the additional task of trying to interpret the language of Congress in its Universal Military Training and Service Act of 1948 as well as its Selective Service Act of 1967. And in all this debate about legislative language and legislative intent, the import of religious conscience itself was at stake.

In the 1965 case of *United States v. Seeger*, the Court explored the breadth of the word *religion*, for Congress had specified exemption from the military draft would be granted only to "those persons who by reason of their religious training and belief are conscientiously opposed to participation in war in any form." By 1965 the nation was manifestly pluralistic in its forms of "religious training and belief," a fact that the Court explicitly recognized. And though Congress had even in its provision for exemption used the term *Supreme Being*, the Court decided to take that not to mean any specific theistic system of belief. Rather, as Justice Douglas said in his concurring opinion, "any person opposed to war on the basis of a sincere belief, which in his life fills the same place as a belief in God fills in the life of an orthodox religionist, is entitled to exemption under the statute." To this remarkably liberalized interpretation, there were no dissents in 1965.

Five years later, however, the Court (in *Welsh v. United States*) began to pull back, as the justices divided five to three on the question of how broadly this matter of conscience could be interpreted. First, did "conscientious" objection always and necessarily have a religious base? Second, could one object, not to war in general, but only to a particular war, doing so on "conscientious" grounds, not political ones? Third, and always the hardest question of all, how was the line to be drawn between the requirements of national interest on the one hand and the protections of free exercise of religion on the other? A majority of the Court decided that people should be exempted from military service if their "consciences, spurred by deeply held moral, ethical, or religious beliefs, would give them no rest or peace if they allowed themselves to become a part of an instrument of war."

For the minority of the Court, however, this was stretching the language of both Congress and the Constitution much too far. Religion has been given a privileged position by both, the dissenters argued, and the Court should not so dilute the meaning of the word as to have it cover every conceivable "sincere belief." A year later the Court pulled back even further, holding that not all dissent and disagreement about war, especially about a particular war (in this instance, Vietnam), was the equivalent of a truly conscientious objection. The nation must be careful, the Court stated, to see that those drafted for military service are not chosen "unfairly or capriciously"; otherwise, "a mood of bitterness and cynicism might corrode the spirit of public service."

The justices of the Supreme Court, like Americans more generally, have repeatedly faced a double bind. On the one hand, they have to take the matter of national solidarity with the utmost seriousness, whether the issue is saluting the flag or exemption from military service. On the other hand, they must respect the right of all Americans to the free exercise of religion. And then the justices must confront the hard reality that such freedom will often collide with the apparent interests of the state. Holding these competing principles together in a wise relationship has long been a great constitutional balancing act.

THE SCHOOLS, PUBLIC AND PRIVATE

In public schools the issue with respect to religion has been primarily curricular: what can be taught or recited in the classroom. In private schools the issue with respect to religion has been primarily financial: what can be paid for in the sectarian or parochial school by the tax monies of all citizens. Both issues not only have proved troublesome to the courts but also have aroused widespread public passion and involvement in a way that few other policy questions have managed to do in times of peace.

In the public schools, controversy in the last four decades has swirled most intensely around two concerns: (1) prayer and Bible reading; and (2) creationism or "creation science." The first of these has a long history since, as has been previously noted, public schools grew up in the midst of a Protestant ethos that not only allowed but encouraged Bible reading, praying, and hymn singing as a routine part of the schoolday. Not until the 1960s, however, did the U.S. Supreme Court deal directly with these issues, though they had earlier reviewed such matters as "released time" (sectarian instruction offered on school property) and "dismissed time" (sectarian instruction offered elsewhere than on school property).

In 1962 the case of *Engel v. Vitale,* making its way up the judicial ladder from the state of New York to the U.S. Supreme Court, concerned the recital of a prescribed prayer, written by the regents of the state, that was required in every public school classroom in New York. Two facets of this case were most striking: one, the decision that such a practice was unconstitutional and must therefore cease was virtually unanimous (a single dissent only); and two, the public outcry in condemnation of the decision was enormous and unrelenting.

The majority opinion itself, delivered by Justice Hugo Black (1886–1971), stated that the New York practice violated that other prohibition of the First Amendment, the Establishment Clause: "Congress shall make no law respecting the establishment of religion." The New York practice, Black wrote, was "wholly inconsistent" with this constitutional clause since the state was engaged in promoting "a solemn avowal of divine faith and supplication for the blessings of the Almighty." If the constitutional language has any meaning at all, Black declared, it "must at least mean that in this country it is no part of the business of government to compose official prayers for any group of the American people to recite as a part of a religious program carried on by government." After reviewing the history of religious freedom in America, Black acknowledged that the nation's religious heritage was a rich and vital one. But the Court's decision, he emphasized, showed no hostility toward either religion or prayer. On the contrary, the aim of both the First Amendment and of the Court in this case was "to put an end to governmental control of religion and of prayer" and not "to destroy either." "It is neither sacrilegious nor antireligious," Black concluded, "to say that each separate

"WHAT DO THEY EXPECT US TO DO— LISTEN TO THE KIDS PRAY AT *HOME*?"

90. Passions ran high over the Supreme Court rulings on prayer, as this 1963 cartoon by Herbert Block suggests. From *Straight Herblock* (Simon & Schuster, 1964). Reprinted with permission of the *Washington Post*.

government in this country should stay out of the business of writing or sanctioning official prayers," leaving "that purely religious function to the people themselves and to those the people choose to look to for religious guidance."

Protestations to the contrary notwithstanding, large segments of the public cried out that the decision was indeed antireligious, sacrilegious, atheistic, and perhaps even Communist inspired. Political figures generally condemned the decision, though President Kennedy was a conspicuous exception. Religious leaders of many stripes vented their outrage. "I am shocked and frightened," Francis Cardinal Spellman (1889–1967) declared, "that the Supreme Court has declared unconstitutional a simple and voluntary declaration of belief in God by public school children." "God pity our country," said Billy Graham, "when we can no longer appeal to God for help." The Supreme Court, said Episcopal bishop James A. Pike (1913–1969), "has just deconsecrated the nation." All of the Hearst newspapers expressed their strong disapproval, along with such major dailies as the *Boston Globe*, the *Chicago Tribune*, and the *Los Angeles Times*. Headlines, editorials, sermons, and syndicated columns sang a loud chorus of condemnation.

To be sure, other voices were raised, a bit more quietly at first. Several Protestant theologians praised the opinion for protecting "the integrity of the religious conscience and the proper function of religious and governmental institutions." Baptist spokespeople from both north and south approved of the decision, though they acknowledged that at the grassroots level much grumbling would be heard. The American Jewish Committee joined with the Synagogue Council of America and many other Jewish organizations, both local and national, in filing a friend-of-the-court brief in opposition to the use of the Regents Prayer. Martin Luther King Jr. pronounced the decision to be "sound and good, reaffirming something basic in the nation: separation of church and state." Many major newspapers editorially backed the court, including the *New York Times*, the *Washington Post*, and the *St. Louis Post-Dispatch*. The *Christian Science Monitor* wrote that "both religion and government are stronger when each stands on its own feet." The Court had announced its decision on June 25, 1962, as its regular term came to a close; in that way, the country would have the whole summer to adjust to the new reality. It turned out to take much longer than that.

The following year the Court did little to heal the wounds or settle the dust when in *Abington v. Schempp* it went on to say that ritual Bible reading and recitation of the Lord's Prayer in the public schools were likewise unconstitutional. There the Court made clear a distinction between the practice of religion on the one hand and the study of religion on the other; the former was clearly unconstitutional so far as governmental agencies or offices or schools were concerned, but the latter was appropriate and should even be encouraged. The Bible could be studied, religion could be studied, the role of religion in American life could be studied, but "the exercises here do not fall into those categories. They are religious exercises, required by the states [Maryland and Pennsylvania] in violation of the command of the First Amendment." Those opposed to the 1962 decision were not soothed by the 1963 one; those supporting the 1962 decision were not stimulated in 1963 to do much about instituting a genuine program of study about religion in the public schools.

Reactions to these two major Supreme Court judgments took a variety of forms. One reaction indicated that the law of inertia was more powerful than the law of the land; that is, many school districts continued, as before, with daily prayers and reading of the Bible. Another reaction was, of course, to comply with the rulings. Still another was to try in some way to clip the wings or restrict the power of the Court; one congressman from Texas even introduced a bill that would empower Congress to override (by a two-thirds vote) any ruling of the Court with which it disagreed. But the most sustained reaction of all, continuing for decades, was to propose an amendment to the Constitution that would have the effect of negating the 1962 and 1963 decisions. Wordings would vary and political alignments would shift, but the campaign continued.

Soon after the 1962 decision about 150 different amendment proposals were put forward in Congress. This does not count, of course, the many suggestions offered outside those legislative halls. Congressman Frank Becker of New York gathered much support for what came to be called the "Becker amendment," which would make prayer and Bible reading constitutional, "if participation therein is on a voluntary basis, in any governmental or public school institution, or place." Such an amendment was necessary, Becker explained, "if we are to prevent the advocates of a godless society to accomplish in the United States that which the Communists have accomplished in Soviet Russia." But another New York congressman, Emmanuel Celler, held hearings before his House Judiciary Committee that succeeded in showing much public resistance, including that of major religious bodies, to such an amendment. The Becker amendment never came to a vote.

In the Senate Everett Dirksen (1896–1969) of Illinois introduced a similar amendment that did come to a vote in September of 1966. There it was narrowly defeated, but the cause did not die. Other amendments were proposed in the 1970s and in the 1980s when no less a figure than President Ronald Reagan himself introduced an amendment, the wording of which had over the years been refined and clarified. "Nothing in this Constitution," it read, "shall be construed to prohibit individual or group prayers in public schools or other public institutions." At the same time, however, "No person shall be required by the United States or by any state to participate in prayer." After weeks of debate and rapt public attention, the Senate in March of 1984 voted: fifty-six for and forty-four against the Reagan amendment. But since a two-thirds vote is required for a constitutional amendment, the measure lost. One indication of the intense interest, however, was the fact that all one hundred U.S. senators were present for this crucial count.

Since the 1980s conflicts have continued to rage over prayer in the public schools. Highly publicized cases have emerged involving student-led prayer before football games as well as organized prayer at other school assemblies such as graduation ceremonies. Increasingly, the issue has come to center on the extent to which student-conducted prayer is to be considered a voluntary rather than an officially sanctioned activity. Does the pigskin piety of the Texas public schools, as some have dubbed the prayers before football games there, fall into the category of a student-initiated practice, or does it carry the weight of administrative endorsement? Are such activities a matter of free expression or a matter of establishment? In June 2000 the Supreme Court in *Santa Fe Independent School District v. Doe* ruled in a six-to-three decision that such student-led prayers at football games constituted a breach of church-state separation. Predictably enough, public response was intense and divided. With attention shifted to the initiatives of students, consensus about how to draw the line between acceptable and unacceptable devotional activities in the public schools has proven as fugitive as ever.

The other religious contest in which public schools have been embroiled concerns the curriculum itself: What books are required or recommended, what philosophies are espoused or rejected, what course of study are all students obliged to pursue? Some school districts have engaged in censorship on religious grounds, arguing that certain books (*Cinderella,* for instance) may deal in "occultism, secular humanism, evolution, disobedience to parents, pacifism, and feminism." Other districts have been presented with parental petitions to excuse their children from certain required courses, to permit home instruction, or to create a separate curriculum. The most heated debates, however, have centered on science courses in which Darwinism is taught not as theory but as fact with no alternative explanations for the origins of life being offered.

The alternative most frequently proposed has been a religious explanation of those origins, an explanation based to a large degree on the book of Genesis and bearing the name "creationism." In January 1982 the U.S. district judge in the state of Arkansas declared a law titled Balanced Treatment for Creation-Science and Evolution-Science Act to be in violation of the establishment clause of the First Amendment. The court found this law unconstitutional since it amounted to government sponsorship and support for a particular sectarian point of view. The creationists, said the judge, "take the literal wording of the Book of Genesis and attempt to find scientific support for it." Since this law has the effect of advancing religion, he argued, it cannot be found constitutional. Many prominent religious groups in Arkansas (Catholics, Methodists, Presbyterians, Union of American Hebrew Congregations, and so on) joined in the legal action to have this law overturned. But as the judge pointed out in his conclusion, whether the supporters of the act constituted a minority or a majority was irrelevant to his finding. "No group, no matter how large or small, may use the organs of government, of which the public schools are the most conspicuous and influential, to foist its religious beliefs on others."

Subsequently, the U.S. Supreme Court was asked to consider an even older Arkansas law that prohibited teachers in the public schools and the public universities from teaching any theory suggesting that humans evolved from some other form of life. The Court agreed unanimously that the 1928 law was as defective as the 1961 "balanced treatment" act, for it, too, advanced the narrow religious interest that "the Book of Genesis must be the exclusive source of doctrine as to the origin of man." This was not religious neutrality, the Court pointed out, but religious favoritism. "Plainly, the law is contrary to the mandate of the First, and in violation of the Fourteenth, Amendment to the Constitution."

Then in 1986 and 1987 a creation-science initiative from the state of Louisiana was the subject of Supreme Court argument and action as another "balanced treatment" law came up for review. In *Edwards v. Aguillard* the Court said—but not unanimously—that the history of legislative action in Louisiana clearly demonstrated that its purpose was "to provide persuasive advantage to a particular religious doctrine that rejects the factual basis of evolution in its entirety." Its constitutional defectiveness lay in advancing a specific religious doctrine. Two dissenters, however, argued that the law had a secular basis as well as a religious one and that this purpose must be recognized. "The people of Louisiana, including those who are Christian fundamentalists," the dissenters noted, "are quite entitled, as a secular matter, to have whatever scientific evidence there may be against evolution presented in their schools." If there is no such scientific evidence, said Chief Justice William Rehnquist and Associate Justice Anthony Scalia, that was another question but one that the Supreme Court did not have before it the evidence to decide.

Judicial rulings have gone against creationism repeatedly but not with perfect unanimity. One consequence of the public discussion has been a new awareness that Darwinism is indeed only a hypothesis or theory, though admittedly the highly favored theory of the worldwide scientific community. Another consequence, of course, has been to arouse in certain circles still more resentment against the public schools, with a growing number of parents, on religious grounds, turning to private education or home schooling. Indeed, the turn of conservative Christians toward private Christian academies and home schooling has been one of the most visible results of the Supreme Court decisions of the last forty years. But private education, no less than public, managed to inspire much litigation and much discussion about that metaphoric wall of separation.

Within the realm of private education, the leading issues remained financial. And these money questions could and did take a bewildering variety of forms. Though historically the public versus private education issue has been seen as largely a Protestant versus Roman Catholic issue, in recent decades the contest has become considerably more complex than that. The Supreme Court, moreover, has felt it necessary to invent a whole new set of guidelines in an effort to determine whether or not the Establishment Clause of the First Amendment is being violated. The simple phrase that "Congress shall make no law respecting an establishment of religion" has proved inadequate for the many contemporary queries regarding textbook purchases, salary subsidies, construction loans, tax credits, voucher plans, financial help in buying maps or projectors or standardized tests, or whatever. To get through this maze, the Court needed a compass or at least a clear grid with coordinates sharply delineated.

So the Court asked itself, as case after case fell into its lap, a series of questions: Does this particular law benefit mainly the child or the church school? Does this law have a prevailingly secular purpose? Whatever the purpose of a given law, is the effect of that law to advance or inhibit religion? Or is it neutral with regard to religion? Further, does the administration of the law require government (federal or state or local) to become "excessively entangled" with religion? And finally, is such a law likely to unify the body social or to divide it by fanning the flames of religious passion? With such an array of questions and with such an array of cases, it will probably come as no surprise that the Court had difficulty making up its mind or reaching any degree of unanimity in its decisions. (In one 1977 case arising from Ohio, the justices issued seven separate dissents to one or more parts of the decision!)

The modern story begins with the famous case of *Everson v. Board of Education* that the Court heard in 1947. The case is famous for several reasons: one, it explicitly applied the Establishment Clause (by way of the Fourteenth Amendment) to the states; two, it began, with its five-to-four decision, a tradition of a much-divided court in cases related to religious schools; and three, it used the strongest separationist language one could readily imagine yet decided in favor (by the slimmest majority, to be sure) of a practice that to the dissenters seemed the opposite of separation in matters of church and state. The facts of the case can be briefly stated. A New Jersey law authorized school districts to use public transportation (instead of their own school buses), reimbursing the children for the bus fares. In one township in the state, children riding the public buses to parochial schools were also reimbursed. The question: Was this latter practice constitutional?

Justice Hugo Black, speaking for the majority of five, concluded the Court's opinion in these words: "The First Amendment has erected a wall between church and state. That wall must be kept high and impregnable. We could not approve the slightest breach." Then, the surprise: "New Jersey has not breached it here." The dissenters, shaking their heads in disbelief, declared that the majority's advocacy of "complete and uncompromising separation of Church from State" seemed "utterly discordant with its conclusion." The long dissenting opinion, reviewing the history of church-state separation, and especially of James Madison's "Memorial and Remonstrance," concluded that the issue was not how much money was being spent to transport children to parochial schools, how modest the accommodation offered here really was. "Now as in Madison's day it is one of principle, to keep separate the separate spheres as the First Amendment drew them; to prevent the first experiment upon our liberties; and to keep the question from being entangled in corrosive precedents." Anyone reading the full text of both majority and dissenting opinions could only conclude that a rough road lay ahead.

And so it did. As the cases tumbled in during the sixties, seventies, and eighties, the Court divided again and again; state legislatures tried again and again to find other avenues for financial assistance to parochial schools. In a New York case in 1968 a majority of six justices agreed that a

91. Roman Catholic parochial schools raised church-state issues at a number of points, including arrangements for busing and textbooks. Here a group of sixth graders receive instruction from a nun at a parochial school on Staten Island, New York, in the early 1960s. *National Catholic Educational Association*

state law that would lend textbooks free of charge to all students in grades seven through twelve, including parochial school students, was in fact constitutional. Dissenters, mincing no words, pronounced the New York law "a flat, flagrant, open violation of the First and Fourteenth Amendments." That law called "for furnishing special, separate, and particular books, specially, separately, and particularly chosen by religious sects or their representatives for use in their sectarian schools." Under those circumstances, the dissenters said, the New York law must be declared unconstitutional. No, said six; yes, said three.

In a case from Pennsylvania heard in 1974 *(Meek v. Pittenger)*, the Court divided once again six to three, but this time the majority of six moved in the direction of restricting the use of public monies for parochial schools. Helping with textbooks was ruled acceptable, but helping with many other "auxiliary services"—counseling, remedial classes, testing—was not acceptable. But the complexity of the case began to resemble a theater of the absurd as "Mr. Justice Brennan concurred in part and dissented in part" and filed an opinion in which two other justices joined. "Mr. Chief

92. A program of religious instruction was offered just off the campus of the public schools in Fort Wayne, Indiana, in 1964. *Religious News Service*

Justice Burger concurred in the judgment in part and dissented in part and filed opinion. Mr. Justice Rehnquist concurred in the judgment in part and dissented in part and filed opinion" in which another justice joined. Did anybody know which way the compass pointed, or did magnetic north just keep jumping around?

Of course, when the Court is so badly divided, it is a fairly good sign that society is divided as well. Public schools in the 1960s and beyond came under increasing criticism from many segments of society. Private schools, meanwhile, ceased to be the preserve mainly of Roman Catholics, as many traditional supporters of public schools now—for a variety of reasons—began to develop schools of their own. Sometimes the issue was religion, sometimes morals or safety, sometimes quality of education and curricular content, sometimes ethnicity or race or social class. By the 1980s the issues had become much more complex than those relating just to sep-aration of church and state, though that surely remained. Also by the 1980s the efforts to find more suitable or judicially acceptable means for publicly supporting private education had won some significant victories.

One notable and surprising victory pertained to a Minnesota case that the Court decided in 1983. In *Mueller v. Allen* the Court examined a state law that permitted all parents to deduct from their taxes between five and seven hundred dollars per child for tuition, textbooks, and transportation to any school, public or private. Perhaps the only thing predictable about this case was that the justices would be divided, and so they were, five to four, with the majority finding the Minnesota law permissible because any aid that reached the parochial schools did so as a result of individual parental decision and not as an "imprimatur of state approval." Dissenters pointed out that 90 percent of all students attending private schools went to schools permeated with religious instruction and that no effort had been made to restrict the public monies to secular rather than religious uses. Also, it was noted that the decision in this case contradicted earlier judgments of the Court.

That the dissenters were correct in that last point should come as no surprise. For the justices recognized more than once that whether they voted with the majority or the minority, they followed no crystal clear or steady direction. One justice confessed in 1977 that the Court's decision in the whole arena of parochial education "often must seem arbitrary." But another justice, trying to put the best face on the situation, said in 1980 that the Court "sacrifices clarity and predictability for flexibility." Flexibility might also be called inconsistency, for the patterns were admittedly often difficult to discern. The appointment of each new justice, the election of each new president, the makeup of each new Congress aggravated the difficulties and sometimes confounded the nation.

MATTERS OF LIFE AND DEATH

As strongly as citizens have felt about such issues as saluting the flag or praying in the public school or funneling tax monies to the private school, Americans have encountered controversies even more inflammatory, even more divisive. These controversies tended to be more personal and private, yet their resolution was repeatedly sought in very public ways. Contending parties have argued their respective points of view not just in the churches or the courts or the schools, but also in the streets, where violence sometimes has replaced debate.

State and federal courts have been required to deal with laws concerning contraceptive devices and birth control instruction. They have had to adjudicate cases of euthanasia or "mercy killing," cases made more complex by the modern technical ability to sustain biological life long after life of any discernible quality has ceased. In the case particularly of Jehovah's Witnesses, the courts have had to remove a child temporarily from the custody of the parents so that a life-saving blood transfusion might be administered. In the case of faith healing, and especially if a person died without conventional medical assistance being made available, questions of criminal neglect demanded legal resolution. Cities have been restrained by religious pressure groups from fluoridating their water systems. Vaccinations against smallpox or polio have become church-state controversies. The morality of suicide and of capital punishment has repeatedly emerged as a subject for theologians, politicians, ethicists, and others to debate; here, too, sometimes the theoretical discussions have spilled over into passionate demonstrations. Now stem cell research and cloning grip both religious and scientific communities as ethical and legal conundrums.

One subject, however, has outbid all others in the degree of public attention it has received and the vigor on opposing sides it has aroused. Abortion, like many of the issues noted above, is not a church-state question in the sense that the First Amendment always provided the grounds for judicial opinion. But abortion, like those other matters, is a religious question in the sense that churches and voluntary religious associations have appeared repeatedly as antagonists or litigants or lobbyists. And with respect to the abortion controversy in particular, some observers have gone so far as to refer to it as a religious war, the critically divisive issue in a larger culture war. While this dichotomizing of American culture underestimates the strength (and the anguish) of the middle ground, it is no exaggeration to say that religion has been thoroughly caught up in this pivotal matter.

In the 1960s and 1970s the move to eliminate criminal penalties for abortion gained much religious support, particularly among Protestants and Jews. A professor at the Episcopal Theological School in Cambridge in his capacity as director of the Association for the Study of Abortion led much of the "pro-choice" reform, aided by the official statements of such denominations as the United Church of Christ in 1971 and the United Methodist Church in 1972. Many evangelical and fundamentalist Protestants joined the ranks of the "pro-life" forces, as did the Church of Jesus Christ of Latter-day Saints. But through much of the continuing controversy, the Roman Catholic Church has been seen as the most consistent and powerful foe of abortion.

In 1973 the Supreme Court at last agreed to hear an abortion case, and the result in *Roe v. Wade* did little to mend the social and religious divisions. Indeed, that 1973 case has become a rallying point for both critics and supporters of the Court's decision. The Court began by recognizing that this was an issue of utmost complexity and deepest conviction. "One's philosophy, one's experiences, one's exposure to the raw edges of human existence, one's religious training, one's attitude toward life and family and their values, and the moral standards one establishes and seeks to observe, are all likely to influence and to color one's thinking and

93. Demonstrators picket in front of St. Patrick's Cathedral in New York City in 1967 to protest Roman Catholic opposition to abortion rights. *Library of Congress*

conclusions about abortion." The Court then reviewed at great length historical attitudes regarding abortion from the ancient world up through English Common Law and early American law. The Court also evaluated the official pronouncements of such agencies as the American Medical Association, the American Public Health Association, the American Bar Association, the Roman Catholic Church, the National Council of Churches, and others. As a result of this extensive review, the Court decided that in the first trimester of pregnancy the decision about abortion

94. Roman Catholics and Eastern Orthodox Christians join in opposition to abortion in a March for Life in Washington, D.C. *St. Tikhon's Orthodox Theological Seminary*

"must be left to the medical judgment of the pregnant woman's attending physician." In the second trimester the state may, if it so chooses, "regulate the abortion procedure in ways that are reasonably related to maternal health." And in the final trimester, the state may, if it chooses, regulate or even prohibit abortion except where it is judged necessary "for the preservation of the life and health of the mother."

One of the two dissenters in this case, Justice William Rehnquist (now chief justice) argued that the issue should be left in the hands of the states rather than the federal government. That dissent gained the broad support of conservatives, who soon took aim especially at the involvement of the federal government in subsidizing and funding abortions. Legislative lobbying, constitutional amendment proposals, and popular demonstrations all followed in the wake of *Roe v. Wade*. Protests sometimes turned violent and have included the bombing of abortion clinics and the murder of physicians who perform abortions. During his eight years in office President Reagan identified closely with the pro-life forces, declaring January 22 (the anniversary of *Roe v. Wade*) as National Sanctity of Human Life Day. When demonstrations opposing abortion were held on that day, counterdemonstrations (sponsored, for example, by the National Organization for Women) contended for a woman's right to seek an abortion.

In presidential campaigns as well as in state and local races, abortion has remained a hot-button issue, for some the single issue upon which to base one's vote. In appointments to the Supreme Court as well as to all lower federal courts, the prospective jurist's views on abortion often overshadow everything else. In the last decade, though, signs of a more constructive dialogue have appeared, evident in such grassroots organizations as the Common Ground Network for Life and Choice and the National Association for Community Mediation. By focusing on broad areas of agreement—preventing teen pregnancies and reducing the number of abortions, for example—such groups hope to bring people together across the divide, at least for civil exchanges. As one local leader of the Common Ground Network in Buffalo, New York, reported of the abortion debate there, "Members of the same family, the same church, couldn't even talk about it. We thought, 'We have to find a way to talk about something so divisive.'" Though President Bill Clinton shared in the Common Ground rhetoric, as did Vice President Al Gore, the abortion debate remains a wrenching religious and social issue with far greater potential to divide than unify. With the new millennium, the courts have hardly seen the last of this battle.

NATIVE AMERICANS AND RELIGIOUS FREEDOM

One of the most important and contentious church-state debates in recent decades has concerned the religious freedom of Native Americans, especially the freedom to use the cactus peyote in religious ceremonies. Just as missionaries and government officials felt on the brink of triumph in their programs of assimilation and conquest, a new religious movement, centering on the ritual ingestion of peyote, came to the fore among Plains Indians at the end of the nineteenth century and soon spread much more widely. Peyote had long been in use among tribes in northern Mexico and southern Texas, employed in healing ceremonies, visionary practices, and divination; indeed, Roman Catholic missionaries had noted and decried its ritual use from the time of initial contact in the sixteenth and seventeenth centuries. When the peyote religious movement took off among tribes all across the western United States after 1900, missionaries responded with predictable alarm. The claim made by most native practitioners that peyotism was closely allied with Christianity, indeed that it was a Native American Church, only inflamed missionary anger. As one Protestant minister wrote in 1932, "Peyote is a false religion and the claim that its devotees worship the Father, the Son, and the Holy Spirit, is sacrilegious. Therefore, Christians must view it as evil. . . . A religion proves its value or its worthlessness by what it does or fails to do for its worshippers. Indian religions *do not save* their followers."

As early as 1897 and increasingly by the 1910s, missionaries and their supporters lobbied for legislation to suppress the peyote religion. With temperance crusades and prohibition on the national agenda, the use of peyote was a clear target for reformers who were sure that it was far more dangerous to the moral and physical well-being of its partakers even than alcohol. Yet Native Americans, with the help of allies such as the anthropologist James Mooney (1862–1921), staved off legislation at the time, mounting an impressive campaign to incorporate the movement as a denominational organization and to demonstrate that the moral tone of the Native American Church was in keeping with wider religious values of the day (including the group's own thoroughgoing advocacy of temperance). The supportive commissioner of the Bureau of Indian Affairs, John Collier (1884–1968), seemed to cap the victory in 1934 when he declared that "no interference with Indian religious life or ceremonial expression will hereafter be tolerated. . . . The fullest constitutional liberty in all matters affecting religion, conscience, and culture is insisted on for all Indians." The Native American Church grew rapidly, becoming the most successful pan-Indian religious movement of the twentieth century and now counting about 25 percent of Native Americans among its followers.

Those early successes did not settle the church-state matter, however. In the 1960s, as leaders of the counterculture gave drug use increasing cachet and often drew on Native American traditions to justify their own experimentation, questions about the legitimacy of the Native American Church were pressed again. Could the state afford to make a selective exemption from its narcotics laws for the sake of free religious expression? In 1962 three Navajo Indians were arrested near Needles, California, for using peyote as part of their religious ritual. Found guilty of violating state law that prohibited the drug, they appealed to the California Supreme Court. That court in 1964 found in favor of the Navajos and their religious freedom, the court noting that the theology of the Native American Church "combines certain Christian teachings with the belief that peyote embodies the Holy Spirit and that those who partake of peyote enter into direct communion with God." This was not traditional Christianity, to be sure, but then in a pluralistic society such as ours, said the court, pressures for religious conformity must be resisted: "The varying currents of the cultures that flow into the mainstream of our national life give it depth and beauty." The state has an "interest" in enforcing its laws against narcotics, but the state has an even weightier interest, the court concluded, in permitting a ritual that involves "the very essence of religious expression."

Legal opinion continued to tilt toward the Native American Church in the 1970s, and in 1978 the U.S. Congress took another important step toward full legitimation when it passed the American Indian Religious Freedom Act. That such an act was necessary almost two hundred years after the Bill of Rights had guaranteed religious freedom to all Americans is powerful commentary on the suppressions that Indians had long endured. In 1924 formal citizenship had been belatedly granted to Native Americans, and in 1978 that citizenship began to be taken more seriously. Congress declared official U.S. policy now to be "to protect and preserve for American Indians their inherent right of freedom to believe, express, and exercise the traditional religions of the American Indian, Eskimo, Aleut, and native Hawaiian, including but not limited to access to sites, use and possession of sacred objects, and the freedom to worship through ceremonials and traditional rites." Under this protective umbrella, Native Americans have reclaimed burial sites and sacred relics and have again been guaranteed access to ancestral sacred places.

Despite this act of Congress in 1978, the peyote sacrament in the Native American Church became again the object of much legal dispute in the 1980s and 1990s. In Oregon Alfred Smith, a counselor in a drug and alcohol rehabilitation center and a member of the Native American Church, was fired from his job in 1984 when he refused to stop participating in the peyote rituals. Denied unemployment benefits by the Oregon Employment Division as a result of state laws prohibiting the use of certain controlled substances, including peyote, Smith countered with a lawsuit claiming that the constitutional guarantee to the free exercise of religion had been violated. Smith was vindicated in the Oregon Supreme Court in 1988, but *Employment Division v. Smith* ended up before the U.S. Supreme Court in 1990, and there Justice Anthony Scalia led the court in a five-to-four decision to reverse the lower court's ruling. No longer did the state have to prove, Scalia argued, a "compelling interest" when a law of general applicability burdened the free exercise of religion. The Oregon law making peyote a controlled substance was a valid and neutral law, and the state was under no obligation to create an exemption to such regulations simply because they indirectly impeded religious practice.

That decision both shocked and galvanized members of the Native American Church, but it also rallied other religious leaders and civil libertarians to a defense of the "compelling interest" test. The Smith decision immediately intensified the battles on the legislative side, and one result was that Congress passed the Religious Freedom Restoration Act of 1993, which explicitly restored the standard for the protection of religious liberty and free exercise that had reigned previous to the Smith case. In turn, though, the Supreme Court struck down that act as unconstitutional in a six-to-three decision in 1997 (*City of Boerne, Texas, v. Flores*), arguing that Congress had overreached its legislative powers. And so the conflict rages on, with many Native American Church members turning increasingly to state legislatures to continue their long fight for the guarantee of religious freedom. As the country moves into the new millennium, the religious practices of Native Americans remain front and center in working out the meaning and extent of religious liberty for the nation as a whole.

CHAPTER 17

Justice, Liberation, Union

When thirteen quarreling colonies managed to agree on the cause of independence from Britain and when, a few years later, thirteen jealous states managed to agree on a Constitution, the question of national unity might appear to have been settled. Two hundred years later, however, the American pledge of "one nation, under God, with liberty and justice for all" remained far more a matter of visionary faith than an empirical fact. Some even questioned whether it was still an article of faith, and others wondered what unity could possibly mean in a society so rife with divisions based on race, ethnicity, gender, sexuality, and creed. And while some churches continued to travel an ecumenical path blazed in the first half of the twentieth century, the mending of old ecclesiastical divisions still left most of the larger social issues of reconciliation, racial and otherwise, very much a work in progress.

RELIGION, SOCIAL JUSTICE, AND CIVIL RIGHTS

The most pressing religious crusades of the 1950s and 1960s concerned civil rights, initially and dramatically aimed at improving the status of the nation's African American citizens. The leader of this crusade was a black Baptist minister, Martin Luther King Jr. (1929–1968). But his crusading army included far more than Baptists or African Americans, as Protestant clergy of many communions, Catholic priests and nuns, and Jewish rabbis and congregants all joined in marching and in praying in the interest of "liberty and justice for all." In solidarity and resistance, they also endured abuse, arrest, imprisonment, attack dogs, fire hoses, beatings, and even death.

A native of Atlanta, Georgia, King attended Morehouse College in his hometown then went north for ministerial study at Crozer Theological Seminary in Chester, Pennsylvania. Then he moved still farther north to

95. With respect to civil rights, both the nation and its churches turned a corner in the 1950s and 1960s. This march on Selma, Alabama, in 1965 brought together priests, rabbis, nuns, and ministers in their support of Martin Luther King Jr. and his larger cause of justice. *Religious News Service*

work on a Ph.D. in systematic theology at Boston University. Returning to the South in 1954, King accepted the position of pastor of the Dexter Avenue Baptist Church in Montgomery, Alabama. There, almost by accident, he found himself in the eye of a gathering storm. Toward the end of 1955 one black citizen of the city refused to accept the pattern of blacks sitting only in the rear of the public buses. When, after a long and tiring day, Rosa Parks boarded the bus to find all seats in the rear already taken, she simply sat in the first available seat toward the front. She declined to move. But by not moving that day, she moved a whole people as the Montgomery bus boycott was born.

African Americans, the major patrons of the city's public transportation system, agreed under King's leadership not to ride the buses again until this pattern of segregated seating was abolished. The black community gradually came to recognize, King noted, "that it was ultimately more honorable to walk the streets in dignity than to ride the buses in humiliation." The nonviolent protest, lasting more than a year, resulted in victory

96. Martin Luther King Jr. and Malcolm X greeted each other at a meeting in Washington, D.C., in 1964. A potential coalition became impossible when Malcolm X was assassinated a year later, with King's assassination following three years after that in 1968. *Religious News Service*

on that small point, but it also thrust King into a role of national leadership that would last for the remaining years of his life.

Marchers moved from Montgomery to Selma; from Meridian, Mississippi, to Jackson; from St. Augustine, Florida, to Atlanta, Georgia; then to the black ghettos of northern cities as well. In Birmingham King was arrested in the spring of 1963 and jailed along with other religious leaders who had joined him in public protest. From that jail King wrote a letter to some Atlanta clergy who had complained about activities that took King far from his own church in Montgomery and his pastoral responsibilities there. Why, they had asked, was King in Birmingham (redubbed by some Bombingham because of the violence of resistance to integration and civil rights)? He was there, King replied, because that was where injustice could be found, and "injustice anywhere is a threat to justice everywhere." Comparing himself to ancient prophets who took their message everywhere God led them to go, and to the early Christian apostle Paul (who also ended up in jail), King declared that he was "compelled to carry the gospel of freedom beyond my own hometown."

King carried that gospel most powerfully to Washington, D.C., when in August of 1963 he led a march of tens of thousands to the mall near the monument erected in honor of the nation's first president. There King spoke not only to the thousands assembled but also by way of television to the millions far from the capital. And he spoke to the national soul, reminding them that his dream of justice was fundamental to the American dream. It was a dream of a day when the "jangling discords of our nation" shall be transformed "into a beautiful symphony of brotherhood." It was a dream of a day when "all of God's children will be able to sing with new meaning, 'My country, 'tis of thee, sweet land of liberty, of thee I sing.'" On that grand day it will at last be possible, King proclaimed, for "all of God's children, black men and white men, Jews and Gentiles, Protestants and Catholics . . . to join hands and sing in the words of the old Negro spiritual, 'Free at last! Free at last! Thank God almighty, we are free at last.'" In King's inspiring oratory the religious vision of a beloved community merged with the political lexicon of democratic freedom.

The next year, following the assassination of President John F. Kennedy, Congress passed a civil rights bill, a process in which the leadership of Martin Luther King Jr. made a powerful difference. The visible presence of so wide a spectrum of religious participation in the movement had also been critical. So had the increased lobbying by such agencies as the National Catholic Welfare Conference, the National Council of Churches, and B'nai B'rith, along with its offspring, the Anti-Defamation League. Then in Memphis, Tennessee, three days before Palm Sunday of 1968, King himself fell before an assassin's rifle shot. Though his life ended, the push toward the Promised Land of racial justice did not. That determination was evident in the words of one of the religious anthems of the movement: "Keep your eyes on the prize, hold on, hold on. Freedom's name is mighty sweet. . . . The only thing we did wrong, stayed in the wilderness a day too long. But the one thing we did right, was the day we started to fight. . . . We're gonna ride for civil rights, we're gonna ride both black and white. We've met jail and violence too, but God's love has seen us through."

In 1969, the year after King's death, Father Theodore M. Hesburgh of the University of Notre Dame agreed to serve as chair of the federal government's Civil Rights Commission; it was more than an honorary position as Hesburgh stood out as a courageous spokesman for civil rights. In that same year Chicagoan James Forman issued a "Black Manifesto," which challenged the nation's religious institutions to cleanse themselves of all institutional racism and begin to repair the damage done to millions of their fellow citizens. In that year, too, a young African American theologian, James H. Cone, joined the faculty of Union Theological Seminary in New York City. He emerged in the 1970s as a leading spokesman for a new kind of religious thinking, a black theology called forth by "the failure of white religionists to relate the gospel of Jesus Christ to the pain of being black in a white racist society."

In his book *A Black Theology of Liberation*, published in 1970, Cone argued that "there can be no Christian theology which is not identified unreservedly with those who are humiliated and abused." Since Cone felt this description applied especially to the black experience in America, he believed that from the African American community could come a revived New Testament Christianity that identified not with the rich and powerful, but with the poor and oppressed. The dominant theology in the United States, Cone wrote, has been "a theology of the white oppressor, giving religious sanction to the genocide of Indians and the enslavement of black people." That was why blacks must seize upon a new kind of theology, a theology of liberation, which will see the Christian gospel "as inseparable from the necessary power to break the chains of oppression." The Exodus from Egypt under Moses stands, Cone explained, as God's first liberating event, freeing men and women from a cruel bondage. The resurrection of Jesus was another kind of emancipation, freeing all from the fear and sting of death. As the National Committee of Black Churchmen declared in 1969, "Jesus is the Liberator!" "The demands that Christ the Liberator imposes upon all men requires all blacks to affirm their full dignity as persons and all whites to surrender their presumptions of superiority and abuses of power."

Cone's black theology proved more a theological overture than a finale. Soon leading African American women, such as ethicist Katie Cannon in dialogue with novelist Alice Walker, were developing their own theological voices of liberation in a movement known as Womanism. "Black women," Cannon wrote, "are the most vulnerable and the most exploited members of the American society. The structure of the capitalist political economy in which Black people are commodities combined with patriarchal contempt for women has caused the Black woman to experience oppression that knows no ethical or physical bounds." Growing up in the segregated confines of North Carolina, Cannon saw clearly the double entrapment of African American women in the constructions of race and gender. As one response, she has spun a theology of resistance out of the ethical wisdom of black women themselves. Cannon, among others, has insisted that neither white feminism nor black theology should presume to speak for women of color and their own dream of justice.

The civil rights movement among African Americans, along with its theology of liberation, was mirrored in the growing efforts on the part of other minorities to find their voice and achieve power in the public spheres of religious and political life. Hispanics, comprising more than one-fourth of all America's Catholics, gained representation and recognition slowly within Roman Catholicism, as in the wider society. Among the leading proponents of a new activism was the Catholic layman Cesar Chavez (1927–1993), who, beginning in the 1950s, tried to organize the migrant Mexican laborers in California. He eventually did so effectively enough to win support well beyond the laboring ranks themselves, linking arms with such civil rights stalwarts as Senator Robert Kennedy and Coretta Scott King. By 1975 polls indicated that 17 million Americans were boycotting grapes in support of Chavez's United Farm Workers. Through long fasts, hard-edged strikes, and marches under the banner of Our Lady of Guadalupe, Chavez passionately and continually applied Catholic social teachings to the contemporary economic order.

In 1970 Chavez was invited to San Antonio, Texas, to witness Patrick Flores become the first Hispanic elevated to the office of bishop in American Catholicism. Out of 225 bishops in the Catholic Church at that time, one was Hispanic—hardly a tidal wave or a case of proportional representation, but at least one small step forward had been taken. In 1979 Flores, the son of migrant farm workers, became the first Mexican American to be elevated to archbishop. Serving the Archdiocese of San Antonio, with more than 700,000 Catholics in its bounds, Flores remains among the most respected and powerful religious leaders in the country.

Another important step toward inclusion and fuller recognition included the National Hispanic Pastoral Conferences (Encuentros), which began to be held in 1972. At the second such conference (Segundo Encuentro Nacional Hispano de Pastoral) in 1977 the pope lent his blessing, and the president of the National Conference of Catholic Bishops convened the group with the assurance that the church would do all that it could, "as a matter of strict justice, to help people in their struggle to overcome everything which condemns them to a marginal existence." By 1980 the number of Hispanic bishops had grown from one to twelve, and a Secretariat for Hispanic Affairs had become a regular part of the United States Catholic Conference.

97. El Sanctuario de Chimayó in New Mexico has emerged as one of the leading pilgrimage sites in the nation. Every year tens of thousands journey there to seek cures, offer penance, give thanks, and receive blessing. While it remains a predominantly Mexican American Catholic site of devotion, its attraction beyond those circles indicates the growing influence of Hispanic religious practice on American religious life more generally. *Library of Congress*

In 1983 the nation's bishops issued a pastoral letter on "The Hispanic Presence: Challenge and Commitment," which revealed a new level of consciousness in the Catholic community. No longer should Spanish-speaking parishes have priests who spoke English only. No longer should liturgy fail to reflect and incorporate the contributions of Hispanic artists and musicians. No longer should the priesthood be seen as the privilege of a very few. "We call upon Hispanic parents," the bishops said, "to pre-

98. Each year Jesus shoulders the cross on his way to Calvary during a Holy Week festival in San Antonio, Texas, and helps turn the streets of the contemporary city into a theater of Mexican American Catholic devotion. *Sarah Curran*

sent the life and work of a priest or religious as a highly desirable vocation for their children, and to take rightful pride in having a son or daughter serve the church in this way." And no longer should justice be denied to the Hispanic population at large. The bishops spoke specifically in 1983 of "those social concerns which most directly affect the Hispanic community, among them voting rights, discrimination, immigration rights, the status of farmworkers, bilingualism and pluralism." These, said the hierarchy, "are social justice issues of paramount importance to ministry with Hispanics and to the entire Church."

By the late 1980s and 1990s Catholic leaders were speaking not only about issues of inclusion and representation but also of a larger Hispanicizing or "browning" of American Catholicism. Latinos had become crucial players in all aspects of Catholic life, from popular devotionalism to art to foodways to feast days to pilgrimage sites. The prominence of Father Virgilio Elizondo, rector of San Fernando Cathedral in San Antonio, shows that diffuse influence. The son of Mexican immigrants, he has become a major interpreter and proponent of Latino religious thought, practice, and culture. He was listed, for example, among *Time* magazine's top 100 innovators for the new millennium. Sharing in the larger civil rights conviction of holding the United States to its own charter, Elizondo keeps prodding "this country out of its white and English-only self-righteousness." "We believe firmly in the great American dream of liberty and justice for all. . . . Is it too much to ask America to truly be America?"

The future that Elizondo imagines is thoroughly *mestizo*, a society of cultural, racial, and religious mixing. Both American Christianity and the wider United States, he concludes, will be shaped ever more deeply by its encounter with Mexican and Mexican American religious cultures. Elizondo's vision of the future seems right on the mark: Mexican Day of the Dead celebrations cross the border and grow in cultural prominence: Harvard Divinity School, once an Anglo-Protestant bastion, set up its own altar of memorials in the late 1990s; Chimayó, a local Catholic shrine in New Mexico, is emerging as an international pilgrimage site for those seeking cures from heaven and from the very power of the sanctuary's soil; the sacred theater of Mexican American Catholics, dominating the public streets of San Antonio during Holy Week, invites pilgrims and spectators to share in the drama of Christ's road to Calvary. Indeed, as the U.S. census data for 2000 indicates, Hispanics are now poised to surpass African Americans as the nation's largest minority group. Within the loose census category of Hispanic, which spans immigrant groups from the Caribbean to South America, those of Mexican ancestry make up about 60 percent of the nation's 35 million Latinos. Elizondo's *mestizo* future is already present.

GAY RIGHTS AND WOMEN'S RIGHTS

Confronting the realities of discrimination and inequality in the latter half of the twentieth century meant extending attention to issues of gender and sexuality. As with the struggles for civil rights and social justice for African Americans and Hispanics, the drive for women's equality and for gay rights has both energized and fractured America's religious institutions. In the late twentieth century the ordination of women and gays was a consistent flash point of controversy. Issues related to gender and sexuality dominated discussion across a wide religious spectrum, compelling every tradition to reconsider its commitments and to reexamine its historical positions.

In late June 1969 the New York City police raided the Stonewall Inn, a club frequented by gays in Greenwich Village, on the charge that it was operating without a liquor license. A violent confrontation between police

99. The Reverend Troy Perry, founder of the Metropolitan Community Church, has long been a leading voice for the full inclusion of gays and lesbians in the Christian community and the wider society. *Universal Fellowship of Metropolitan Community Churches*

and patrons ensued, and the sparring and taunting quickly spilled out into the streets. The Stonewall riots and protests served as an important spark for a new liberation movement, one dedicated to protecting and ensuring the civil rights of gays and lesbians. A few months earlier, in October 1968, Troy Perry, an openly gay minister of a deeply evangelical background, took a step that gave some inkling of the religious dimensions of the movement. Gathering a small group of worshipers together in his home in Los Angeles, he inaugurated a gay and lesbian Christian fellowship. In 1972 Perry published the first of his autobiographies, *The Lord*

Is My Shepherd and He Knows I'm Gay, chronicling his early years as a Pentecostal and Baptist preacher and the eventual revoking of his ministerial license as a result of his homosexuality. The book served also as a manifesto of his new ministry and his vision for a transformed church that was openly accepting of gays and lesbians and that was carefully attentive to the pastoral needs of those so long scorned and condemned. Over the next three decades the group Perry founded in Los Angeles grew into a small denomination, the Universal Fellowship of Metropolitan Community Churches (UFMCC), with dozens of churches across the country and more than 40,000 adherents.

The kind of Christian inclusivity for which the UFMCC stands has often met with profound hostility. Local congregations from Los Angeles to Nashville to Baltimore have been the targets of arsonists and vandals, and many of the denomination's clergy have been assaulted and threatened. Violence against gays and lesbians has remained rampant across the country—most notoriously in the murder of Matthew Shepard, a young gay man tied to a fence and tortured in Laramie, Wyoming, in October 1998. Not surprisingly, combating hate crimes has stayed high on the social and political agenda of the UFMCC. Troy Perry has joined forces, for example, with Jesse Jackson, veteran Baptist preacher and social activist, to rally for hate crimes legislation, a legal provision that took on new urgency among civil rights advocates after the murder of James Byrd, who was dragged to his death behind the pickup of three white racists in Texas in June 1998. The partnership of Perry and Jackson, reminiscent of the wider alliances formed in the civil rights movement, shows a new religious coalition emerging on the left that supports federal protections against hate crimes and that stands in solidarity with gay and lesbian Christians. As one UFMCC official said in an address in 1998 before the National Council of Churches, "There are over 13 million gay and lesbian, bisexual, transgendered people living in the United States today. Thirteen million. We will not simply go away. . . . 'Homosexuality' will not just disappear from the Church either. No matter what people do to so many of us, gay and lesbian people—they will not separate us from our love of Jesus Christ or from our belief that God created us and had a plan for us as a people of dignity through His love and Grace."

Beyond confronting the violence against gays and lesbians in American culture, religious groups have faced a number of other agonizing issues related to the full participation of homosexuals in their communities. Two issues in particular have stood out for their level of contestation: the ordination of gays and lesbians to the ministry and the ceremonial blessing of same-sex unions. Just how contentious these issues have become is evident in the saga of Jimmy Creech. As a United Methodist minister in North Carolina, Creech became a local leader in the late 1980s of the Raleigh Religious Network for Gay and Lesbian Equality. Supporting an array of antidiscrimination measures, Creech lobbied for the legal recognition of gay relationships, for the rights of adoption for gay parents, for the repeal of antisodomy laws, and for a compassionate community response to the AIDS crisis. Creech, like many other activists, extended the logic of the larger civil rights movement to an attack on the "heterosexism" of American civil and religious institutions. "We know that racism is a sin, an offense against God," Creech exhorted. "Heterosexism is just as sinful, just as offensive to God."

A longtime supporter of both gay ordination and same-sex unions, Creech made the national spotlight in 1997 when he conducted "a holy union ceremony" for a lesbian couple at a Methodist church in Omaha, Nebraska. The stage had been set for a public showdown by the General Conference of the United Methodist Church, which had formally voted against the ordination of homosexuals in 1988 and against the celebration of union ceremonies for gay couples in 1996. Creech was brought to church trial, initially acquitted in the Omaha case, but then found guilty in November 1999 for continuing to perform same-sex union ceremonies. The ordeals of Jimmy Creech carried some of the fanfare of the Scopes trial of 1925, with pickets and protests arrayed on both sides and with the national news media offering a flurry of coverage. Stripped of his ministerial credentials in his own church, Creech moved to the UFMCC, where he has continued his campaign of civil disobedience and social action to stop the "spiritual violence" committed by church bodies against gays and lesbians. While officially free of Creech, the Methodists, like most other denominations, were hardly free of the deep divisions that marked the issues of gay ordination and same-sex unions. Some groups, such as Reform Jews and Unitarian-Universalists, had clearly staked out a progressive position on these issues, and some, such as Southern Baptists, had consolidated their opposition, but for most religious bodies, schism rather than reconciliation seemed the drumbeat of the new millennium.

If conflict has run high over the movement toward gay liberation, controversy has been equally intense over women's liberation and its religious implications. The drive for women's rights has been a long one, filled with frustration and disappointment, and religion has not always been in the vanguard. Instead, religion has often been the restraining anchor, the unyielding institution, the bastion of male domination reinforced by centuries-old traditions and buttressed by a "thus saith the Lord." But as in other movements for civil rights, religion has also been a fertile source of women's resistance. Women have led religious movements of their own, have dominated church membership rolls, and have exercised leadership in such disparate areas as missions, religious education, temperance reform, and health services. Yet most doors to women's wider participation have not opened easily, and some have not opened at all.

Since the 1960s and 1970s gender-inclusive language has been a particularly fecund area of controversy and innovation. Standard liturgies and traditional Christian hymns have regularly used the male pronoun not only for God but also for all the people of God. Hymns such as "Rise Up, O Men of God," "Faith of Our Fathers," or "Good Christian Men Rejoice" have increasingly proven less than stirring to those who hear in such words only continued patriarchal domination and sexist exclusion. As feminist theologian Rosemary Radford Ruether has pointed out, the ruling group uses language to define reality in its own terms, reducing the subordinate group to a point of near invisibility. "Women," says Ruether, "more than any other group, are overwhelmed by a linguistic form that excludes them from visible existence." In speaking only of the "fatherhood of God" and the "brotherhood of man," religion reflects and also helps construct the social reality of male power and privilege. In this line of thought, the rhetoric of sexuality serves as "both a mirror and a legitimation of the oppressing and eclipsing of women." Thus it is time, wrote one author, to move *Beyond God the Father;* it is time, wrote others, to know again *The Once and Future Goddess* or *When God Was a Woman.*

In seeking to revise gender talk about God, women have sought to transform the very language and liturgies that religious communities employ, and such transformations have been the source of both tremendous creativity and tremendous opposition. The scope of the division became especially evident after the "Re-Imagining Conference," a major gathering of feminist theologians and churchgoing women held in Minneapolis in November 1993. Centered on furthering the development of Christian feminist spirituality and ritual, the Re-Imagining event became renown (or, from the opposing perspective, notorious) for its celebration of the worship of Sophia or Wisdom as an ancient feminine aspect of the divine. Proponents suggested that "Fairest Sophia," long suppressed within the patriarchal traditions of orthodox Christian piety, now needed to be recovered as a feminine face of God and actively incorporated into the eucharistic rituals and prayers of the church. Such explorations drew the sustained fire of various evangelicals and conservatives, who saw the issue as a matter not of equality but of apostasy, and their counter-rhetoric often took on an inquisitorial quality. Earl G. Hunt, a retired Methodist bishop, went so far as to claim that "no comparable heresy has appeared in the church in the last fifteen centuries." A few years later one still-outraged critic, under the banner headline "Invasion of the Sophia Women," dated the "the organized Feminist/Lesbian take-over of the mainline denominations" to the Re-Imagining Conference in 1993. Revising religious language and liturgy to reflect the values of gender equity and inclusion has proven a tough, conflict-ridden proposition.

If anything, gender conflicts are even more acute when dealing not with symbols but with the realities of authority, of office and power. How many women are on governing boards of denominations and seminaries, of local churches and synagogues? How many women have been accepted as equals in the professional ministry of the several denominations? Or, to raise the ante, how many women have broken through the "stained-glass ceiling" into positions of leadership at big-steeple churches? Issues of women's ordination dominated all others from the 1960s through the 1980s, and even in the 1990s the biggest debate in the largest Protestant denomination, the Southern Baptists, remained tightly focused on women's ordination and the reservation of the power of the senior pastor position for men alone.

Some Protestant groups—for example, the Pentecostal and Holiness bodies—had a long tradition of female preaching. Quakers with their tradition of no professional clergy listened to male and female alike, as the Spirit moved, and early Methodists and Freewill Baptists had inherited a modicum of that Quaker openness to women preachers and exhorters. In Christian Science the number of female practitioners greatly outnumbered the male, and in some other religious bodies, such as the Spiritualists and Freethinkers, gender equity had been pursued, sometimes idiosyncratically, sometimes systematically. But in the majority of religious groups the leadership of women did not come easily, and steps taken in that direction were anything but easy.

When, for example, the Episcopal Church in 1976 ruled that women could be ordained priests, a dozen or more churches soon broke away from the parent body, forming a separate diocese for those who "wish to remain faithful to the traditional Church." "Most of the reasons the church gave for ordaining women," the dissenters explained, "are on a sociological plane, not a theological plane." Equality between the sexes, they also argued, did not imply identity of function for the sexes. Meanwhile, the Episcopal Church continued to ordain women priests and then, in 1989,

100. Amid much controversy and some schism, the Episcopal Church in the 1970s began ordaining women to the priesthood; here three such recently ordained priests join in celebrating communion in New York City in 1974. *Religious News Service*

confirmed the election of the first female bishop in the church, Barbara C. Harris. Here, too, the action was met with resistance and many expressions of displeasure, yet the Episcopal Church as a whole appears steady in its course of making available more and more opportunities for women to enter the professional ministry at all levels.

Within Lutheranism the progress has been uneven as separate segments have moved toward the ordination of women at varying speeds. The Lutheran Church in America in 1966 called for a "reexamination of all stereotyped cultural and social differences between man and woman, to determine those that are relative and outmoded and consequently irrelevant and even harmful to the church's ministry." In the late 1960s three large Lutheran groups held an Inter-Lutheran Consultation on the Ordination of Women. Two of the three groups had approved such ordination by 1970, but the third, the more conservative Lutheran Church–Missouri Synod, did not. That group preferred to debate not whether women could become ministers but whether they could attend business meetings of the church and, if they could attend, whether they could be granted the right to vote. In 1969 this synod agreed that the oft-quoted scriptural injunction for women to "keep silent" in church did not necessarily apply to congregational meetings, but it did apply to holding the pastoral office.

Some denominations, rather than taking steps in the direction of female ordination and greater leadership opportunities for women, have taken steps in the opposite direction. The Southern Baptist Convention had ordained women as early as 1964 and by the mid-1980s had ordained over 400 women. By that time, however, ordaining women to the ministry had become highly controversial, with an increasingly conservative leadership becoming ever more outspoken in opposition to such action. At its 1984 annual meeting, in a crucial fundamentalist move, the Southern Baptist Convention declared that women should not assume a role of authority over men. Women were to be excluded from the pastoral ministry to "preserve a submission God requires because the man was first in creation and the woman was first in the Edenic fall." In 1986 the convention's Home Mission Board voted not to grant funds to any church that employed a woman pastor, and then in 1998 the convention capped its reactionary turn by declaring that women were to practice "gracious" submission to their husbands' leadership. By then the conservatives had control of the denomination's leading seminaries, including Southern Theological Seminary, the flagship in Louisville, Kentucky, where the faculty had been purged of tenured women such as theologian Molly Marshall.

Though beleaguered, moderate Southern Baptists have kept up the pressure in support of women's ordination and women's leadership. In 1998 William Self, a leading Georgia Baptist and a member of the moderates' Cooperative Baptist Fellowship, said that he found the actions of the Southern Baptist Convention limiting the roles of women in church and society so offensive that he thought the denomination owed "every woman an apology." Having opposed the 1984 resolution against the ordination of women "with all my heart," Self was, by 1998, embarrassed by his denomination's redirection. "I think our wives and daughters must hear an apology from all of us. They must hear and know that they can be all that God wants them to be. Parents, when you bring your children to this church and put them in our Sunday school, you will not hear anyone tell your daughter that she can't be all that God intended for her to be. She can grow up to be anything that God has ordained her and called her to be." And then Self followed with a bit of his own autobiography that was revealing of wider Baptist experience. "I grew up with a strong-minded mother, I married a strong-minded woman whose mother was a strong-minded woman. Churches have always been run by women. I cannot imagine intelligent, right-minded women being subservient to men." Self's heartfelt engagement with these issues indicates how much poignancy and power they still carry in Southern Baptist circles.

In Roman Catholicism the question of the ordination of women has been highly visible and the resistance, to this point, highly successful. Nonetheless, slow changes are under way. In 1972 the Leadership Conference of Women Religious was organized in the United States, a body that represented about 90 percent of all sisters and nuns in this country. Two years after its organization the conference supported "the principle that all ministries in the Church be open to women and men as the Spirit calls them." In 1976 hundreds of Catholic women organized a Women's Ordination Conference to protest "a priesthood that is elitist, hierarchical, racist, classist." Taking a strong stand on behalf of equal *rites* for Catholic women, this group and others associated with it contended that "what is central to the historical Jesus is his humanity and not his maleness."

The following year, however, the road became bumpy when the Vatican released its "Declaration on the Question of the Admission of Women to the Ministerial Priesthood." Christ was a male, the report solemnly explained, and he called as apostles only males, and moreover, one can find no evidence of an intent to widen the ministry to include females. With these words the declaration affirmed, as Rosemary Ruether observed, "some mysterious sacramental bond between Christ, maleness, and priesthood." But, as Ruether also pointed out, the Vatican statement was met with a mixture of incredulity and ridicule, the end result being that the numbers of Catholics in this country that favored the ordination of women actually went up, not down. By the 1990s more than 60 percent of the American Catholic laity favored the ordination of women to the priesthood.

Meanwhile, the Roman Catholic Church confronted special problems with respect to the thousands of nuns that served in one capacity or another in the United States. Two problems stood out. The first was that the general trend toward gender equality and female liberation caused many nuns to chafe under the severe restrictions of dress, behavior, and male authority. Some small orders disbanded as entities under church discipline, and thousands of individual nuns left the cloister to serve as church administrators, prison chaplains, social workers, professors, and even holders of public office. The second problem was the declining attractiveness of the convent as a religious vocation for Catholic young women. The number entering any order declined sharply from over 30,000 in the years from 1958 to 1962 to fewer than 3,000 in the years between 1976 and 1981. In 1960 the total number of sisters in America was about 170,000; by the late 1980s that number had fallen to a little over 100,000.

The Catholic Church also managed to create more problems for itself on women's issues when in 1968 Pope Paul VI issued an encyclical entitled *Humane Vitae* ("On Human Life"). Contrary to wide expectation, this encyclical did not moderate or modify the church's historic position with respect to contraception but strongly reaffirmed the long-standing prohibitions against any form of birth control outside abstinence. "Each and every marriage act," the papal letter declared, "must remain open to the transmission of life." Repeated surveys in the United States revealed that Catholics practiced birth control at about the same rate as non-Catholics in similar economic or social classes. Not too surprisingly, then, criticism of *Humane Vitae* abounded, and where it was not criticized its prohibitions were often simply ignored. Theologians at the Catholic University of America were quick to point out that the encyclical was not "an infallible teaching" and that like many other positions taken by the church in the past, this one, too, could prove to be "inadequate or even erroneous." Such moderating voices notwithstanding, many American Catholic women found themselves on a collision course with the Vatican over issues that involved control of their own bodies, whether the issue was taking the Pill, getting an abortion, or engaging in premarital sex.

As was the case with Lutheranism, Judaism found itself moving with uneven step toward a full clerical equality for women. Reform Judaism made the initial breakthrough when it ordained its first female rabbi in 1972. Rabbi Sally Priesand spent eight years preparing for that moment, preparing, as she wrote, "for a profession that no woman had yet entered." The happiness of the event in 1972 was somewhat diminished by the resistance of many congregations to hire or even interview her. But then the Stephen Wise Free Synagogue in New York City offered her the position of assistant rabbi, and that was "a blessing in the true sense of the word." She committed herself, she noted, to the survival of the Jewish tradition, "knowing that Judaism had traditionally discriminated against women [and] that it had not always been sensitive to the problems of total equality." But, said Rabbi Priesand, Judaism has "tremendous flexibility," this enabling the tradition to survive for so many centuries and likewise enabling her to work toward "the necessary changes which will grant women total equality within the Jewish community."

At the leading institution of Conservative Judaism, the Jewish Theological Seminary of New York City, the faculty in 1979 voted to postpone "indefinitely" the question of ordaining female rabbis. Indefinitely turned out to last only four years as that same faculty in 1983 voted thirty-four to eight to open the doors for such ordination. By that time Reform Judaism had ordained over sixty young women and the small Reconstructionist branch over a dozen. Resistance among Conservative rabbis to the 1983

101. In 1972 Reform Judaism ordained its first female rabbi—Sally Priesand, standing in the center—and since then has become fully inclusive of women rabbis. *Religious News Service*

decision took the form of vocal reproof rather than schism, one rabbi pleading for "a great deal of compassion lest we fall into the kind of polarization that exists among our friends in the Orthodox world."

That "Orthodox world," both in Israel and in America, did present a much more daunting picture, at least so far as the ordination of women was concerned. Orthodoxy in America stood firm against ordination, but that did not mean that no winds of feminism blew there. Blu Greenberg, married to an Orthodox rabbi and mother of children being raised in the Orthodox tradition, wrote in 1981 of her gradual realization of how total the male domination in that branch of Judaism had been. Under the stimulus of the feminist movement of the 1960s, she reported, "I became sensitized to issues and situations that previously had made no impression upon me." But the feminist engagement with Orthodoxy has remained tough going for many. Vanessa Ochs, writing of her complex pursuit of the Orthodox way of learning, is finally at a loss to explain the wisdom of the rabbis for whom the study of Torah was a male preserve. "The words of the Torah should be burnt," one rabbi had said, "rather than be taught to women." "If these sages have divine sanction," Ochs concludes, "how poorly that divinity esteems me."

In one case after another, American religious institutions in the closing years of the twentieth century confronted the issues of equity and justice that the movements for women's rights and gay rights raised so dramatically. Those causes stirred deep scriptural debates and crises of authority in the culture. What, after all, did the Bible say (and not say) about equality and sexuality? These movements raised as well fundamental questions about the organization of the family, about parenting and home life, and about the intimate relationship of couples, all of which were issues that went to the core of religious traditions and institutions. That America's religious bodies seemed ill equipped to resolve these monumental issues was hardly surprising. Yet the rancor itself is in some ways encouraging. As with the civil rights movement, overt struggle and engagement are far better than silence and invisibility.

UNIONS AND REUNIONS

With all the conflict and separation based on race, gender, class, and sexuality, American religion in the latter half of the twentieth century also evidenced divisions based on religion itself. Schisms and separations appeared, decade by decade, to grow only more flagrant, more irreversible. Denominations, already representing countless divisions in themselves, divided even further, and the search for a pattern in that multicolored quilt known as religion in America might have appeared bewildering. But there is another side to that story of fragmentation, especially in the last half century, and that side also deserves some recognition.

Aside from such broadly cooperative groups as the National Association of Evangelicals formed in 1942, the World Council of Churches founded in 1948, and the National Council of Churches, whose old federated structure was revised in 1950, many denominations in the middle and late twentieth century took steps that led to actual merger. The Congregational Christian Churches (the result of an earlier union in 1931) in 1957 merged with the largely German Evangelical and Reformed Church to form what is now called the United Church of Christ. The Methodists, having brought their southern and northern sections together in 1939, joined with a German Methodist group in 1968 to form the United Methodist Church. Both Congregationalism and Methodism, strengthened by mergers, nonetheless found themselves weakened by a slow but steady decline in membership, that quarter century of decline only recently leveling off.

Presbyterians, divided earlier by questions of revivalism, education, slavery, and ordination, managed in 1983 to bring together the northern and southern halves of a denomination that split just prior to the Civil War. The resulting body, taking the name of the Presbyterian Church (U.S.A.) built upon an earlier union (1958) between northern Presbyterians and a Scottish communion called the United Presbyterian Church of North America. A quarter century after that merger, the even larger and more significant one took place, creating a church of over 3 million members, by far the largest representative of that ecclesiastical family in America. Not all Presbyterians joined in the new church, to be sure; the Presbyterian Church in America, for example, held its membership of less than a quarter million to a more conservative stance, both theologically and socially.

Lutheranism had been divided not so much by such issues as slavery and revivalism as by its countries of origin and its periods of immigration. But modern mergers have overcome many of those historic separations. In 1960 the American Lutheran Church (ALC) gathered together Midwesterners of German, Norwegian, and Danish extraction; then two years later the Lutheran Church in America (LCA) represented a union of German, Danish, Finnish, and Swedish elements. The former with a membership of over 2 million and the latter with a membership of just under 3 million then pulled off still another merger in 1988 to create the Evangelical Lutheran Church in America. Also joining in this splash of ecumenicity was a smaller group that in the turmoil of the 1970s had separated from the more conservative Lutheran Church–Missouri Synod. Church historian Martin E. Marty, a member of that smaller group and a leader in the complex negotiations for merger, described the final vote of approval as the "most decisive day" for Lutheranism in North America. Mergers in and of themselves are not destiny, to be sure, but they increase the possibility that an emboldened, unified, historic tradition might have a definable public voice in American culture.

The most ambitious effort to shape the destiny of institutional religion in America, launched with much fanfare in 1960, took the name of the Consultation on Church Union (COCU). For more than a quarter of a century, earnest and sometimes tense negotiations have taken place among Methodists (both black and white), Presbyterians, Episcopalians, Disciples of Christ, Congregationalists (under the name of United Church of Christ), and from time to time other denominations as well. Dialogue began in the early years with considerable enthusiasm and high optimism that an actual merger of 20 million or more American Protestants might take place sometime in the 1970s.

By the 1980s, however, both optimism and enthusiasm waned as delegates to the successive plenary sessions solved one problem only to find several others immediately taking its place. Some theological agreement was reached in 1984, but ecclesiastical hurdles (the power of bishops, the relationship with worldwide denominational fellowships, and the like) remained. In the late 1980s COCU pulled back from the idea of full merger to what was called "Covenant Communion." Under the terms of this proposed agreement, the several member denominations would ordain clergy jointly, hold baptismal services in common, and cooperate in such areas as foreign missions and domestic social agenda. Each church would continue, however, to govern its internal affairs and to maintain close ties with such transnational bodies as the Anglican Communion and the World Alliance of Reformed Churches. Forty years into its mission, COCU still retains its ecumenical vision, but as members of the consultation confessed in January 1999, "we have not always been certain of the road toward visible unity in Christ, or patient with the pace of our journey." Many members, though, held out hope for a more visible reconciliation of competing ministries in the first decade of the new millennium.

Perhaps the most dramatic strides in the last quarter century or so have come from a source that in many respects was the least expected: the Roman Catholic Church. Part of the turnaround was due no doubt to the personality and charm of Pope John XXIII, but changes were institutional no less than personal. Beginning with John's creation of a Secretariat for Promoting Christian Unity in 1960, the Catholic Church has repeatedly demonstrated a desire for dialogue as well as an openness to mutual instruction. Vatican II issued its decree on ecumenism in 1964, this important document signaling, in the words of one Protestant observer, "the beginning of a new era in the relation of the Churches to one another." That it was a new era quickly became evident as steps were taken to enlarge Catholic participation in the World Council of Churches, as Pope Paul VI received the Archbishop of Canterbury in 1966 and in 1967 journeyed to Istanbul to pay an official visit to Patriarch Athenagoras I. In 1975 Paul canonized the first American-born saint, Elizabeth Seton (1774–1821), paying respectful tribute to her upbringing in New York City as an Episcopalian. In that same year he addressed a committee charged with special responsibility for improved Christian-Jewish relations, urging that "a true dialogue may be established between Judaism and Christianity." What Vatican II delivered in 1964 set the tone for decades to come; much was done, even if much remained to be done.

John Paul II, who ascended to the papal office in 1978, through his extensive travels and countless meetings continued the ecumenical efforts among the Orthodox, the Protestants, and the non-Christians as well. In 1979 he, too, made the pilgrimage to Istanbul, assuring Patriarch Dimitrios I that the thousand years of common history between East and West (before the final schism in 1054) should be sufficient basis for greater unity "between our sister-Churches." Dimitrios responded, "Your coming here, full of Christian charity and simplicity, means more than a mere meeting between two local bishops." East and West might perhaps be one again: "We believe that at this moment the Lord is present among us here." In that same year John Paul II addressed ecumenical leaders gathered in Washington, D.C., welcoming "the opportunity to embrace you, in the charity of Christ, as beloved Christian brethren and fellow disciples of the Lord Jesus." Such irenic gestures toward the Eastern Orthodox churches have continued to be a common part of the pontificate of John Paul II.

But apart from these highly visible papal visits and papal words, dialogues were more quietly begun between Roman Catholics and the Lutheran World Federation in 1965; with the Anglican Communion and the World Methodist Council in 1966; with the World Alliance of Reformed Churches in 1968; and with Pentecostals in 1972. Meanwhile, Protestants were themselves carrying on quieter dialogues away from the public spotlight: Lutherans with Reformed; Episcopalians with the Orthodox; the United Church of Christ with the Disciples of Christ; the Churches of Christ with the Disciples of Christ; and the Methodists with the Episcopalians. These inconspicuous exchanges were still bearing fruit right through the 1990s and into the new millennium. For example, in 1998 the Lutherans and the Catholics managed to come to an agreement on the age-old source of their disagreement, the doctrine of justification by faith alone. And in 2000, after years of negotiation, the Episcopal Church and the Evangelical Lutheran Church entered into full communion with each other.

Yet, for all these unions and reunions, several dark clouds dotted the ecumenical horizon. The National Council of Churches (NCC) and the World Council of Churches (WCC), under critical scrutiny from such media sources as *Reader's Digest* and *60 Minutes*, took a beating in the 1980s and 1990s for their left-leaning political, theological, and economic stands. In 1992, for example, the NCC jumped into the fray over the five hundredth anniversary of Columbus's discovery of America, presenting the explorer not as a daring Italian Catholic mariner but as an arch villain in a drama of colonialist invasion and genocide. The council's efforts to turn the celebration into an occasion of repentance seemed to provoke more bewilderment than serious reflection or sorrow. By the late 1990s both the NCC and WCC faced massive financial crises and severe cutbacks in programs, making the apparent future of such ecumenical bodies less than bright.

And, not to be forgotten, the issues that divided the various churches ripped apart their ecumenical councils as well. When the Universal Fellowship of Metropolitan Community Churches approached the National Council of Churches about membership in 1982 and 1983, the fragility and limits of church unity became crystal clear. The council, wary of further alienating its diverse constituencies, especially the Orthodox churches, kept postponing action, finally voting against "observer status" for the UFMCC in 1992. In the battle-strewn landscape of American religion, even the ecumenical movement offered little rest to those weary of the divisions over human sexuality.

CHAPTER 18

Politics and Pluralism

The 1960s and early 1970s represented a high point of liberal religious activism—from the successes of the civil rights movement to the birth of the gay rights and women's rights movements to the protests of the war in Vietnam. That activist legacy survived into the 1980s and 1990s, but much of its political thunder was stolen through the organized resurgence of conservative Protestantism. Now it was the religious right, not the religious left, that captured the bulk of the nation's attention. At the same time, the revision of immigration laws in 1965 led to a fundamental shift in immigrant demographics, and the religious patterns of the United States, for so long seemingly decipherable within Christian and Jewish frameworks, became ever more diverse. That widening pluralism—Muslim, Buddhist, Hindu, Sikh, among others—had transformed the basic shape of American religion by the turn of new millennium and portended still greater changes ahead.

Pluralism, though, also remained a matter of home-grown sects, as the nation continued to grapple with new religious movements. Such movements, which for so long had found America's voluntaristic and democratized milieu a fertile seedbed, only grew more visible and variegated after the 1960s. At the same time, religious identity itself became increasingly plural as spiritual seekers tried on a whole series of devotional options and esoteric practices. Spirituality, experiencing a great boom in the last decade or so of the century, was itself an eclectic, pluralistic construct, embracing everything from Gregorian chants to Jewish mysticism, channeling to yoga, Buddhist meditation to shamanic drumming.

RELIGION AND POLITICS

In the 1960s so much had galvanized the activism of religious liberals and progressives, and nothing more so than the long-lasting Vietnam War

(1964–1973). The longer the war continued and the greater the escalation of American military presence, the more uneasy or critical many segments of the American public, including the religious public, became. In 1965 an organization called Clergy and Laymen Concerned About Vietnam was formed to give stronger voice to the religious protests against the war. In 1966 the nation's Catholic bishops warned of the "grave danger that the circumstances of the present war in Vietnam may, in time, diminish our moral sensitivity to its evils." In 1967 the United Presbyterian Church affirmed that "there is no moral issue more urgently confronting our Church and nation than the war in Vietnam. The hour is late; the Church dare not remain silent. We must declare our conscience." Many did declare their consciences, marching in the streets, protesting on the Washington Mall, disrupting university campuses from coast to coast, and urging church as well as synagogue to forthright action. With the number of American dead and wounded soaring to over 200,000 by the war's end, the ghosts of that military deployment have long haunted the American soul.

The antiwar protests that Vietnam precipitated made peace activism a primary component of the religious left's identity. Much of the leadership came from the Catholic left. The Trappist monk Thomas Merton (1915–1968) took an early stand on behalf of nonviolence and, with his plentiful and popular writings, served as a spiritual guide within the wider peace movement. Even greater attention came to a Jesuit father, Daniel Berrigan, and his brother in the Josephite order, Philip, when they encouraged resistance to the military draft and especially when in 1968 they burned draft board records in Catonsville, Maryland. Both men, arrested and jailed by the government and censured by ecclesiastical superiors, proved an embarrassment to church authorities and to much of the Catholic constituency. What, they asked, did these dissident Catholics think they were doing in resisting the war so dramatically?

Wary of the protests and subversive activities of the Catholic left, America's Catholic bishops initially held themselves aloof, but eventually they came to share in much of the peace movement's larger critique of nuclear proliferation and deterrence. In 1983 the nation's bishops disturbed many with their pastoral letter "The Challenge of Peace: God's Promise and Our Response." The letter adopted a critical tone, critical even of the United States, that disturbed conservative Catholics who thought their bishops were meddling in politics and matters beyond their ken. "We fear," wrote the bishops, "that our world and nation are headed in the wrong direction." The situation was grim, the bishops said, and what it called for was not larger stockpiles of atomic weapons but a "moral about-face." Somehow the nation and the world "must summon the moral courage to say No to nuclear conflict," the bishops concluded, "No to weapons of mass destruction; No to an arms race which robs the poor and the vulnerable; and No to the moral danger of a nuclear age which places before humankind indefensible choices of constant terror or surrender." The time had come for peacemaking, not as mere political policy, but as "a requirement of our faith."

The protests in the early to mid-1980s on behalf of a nuclear freeze were a crescendo of this movement on the religious left. In 1982, the year before the Catholic bishops' pastoral letter, about 1 million people took to the streets of New York City to protest nuclear armaments, especially President Ronald Reagan's support for the production and deployment of the MX missile system. That demonstration, one of the largest in American history, was followed the next year with the television dramatization of nuclear Armageddon in *The Day After*, which drew the biggest TV audience of the year. The issue was clearly in the forefront of public consciousness, and that intensified awareness presented an opening for religious activists and reformers, some of whom boldly imagined themselves as the new abolitionists. Pushing for a halt on the testing and production of nuclear weapons, grassroots peace groups saw a nuclear freeze as a way to bring an end to the arms race and to stave off the unfathomable destructiveness of nuclear warfare. Other political issues in the 1980s struck deep religious chords on the left, such as the sanctuary movement, in which local churches sought, against the will of the American Immigration and Naturalization Service, to provide a haven for Salvadoran and Guatemalan refugees fleeing the civil strife in their homelands. Still, no other political cause of the period generated greater religious resonance and reaction than that of nuclear disarmament.

The nuclear threat also played into another leading issue on the religious left, that of environmental protection. Nuclear power plants, with their radioactive wastes and potential for catastrophe, were the target of various ecological warnings and protests, and that resistance was interconnected with a much larger "greening" of American religion and theology. Building on deep-rooted conservationist and preservationist legacies, the environmental movement gained new momentum in the decades following the 1960s, taking on issues that ranged from air, water, and noise pollution to chemical pesticides and energy resources to biodiversity and global warming. In 1962 Rachel Carson's bellwether work, *Silent Spring*, detailed the baneful effects of pesticides, and two years later the Faith-Man-Nature group, a consortium of theologians and conservationists, came together to explore the religious dimensions of environmental issues and to articulate a theology of stewardship for God's creation. To those ends, the group published a manifesto called *Christians and the Good Earth* in 1968.

On April 22, 1970, the first Earth Day was held and shared in the larger culture of protest that had come to the fore through the civil rights and antiwar movements. Along with teach-ins on pollution and recycling, citizens participated in a carnivalesque air of costuming and playful destruction (the ritualized bashing of gas-guzzling cars, for example). Religious institutions offered substantial support for this ecological festival; the National Council of Churches, for example, offered its official support and endorsement of Earth Day. "The Church must begin talking a theology of ecology," preached Episcopal bishop Paul Moore Jr. in the Cathedral of St. John the Divine in New York City. And religious groups increasingly did, evident in a proliferation of publications on the theme, such as H. Paul Santmire's *Brother Earth* (1970), John B. Cobb's *Is It Too Late? A Theology of Ecology* (1972), Matthew Fox's *Creation Spirituality* (1988), and Sallie McFague's *Models of God: Theology for an Ecological, Nuclear Age* (1989). Environmentalism has continued to stir the religious left especially, evident even with such prominent politicians as former vice president Al Gore, whose *Earth in the Balance* (1993) preached the ecological gospel. By the 1990s the religious measure had become *environmental justice:* attentiveness to protecting the environment combined with a social awareness of the ways in which the neighborhoods of the poor and the marginalized are left especially vulnerable to dangerous wastes and polluted air.

The religious left still has plenty of vigor at the dawn of the twenty-first century. Indeed, some have pointed to the nomination of Senator Joseph Lieberman as Al Gore's running mate in 2000 as bringing the religious left back into the national spotlight. Lieberman, an Orthodox Jew who came of age in the civil rights struggles of the 1960s, spoke passionately during the campaign on the fundamental role of religion in American civic life. "I hope," he said of his candidacy, that "it will enable people, all people who are moved, to talk about their faith and about their religion, and I hope it will reinforce a belief that I feel as strongly as anything else, that there must be a place for faith in America's public life." Arousing the suspicions of some secularists and civil liberties groups (including the Anti-Defamation League), Lieberman argued against any formulation of liberalism that substituted "freedom from religion" for "freedom of religion." For those on the religious left who had grown "tired of the religious right getting the last word in religion," it seemed about time that the religious dimensions of social progressivism get a larger hearing again. Yet political fortunes are notoriously fickle, and none more so than the hair's-breadth defeat of the Gore-Lieberman ticket. The supposed revival of the religious left during the 2000 campaign was, in many ways, just another media bubble. Yet the issues that propel grassroots activism—the environment, feminism, civil rights, acceptance of gays and lesbians, economic justice—remain, and so do the various religious organizations, whether Church Women United or the Network for Environmental and Economic Responsibility, that make such issues their own.

In the domain of religion and politics, the dominant story of the last quarter of the twentieth century was not the post-1960s legacy of the religious left but instead the rise of the new Christian right. As a movement, it has generated high hopes for the redemption of the United States as a Christian nation and at the same time has provoked soaring fears of theocratic intolerance. The resurgence of evangelical Protestantism as a political force sneaked up on a lot of pundits, but by the late 1970s the significance of the phenomenon was lost on few of them. In 1979 a mighty triumvirate of new organizations emerged: the Moral Majority, led by Jerry Falwell, a Baptist minister in Lynchburg, Virginia; the Christian Voice, with headquarters in Pasadena, California, and with strong congressional representation in Washington, D.C.; and the Religious Roundtable of Arlington, Virginia, directed by a Texas evangelist, James Robison. These groups shared similar if not identical agendas; they also shared ties with the political right, both nationally and at the local levels. They united in promoting prayer in the public schools, in opposing abortion, in condemning homosexuality, in despairing over the growth of "secular humanism," in supporting at least equal time for the teaching of creationism, and in promoting in whatever way possible a "return" to a Christian America. They also united in such events as a "Washington for Jesus Day," which was held in 1980 on the Washington Mall, with the speakers reflecting both political and religious conservative ranks.

The agenda of the Christian right has taken much of its shape from the conservative wing of the Republican Party. These forces combined, for example, to oppose nuclear test ban treaties, the Equal Rights Amendment, affirmative action, the National Endowment for the Arts, school busing, and gays in the military. At the same time, they combined to support increased spending on national defense, school vouchers, and tax relief for families (such as the elimination of the marriage tax penalty). Christian lobbying groups wielded increasing power throughout the

102. The Reverend Jerry Falwell, founder of the Moral Majority, addressed huge congregations in his Baptist Church in Lynchburg, Virginia; his television audience was estimated to be as high as 4 million at the peak of popularity. *Religious News Service*

1980s and 1990s, claiming credit for conservative victories and liberal defeats in various elections at national, state, and local levels.

The banner group of the early to mid-1980s had been Falwell's Moral Majority, which closed down in 1989 at a moment when even its partisans felt temporarily beleaguered by a series of scandals involving TV evangelists such as Jim Bakker and Jimmy Swaggart. Having accomplished his mission of politically activating America's conservative Christians, Falwell retired from the front lines of the fray and settled into a role of elder statesman of the movement he had helped launch. The same year that witnessed the demise of the Moral Majority also saw the birth of the next banner group of the movement, the Christian Coalition. Founded by the TV preacher and presidential candidate Pat Robertson, the group has concentrated its resources especially on "voter education" through the distribution of voting guides tilted to the family issues long dear to the religious right. By the year 2000 the group claimed to be distributing some 70 million guides across all fifty states. Though Robertson himself stepped down from the presidency of the coalition in late 2001, the organization remains a flagship of the religious right.

The Christian Coalition, if formidable as a grassroots organizer of the religious right, has had plenty of company in setting the pro-life, pro-family agenda. Three other groups that remain highly visible are the American Family Association (organized in 1988 out of the National Federation for Decency, which itself had been dreamed up in 1977 by an evangelical pastor, Donald Wildmon, to combat the "filth" of the popular media), Focus on the Family (founded by childhood-development expert and radio magnate James Dobson in 1977), and the Family Research Council (a Washington-based offshoot of Dobson's empire, long headed by Reagan acolyte Gary Bauer, who himself became a Republican presidential candidate in 2000). Also of particular note are the activities of Concerned Women of America, a coalition under the leadership of Beverly LaHaye, a longtime foe of the feminism of the National Organization for Women and a promoter of "Bible-based family values." For membership, money, and mailing lists, LaHaye's group is the envy of other public policy groups concerned with women's issues.

On the men's side, the pro-family agenda has gained expression in Promise Keepers, a group founded in 1991 by the college football coach Bill McCartney. Part old-time revival and part men's support group, the Promise Keepers organization is hardly a public policy institute, but its understanding of family meshes well with the larger emphases at the heart of evangelical conservatism. Through its popular rallies (which peaked in October 1997 with a massive gathering on the Mall in Washington under the theme "Stand in the Gap"), the Promise Keepers have placed being a better husband and a more attentive family man at the heart of the Christian life. Even as they aroused considerable secular suspicion as an antifeminist movement, the Promise Keepers staked out a position on the devotional wing of evangelical Christianity and made it hard for their critics to pigeonhole them as sinister soldiers of patriarchy. The Promise Keepers, though attractive predominantly to white audiences, have also thrown their liberal critics off balance through searching explorations (and enactments) of racial reconciliation.

The power of the Christian right as well as the limits of its power perhaps can be seen best in the presidential elections of the last twenty-five years. The 1976 campaign pitted the Georgian Jimmy Carter against the Nebraska-born but Michigan-raised Gerald Ford. The incumbent president, Ford had come into the White House not by direct election of the people but through the resignation of Richard Nixon in 1974 from the presidency. That resignation, amid the scandals associated with Watergate, had raised ethical questions of the highest order and religious questions as well in what many saw as a fundamental breach of faith. Both Ford and Carter were conservative Protestants, the former an Episcopalian (but with a son studying for the ministry in a conservative seminary in Massachusetts), the latter a Southern Baptist who had no difficulty associating himself with born-again religion.

103. Pope John Paul II, the first Roman Catholic pontiff to visit the U.S. capital, is shown here in 1979 with President Jimmy Carter, a Southern Baptist who ran afoul of the growing religious right. *Religious News Service*

Curiously, however, on most political issues the Southern Baptist was more liberal than the northern Episcopalian. A faithful deacon in the local Baptist church in Plains, Georgia, a dedicated Sunday school teacher, and a devoted student of the Bible, Jimmy Carter surprised many by his theological sophistication (Reinhold Niebuhr was a favorite), his strong dedication to separation of church and state (thus losing him the support of the Christian right), and his passionate commitment to human rights, not only within the borders of the United States but all around the world. The *New York Times* commented, regarding the 1976 campaign, that "Jimmy Carter's open espousal of his Christian beliefs ... has raised the issue of religion's place in politics more arrestingly than in any Presidential race since John F. Kennedy's in 1960." Early in the campaign many liberals were nervous about a candidate who apparently took his Christian commitments so seriously; late in the campaign, however, many conservatives found Carter much too liberal for their taste. The nascent religious right officially backed many "Christian" candidates in 1976; Jimmy Carter, who won, was not among them.

In 1980 a new political figure, so far as national politics was concerned, strode forward: Ronald Reagan, by profession an actor but more recently a two-term governor of California. In the race between the Southern Baptist churchman, Carter, and the southern California communicator, Reagan, the mantle of religious blessing ostensibly belonged to Carter. It was Reagan, however, who claimed the attention and the affection of the Christian right as he called for a moment of silent prayer at the 1980 Republican National Convention, as he repeatedly urged a spiritual revival upon the nation, and as he criticized the Supreme Court's "misinterpretation" of the First Amendment. By the time the election was held, Carter was no longer honored as the Bible-believing, church-attending, born-again Christian. That role had been assigned instead to Reagan, who had grown up in a mainline Disciples of Christ church (and attended a denominational college) but who had been an inconsistent churchgoer in later life.

In his first term as president Ronald Reagan and the Christian right drew even closer together. The president presided at National Prayer Breakfasts, addressed the National Religious Broadcasters Conventions, and spoke to gatherings of the National Association of Evangelicals. In 1982 he proposed a constitutional amendment that, in his words, would "restore the simple freedom of our citizens to offer prayer in our public schools and institutions." "I am confident," the president added, "that such an amendment will be quickly adopted, for the vast majority of our people believe there is a need for prayer in our public schools and institutions." Early in 1983 Reagan spoke to the National Religious Broadcasters of his respect for and confidence in the Bible. "Within the covers of that single book," he said, "are all the answers to all the problems that face us today." In that year he agreed to serve as honorary chairman for what was proclaimed as the "Year of the Bible." In 1984, on the anniversary of the Supreme Court decision with respect to abortion, President Reagan proclaimed the National Sanctity of Human Life Day, affirming that abortion had denied to the unborn "the first and most basic of human rights, and we are infinitely poorer for their loss."

In the campaign later that year between the incumbent president and Walter Mondale, two Protestants again headed their respective party's tickets. So thoroughly had the Reagan cause become identified with the cause of the Christian right that an irritated Walter Mondale observed that "most Americans would be surprised to learn that God is a Republican." Mondale also warned that the alliance between Reagan and the religious right threatened to "corrupt our faith and divide our nation." The son of a minister and son-in-law of another, Mondale was no stranger to the nation's Protestant heritage, but he did not believe that political campaigns should become the equivalent of religious crusades. "Policy debates," he told a B'nai B'rith gathering in the fall of 1984, should not be transformed into "theological disputes." And yet that was exactly what was happening, and Mondale was at a loss to stop it. He could only fume when one publication of the religious right, the *Presidential Biblical Scorecard*, all but branded him "antifamily and unchristian."

In 1984 not all attention was given to the top of the ticket. For the first time a major party (the Democrats) had nominated for the office of vice president a woman, Geraldine Ferraro. As a Roman Catholic, Ferraro indicated that though personally opposed to abortion, she supported the 1973 Supreme Court decision as a matter of public law, and that stance became the object of both noisy demonstrations in the streets and official rebuke in the quieter corridors of the church. The archbishop of New York, John J. O'Connor (1920–2000), did not rebuke the vice presidential candidate directly but noted that "some needs are so crucial that they require the best leadership this country can provide." For himself, he said, "I am passionately convinced that no need is more crucial than to protect the rights of the unborn." On that issue, the Democratic Catholic compared ill with the Republican Protestant, costing the former votes despite the effort of New York's governor Mario Cuomo, also a Roman Catholic, to come to Ferraro's rescue. In a major address at Notre Dame University he declared, "Although we believe abortion is wrong, we may and do honorably disagree among ourselves on specific legal political remedies." No one, though, could rescue the Democratic ticket. The Reagan-Bush ticket won decisively and in the process carried 80 percent of the white evangelical vote. The salad days of the Christian right were at hand.

The campaign of 1988 kept religion in the forefront of the news. Two ordained clergymen ran for the presidential office, civil rights veteran Jesse Jackson on the Democratic side and broadcasting mogul Pat Robertson on the Republican side. Both were Baptists, but there the similarities ended. Jackson focused on poverty and homelessness, the inequities that women and minorities still faced, and the victims of the AIDS crisis, while Robertson wanted to fight Communism, end legalized abortions, and promote

104. The Reverend Pat Robertson filed his candidacy for the presidency in Columbia, South Carolina, in 1988 and later went on to spearhead the founding of the Christian Coalition. *Religious News Service*

school prayer. Robertson, the well-educated son of a U.S. senator, was a great hope of the religious right, but his past as TV evangelist was hard to elude even in his new CEO dress. His broadcast musings to the faithful caught up with him (much as they did again later when he and Jerry Falwell mused together about the tragedy of September 11 as God's punishment on a sinfully liberal nation). For example, Robertson had dismissed the whole idea of the separation of church and state as a Soviet invention and had also argued that only Christians (and those Jews who "trust the God of Abraham, Isaac, and Jacob") were qualified to rule, "to take dominion," and to institute a reign of the righteous. Robertson's run for the White House eventually fizzled out, and while he continued to hold a place on the national political stage, he also sought a more realistic road to power and morally righteous legislation through creation of the Christian Coalition. Jackson's campaign was haunted, too, by past statements—in this case, what Jackson had said about Jews and New York City as "Hymie

105. The Reverend Jesse Jackson, longtime civil rights activist, campaigned for the presidency, often from church pulpits, in 1988. Since that unsuccessful bid he has continued his public visibility in many venues, including as a champion of legislation against hate crimes. *Religious News Service*

Town." Those Jewish tensions were made worse by Jackson's delicately balanced relationship with Louis Farrakhan and the Nation of Islam; he tried to spurn Farrakhan's anti-semitism while affirming his social critique of racism.

In the end the presidential ticket in 1988 included neither Jackson nor Robertson but instead pitted an Episcopalian against a candidate reared in the tradition of Greek Orthodoxy. Episcopalianism would be no novelty for the White House, but Eastern Orthodoxy—for so long hardly visible on the political stage in this country—surely would have been. However, the longtime Episcopalian George Bush triumphed over the Massachusetts governor, Michael Dukakis, in an election that, like the one in 1984, was not close. Bush, who had shored up his alliances with the religious right and who had early won the hearty endorsement of Jerry

Falwell, helped his cause by selecting as his running mate Dan Quayle, whose family and whose wife's family were identified with conservative religious causes. President Bush's religious roots went deep, as a vestryman of St. Anne's Episcopal Church in Kennebunkport, Maine, and as a regular communicant in St. Martin's Episcopal Church in Houston, Texas. Yet it was a tradition-minded Protestant heritage that was little at home with evangelical populism, and the centrist Bush never quite jelled as president with the Christian right in the way that his predecessor had.

The impact of the religious right continued to be apparent in the presidential politics of 1992. Robertson's Christian Coalition made its presence felt at the Republican National Convention; Randall Terry, founder of a radical antiabortion group called Operation Rescue, pronounced that a vote for Democrat Bill Clinton, a Southern Baptist, amounted to a sin in the eyes of God; and the fiery commentator-turned-candidate Patrick Buchanan claimed that the United States was in the midst of a cultural war that conservative Christians had to win. Despite the setback dealt them in Clinton's victory, leaders of the religious right felt vindicated in the midterm elections in 1994, helping to hand Republicans clear control of Congress. Many saw the Republican victories of 1994 as a validation of the "stealth" tactics of the Christian Coalition as they were worked out under the guidance of strategist Ralph Reed. "We've learned to move under radar in the cover of night with shrubbery strapped to our helmets," Reed said of his grassroots efforts to mobilize Christian conservatives.

The two-term Clinton administration regularly elicited such images of warfare from the religious right, and at no point more fiercely than in the sex scandal involving White House intern Monica Lewinsky. When the Republicans finally lost the battle for the president's removal from office and when Clinton's popularity remained high, many religious conservatives were ready to despair over the moral state of the nation. The congressional victories in 1994 had come to naught; Senator Robert Dole, a Methodist from Kansas, had proven a lackluster Republican candidate for the presidency in 1996 and had lit only modest fires for the Christian right; and Clinton rode through the scandals of his administration with a pack of ministers at his side as spiritual advisers and confidantes. Meanwhile, the president's wife, Hillary Rodham Clinton, turned her trials and tribulations as First Lady into a platform for a successful senate bid of her own in New York. Her religious vision, a social gospel activism nurtured in her United Methodist youth group in Park Ridge, Illinois, ran directly counter to much that the religious right stood for. The successes of the Clintons suggested that the Christian right, for all the fanfare of the previous twenty-five years, was as often as not on the losing end of the "culture war" that Patrick Buchanan had declared.

Still, this was a fight with many, many rounds left to go, as the inauguration of Republican George W. Bush in 2001 made plain. In a Southern Baptist–United Methodist rematch (Clinton vs. Dole in 1996 carried the same denominational affiliations), the Methodist Bush prevailed over the Baptist Gore. Though the religious right was kept on the sidelines at the Republican Convention to project a more centrist image, Bush is clearly the most powerful ally that the Christian right has had since Reagan. George W. Bush, unlike his father, shares the conversionist vernacular of popular evangelicalism and speaks it fluently. "My relationship with God

106. President George W. Bush, speaking during the 2000 campaign at a Teen Challenge event in Colfax, Iowa, is framed by a mural of Jesus. His comfort level in such settings comes from his own experience that "faith changes lives." *Agence France-Presse*

through Christ has given me meaning and direction," he told a church group in 1999. "My faith has made a big difference in my personal life and my public life as well." Long talks with evangelist Billy Graham in the mid-1980s were instrumental in his recommitment to the faith, and he counts pastor Tony Evans, a favorite with the Promise Keepers, among his spiritual advisors. His profound confidence in faith-based organizations to deliver social services stems from his own personal experience with the way "faith changes lives." With George W. Bush, the religious right may finally have a political leader who not only talks the talk (as Reagan did) but actively pursues the evangelical walk in his public life as a statesman.

RELIGIOUS PLURALISM SINCE 1965

Pluralism, in many ways, has been the great theme of American religion from the beginning. As a pre-Columbian land of tribal religions, the continent had been incredibly complex in its religious varieties and cultural differences. While much of that diversity had been destroyed through the violence of European colonization, much of it survived contact and flourished through recombination and revitalization over the next four centuries. This is still a land of richly textured native traditions, some blended with Christianity, some pan-Indian in scope (such as the Native American Church), and some wholly resistant to the cultures of conquest. In the course of time, British North America and then the United States became markedly Protestant, but Protestantism itself was always a deceptive label that all too easily masked the profound ethnic diversity and religious conflict within it. The welter of groups in early Rhode Island, Pennsylvania, and elsewhere made that divisive Christian pluralism plain from the start. Soon Roman Catholicism, Judaism, and Eastern Orthodoxy revealed with great clarity the limits of any Protestant narrative about the nation's religious direction. The tripartite formulation of "Protestant-Catholic-Jew" was always inadequate to name American religious pluralism; such a unifying construct was rendered intelligible only by overlooking a multitude of sects, seekers, immigrant minorities, and indigenous traditions. After 1965 any narrowly Christian and Jewish story line about religious pluralism became utterly outworn as the United States emerged, by scholar Diana Eck's accounting, as "the world's most religiously diverse nation."

The stunning demographic shifts of the last three decades are everywhere evident. By the late 1990s Asian immigrants, whose movement to the United States had long been stifled through a series of exclusions and restrictions between 1882 and 1924, grew to over 10 million and constituted the fastest growing population in the nation (a 43 percent increase in the 1990s alone). With these new Asian Americans came a mix of religious traditions—Buddhist, Taoist, Confucian, Muslim, Hindu, Jain, and Sikh. While these new immigrants are clearly bringing varied religious traditions to the fore in the United States, they are also changing the face of American Christianity through the presence of, for example, Vietnamese Catholics and Korean Presbyterians. Christianity in America is no longer just European, African, and Hispanic but increasingly Asian as well. There are now, for example, well over 2,000 Korean Christian congregations in the United States. In many old-line Protestant churches, Korean immigrants represent a renewed evangelical leaven. Those who were once the object of American foreign missions have come to American shores to resurrect that Protestant spirit of testimony and witnessing.

The diversity of Asian American religions, let alone the wider immigrant diversity of the last thirty-five years, is not readily summarized. For example, in trying to explore American Hinduism, one faces an internally diverse and highly populous religious tradition, the third largest of the world religions after Christianity and Islam. The classical religious practices (*yogas*) of Hinduism were introduced to the United States through the work of Swami Vivekananda and the Vedanta Society at the end of the nineteenth century, but the Vedanta centers remained small, largely highbrow groups without a substantial following (currently only about 3,000 members nationally). Immigration from India was only a trickle early in the twentieth century, but, as with other groups, immigration from South Asia picked up dramatically after 1965. By the turn of the new millennium, there were more than 200 Hindu temples and sites dotting the American landscape, with particular population centers being found in New York and New Jersey but also in the San Francisco, Chicago, and Houston areas. Hinduism remains the principal vehicle by which immigrants from South Asia make their religious claim upon the nation; there are now over 1 million Hindus in the United States. But other religious traditions from India, especially Jainism (with about 60 temples and centers) and Sikhism (with about 80 temples and centers), are also rapidly transporting additional Indian subcultures to the United States.

Various Hindu-inspired movements have captured the American religious imagination since the 1960s, from the Transcendental Meditation of the Maharishi Mahesh Yogi to the ashram of Bhagwan Shree Rajneesh in Antelope, Oregon, in the 1980s. The popularity of such gurus remains an important feature of American-style Hinduism, indicative of a wider counterculture of spiritual seeking that has become especially prominent

107. The formal consecration of a Hindu temple in Ashland, Massachusetts, attracted hundreds of pilgrims and onlookers. *The Pluralism Project, Harvard University*

since the 1960s. Yet the media's fascination with such colorful figures and their American followings should not obscure the hard work of immigrants to build their own temples and to re-create Hindu worship and festivals in the United States. Sometimes, though, the Euro-American interest in Hindu religious practices (such as meditation and chanting) has converged with the need of new immigrants to find a place to worship in their new country. In this way some of the temples of the International Society for Krishna Consciousness (or Hare Krishnas, a youth-centered movement founded in the 1960s) have become meeting grounds for Euro-American converts and new Hindu immigrants. In Denver, Los Angeles, Chicago, and Dallas, Hare Krishna temples serve both populations. As one new immigrant from India explained about his attendance at a Hare Krishna temple in Denver, "Why should I feel funny there? They practice Hinduism. They're Hindus. What's the difference?"

Just as Spanish missionaries in the colonial world sought to reconsecrate the American landscape on Catholic terms, so Hindu immigrants are remapping the sacred geography of the United States. Pilgrimage to sacred places is a central ritual of Hinduism in India, and these journeys often take devotees to rivers for purification. The confluence of the Yamuna, Ganga, and Sarasvati Rivers in India marks one of the most important pilgrimage sites for Hindus, and some of the ancient sacredness of that place has been re-created in Pittsburgh through the auspicious joining of the Allegheny, Ohio, and Monongahela Rivers in that American city. Likewise, Hindus in Pittsburgh chose a hilltop for the building of the Sri Venkateswara Temple, a geographic placement that was carefully selected to mirror the geography of the temple's original counterpart in southern India. The temple in Pittsburgh opened in 1977 and by the next decade was attracting more than 20,000 pilgrims a year from across the country. Soon other Sri Venkateswara Temples, dedicated to Lord Vishnu, were built in Illinois, Wisconsin, California, and New Jersey, and these began to attract their own pilgrims. For those immigrants cut off from the sacred sites of India, the gods and goddesses are finding new residences and new rivers closer to these new American pilgrims.

The new immigration since 1965 has also transformed the American experience with Buddhism. Even more than Hinduism, Buddhism long had a cultural cachet with those Americans alienated from the prevailing religious ethos of the nation. By the end of the nineteenth century there were even enough Buddhist seekers and sympathizers in fashionable New England circles for the Episcopalian priest Phillips Brooks to remark with exaggeration and annoyance that "a large part of Boston prefers to consider itself Buddhist rather than Christian." The modish quality of that American engagement has continued to flourish in popular culture, from Jack Kerouac's Beat Zen of the 1950s to the Hollywood conversions of Richard Gere and Tina Turner. In *The Dharma Bums* (1958) Kerouac could equate Zen Buddhism with "a great rucksack revolution" of young Americans hitchhiking across the nation, listening to poetry, and cavorting at orgiastic parties. After 1965, though, the growing number of immigrants, who brought with them the Buddhist knowledge that comes from the cradle, made many Euro-American dilettantes look increasingly naive. The new immigration did not dissolve the cultural linkages that some Americans had made between Buddhism and romantic individualism or between Buddhism and youthful alienation, but it certainly made those connections more problematic. As Kerouac had written of one of his leading characters, "Strangely Japhy wasn't interested in the Buddhism of San Francisco Chinatown because it was traditional Buddhism, not the Zen intellectual artistic Buddhism he loved."

The impact of the new immigration on American Buddhism is palpable. Vietnamese, Cambodian, Laotian, and Thai Buddhists all opened many temples in the United States in the 1980s and 1990s; by 1991 Cambodian Buddhists by themselves, with a population of about 160,000, had

108. Hsi Lai Temple in Hacienda Heights, California, is the largest Buddhist temple in the hemisphere. Here a group of nuns process in an ordination ceremony at the temple in 1992. *The Pluralism Project, Harvard University*

founded 41 temples. Sri Lankan, Tibetan, Korean, Japanese, and Chinese Buddhists only add to the diversity and complexity. In Los Angeles alone there are more than 300 Buddhist temples, and by one estimate more than 1,500 temples and meditation centers now mark the American landscape. In Hacienda Heights, California, Taiwanese Buddhists have built Hsi Lai Temple, the largest Buddhist temple in the Western Hemisphere, and not far from the temple they have created their own Buddhist university under the same name. *Hsi Lai* itself means "coming to the West," and the thirty-million-dollar temple on fourteen acres in Hacienda Heights is, indeed, a powerful architectural statement that Buddhism has arrived in America.

Not that the arrival has been without controversy in Hacienda Heights or elsewhere. Angry neighbors tried to thwart the building of Hsi Lai Temple through zoning laws, and some onlookers, skeptical about the Americanness of these recent immigrants, jeered at the Buddhist float in the local Independence Day parade. Nativist violence in American culture still often turns a lot uglier than that, as was the case with the Laotian Buddhist temple in Rockford, Illinois, which was fired upon and vandalized, the refugee community being harshly scapegoated for the social and economic ills of the area. In another episode the Cambodian Buddhist center in Portland, Maine, was robbed in 1993; on the wall the thieves had scribbled, "Dirty Asian, Chink, Go Home." The vandals were never apprehended. As one of the leaders of the community said at the time, "You know our center is not a luxurious place, but we love it, take care of it as our heart and soul. . . . This is why my tears keep dropping when I talk about [the] vandalism."

Such nativist hostility and religious suspicion are familiar to another group that has grown dramatically since 1965, American Muslims. Already at the end of the nineteenth century a prominent American convert to Islam, Mohammed Alexander Russell Webb (1846–1916), complained that "there is no system that has been so willfully and persistently misrepresented as Islam, both by writers of so-called history and by the newspaper press." Distrust and antagonism were, indeed, deep rooted; the Prophet Muhammad had been represented for centuries in Western culture as a great impostor, and the Muslim Turk had been perceived for a similarly long duration as the great enemy of European Christendom. Recent conflicts over the last quarter century in Iran, Lebanon, Libya, Iraq, and Afghanistan have only inflamed those ancient hatreds and given them a distinctly American spin, and clearly none more so than in the ongoing battle with Osama bin Laden's network of terror. The common media image of Islam is one of fanaticism, holy war, and extreme fundamentalism, and American Muslims feel recurrently maligned or profiled by such negative stereotypes. As one Muslim immigrant explained, "I don't volunteer saying I am Muslim. And it is not because I am not proud of being Muslim—I am. It is just the propaganda in the United States. . . . By saying you are a Muslim, you are a bad guy [to Americans]."

American incivility is a common experience for Muslims in the United States, but the harassment is often far worse than the discourtesies that come from cultural ignorance. As has been the case for recent Hindu and Buddhist immigrants, incivility has all too frequently edged into violence. In the wake of the bombing of the Murrah Federal Building in Oklahoma

City in 1995, American Muslims lived in fear of retaliation, as all too many Americans rashly assumed that the perpetrators must be Islamic terrorists. American Muslims reported more than 200 cases of harassment and vandalism in the wake of that tragic bombing. In 1985 arsonists fire-bombed a mosque in Houston; in 1994 a new mosque in Yuba City, California, burned to the ground, and again arsonists were to blame; and in 1995 three more mosques (one each in Illinois, North Carolina, and South Carolina) were torched. As with Catholics earlier, and with Jews, gay Christians, and African American Christians, the religious property of Muslims has become the object of nativist attack. Arsonists, in effect, give tangible expression to the fiery sentiments of one Chicago-area woman who announced at a public hearing in the summer of 2000 about the prospect of a new mosque in town: "One nation under God, and that's a Christian God. These people have absolutely no right to be here." After the immense national tragedy of September 11, 2001, it became even harder to hold such animosities in check. "We must remember," exhorted Nathan Baxter, dean of the Washington National Cathedral, "that evil does not wear a turban, a tunic, a yarmulke, or a cross. Evil wears the garment of a human heart woven from the threads of hate."

These latest episodes of religious intolerance and violence on American shores have not slowed the rapid growth of Islam in the United States. That recent upsurge is built on the solid foundations of a long-standing Muslim presence in America. The religion's first extensive American embodiment was among African slaves, who because of the prior spread of Islam in Africa sometimes brought this faith with them. Omar ibn Said (1770–1864), a Muslim captured in West Africa and sold into slavery in 1807, spent much of his life as a slave in the Carolinas. In an autobiographical account written in 1831, Said recalled his Muslim practices in Africa: "Before I came to the Christian country, my religion was the religion of Mohammed, the Apostle of God—may God have mercy upon him and give him peace! I walked to the mosque before day-break, washed my face and head and hands and feet. I prayed at noon, prayed in the afternoon, prayed at sunset, prayed in the evening. I gave alms every year." By the end of the nineteenth century small immigrant communities of Lebanese and Syrian Muslims had supplemented this initial group of African Muslims. There was also a smattering of Euro-American converts, such as Mohammed Webb, who even started his own publishing house and magazine to promote Islam in the United States.

The history of a Muslim presence among African slaves in the antebellum United States gives a deeper historical resonance to the journeys of

109. Islam has emerged as a growing religious option for African Americans in the last half century, evidenced in this group of black men attending worship at a Philadelphia mosque in the 1970s. *Urban Archives, Temple University, Philadelphia, Pennsylvania*

those African Americans who, in increasing numbers over the last two generations, have turned to Islam. Some of those African Americans have embraced the black separatist movement, the Nation of Islam, led by Elijah Muhammad (1897–1975) as Messenger of Allah from 1934 to 1975 and subsequently by Louis Farrakhan as the movement's chief minister.

Along with some orthodox Islamic elements, the Nation of Islam has emphasized its own message of self-determination, economic empowerment, moral discipline, and African American unity against the devil of white oppression. While the Nation of Islam has attracted thousands of followers and has cultivated especially successful prison ministries and educational programs, the majority of African American converts to Islam have followed the path of Elijah Muhummad's son, W. D. Muhammad, who has emphasized orthodox Sunni Islam. It was a pilgrimage into orthodox Islam that the activist Malcolm X (1925–1965) also traveled at the end of his life. By 1999 there were some signs of a budding reconciliation of these two dominant strands of African American Islam as Imam W. D. Muhammad joined Minister Louis Farrakhan for a thronged celebration in Chicago that looked forward to a united community. While estimates of the number of African American Muslims vary widely—from 500,000 to 1.5 million—most counts suggest that they make up 25 to 30 percent of the American Muslim population, a significant portion, to be sure.

One study in 2001 counted over 1,200 mosques and Islamic centers dotting the United States, a gain of 25 percent over the count in 1995. The survey also offered further confirmation that 30 percent of those affiliated with mosques in the United States are African Americans, while 33 percent are of South Asian background (Indian and Pakistani, most prominently) and 25 percent from the Middle East (Lebanese, Syrian, Palestinian, and so forth). By this study's estimate, about 2 million Muslims are connected to these 1,200 mosques and centers, but another 2 to 3 million Muslim immigrants are estimated to be living in the United States, unaffiliated with an organized religious community. By all counts, Islam is fast on its way to surpassing Judaism as America's second largest faith after Christianity. There are already more Muslims in the United States than Presbyterians or Episcopalians, to name two longtime Protestant standard-bearers. Such numbers have translated increasingly into tokens of official public recognition: a Muslim leader, for example, recited a prayer for the opening of a session of Congress in 1991, Captain Abdul-Rasheed Muhammad became the first Muslim chaplain in the U.S. military in 1993; Chicago Mayor Richard Daley proclaimed an Islam Appreciation Day in 1994; and in 2001 the U.S. Postal Service issued a stamp in honor of a Muslim feast day. As one immigrant said, "When big shots get on a podium all over the United States, I would like the day to come when they all will say 'Catholics, Protestants, Jews, and Muslims.' I would love to see Islam included every single time that someone speaks

110. Mosques and Islamic centers, like this one in Plainfield, Indiana, now dot the whole country—from New Jersey to Oklahoma, from California to Massachusetts—as Islam has grown to rival Judaism as America's second largest faith after Christianity. *Islamic Society of North America*

about religions in America." The list measuring religious inclusiveness, of course, gets longer all the time.

As with new Hindu, Sikh, Jain, and Buddhist immigrants, Muslim immigrants face pressures of change and acculturation. What does it mean to be Muslim in America's pluralistic, voluntaristic, consumerist, alcohol-indulgent milieu? Can the American workplace be accommodated to Muslim practices of praying five times daily? Should the Muslim prayer leader or imam become a professional role, a staff position, to parallel the American ministries of rabbis, priests, and pastors? Is it permissible for American Muslims to observe that grand cultural holiday and holy day, Christmas? As one adaptive immigrant explained, "It is important to get involved with American society, and if you don't celebrate Christmas and if you don't celebrate Thanksgiving, to me really you are telling those people you are not part of American society, you are something else." Another, by contrast, recalls his mother's insistent clarifications about the allures of America's popular holiday icons: "There is no Santa in our religion, this isn't our religion," she explained.

Such questions about change and tradition envelop every aspect of immigrant life, from work to marriage to family life to food to religious activities at the mosque or community center. Take, for example, another much-debated issue: Are traditional patterns of dress still obligatory for Muslim women living now within a new culture of fashion and sexual

111. American Muslims break ground on the Islamic Center of New England at an interfaith ceremony in 1991. *The Pluralism Project, Harvard University*

freedom? In styling her own habits of dress, one young American Muslim woman expresses a mix of alienation and pride, accommodation and persistence, characteristic of the negotiations that immigrants so often have faced. "Women are always encouraged in and out of the mosque to cover their hair and wear long dresses," she says. "Now I think women who go to the mosque to pray should be covered. . . . But how women dress outside of the mosque is their own private business. I don't want to go to college with my head covered, and wearing a short skirt does not make me a bad Muslim. I am a Muslim and I am proud to say it, but . . . I want to blend in as far as my clothes go. I want to look normal." Such are the everyday negotiations of religious identity and difference with which immigrants live.

These excursions into the religious pluralism of the post-1965 era are but samplings of a rapidly changing religious landscape. To these leading examples we might add many others, including the blossoming of American Baha'is from a membership of a few thousand before 1965 to nearly 150,000 at the turn of the millennium. This nineteenth-century religious movement had its roots in Iranian Islam, out of which grew a prophetic vision of universality that aimed to restore a oneness to all the religions and peoples of the world. Intensely persecuted in Iran, Baha'is first brought their global vision of religious and racial reconciliation to the United States at the end of the nineteenth century. Only after 1965, as American doors to immigration were opened wider and as Iranian persecution renewed its ferocity, did the Baha'is become a more sizable presence in the United States. As a modern religious movement growing out of a disaffection with religious exclusiveness and narrowness, the Baha'is offer a living commentary on the primary importance of mediating religious, racial, and cultural differences.

The pluralism of the post-1965 era has grown not only as a result of immigration but also because America offers a voluntaristic religious marketplace in which new religious movements can be born and thrive. Here, as with American encounters with recently arrived Muslims, Buddhists, and Hindus, wariness and conflict are common. Especially since the mass suicide in Jonestown, Guyana, in 1978 in which Jim Jones and more than 900 followers went to their deaths, the American public has been on guard against cults and communes. Jim Jones founded the Peoples Temple as a racially inclusive church in Indianapolis in the 1950s and then moved it to northern California in the 1960s. As a communal religious experiment actively espousing racial justice, the Peoples Temple shared much with the wider counterculture and civil rights movement of the era, only to take a violently authoritarian turn as Jones's religious vision grew more apocalyptic and paranoid. After an ambush of Congressman Leo Ryan and four others who had come to Guyana to investigate allegations of terrifying coercion and child abuse at the agricultural commune, the stage was set for Jones's cyanide-poisoned punch. "The time has come for us," he told his followers, "to meet in another place."

After Jonestown, new religious movements looked highly fearful and dangerous, and the "cult" label was wielded with growing abandon and alarm. What were the limits of religious toleration and pluralism? Should not the government vigorously pursue cult leaders for everything from tax evasion (as it did with Sun Myung Moon, leader of the Unification Church, in the early 1980s) to immigration fraud (as it did with the Bhagwan Shree Rajneesh, guru of Rajneeshpuram, Oregon, in the mid-1980s) to polygamy (as it has with ongoing brushes with fundamentalist Mormons)? No doubt the most glaring example of a showdown with a sectarian religious movement was the government assault on the Branch Davidians in Waco, Texas, in 1993. After a fifty-one-day standoff, federal agents, using M-60 tanks and Bradley vehicles, forced the issue, turning the religious compound into an inferno that left seventy-four Branch Davidians dead, including twenty-one children. Sensational media stories about cult violence and sexual abuse whipped the flames, and government negotiators failed completely to enter into the exegetical world of biblical apocalypse that motivated the group's leader, David Koresh. The siege at Waco revealed the perils of dealing with religious difference out of simplistic cultural stereotypes about cults: FBI agents easily turned a deaf ear to Koresh's "Bible babble" and relished instead demonizing stories of sexual perversions and paramilitary obsessions. The Branch Davidian crisis, raising serious questions about America's experiment with religious freedom and pluralism, makes especially apparent the dangers of the state imagining itself as a cult buster.

Tensions with law enforcement authorities have simmered with another new religious movement, the Church Universal and Triumphant, led by Elizabeth Clare Prophet and based since the late 1980s on a massive ranch in Montana. Prophet's husband was indicted on a weapons charge, but federal authorities eventually negotiated the voluntary relinquishment of firearms at the church's Royal Teton Ranch. While Elizabeth Clare Prophet's movement has thus been caught up in the larger cult scare of the 1980s and 1990s, she is also interesting as one gauge of the wider religious eclecticism of the era. Born and raised in Red Bank, New Jersey, Prophet sampled a wide variety of Christian options as a youth and also moved through the mind-cure teachings of Mary Baker Eddy and the positive thinking of Norman Vincent Peale. Still seeking a clear religious awakening, she became a "channel" or messenger for enlightened spiritual beings that she identified as the Ascended Masters. One in particular was to be her guide, Saint Germain, "the oldest friend I had ever known." A self-described mystic and spiritual teacher, Prophet includes among her "favorite topics" soul evolution, angels, karma, reincarnation, mystical Christianity, Kabbalah or mystical Judaism, Hinduism, and Buddhism. Prophet, who also styles herself as Guru Ma to her followers, is admittedly a rather acute example, but the sort of spiritual eclecticism that she embodies has become increasingly common among a generation of spiritual seekers.

Religious pluralism is now something that many Americans encounter within themselves as much as beyond themselves. "One day I woke up and wondered: maybe today I should be a Christian, or would I rather be a Buddhist, or am I just a *Star Trek* freak?" So one woman glibly told a sociologist in a recent study of contemporary American spirituality. Or, as the feminist spiritual writer and scholar Carol Lee Flinders relates more seriously, "I cannot describe my spiritual practice as Buddhist . . . or as Hindu or Catholic or Sufi, though I feel that in a sense it is all of these."

How to Think Like a Genius

UTNE·READER

THE BEST OF THE ALTERNATIVE MEDIA   JULY-AUGUST 98

Designer God
In a mix-and-match world, why not create your own religion?

Sex Food
Isabel Allende

Science and Soul
Ken Wilber

The Velvet Planet
Václav Havel

Mothers of Invention
Maya Angelou, Julia Cameron, Frank Zappa

112. Spirituality has become one of the great religious booms of the last decade or so as a culture of religious seeking has created a mix-and-match effect in the religious identities of a growing number of Americans. *Utne Reader*

Religious identities have become more porous in the last generation as the firmness of denominational markers have eroded, as the pluralism of the new immigration makes itself felt, as the rates of intermarriage rise, as religion becomes part of a global culture of commodities, and as private spirituality is valued at the expense of institutional religion. Sociologist Wade Clark Roof presents this modern American religious seeking as an integral part of "a quest culture" that yearns for wholeness, reintegration, and meaning, even as stable answers to those desires prove elusive.

Contemporary American religion, matching contemporary understandings of the self, has become increasingly protean and fluid, a hit-and-miss jumble of religious options. America's vast religious marketplace—its cornucopia of therapies, advice books, spiritual techniques, retreat centers, angels, Christian diets, and small groups—now shapes religious identities in its own multiplicitous and ever-shifting image. To be sure, religious pluralism in the United States remains primarily an issue of the relationship between self and other; that is, how will Christians get along with Muslims, or how will Hindus relate to Sikhs? But religious pluralism has also become, in a world of sampling and seeking, a question about the interior relationship among divided and perplexed selves. As the Quaker spiritual writer Thomas Kelly writes, "Each of us tends to be, not a single self, but a whole committee of selves."

Many find these mutable and mixed religious identities cause for alarm more than celebration. Frederica Mathewes-Green, a onetime seeker who has discerned a stable religious identity by anchoring herself in the traditions of Eastern Orthodoxy, remarks, "One of the best pieces of spiritual advice I ever received came early"; "it was that I should give up the project of assembling my own faith out of the greatest hits of the ages." John Daido Loori Roshi, abbot of the Zen Mountain monastery in Mount Tremper, New York, is still more critical and suspicious of this tendency to create "a self-styled practice from fragments appropriated from various religions." Most of the time, he insists, such "hybrid religious paths are a reflection of our cultural trend of greediness and consumerism." In these boom times for spirituality, many commentators see a sensibility of immediate gratification and diverting entertainment so characteristic of a modern consumer culture. "A tree without deep roots," warns Father Thomas Keating, a Catholic monk, "can be blown over by a fairly mild wind." At the beginning of the new millennium, more and more Americans have come to see religion as a domain that offers a smorgasbord of options from which to pick and choose. At the same time, though, many other Americans doubt that gathering up various dollops of spirituality from this great potluck of religious practices and teachings will satisfy the spiritual hunger that so many seekers say they experience.

The recent sociological tale about spiritual seeking is hardly a new story. "We are living in a time of intense spiritual desire," wrote one commentator on the American scene a century ago in 1901, and the same could have been said of the heady religious atmosphere that engulfed the new republic a century before that. Any New Age of religious questing in American religion is also part of an age-old religious journeying in the culture. "Americans seem to be in their own land as pilgrims, prodded by a dream," the French philosopher Jacques Maritain wrote in 1958 in his *Reflections on America.* The Romanian-born poet Andrei Codrescu put it more playfully when he observed in 1993 that "the spiritual pastime of every American" is "getting born again, over and over." "I once wrote a book called *Friends I Lost to Gurus,*" Codrescu relates. "It was about my God-crazy friends who migrated from one teacher to another in the sixties and the seventies, donning robes and shedding habits, changing diets, languages, and hair styles in search of that indefinable something that's still driving people everywhere and nowhere but always away from wherever they came from." Like Walt Whitman and Jack Kerouac before him, Codrescu, a Jewish exile from Communist Romania, has traveled the "open road" of America and has found there a robust religious pluralism and a vibrant spiritual autonomy. These, indeed, have proven to be the hardy and lush perennials of the American garden.

Suggested Reading for Part 4: Religious Transformation from World War II to the New Millennium

Interpreting the religious history of the last half century is an endeavor in which historians, sociologists, and ethnographers share. For a leading historical project, see Martin Marty's still-unfolding multivolume account, *Modern American Religion* (Chicago, 1986–). For a banner sociological treatment, see Robert Wuthnow, *The Restructuring of American Religion: Society and Faith Since World War II* (Princeton, 1988). Also of note are the studies of Robert S. Ellwood, including *1950, Crossroads of American Religious Life* (Louisville, 2000), and *The Fifties Spiritual Marketplace: American Religion in a Decade of Conflict* (New Brunswick, 1997).

For guidance through the broad-ranging literature on the postwar court battles, see the relevant bibliographic essays in John F. Wilson, ed., *Church and State in America: A Bibliographical Guide*, 2 vols. (Greenwood, CT, 1986–1987). See as well the luminous studies of John T. Noonan Jr., *The Believer and the Powers That Are* (New York, 1987), and *The Lustre of Our Country: The American Experience with Religious Freedom* (Berkeley, 1998). On free exercise issues generally, see Dean Kelley, ed., *Government Intervention in Religious Affairs* (New York, 1982), and Milton R. Konvitz, *Religious Liberty and Conscience* (New York, 1968). The 1940s episode involving Jehovah's Witnesses and the American flag is covered in illuminating detail by David R. Manwaring in his *Render unto Caesar: The Flag-Salute Controversy* (Chicago, 1962). Also see the more recent work of Shawn Francis Peters, *Judging Jehovah's Witnesses: Religious Persecution and the Dawn of the Rights Revolution* (Lawrence, KS, 2000). Excellent background on the conscientious objection issue that became so heated in the early 1970s may be found in Peter Brock's *Pacifism in the United States* (Princeton, 1968).

Issues raised in the general area of religion and the public schools are explored in Warren A. Nord, *Religion and American Education: Rethinking a National Dilemma* (Chapel Hill, 1995). Creationism has received much recent attention, but see preeminently Ronald L. Numbers, *The Creationists* (New York, 1992). On the abortion issue, see Kristin Luker, *Abortion and the Politics of Motherhood* (Berkeley, 1984). For the range of political and social battles being fought, often along religious lines, see James Davison Hunter, *Culture Wars: The Struggle to Define America* (New York, 1991). A full history of gay issues in the American churches has yet to be written, but much of the intensity of the conflict, personal and institutional, is captured in Troy D. Perry, *Don't Be Afraid Anymore: The Story of Reverend Troy Perry and the Metropolitan Community Churches* (New York, 1990). On recent struggles over religious freedom for Native Americans, see Carolyn N. Long, *Religious Freedom and Indian Rights: The Case of Oregon v. Smith* (Lawrence, KS, 2000). On the peyote movement more widely, see Omer C. Stewart, *Peyote Religion: A History* (Norman, OK, 1987).

The civil rights movement, along with religion's involvement at several levels, may be explored through biographical studies of key figures as well as in a topical fashion. On Martin Luther King Jr., see, for example, Stephen B. Oates, *Let the Trumpet Sound: The Life of Martin Luther King, Jr.* (New York, 1982); David L. Lewis, *King: A Critical Biography* (New York, 1970); and a useful compilation of King's major writings, edited by James M. Washington, *A Testament of Hope* (San Francisco, 1986). On the pursuit of liberationist themes in black religious thought, see Gayraud S. Wilmore and James H. Cone, eds., *Black Theology: A Documentary History, 1966–1979* (Maryknoll, NY, 1979), and these can be traced out more broadly in Milton C. Sernett, ed., *African American Religious History: A Documentary Witness*, rev. ed. (Durham, 1999). On the everyday theological dimensions of the civil rights era, see the stellar work of Charles Marsh, *God's Long Summer: Stories of Faith and Civil Rights* (Princeton, 1997).

For a guide to the literature on religion among Latinos, see Anthony M. Stevens-Arroyo, ed., *Discovering Latino Religion: A Comprehensive Social Science Bibliography* (New York, 1995). On Mexican American Catholic history and culture, see Jay P. Dolan and Gilberto M. Hinojosa, eds., *Mexican Americans and the Catholic Church, 1900–1965* (Notre Dame, 1994), and Virgilio Elizondo, *The Future Is Mestizo: Life Where Cultures Meet*, rev. ed. (Boulder, 2000). Also useful is Jay P. Dolan and Allan Figueroa Deck, eds.,

Hispanic Catholic Culture in the U.S.: Issues and Concerns (Notre Dame, 1994). For a finely wrought ethnography of one immigrant community's shrine, see Thomas A. Tweed, *Our Lady of the Exile: Diasporic Religion at a Cuban Catholic Shrine in Miami* (New York, 1997).

On women and religion in contemporary American society, the choices are many and various. For a spectrum of leading possibilities, see Margaret Lamberts Bendroth, *Fundamentalism and Gender, 1875 to the Present* (New Haven, 1993); Karen McCarthy Brown, *Mama Lola: A Vodou Priestess in Brooklyn* (Berkeley, 1991); Mark Chaves, *Ordaining Women: Culture and Conflict in Religious Organizations* (Cambridge, MA, 1997); Lynn Davidman, *Tradition in a Rootless World: Women Turn to Orthodox Judaism* (Berkeley, 1991); R. Marie Griffith, *God's Daughters: Evangelical Women and the Power of Submission* (Berkeley, 1997); Cynthia Eller, *Living in the Lap of the Goddess: The Feminist Spirituality Movement in America* (New York, 1993); and Robert A. Orsi, *Thank You, St. Jude: Women's Devotion to the Patron Saint of Hopeless Causes* (New Haven, 1996).

For perspective on the emergence of the Christian right, see Joel A. Carpenter, *Revive Us Again: The Reawakening of American Fundamentalism* (New York, 1997); Susan Friend Harding, *The Book of Jerry Falwell: Fundamentalist Language and Politics* (Princeton, 2000); Mark Noll, *Religion and American Politics* (New York, 1989); David E. Harrell Jr., *Pat Robertson* (San Francisco, 1988); Nancy Tatom Ammerman, *Bible Believers: Fundamentalists in the Modern World* (New Brunswick, NJ, 1987); William Martin, *With God on Our Side: The Rise of the Religious Right in America* (New York, 1996); and Christian Smith, *Christian America? What Evangelicals Really Want* (Berkeley, 2000).

On the growing pluralism in American religion, see Diana L. Eck, *A New Religious America: How a "Christian Country" Has Become the World's Most Religiously Diverse Nation* (San Francisco, 2001); R. Stephen Warner and Judith G. Wittner, eds., *Gatherings in Diaspora: Religious Communities and the New Immigration* (Philadelphia, 1998); Raymond Brady Williams, *Religions of Immigrants from India and Pakistan: New Threads in the American Tapestry* (Cambridge, MA, 1988); David K. Yoo, ed., *New Spiritual Homes: Religion and Asian Americans* (Honolulu, 1999); Thomas A. Tweed and Stephen Prothero, eds., *Asian Religions in America: A Documentary History* (New York, 1999); Richard Hughes Seager, *Buddhism in America* (New York, 1999); Yvonne Yazbeck Haddad and Jane I. Smith, eds., *Muslim Communities in North America* (Albany, 1994); Yvonne Yazbeck Haddad and Adair T. Lummis, *Islamic Values in the United States: A Comparative Study* (New York, 1987); and Jane I. Smith, *Islam in America* (New York, 1999).

For an excellent study of the Branch Davidians and new religious movements, see James D. Tabor and Eugene V. Gallagher, *Why Waco? Cults and the Battle for Religious Freedom in America* (Berkeley, 1995).

Sociologists have led the work on contemporary American spirituality. See especially Robert Wuthnow, *After Heaven: Spirituality in America Since the 1950s* (Berkeley, 1998); Robert Wuthnow, *Creative Spirituality: The Way of the Artist* (Berkeley, 2001); Robert Wuthnow, *Sharing the Journey: Support Groups and America's New Quest for Community* (New York, 1994); Wade Clark Roof, *A Generation of Seekers: The Spiritual Journeys of the Baby Boom Generation* (San Francisco, 1993); and Wade Clark Roof, *Spiritual Marketplace: Baby Boomers and the Remaking of American Religion* (Princeton, 1999). For historical perspective, as well as a collection of documents, see Catherine L. Albanese, ed., *American Spiritualities: A Reader* (Bloomington, IN, 2001). For highly perceptive ethnographies of two different groups of contemporary spiritual seekers, see Michael F. Brown, *The Channeling Zone: American Spirituality in an Anxious Age* (Cambridge, MA, 1997), and Sarah M. Pike, *Earthly Bodies, Magical Selves: Contemporary Pagans and the Search for Community* (Berkeley, 2001).

General Bibliography

Since many of the most relevant titles have already been listed in the four Suggested Reading sections, this short bibliography will be limited to more general works on religion in American history and culture. For documentary readings from primary sources, see Edwin S. Gaustad, ed., *A Documentary History of Religion in America*, 2 vols., rev. ed. (Grand Rapids, 1993) and Colleen McDannell, ed., *Religions of the United States in Practice*, 2 vols. (Princeton, 2001). Both offer helpful supplements to a general history of religion in American culture by pulling together an array of primary materials. For more specialized collections of documents, see Rosemary R. Ruether and Rosemary S. Keller, eds., *Women and Religion in America*, 3 vols. (San Francisco, 1981–1986); John Tracy Ellis, ed., *Documents of American Catholic History*, rev. ed. (Chicago, 1967); and Jonathan D. Sarna and David G. Dalin, eds., *Religion and State in the American Jewish Experience* (Notre Dame, 1997). Also still of use is H. Shelton Smith, Robert T. Handy, and Lefferts A. Loetscher, eds., *American Christianity: An Historical Interpretation with Representative Documents*, 2 vols. (New York, 1960–1963).

Two basic readers geared to introducing the range of contemporary scholarship across the whole span of American religious history are David G. Hackett, ed., *Religion and American Culture* (New York, 1995), and Jon Butler and Harry S. Stout, eds., *Religion in American History* (New York, 1998). Four essay collections of the late 1990s, taken together, offer a good sense of trends in the most recent scholarly literature: D. G. Hart and Harry S. Stout, eds., *New Directions in American Religious History* (New York, 1997); Thomas A. Tweed, ed., *Retelling U.S. Religious History* (Berkeley, 1997); David D. Hall, ed., *Lived Religion in America: Toward a History of Practice* (Princeton, 1997); and Peter Williams, ed., *Perspectives on American Religion and Culture* (Malden, MA, 1999). And then add two from the new millennium to help complete the picture of the recent scholarship: David

Morgan and Sally M. Promey, eds., *The Visual Culture of American Religions* (Berkeley, 2001), and Bruce David Forbes and Jeffrey H. Mahan, eds., *Religion and Popular Culture in America* (Berkeley, 2000).

On the encyclopedia front, Charles H. Lippy and Peter W. Williams have edited a comprehensive three-volume *Encyclopedia of the American Religious Experience* (New York, 1988) that remains a standard. For still wider coverage of the welter of religious groups and creeds in the United States, see J. Gordon Melton, *Encyclopedia of American Religions,* rev. ed. (Detroit, 1998). Also a handy reference is the *Encyclopedia of American Religious History* (New York, 1996), edited by Edward L. Queen II, Stephen R. Prothero, and Gardiner H. Shattuck Jr. Biographical guidance may be found in Henry W. Bowden, *Dictionary of American Religious Biography* (Greenwood, CT, 1977), and in the new *American National Biography,* 24 vols. (New York, 1999).

For geographical and demographic assistance in mapping the history of religion in America, the most comprehensive guidebook is Edwin S. Gaustad and Philip L. Barlow, *New Historical Atlas of Religion in America* (New York, 2000). Two other resources of note are Roger Finke and Rodney Stark, *The Churching of America, 1776–1990: Winners and Losers in Our Religious Economy* (New Brunswick, NJ, 1992), and Bret Carroll, *The Routledge Historical Atlas of Religion in America* (New York, 2000).

For current statistics on religious membership, consult the *Yearbook of American and Canadian Churches,* published and updated each year by Abingdon Press of Nashville, Tennessee. Most religious groups also now have Web sites from which one can usually garner basic information on membership statistics, creedal statements, current initiatives, publications, thumbnail histories, and contact information. Standard Internet search engines yield a wealth of these sites. For a small sampling of especially useful Web sites on American religion and culture, see the following:

www.materialreligion.org
on religious artifacts

www.wabashcenter.wabash.edu
on teaching resources

www.northstar.vassar.edu
on African American religious history

www.arda.tm
on sociological data

are.as.wvu.edu
on the American religious experience broadly construed

www.wheaton.edu/isae
on evangelical Protestantism

www.ajhs.org
for the American Jewish Historical Society

www.fas.harvard.edu/~pluralsm
on the new religious pluralism

www.iupui.edu/~raac
on recent research and conferences at one prominent center

www.nd.edu/~cushwa
for American Catholic studies

Index

Page numbers of photographs appear in italics.